Nineteenth-century Cape Town, the capital of the British Cape Colony, was conventionally regarded as a liberal oasis in an otherwise racist South Africa. Longstanding British influence was thought to mitigate the racism of the Dutch settlers and foster the development of a sophisticated and colour-blind English merchant class. Vivian Bickford-Smith skilfully interweaves political, economic and social analysis to show that the English merchant class, far from being liberal, were generally as racist as Afrikaner farmers. Theirs was, however, a peculiarly English discourse of race, mobilised around a 'Clean Party' obsessed with sanitation and the dangers posed by 'un-English' Capetonians in a period of rapid urbanisation brought about by the discovery of diamonds and gold in the interior.

This original contribution to South African urban history draws on comparative material from other colonial port towns and on relevant studies of the Victorian city.

Ethnic pride and racial prejudice in Victorian
Cape Town

African Studies Series 81

The old Town House, Greenmarket Square, decorated for Queen Victoria's Jubilee, 1897

Ethnic pride and racial prejudice in Victorian Cape Town

Group identity and social practice, 1875–1902

Vivian Bickford-Smith

University of Cape Town

CAMBRIDGE
UNIVERSITY PRESS

Published by the Press Syndicate of the University of Cambridge
The Pitt Building, Trumpington Street, Cambridge CB2 1RP
40 West 20th Street, New York, NY 10011–4211, USA
10 Stamford Road, Oakleigh, Melbourne 3166, Australia

First published 1995

Printed in Great Britain at the University Press, Cambridge

A catalogue record for this book is available from the British Library

Library of Congress cataloguing in publication data
Bickford-Smith, Vivian.
Ethnic price and racial prejudice in Victorian Cape Town: group identity and
social practice, 1875–1902 / Vivian Bickford-Smith.
    p.   cm. – (African studies series; 81)
includes bibliographical references.
ISBN 0 521 47203 2
1. Cape Town (South Africa) – Social life and customs. 2. Cape Town (South
Africa) – History. 3. Racism – South Africa – Cape Town – History. I. Title.
II. Series.
DT2405.C3657B53   1955
968.7′355–dc20   94–12143   CIP

ISBN 0 521 47203 2 hardback

CE

Contents

Illustrations

Frontispiece: The old Town House, Greenmarket Square, decorated for Queen Victoria's Jubilee, 1897

Maps

Plates

Tables

Preface

David Kennedy, a professional singer from Scotland, visited Cape Town in 1879. He saw a city that was 'dusty and dirty by day, and unsavoury by night'. He described the local population: 'English, Dutch, Malays, Mozambiquers, Indians, Kafirs and "Cape Town Boys" ... all shades of colour ranging from deepest negro night, through twilight of half and quarter castes, to pure white European.'[1]

Kennedy had indirectly raised two topics that were likely to be of considerable interest to his readers back in Victorian Britain: urban problems and the question of 'race'. Both are central themes of this book. In writing colonial urban history I will be exploring the connections between them.

The question of the historical efficacy of 'race', or what I will call ethnicity, has not unnaturally been the subject of considerable debate in South African historiography in the last two decades, as my introduction will relate. What I briefly wish to acknowledge in this preface is the existing corpus of work on South African urban history. In particular I would like to draw attention to some of the unpublished or little-known work on Cape Town, without which this book could not have been written.

Until the second half of the 1970s, it would be difficult to say that a South African urban historiography, resembling that extant for Britain or America, existed at all. Those studies where towns were either the setting or the overt object of the historian's attention could largely be divided into two categories: the antiquarian and the municipal history.[2] A few exceptions to this categorisation existed, notably Maynard Swanson's observations on the origins of segregation in Durban and David Welsh's chapter on the growth of cities in the *Oxford History of South Africa*.[3]

This situation changed somewhat in the 1970s. This was partly because a vigorous neo-Marxist critique of South African historiography focused attention on processes such as the rise of capitalism and class formation in that country's past. In turn this meant that attention was focused on

Kimberley and Johannesburg, the leading centres of capital accumulation in the late nineteenth century. Gathering pace from the late 1970s, a body of papers, theses and books have appeared, chiefly from the School of Oriental and African Studies in London and the University of the Witwatersrand in Johannesburg. These works began to reveal the social history of Kimberley and the Rand and, *inter alia*, something of the interplay between 'race' and class in these places.[4]

For Cape Town, Swanson followed up his paper on Durban with another in 1977 which examined the origins of the segregation of Africans in this city as well as in Port Elizabeth.[5] Shirley Judges produced an impressive MA thesis on poverty in the 1830s and 1840s.[6] A paper by Edna Bradlow looked at the same topic for the mid-1870s.[7]

But it was the University of Cape Town (UCT) workshops, initiated by Robin Hallett in 1978, that really accelerated the process of remedying some of the deficiencies in our understanding of the city's past. These workshops, like the contemporaneous ones at the University of the Witwatersrand, were undoubtedly inspired – in the wake of the urban uprisings of 1976 – by what Dyos saw as the purpose of urban history: to offer to ordinary people an understanding of their historical predicament and to enable the historian to take a city and explain its present condition in terms of the forces that have made it.[8] The academic side of this process has involved the publication of *Studies in the History of Cape Town* and the production of numerous theses and research papers in the 1980s and 1990s.[9]

This volume draws heavily on this research. Particularly helpful has been the work of Elizabeth van Heyningen, on health and social welfare, and Christopher Saunders on the experience of Africans in Cape Town.[10] Major lacunae still include the paucity of work on the city's economy and statistical studies in general that would reveal marriage, property ownership, wages and cost of living patterns for the late nineteenth century.

An additional weakness of Cape Town historiography has been its lack of cohesiveness when compared to the work on Kimberley and the Rand. This is largely, one suspects, because Cape Town researchers have not been united by a Marxist or neo-Marxist theoretical perspective. Marxist analysis, when applied to the social history of the mining centres, has given a certain unity and sense of purpose to ostensibly very diverse material. Marxist analysis has also meant that this material has been linked to broad developments within the South African political economy, such as the rise of industrial capital.

Such linkage is much less apparent in the bulk of the Cape Town material. One exception has been provided by two papers by Robert

Ross, of Leiden University, who has also been a contributor to the UCT workshops. Ross's all too brief 'Cape Town: Synthesis in the Dialectic of Continents' examined the functions, economic activity, demographic growth and social structure of Cape Town in the eighteenth and early nineteenth centuries. Although his study only briefly touched on post-emancipation Cape Town, Ross made the important assertion that no clear distinction between White and Black Capetonians was possible in the nineteenth century 'because the sharp contradiction between master and servant, so characteristic of the South African countryside, was also absent'.[11] His similarly brief, yet suggestive 'Structure and Culture in Pre-industrial Cape Town: A Survey of Knowledge and Ignorance' is aptly titled and provided an implicit agenda of work to be done in this field.[12]

Despite the advances that have been made in the last decade, the historiography of Cape Town remains patchy. Andrew Bank on slavery in the early nineteenth century, John Western's *Outcast Cape Town,* which examines residential segregation instigated by the National Party in the 1950s, and Josette Cole's *Crossroads*, on the eponymous squatter community in the late 1970s and early 1980s, remain the only published academic monographs on the city for any period.[13] There is no equivalent, for colonial Cape Town, of the works of Worger and Turrell on Kimberley, or Van Onselen on Johannesburg. This book, hopefully, will begin to fill this gap.

Notes

1 D. Kennedy, *Kennedy at the Cape: A Professional Tour Through the Cape Colony, Orange Free State, Diamond Fields and Natal* (Edinburgh, Edinburgh Publishing Company, 1879), pp. 9–10.

2 Some examples from both antiquarian and municipal genres of Cape Town histories from which I have gathered pickings for this book are: antiquarian – L. Green, *Growing Lovely, Growing Old* (Cape Town, Howard Timmins, 1975); C. Pama, *Bowler's Cape Town, Life at the Cape in Early Victorian Times, 1834–1868* (Cape Town, Tafelberg, 1977); and municipal – P. W. Laidler, *The Growth and Government of Cape Town* (Cape Town, Unie-Volkspers, 1939); M. Marshall, 'The Growth and Development of Cape Town' (MA thesis, UCT, 1940); R. F. M. Immelman, *Men of Good Hope* (Cape Town, Chamber of Commerce, 1955); J. Shorten, *Cape Town* (Johannesburg, Shorten, 1963); and H. W. J. Picard, *Grand Parade* (Cape Town, Struik, 1969). In addition there was also the rather spartan thesis of J. Whittingdale, 'The Development and Location of Industries in Greater Cape Town' (MA thesis, UCT, 1973).

3 See M. Swanson, 'Reflections on the Urban History of South Africa: Some Problems and Possibilities, with special reference to Durban', in H. L. Watts

(ed.), *Focus on Cities: Proceedings of a Conference Organised by the Institute for Social Research, at the University of Natal, Durban, 8–12 July 1968* (Durban, Institute for Social Research, University of Natal, 1970), pp. 143–9; and D. Welsh, 'The Growth of Towns', in M. Wilson and L. Thompson (eds.), *The Oxford History of South Africa* vol. II (Oxford, Clarendon Press, 1971), pp. 172–243.

4   See for example B. Bozzoli (ed.), *Labour, Townships and Protest: Studies in the Social History of the Witwatersrand* (Johannesburg, Ravan, 1979); B. Bozzoli (ed.), *Town and Countryside in the Transvaal: Capitalist Penetration and Popular Response* (Johannesburg, Ravan, 1983); B. Bozzoli (ed.), *Class Community and Conflict: South African Perspectives* (Johannesburg, Ravan Press, 1987); C. Van Onselen, *Studies in the Social and Economic History of the Witwatersrand 1886–1914* vol. I, *'New Babylon'* (Johannesburg, Ravan Press, 1982) and vol. II, *'New Nineveh'* (Johannesburg, Ravan Press, 1982). On Kimberley see R. V. Turrell, *Capital and Labour on the Kimberley Diamond Fields, 1871–1890* (Cambridge, Cambridge University Press, 1987); and W. H. Worger, *South Africa's City of Diamonds: Mine Workers and Monopoly Capitalism in Kimberley, 1867–1895* (Craighall, AD. Donker, 1987).

5   'The Sanitation Syndrome: Bubonic Plague and Urban Native Policy in the Cape Colony, 1900–1909', *Journal of African History*, 18, 3 (1977), 387–410.

6   'Poverty, Living Conditions and Social Relations – Aspects of Life in Cape Town in the 1830s' (MA thesis, UCT, 1977).

7   'Cape Town's Labouring Poor a Century Ago', *South African Historical Journal*, 9 (1977), 19–29; also useful, for the period in between, is her 'Emancipation and Race Perceptions at the Cape', *South African Historical Journal*, 15 (1983), 10–33.

8   See B. M. Stave, 'In Pursuit of Urban History, Conversations with Myself and Others: A View from the United States', in D. Fraser and A. Sutcliffe (eds.), *The Pursuit of Urban History* (London, Edward Arnold, 1983), p. 418.

9   *Studies in the History of Cape Town* vols. I and II (1979); vol. III (1980); vol. IV (1981); vol. V (1984); vol. VI (1988); and vol. VII (1994). All are published by the Centre for African Studies at the University of Cape Town. Among works not published in *Studies*, of particular use for this book were: E. B. Van Heyningen, 'Public Health and Society in Cape Town, 1880–1910' (Ph.D. thesis, UCT, 1989); D. P. Warren, 'Merchants, Commissioners and Ward Masters: Politics in Cape Town, 1840–1854' (MA thesis, UCT, 1986); and A. Bank, 'Slavery in Cape Town, 1806–1834' (MA thesis, UCT, 1991). Many other theses will also be cited as references in the course of this book.

10 C. Saunders, 'The Creation of Ndabeni: Urban Segregation and African Resistance in Cape Town', *Studies*, I (1979), 165–93; E. van Heyningen, 'Cape Town and the Plague of 1901', *Studies*, IV (1981), 66–107.

11 R. Ross and G. J. Telkamp (eds.), *Colonial Cities: Essays on Urbanism in a Colonial Context* (Leiden, Martinus Nijhoff, 1985), pp. 105–21; the quotation can be found on p. 116.

12 R. Ross, 'Structure and Culture in Pre-industrial Cape Town: A Survey of Ignorance and Knowledge', in W. G. James and M. Simons (eds.), *The*

Angry Divide: Social and Economic History of the Western Cape (Cape Town, David Philip, 1989), pp. 40–6.

13   Andrew Bank, *Decline of Urban Slavery at the Cape, 1806 to 1834* (Cape Town, Centre for African Studies, 1991); John Western, *Outcast Cape Town* (Cape Town, Human & Rousseau, 1981); J. Cole, *Crossroads: The Politics of Reform and Repression 1976–1986* (Johannesburg, Ravan, 1987)

Acknowledgements

Newspapers, government publications and the archives of the Standard Bank of South Africa provided the bulk of the primary sources on which this history is based. Newspapers have helped to fill in the gaps created by the absence of other sources often available to the social historian: oral testimony, diaries, or the detailed records of trade unions, businesses and industries. The correspondence columns of Cape Town's various newspapers express the opinions and attitudes of literate Capetonians. Coverage of magistrates' court proceedings often report voices of the illiterate.

Particularly useful were the *Cape Times* and *Cape Argus*. Specific newspapers or journals have provided information on topics dealt with less assiduously by others: the *Lantern* made frequent forays into slummer journalism; the *Cowley Evangelist* reported missionary work in central Cape Town; the *South African News* had detailed reports of trade union activity from 1899; the *South African Spectator* (1901–2) was interested in Black upliftment. Before the *Spectator*, there was unfortunately no newspaper in Cape Town aimed at a Black readership, let alone with a Black editor or owner. Dutch-language newspapers, such as the *Zuid-Afrikaan*, provided only sporadic information on Dutch/Afrikaans attitudes to events in Cape Town. These journals tended to concentrate on broader colonial and rural issues.

Cape government and official publications increase in volume as the years progress. Particularly helpful were the numerous select committee reports of both houses of the Cape parliament and the often voluminous evidence they collected, and the even larger number of government reports. These reports provide regular, often annual, information on institutions under government control such as hospitals, schools and prisons.

The Standard Bank archives contain regular inspection reports for individual branches of the bank which analyse the state of the local economy. The half-yearly reports of the general manager of the bank, together with his correspondence to headquarters in London, comple-

xviii

ment and add to an understanding of fluctuations in the South African and Cape Town economy from the mid-nineteenth century. These archives also provide information on individual account holders, happily unprotected by closed access.

Many archivists and historians helped in finding and making material available for the research on which this book is based. The efforts of the staff of the South African Library and the African Studies Library, UCT, were particularly impressive in this respect. I would also like to mention the help of Barbara Conradie at the Cape Archives and those of the Standard Bank. Many thanks also to James Henry for his kindness in allowing me to use his extracts from the Standard Bank archives. David Lowe, of Cambridge University Library, allowed me to use the newly acquired Rosenthal Collection and explained the mysteries of its extraordinary indexing system.

Jessica Kuper guided the book through the process of production at Cambridge University Press with patience and good humour. I was particularly fortunate to have a copy-editor, Mary Starkey, who was conscientious, extremely sharp and very patient. She spotted errors and made useful suggestions with impressive skill, aided in part by her own South African background. I would also like to thank Marigold Acland, Jayne Matthews and Caroline Drake for their help with co-ordinating the manuscript, and Hilary Bassett for the index.

John Iliffe, of Cambridge University, started me on the thesis that ultimately led to this book and helped me to spend six months at Cambridge which enabled me to all but finish the manuscript. His kindness, wisdom and enthusiasm helped to sustain me through the very long time the whole process involved. I was fortunate indeed to have such a conscientious and skilful mentor.

Shula Marks at London University and John Lonsdale at Cambridge were the examiners of the thesis on which a great deal of this book is based. Their comments to this nervous examinee during the viva were duly taken to heart. I hope that I have managed to do some justice to their insightful and extremely useful criticisms in the intervening years. The considerable transformations from thesis to book were greatly inspired by them.

Robert Ross, of Leiden University, gave very generously of his time in reading the manuscript of *Ethnic Pride and Racial Prejudice* and offered ideas for its improvement. I hope that the conclusion in particular has benefited.

Obviously the blame for any remaining shortcomings in this book is mine.

No writer is unaware of the debts owed to friends and family in the process of getting into print. I have been very fortunate at the Universities of Cambridge, Rhodes and Cape Town to have had colleagues who were also friends. It would be invidious to single out individuals. I owe all of them much gratitude, if some more meals than others. But as they are not at the above universities I do wish to thank Bill Freund, Saul Dubow, Rob Turrell, Jeff Peires, Gavin Lewis and Hilary Sapire for their encouragement. Non-historians Jeremy Jones, Jeanne Fourie, Gavin Stewart, Charles Dingley, Roger Young, the Mills, Chomse and Meadows families, and many others, were hugely supportive, and (mostly) tactful enough not to make too many rude comments about the time that was taken to produce this book.

As to my family, many thanks to all the scattered members of the Bickford-Smith clan. My parents, Anne Hamilton-Gordon and John Bickford-Smith, never queried my strange choice of an academic career. Instead, they made it possible. My father died in September 1993, as this book was already in the hands of the publishers. I would very much like him to have read it. His own life, from being a member of the British Conservative Party to local ANC treasurer, trade union organiser and Legal Aid officer in Cape Town, was a perfect example of changeable social identity. He will be missed.

I have recently gained additional kinship networks through the Pienaars. I am very lucky to have done so. I am particularly fortunate in Claudia. This book is for her.

A note on terminology

If I have used terms such as Black, White, African and Coloured in this book, I do not wish to suggest that they are anything other than ethnic labels or racialised categories. The capitalisation of initial letters is intended to suggest as much. This allows me to cut down on the number of inverted commas. These can be more usefully employed to surround terms more obviously offensive to South Africans today such as 'Kaffir' or 'Native', for which I also use the synonym 'African'. Although 'White' was a common self-description used by nineteenth-century Capetonians, 'Black' was used much less often in this way. I have used 'Black' as a synonym for people described by Whites as 'Other than White' in contemporary censuses. Black, in my usage, is a collective noun for the range of people who thought of themselves, for instance and at times, as Coloured, African, Malay or Indian.

Unless otherwise specified, Cape Town refers to both the municipality of Cape Town and its suburbs.

Abbreviations

AG	Attorney General (CC)
AME	African Methodist Episcopalian (Church)
ANC	African National Congress
APO	African People's/Political Organisation
Bond	*Afrikaner Bond*
BBV	*Boeren Beschermings Vereeniging*
CA	Cape Archives
CBB	*Cape Blue Books*
CC	Cape Colony
CCP	*Cape Command Papers*
CGR	Cape Government Railways
CHB	Cape Harbour Board
CMM	*Cape Monthly Magazine*
CO	Colonial Office
CPA	Coloured People's Association
CPP	*Cape Parliamentary Papers*
CSC	Cape Supreme Court
CT	Cape Town
DEIC	Dutch East India Company
DRC	Dutch Reformed Church
DSAB	*Dictionary of South African Biography*
GH	Government House (CC)
GM	General Manager
GWU	General Workers' Union
HA	Henry Archives
HBC	Archives of the Cape Town Free Dispensary
HOS	Archives of the Superintendent, Old Somerset Hospital (CC)
IAC	Immigration and Labour Department (CC)
IR	Inspection Report
JAH	*Journal of African History*
JSAS	*Journal of Southern African Studies*

LC	Limited Companies (CC)
LO	London Office
MC	Medical Committee (CC)
MLA	Member of the Legislative Assembly
MLC	Member of the Legislative Council
NA	Native Affairs Department (CC)
PWD	Public Works Department (CC)
SACPA	South African Coloured Protection Association
SAHJ	*South African Historical Journal*
SALVR	*South African Licensed Victualler's Review*
SAWMPU	South African Working Men's Progressive Union
SAWMU	South African Working Men's Union
SBA	Standard Bank Archives
SCR	Select Committee Report
SDF	Social Democratic Federation
SGE	Superintendent General of Education (CC)
SPG	Society for the Propagation of the Gospel
Studies	*Studies in the History of Cape Town*
UCT	University of Cape Town
UG	Union Government
Wits	Witwatersrand
WP	Western Province
ZAUK	*Zuid-Afrikaansche Vereeniging van der Kaapstad*
1CT	Cape Town Magistrate's Archives
3CT	Cape Town Municipality's Archives

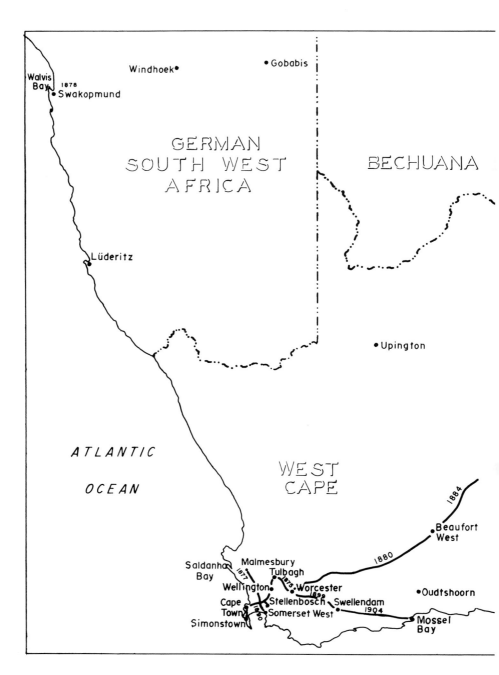

1   The Cape Colony, *c.* 1909

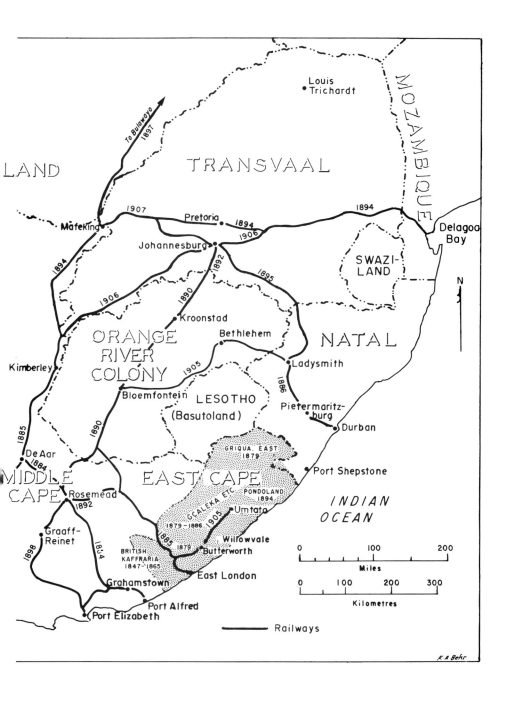

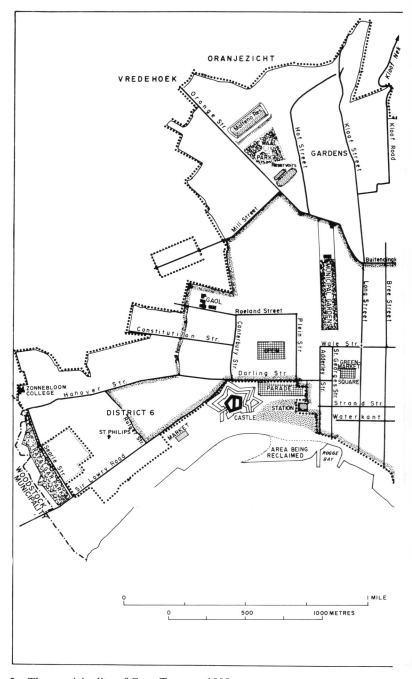

2 The municipality of Cape Town, *c.* 1909

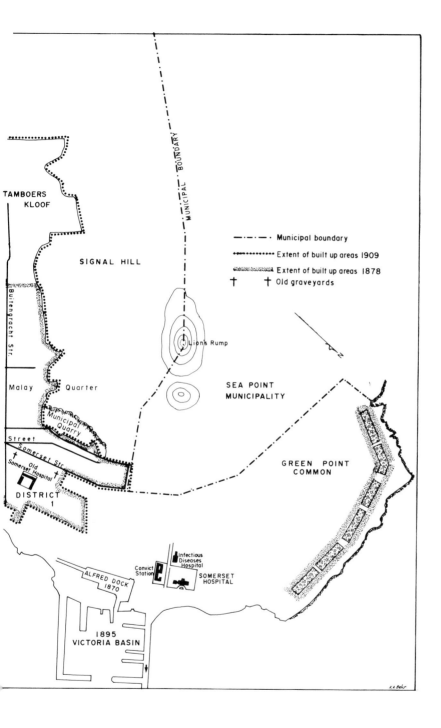

TAMBOERS
KLOOF

Buitengracht Str.

SIGNAL HILL

Lions Rump

Malay   Quarter

Municipal
Quarry

Street

Somerset Str.

Old
Somerset Hospital

DISTRICT
1

SEA POINT
MUNICIPALITY

GREEN POINT
COMMON

MUNICIPAL   BOUNDARY

Municipal boundary

Extent of built up areas 1909

Extent of built up areas 1878

✝   ✝ Old graveyards

N

Infectious
Diseases
Hospital

Convict
Station

SOMERSET
HOSPITAL

ALFRED DOCK
1870

1895
VICTORIA BASIN

K A Behr

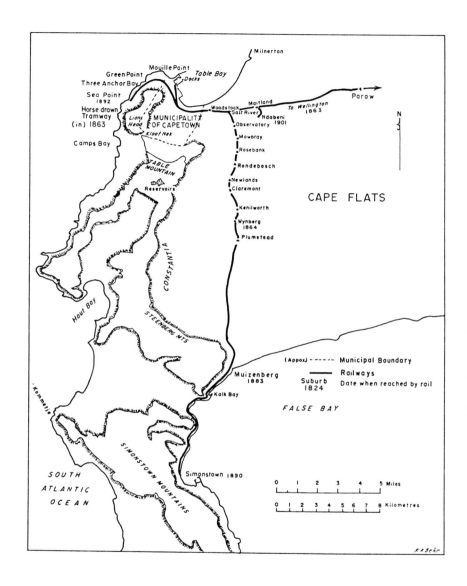

3 The Cape Peninsula, *c.* 1901

1   Introduction

In the early twentieth century the city of Cape Town, the capital of the British Cape Colony, was an exceptional place in southern Africa. At least this was the judgement of the American historian George Fredrickson. He was not referring to the city's size or functions, or even its extraordinarily beautiful setting beneath Table Mountain, on the shores of Table Bay. For Fredrickson, Cape Town's significance lay in 'its traditional toleration of white–Colored intermingling in public places'. The city had a 'special tradition of multi-racialism', and

> fraternization between racial groups in Cape Town remained relatively free and unimpaired by laws or even strong and consistent patterns of customary exclusion until well into the twentieth century.

Such toleration was apparently not extant in other South African cities, or those of the American South, by the 1890s.[1] In his chapter on the growth of towns in the *Oxford History of South Africa*, David Welsh also suggested that Cape Town was unique among South African cities 'in the extent to which it was racially integrated'.[2]

In support of their contentions, both Fredrickson and Welsh quoted from an account of his visit to Cape Town in 1911 by Maurice Evans, an expert on the 'native question'. Here, writing in the third person, he describes his experiences:

> He hears that it is quite a common thing for the European immigrant introduced for railway and mechanical work to marry, even to prefer to marry, women of colour ... he sees a toleration of colour and a social admixture to which he is quite unaccustomed; it is evident on the streets, on the tramcars, in the railway stations, public offices, and in places of entertainment ... impossible in an eastern town such as Durban or Pietermaritzburg ... [in a cinema] ... he will find no distinction made, all and any colour occupy the same seats, cheek by jowl, and sometimes on each other's knees.[3]

Despite the evidence from Evans, the contentions of Fredrickson and Welsh were based on little primary research, as both would undoubtedly acknowledge. Yet many Capetonians today also believe that their city was a haven of ethnic harmony and integration before the coming of Apartheid in 1948. They believe that segregation was something imposed on the city from outside. The culprits were Afrikaner nationalists, of an intolerant northern *voortrekker* tradition. These nationalists, in their administrative fastness of Pretoria, were hostile to the liberal Cape tradition. This tradition, based on equality of all before the law and a non-racial franchise, was epitomised and symbolised by social relations in the southern legislative capital, '*Kaapstad*', the mother city.

After 1948, putting a master plan of social engineering into operation, 'Pretoria' introduced the Acts that destroyed ethnic harmony. The Population Registration Act legally defined people according to race. The Group Areas Act determined where members of each race should live. The Separate Amenities Act became South Africa's comprehensive Jim Crow law. The Mixed Marriages Act, in Orwellian vein, prevented them between people defined as belonging to different races. Only in the 1980s did the nationalists began to see, or were made to see, the error of their ways.

What both academic and popular versions of Cape Town's past have done is to suggest the tantalising possibility that for once there was a colonial town in which the 'distinctive social characteristic' was not 'the fact of race'[4] – a town which was in, of all places, the part of the world that was to become Apartheid South Africa. The initial motivation for this book was to examine this possibility. I wished to explore the extent and limitation of segregation on the basis of 'race' in colonial Cape Town. Living in Cape Town in the 1980s, when government ideology espoused the primordial nature of race and its historical efficacy, I even saw subversive possibilities in the project.

South Africa is now staggering away from institutionalised racism. 'Ethnicity' has replaced 'race' as the acceptable catchword of political pundits and social scientists. But 'ethnic' prejudice can be just as destructive as the 'racial' variety. Both can, and have, fuelled what I would call racism. Therefore a further purpose behind this book is, through a case study, to explain ethnicity and explore its relationship with racism. South Africa's future will be as Bosnian bleak as its past if 'ethnic cleansing', from whatever quarter, replaces the desire for 'racial purity' as social practice.

Ethnicity, like class and community, is a concept that can be used to describe group identity. Group identities, like the concepts that describe them, are socially constructed and subject to change. Group identities do not, as I hope to show, evolve in any linear or predictable way, and should not be reified as primordial or permanent. Therefore particular ethnicities are best explained through historical methodology. Once people are seen by themselves or others as, say, Muslim, working class or from London's East End, this does not necessarily remain the case permanently. Some may reject identities that they once accepted or take on identities they once rejected. Equally 'different' group identities can coexist, reinforce, influence or cut across each other, have greater or lesser salience for the same individual, even in the course of a single day.

It follows that if the terms we use to describe group identities are to have individual analytical value, we should define the different meanings we attach to them. 'Race' and 'ethnicity' are often used interchangeably in the late twentieth century, as 'race' and 'class' were in the nineteenth. 'Race' was a concept frequently used by Capetonians, and visitors to late Victorian Cape Town, to categorise others and themselves. The varied meanings which they attributed to race are best demonstrated in their historical context, and will be.

'Ethnicity' is a modern derivative from *ethnos* the Greek word for nation or people. Even the older English terms 'ethnie' and 'ethnic' were very seldom used in nineteenth-century Cape Town.[5] I will be using ethnicity to mean the perception that a person has of having common ancestry or permanent cultural ties with one collection of people, one ethnic group, rather than another or others. Such perceived difference will be given a collective name such as Afrikaner, Coloured, or Christian. Ethnicity will be conferred or enhanced by informal or formal education as well as by shared activities and symbols.

An ethnicity will be further strengthened when its adherents are encouraged, their ethnicity perhaps given greater and newly invented content, by ethnic mobilisers. These are usually politicians, journalists or teachers who propagate the idea that the group has common interests, history or destiny. Implicitly or explicitly they will suggest that individual interests can be advanced or defended by the collective action of the group.[6]

Much of what I have said about ethnicity applies to other terms for group identities that appear in this book. The two most frequently used are 'community' and 'class'. 'Ethnicity' and 'community' are often used as synonyms. It would seem to be an appropriate distinction to give 'community' a spatial dimension, even if the spatial boundaries of a community are not always absolutely clear and might change over time. Consciousness of belonging to a community has both a real and imagined component in my use of the term. The real component is provided through occupational, kinship and neighbourly ties so that members of a community can have a real rather than purely imagined sense of knowing many, if not all, other members. But there is an element of imagination involved in turning such ties or knowledge into a sense of community, in converting community-in-itself into community-for-itself, so to speak. Some members of a community might be particularly responsible for doing so, to, for instance, defuse potential conflict along class lines. As Belinda Bozzoli has pointed out, a sense of community has often been strengthened in the South African context by an external 'hostile environment'.[7]

Imagination is also a part of class consciousness, but I will use the term 'class' in both the objective and subjective senses of 'class-in-itself' and 'class-for-itself'. I will categorise people according to my perception of their relationship to the means of production, and thereby to one another. But it will be assumed that class only exists as a social identity when people so categorised become aware, in historical situations, of those relationships.

Two other terms central to my analysis and arguments are 'racialisation' and 'racism'. 'Racialisation' I use to describe the process whereby meaning is attached to real or imagined biological and heritable difference in human beings, to 'race'. Often such difference is perceived in lightness or darkness of pigmentation – 'colour'. Sense of belonging to a race is one manifestation of ethnicity. I use 'racial' as a synonym for 'racialised'. 'Racism' occurs when signification attached to difference is predominantly negative. Racialisation and racism can occur whether or not the term 'race' is actually used in elite or popular discourse.[8]

All group identities and their corollary, categorisation of others, are highly situational. Context is crucial. Therefore this book needs to explain Cape Town as a place, needs to be a work of urban history. As such it combines the approaches that Checkland foresaw as dominating the future of this sub-discipline: analysing a city's function; exploring themes such as the economic, social, governmental, spatial and perceptual; but doing so within a focus on a particular city, itself seen within 'grand processes' such as industrialisation and in relation to other cities held to belong to (and differ from) the same 'category'.[9] In providing what one might call an urban profile of Cape Town, it is hoped that this will be useful for comparative purposes with similar studies that exist for both colonial and non-colonial cities within and outside southern Africa.

This book, then, is an exploration of group identities – their causes, contents and practical consequences – within a history of Cape Town. The organising question remains to what extent Cape Town really was an exceptional place in southern Africa in its 'tradition of multi-racialism' and, if so, why? Fredrickson offered an answer to the second part of this question. He argued that a combination of the 'notorious permeability of the colour line' with a 'certain tolerance of miscegenation' had made segregated public accommodation 'not only contrary to local traditions but impracticable'. For Fredrickson the presence of the political and legal Cape liberal tradition, and the absence of Black 'institutional parallelism', explain the lack of segregation in the Cape in general compared to other parts of southern Africa or the American South.[10]

Unfortunately Fredrickson seriously underestimated the extent of segregation in the city before 1948. De facto segregation existed in many amenities, social activities and institutions between 1875 and 1902. Fredrickson's explanation of the 'special tradition' is anyway logically flawed. The existence of the 'notorious permeability of the colour line' was certainly used on occasions to explain why segregation in Cape Town was, or would be, difficult to attain. It probably does help to explain why de jure segregation was delayed in education and some government institutions in the city. But this permeability ultimately did not prevent the introduction of comprehensive segregation in Cape Town by the second half of the twentieth century.

'Contrary to local traditions' explains everything and nothing. It begs the question of why those local traditions existed in the first place. And the Cape liberal tradition did not stop the Native Reserve Location Act of 1902 giving de jure weight to African residential segregation, or the School Board Act of 1905 doing the same for education. As we shall demonstrate, Black 'parallel institutions' did come into being in late nineteenth-century Cape Town.

So we are left wondering why segregation in the city lagged behind the rest of South Africa, and why it took on different forms in different places? I will argue in subsequent chapters that the nature of economic activity and consequent employment patterns in Cape Town, and how this changed over time and differed from other parts of South Africa, is a crucial part of the answer. So is the relationship between ethnicity and divisions of labour in different places, and the timing of outbreaks of war and disease. In the case of cities, function and geographical location could also affect the extent and nature of segregation.[11] As was the case in the American South, so could chronological origins, because 'older towns possessed pre-existing racial patterns that altered more slowly', that could, perhaps, only be altered at considerable expense.[12]

This still leaves the question of why segregation became such an increasingly important feature of Cape Town, and southern African, society between 1875 and 1902. The debate about the origins of segregation dominated South African historiography in the 1970s and early 1980s, and has been described in Harrison Wright's *Burden of the Present*.[13] According to Wright, 'radicals' (typically neo-Marxist revisionists) attacked what they perceived to be the 'liberal' orthodoxy: that economic growth associated with capitalist development was inimical to segregation and vice versa.

The radicals argued that the growth of segregation had served the specific needs of capitalism in South Africa. For them Apartheid ceased to be the economically illogical legacy of the frontier, the creation of Afrikaner nationalism, of the alleged liberal scenario. Instead, intensified racism, culminating in Apartheid, came with discovery of diamonds (1867) and gold (1886): the Mineral Revolution. An ethnic division of labour and segregation were in the interests of, and therefore promoted by, the mining magnates of Kimberley and the Rand. Consequently, from the late nineteenth century, legislation was passed which accomplished two aims. It destroyed the economic independence of African peasant producers so that their labour could be available for, and hyper-exploited by, mine owners, farmers and industrialists. Second, it provided for institutions and practices in South African cities that created an ethnically divided labour force and, specifically, a high degree of control over African labour.

By the mid-1980s, both liberals and radicals had shied away from maintaining that either ethnicity (more often called 'race' in the literature) or class had played the primary role in bringing about segregation.[14] However, Fredrickson, for instance, still saw as crucial the role of 'traditional' attitudes in influencing the response of employers of labour in the era of the Mineral Revolution. Without their inherited prejudices, employers would have 'hired the best individuals for the job regardless of their ancestry'. In contrast, John Cell, while acknowledging the role of 'tradition', argued that it was mining capital that brought about the significantly new institutions of segregation in the late nineteenth century. A further purpose of this book is to examine the relationship between ideology and social practice for Cape Town.[15]

However, it is possible to discern a new and improved analysis of the origins of segregation in South Africa gradually emerging from the dialectic between liberals and radicals. This analysis acknowledges the existence of racism before the Mineral Revolution, in the slave-owning Cape and the constitutions and social practices of the Afrikaner Republics, and the contribution of 'scientific' views about race towards its intensification thereafter. Kimberley was the place where crucial features of urban segregation arose: the labour registration office, migrant labour controlled via a pass system and the labour compound.[16]

Shula Marks, following David Welsh, emphasised the 'rural dimensions of segregation' offered by Natal:

the allocation of reserved lands vested in a Trust for purely African occupation; the control of urban immigration through the registration of casual labour; the use of the Governor as Supreme Chief; the 'recognition' of African customary law; the manipulation of chiefs as agents of the colonial state.[17]

These long-enduring features of segregation were not just invented and imposed by the Natal ruling class, let alone Transvaal mine owners. Nor were they necessarily functional to capital.[18] Instead, they substantially reflected the very real existence of African societies 'with their own traditions and geographical base', whose members could, and did, attempt to resist incorporation or assimilation into colonial society.[19]

Most recently, and in not dissimilar vein, Clifton Crais has offered the Eastern Cape's contribution to segregation. He has showed that it produced colonial Africa's first 'native reserves', passes for 'native foreigners' and earlier urban locations than those of the mining centres. He has powerfully reaffirmed that social relations on the frontier, as well as under slavery, generated racism.[20]

There are still many gaps. They include the absence of a major study on any of the towns of the Cape, *sans* Kimberley, in the nineteenth century: one more reason for this book.

The point is that many parts of what was to become South Africa, including Cape Town, practised forms of segregation in the nineteenth-century and generated racism. They can all, correctly, be offered as providing precedents for aspects of the ideology and practice of Apartheid. But seeking a single origin for twentieth-century practice has been, and would be, a misguided exercise. Equally, different manifestations of segregation, or its extent and limitations, can only be explained by detailed histories of different places. Hence the need for a monograph. Segregation, and racist discourses, were situational, even if they could and did inform one another.

Saul Dubow has convincingly argued that 'segregation' did not become a 'keyword' in the discourse of South African politicians until the twentieth century. He suggests that one of the first occasions it was used was when the Governor opened the Cape parliament in 1902. Sir Walter Hely-Hutchinson said that the government should be 'endowed with larger powers than they now possess to effectively carry out the policy of segregation'.[21]

As with the American South, the precise chronological origins of this ideology in nineteenth-century South Africa have hitherto been obscure.

This monograph attempts to trace and explains its emergence in Cape Town by the 1890s, even if 'separation' rather than 'segregation' was the 'keyword'. Without, I hope, falling prey to the 'idol of origins', I will seek at the same time to demonstrate that in South Africa, as in the American South, Jim Crow was a 'city slicker'.[22] In other words the Separate Amenities Act legalised many practices that had been extant in Cape Town since the nineteenth century, as they had been in other southern African cities.

These practices grew, and came to interact with an ideology of racial separation, in the course of the economic and social changes wrought by the Mineral Revolution. This begins to explain the chronological starting-point of this study. The major diamond discoveries at Kimberley in 1870 were beginning to have a dramatic effect on Cape Town's economy. The information contained in the Cape government census of 1875 is extremely useful in giving a picture of economic activity and social structure at the advent of this change.

During the Mineral Revolution, Cape Town's merchants and businessmen, her dominant class, moved closer to the social practices of their northern counterparts. They did so because they were forced to come to terms with economic and demographic change on a hitherto unprecedented scale. The problems they faced were similar to those that confronted Wiebe's 'middle-class' Americans at roughly the same time: how to maintain social order in a society undergoing rapid urbanisation, immigration and industrialisation. The latter, together with the enhanced possibilities of social mobility, combined to challenge the 'traditional system' of social relations in Cape Town: dominance of White over Black.[23] They found their answer in forms of segregation.

Mirroring a similar development described by Andrews for Buenos Aires, it was during economic booms, rather than depressions, that the challenge was most severe.[24] In consequence it was during the boom years from 1875 to 1882, and especially 1891 to 1902, that new forms of segregation generated within the city were most in evidence. In contrast, Van Onselen has shown for Johannesburg that depression years were more significant in this respect because they led to poor Whites demanding differential state intervention on their behalf.[25] In the 1880s depression in Cape Town the poor united across potential ethnic divides. But the depression helped to change dominant-class attitudes to poverty and the poor. It led many to make distinctions on the basis of racialisation and racism, and thereby promoted the ideology of racial separation.

Dominant-class consciousness in Cape Town in 1875 was informed by White (or 'European') ethnicity. But there was little attempt to separate

Whites from Blacks throughout society. The forms of segregation that existed demonstrated and preserved the power of the dominant class. They did not emphasise White ethnic solidarity across potential class divides.

By 1902, ethnic solidarities that did cut across class divisions tended to be of greater significance than they had been in 1875. English and Afrikaner ethnicity now had meaning for many Capetonians in this respect. So did African ethnicity for those forced into locations in 1901 because they were 'natives'. And in 1902 an organisation was formed to defend the 'Coloured People's social, political and civil rights'.[26]

Ethnicity did not simply replace other forms of group identity. Class and community consciousness continued to interact with and occasionally subsume ethnicity. Working-class and occupational consciousness had their salient moments between 1875 and 1902, and beyond. In the 1880s, for instance, there were several demonstrations and strikes jointly embraced by workers of different potential ethnicities. Some artisan trade unions had White and Coloured members in the 1890s and 1900s. And there was still 'multi-racial' social activity for Evans to witness in 1911.

Writing about group identity and social practice in Cape Town does not mean that we can ignore 'rural dimensions', or what was happening in mining centres. On the contrary, it is only by analysing the connections between the different sectors of the Cape's political economy that it is possible to understand what was happening in Cape Town. Only then does it become clear why the city was indeed an 'exceptional' place in southern Africa in some respects, but so similar in others.

2   The world that commerce made

Cape Town, in 1875, was the capital of Britain's Cape Colony. The British had granted Responsible Government to the Cape only three years earlier, in 1872. The Cape, through conquest and annexation, now extended to the Orange River in the north and the Kei River in the east. The predominantly rural population numbered around 720,000, divided into about 236,000 Whites and 484,000 'coloureds' by the census enumerators. The economic activity that employed the vast majority was farming, either pastural or agricultural.[1]

Located on the Cape Peninsula, Cape Town was still small compared to places such as Melbourne or Buenos Aires, if larger than any other city in southern Africa. Cape Town had a population of some 45,000 people. Thirty-three thousand of these lived in the municipality of Cape Town, contained within a natural amphitheatre of approximately six-and-a-half square miles, formed and dominated by Table Mountain and Signal Hill.

In the sixteenth century the Table Bay area, relatively flat and well watered, had been a place of barter between the Peninsula's Khoisan inhabitants and the crews of ships passing between Europe and the East Indies.[2] In establishing a settlement at the Bay in 1652, the directors of the Dutch East India Company (DEIC) were primarily concerned to maintain the *status quo ante*. The settlers' and Khoisan's failure to achieve this aim has been well documented, and led to the inexorable growth of a Dutch colony at the Cape, complete with imported slaves as well as subjugated Khoisan.[3]

In this process the settlement in Table Valley, Cape Town, continued to serve first and foremost as a trading centre between land and sea, between hinterland and port, port and passing ships. The extent of such trade underpinned the economic and demographic fortunes of the town. Demographic expansion, in turn, increased opportunities for retail and manufacture for local consumption. The town's economy also drew nourishment from Cape Town's further roles as administrative capital and military headquarters, and the concomitant expenditure.[4]

Table 1 *Approximate population of major towns in the Cape Colony, 1806-1904*

	Cape Town	Port Elizabeth	East London	Kimberley	Colony Total
1806	16,000	—	—	—	75,000
1865	27,000	11,300	—	—	470,000
1875	45.000	13,000	2,000	13,600	720,000
1891	79,000	23,000	7,000	29,000	1,500,000
1904	170,000	33,000	24,000	34,000	2,400,000

Based on censuses of the Cape Colony for these years and Ross, 'Synthesis', p. 107.

Although the Cape's economy was by no means stagnant under the Dutch, it was under the British that the Cape was for the first time brought within the ambit of a powerful industrialising economy. The British had both the inclination and the ability to change the nature and capacity of colonial production, with the consequent implications for the accumulation of capital and urbanisation in the new colony. KhoiKhoi labour, under the Dutch reduced to serf status, was made more mobile and responsive to market forces by 1828. Slavery was abolished in 1834 and the ex-slave apprentices freed four years later.[5] Yet for economic growth, for the growth of Cape Town and other places of exchange to take place, there needed to be more than a transformation in conditions of production. The Cape had still to find the product or products that the world market required.

One such product seemed, by the 1840s, to be wool. The rapid rise of British demand for wool took place between 1840 and 1870, and with it a rise in the price of that commodity. Cape merchants and farmers responded by concentrating their attention on the possibilities of maximising this new source of profit.[6]

From the point of view of Cape Town merchants, the problem was that Port Elizabeth and East London, founded by the British, had developed as rivals in competing for expanding agricultural output. Geographical determinism should have ensured that Cape Town was eclipsed as the midlands and Eastern Cape, the logical hinterlands of the other two ports, became the heartlands of wool production. Indeed logic seemed to be winning the day as Port Elizabeth's exports, chiefly wool, took premier position over those of any other Cape port in 1854.[7]

Despite this challenge, Cape Town retained its commercial pre-eminence in the late nineteenth century. This was partly made possible by the town's function as seat of government. Cape Town's mercantile elite (organised since 1822 in a commercial exchange) were at something of an advantage compared to Port Elizabeth's when competing for the favours of the colonial state. Representative Government, granted in 1853, accentuated the advantage. For electoral purposes, it divided the Colony into two sections, east and west, giving the Western Cape, and thus Cape Town, a majority of seats in the legislature.

Responsible Government, in 1872, brought in two-tier government in the form of a Legislative Council and a House of Assembly. Constituencies for the lower house, the House of Assembly, were more akin to those in Britain. After 1874 a simple east versus west divide was further diffused when seven electoral provinces were established as constituencies for the Legislative Council. In addition, competition between East London and Port Elizabeth merchants, particularly over railway building, led to their mutual inability to counter dominant western interests.

Thus Cape Town's infrastructure continued to receive the bulk of government expenditure in the late nineteenth century. It was Cape Town rather than its rivals that secured government money, in part gleaned from Port Elizabeth's enlarged custom, to build a proper harbour between 1860 and 1870. This harbour continued to attract large sums from the government for further improvements until the severe depression of the 1900s.[8] With Cape Town remaining the first port of call for ships on their way to southern Africa from Europe, such expenditure and facilities gave the economy of the town a sound foundation in the late nineteenth century.

But continued government money, and the continued economic well-being of the town, depended very largely on the southern African interior continuing to provide a product that could be successfully marketed overseas. By 1869, after several years of severe economic depression, considerable doubts had been raised in financial circles about the ability of wool to maintain an export-led growth of the colonial economy. Such doubts were dispelled by major diamond discoveries at what became Kimberley in 1870, after initial smaller finds in 1867. The first stage of the Mineral Revolution paved the way for Responsible Government. Both these developments led to the growth of a sophisticated colonial infrastructure.[9]

Between 1873 and 1883 more than 1,000 miles of railway and 7,000 miles of telegraph were constructed. For reasons outlined above, Cape Town's interests were well served by the nature of the resulting network (see map 1). Her effective hinterland was massively increased. In addition, the Cape government spent almost £1,000,000 on improving Cape Town's harbour, compared to the £500,000 and £300,000 expended on East London's and Port Elizabeth's respectively. Thanks also to a special fast-train service, Cape Town by the early 1880s became the main port of entry for the escalating number of passengers to the interior. After initial overspeculation, over-trading and a minor recession in 1876–7, Cape Town merchants were enjoying unprecedented prosperity by the end of the decade.[10]

When the British took over the Cape in 1806 they had inherited a still-small capital of 16,000 people, the only sizeable urban centre in an overwhelmingly rural colony of 75,000. Cape Town's inhabitants were housed in a cluster of buildings between what had been the DEIC's vegetable garden, an aid to the provisioning of passing ships, and Table Bay. The rest of the amphitheatre was occupied by sizeable estates or left unsettled. A few hamlets, future suburbs of Cape Town, lay behind and to the south of the mountain, sandwiched between the latter and an area of sand dunes and marshes, the Cape Flats.[11]

The demographic growth of Cape Town under British rule was steady if undramatic before 1875. The population of the town itself had, after all, only doubled by this date. Yet the composition of the population had undergone some significant changes. In 1806 there was a two-way division of Capetonians into approximately 7,000 free and 9,000 slaves. The former group, predominantly Dutch or German in origin, also included other European immigrants as well as about 1,400 freed slaves and KhoiKhoi. The majority of the slaves, many of whom were Muslims, were from the East, from the area of company activity in the Indies, and from Madagascar and Mozambique. By the late eighteenth century a high proportion were from Africa. At the beginning of the nineteenth century about half the slave population had been born within the colony.[12]

Between 1806 and 1875 the natural increase of this population would appear to have been retarded by three factors: the negative rate of slave reproduction, the sale of Cape Town slaves to the hinterland and frequent severe epidemics.[13] On the other hand, Cape Town's demographic growth gained by migration from elsewhere in southern Africa, and immigration from overseas. To begin with, besides heralding the arrival of their merchants and civil servants, British control of the Cape brought the importation of several thousand 'Prize Negroes', freed from slave ships after 1807. Their numbers were supplemented by the voluntary arrival of workers from Europe, particularly from Britain. Cape Town's population was further bolstered by permanent or seasonal migration of KhoiKhoi, freed slaves and, if to a lesser extent, Africans from the Eastern Cape.[14]

Much of the Cape Peninsula was still being cultivated in 1875. Yet the built-up areas were steadily increasing. Within Cape Town itself, close settlement moved beyond the castle to the east and towards Green Point in the west, into areas that became known as Districts Six and One respectively. Houses crept beyond Buitengracht street and were just beginning the assault on the slopes of Signal Hill. Building had also commenced to the south of the DEIC's gardens, into an area that took its name from the latter (see map 2).[15] The very centre of Cape Town, the Adderley/St George's street area, was in the process of being abandoned as a place of residence and becoming the commercial centre of the city. Shops, warehouses, banks and insurance offices stood as monuments to the God that had created them, merchant capital.[16]

Since 1806 those hamlets to the south of Cape Town had become suburban villages. This development had been facilitated by something of a transport revolution just before the slump of the 1860s. A railway line, built by private capital, reached as far as Wynberg in the south by 1864 and was backed up by a tramway service. The latter also linked Cape Town to Sea Point by 1863 (see map 3). Spread along a fourteen-mile line from Sea Point in the west to Wynberg in the south-east, these suburbs, more *rus* than *urbs*, contained 12,000 people.[17]

All the descriptions by British visitors to Cape Town in the 1870s agree on the city's beautiful physical setting. All agreed that, architecturally, the place looked like an old colonial Dutch town: low, whitewashed buildings with flat roofs and raised *stoeps* (verandas). Less flatteringly, the British novelist, Anthony Trollope, summed up many visitors' accounts and inhabitants' reminiscences of Cape Town in this decade when he described it as 'somewhat ragged'. The streets were unclean and the line of pavements was broken, partly the fault of the *stoeps*. As one Capetonian reminisced fifty years later:

Each street was an almost impassable morass in winter, and a desert of sand and small pebbles in summer, providing effective ammunition for the violent south-easters that bombarded the innocent inhabitants with all the fury of modern machine guns.[18]

In contrast, unreserved praise was heaped upon the city's suburbs. As one visitor put it:

The suburbs of the city are exceedingly beautiful, and here many of the principal inhabitants have built elegant mansions, to which they retire after the business of each day to escape the heat, dust and smells of the town.[19]

Few accounts ventured beyond the main thoroughfares and sylvan delights of the suburbs, to describe the poorer and most densely inhabited parts of the city. One exception was an article that appeared in the *Cape Argus* in 1876. In the best tradition of slummer journalism, its

1 Adderley Street, 1875

author positively revelled in the details of filthy living conditions, poverty and overcrowding. Government select committee reports and census statistics bear out the substance of the article. The city's 33,000 residents were squeezed into under 4,000 houses, almost half of which were small, three rooms or less. The latter were inhabited chiefly by fishermen, artisans, labourers and their families.[20]

Any analysis of economic activity and social structure in Cape Town in 1875 must rely very heavily on the census of that year. Using the census presents a number of predictable problems. The individual returns no longer exist and there is no guarantee that they were entirely accurate. Apparently some Capetonians refused to give the full number of residents in their houses because they feared that the town council might act against 'overcrowding'. Others were wary that the census had tax implications, and therefore did not complete the returns. The council was in charge of collecting census returns.[21] Yet for all the potential pitfalls the 1875 census provides a useful picture of economic activity and social structure in Cape Town at the advent of the Mineral Revolution.[22]

Cape Town's economy in 1875, like that of Melbourne in the 1850s, was dominated by great mercantile firms. Cape Town's included W. Anderson & Co., Wilson & Glynn's and Barry & Nephews. Often dependent on credit from their parent houses or financial backers in England, these companies, granting lengthy credit in their turn, supported retailers serving farmers up country as well as in Cape Town itself. They also supplied the semi-finished or raw materials used in Cape Town's industrial production. In addition many of these wholesale merchants were involved in exporting agricultural commodities, chiefly wool, ostrich feathers, wine and brandy. As a result they were obviously vulnerable to a fall in the international price of these commodities. Moreover they would be hit as farmers' incomes dropped, the latter bought less imports and repayment of credit was delayed all along the line.[23]

The power of these merchants, who numbered about 150 individuals, within Cape Town's economic system was enhanced by their control over local banks, as shareholders and directors. Flush with funds in the early 1870s, Cape Town's mercantile elite invested principally in diamond and insurance shares (they controlled the local insurance companies), which in turn became securities for further bank loans and extensions of their business enterprises after 1875. Investment in residential property appears to have been pursued by the older mercantile families such as the Wichts, who owned 12 per cent of the housing stock before the big building boom of the late 1870s. Despite the dominance of merchant capital within Cape Town's social formation, wholesale merchants directly employed well under 1,000 people, as clerks, accountants or storemen. But the extent of economic activity within the city was inextricably linked to the success or failure of their business ventures.[24]

The retailers of Cape Town and its suburbs came in many shapes and sizes. Some were, as will become evident, the heirs apparent to the dominant position of the wholesalers. Others were not so much of bourgeois class, let alone grand bourgeois, as lumpen proletarians, hawkers and pedlars. Apart from differences of class, retailers could be distinguished typologically. There were 500 who retailed the imported goods of the wholesale merchants and might be directly indebted, literally, to the latter for their start in business. Slightly fewer retailed locally produced food and drink. Such butchers, fishmongers and so on were not directly dependent on the importers for credit or supply of goods and could purchase their wares from fishermen or farmers.

Serving the needs of merchants and retailers, if not actually in their employ, were those people involved in the transportation of goods, or in facilitating their transportation. The 500 individuals obviously in this category ranged from dock officials through to watermen and messengers. But this figure does not appear to have included day labourers employed at the docks in various capacities, and who were presumably numbered in the census among general labourers. The Harbour Board employed, on average, over 100 labourers on maintenance and construction (alongside about 200 convicts). Several hundred more must have been employed in stevedoring and as dock labourers.[25]

Cape Town's demographic expansion, which had increased opportunities for retail, had a similar effect on local industrial activity: overwhelmingly, if not exclusively, the production of food, drink, clothing and shelter. The nature of such production was partly determined by the ability of the wholesale merchants to import finished, or semi-finished, goods into a colony whose low tariffs on such commodities they unsurprisingly supported. To make matters more difficult for putative industrialists, duty still had to be paid on raw materials.

These factors, together with Cape Town's distance from any cheap fuel deposits, meant that factory production was in its infancy. Those factories that did exist were few, small, with minimal mechanisation and thus low in capital value. They produced a motley array of articles such as soap, candles, snuff, biscuits or soda-water, requiring little labour or machinery. On only a slightly larger scale there were half a dozen or so printing, furniture, fishing-boat and coach-building establishments. Apparently an exception to the general pattern was the growing railway workshop at Salt River which became Cape Town's foremost industrial plant by the turn of the century. But this was owned by the Cape government and, at this stage, was confined to the reassembling of railway carriages built in England. Greatest private capital investment was probably in plant-processing of local agricultural products: breweries, distilleries, mills and tanneries. These were located on the Liesbeeck River between Observatory and Newlands in the southern suburbs.[26]

The local production of finished articles of clothing and footwear, when not actually undertaken by independent craftsmen, was seemingly characterised by the putting-out system and a low division of labour.[27] Employing just under 1,500 Capetonians, this was the city's most important industrial activity, ahead of building. The building industry had at its head 34 people described in the census of 1875 as builders, who were presumably employers rather than workers. They could call on over 1,000 artisans, mainly carpenters, masons and painters. These artisans were, in slack times, available to Cape Town's other major industry, fishing.

Only 280 Capetonians described themselves as fishermen to the census enumerators. Yet 245 fishing vessels were active from Table Bay, each of which took, on average, five men. This anomaly is explained by a government report of 1892, which stressed that the structure of the industry had not changed significantly since the 1870s:

In regard to the fishermen themselves, those at Kalk Bay and at places distant from towns usually adopt that calling when young and follow it all their lives; but in Cape Town many of the men are ... half carpenters, masons, or coolies who only go out fishing when they cannot get other work, and even when fishing pays best they frequently prefer to remain on shore lest they be unable to obtain employment when the fish are scarce.[28]

Certainly those fishermen operating from Rogge Bay, where the town met the sea, considered scarcity of fish the norm except in the 'snoek season'. This lasted, roughly, from the end of October to the beginning of February. Only during these months could they save money.[29]

Altogether 12,500 Capetonians were in paid employment in 1875 according to the census, about 7,500 men and 5,000 women. Six thousand people were employed in commerce, the professions and the production of goods. Slightly more, some 6,500, were either labourers whose precise employment was undefined or were in the service industries. Approximately 4,000 of the latter were in domestic service, while another 1,000 were washerwomen and a couple of hundred were employed in hotels, lodging or coffee houses. There were a further 5,400 people in domestic service who received no pay: those listed as housewives.

What was said about fishing and its relationship with the building industry begins to demonstrate the imprecise division of labour in Cape Town's employment pattern. This imprecision is also apparent in dock work, with no simple division of labour between stevedores and those who worked on shore. This was due to the particular system of loading, landing and delivery of goods employed at Cape Town docks. The docks were under the authority of the Table Bay Harbour Board, established by the government. Loading and unloading from ships to quay was either undertaken by the ship's crew or by a landing agent appointed by the Board's dock superintendent. Labourers working for landing agents performed a variety of tasks not necessarily confined to the harbour itself. This was because landing agents doubled up as dock agents appointed by the merchants to move goods from town to harbour or vice versa, work which landing agents *per se* were not allowed to undertake according to Harbour Board regulations.[30]

One of the few clear divisions of labour was between men's work and women's. Women's work, almost exclusively, involved keeping homes clean; making, mending and washing of clothes; and nursing or teaching of children. In other words it involved them in supportive, if not always directly subordinate, roles to men's. The occupational areas that offered women the best chance of more remunerative and potentially independent employment were shop, hotel or boarding-house keeping. But it is safe to say that women's work was generally paid less than men's.[31]

Seasonality and casual employment characterised the Cape Town labour market, as they did that of London in the late nineteenth century, themselves reducing rigidity in patterns of employment. Seasonality, in the form of the weather, obviously affected both the fishing and building industries.[32] In terms of the supply of raw materials, seasonality would also have affected the production of finished goods: the tailoring industry might wait upon the arrival of cloth from Europe; baking, milling or confectionery on the incoming harvest. Fluctuations in production presumably also occurred due to fluctuating consumer demands, for instance before and after the Christmas holiday. It would seem as though employment possibilities were at their peak between about mid-October and mid-February. This was only partly due to the fact that this period covered the dry, snoek and Christmas seasons. Harvest time in the city's hinterland, besides meaning the supply of agricultural produce referred to, also meant employment opportunities in the countryside.[33]

Casual employment was closely linked to seasonality. An employer could attempt to adjust the size of his labour force to his exact requirements when 'the supply of labour was plentiful or the proportion of fixed capital was insignificant'. Thus, if these conditions existed, an employer could react to seasonal or even shorter-term fluctuations in demand. Dock agents, master builders, and many other employers using a proportion of unskilled or semi-skilled labour constantly would want, and might be able, to adjust the size of their workforces. Those casually unemployed in the process would, failing all else, have to scrape a bare living from such residual occupations as shell gathering or rag-and-bone picking. Shebeen, or illegal canteen, running and prostitution were other possibilities in this harbour town. But precisely the fact that such activities were defined by the state as illegal undermined their ability to bring greater security to working-class lives. So did the expensive fees attached to the practice of many legal occupations.[34]

Because of the lack of clarity of the 1875 census categories, it is difficult to delineate Cape Town's social structure in class terms with the kind of precision that Foster used in his study of three nineteenth-century English cities.[35] With the absence of comprehensive research on marriage patterns or friendship groups, and only partial evidence on the wealth of some Capetonians, the task is made even more difficult. The line between grand and petty bourgeois, for instance, must perforce remain somewhat blurred. Yet, while recognising the truth in Engels' statement, one can do a little better than merely stating that Cape Town experienced 'the division of society into innumerable gradations'.[36]

Undoubtedly to be counted among Cape Town's grand bourgeoisie, those who helped form the city's social elite, were many, if not most, of the wholesale merchants and their families. These men belonged to firms with tens of thousands of pounds in capital, and were often extremely wealthy in their own right. In terms of wealth, Cape Town's grand bourgeoisie also included a number of identifiable industrialists and retailers. Although this prematurely raises the question of group consciousness, leading civil servants receiving generous annual incomes of £1,000 or so can also be included among the grand bourgeoisie. So can some professionals and retired individuals of substance.[37]

Foster defined petty bourgeois as including both tradesmen and 'little masters' while excluding 'non-bourgeois' (but also non-manual) occupations such as 'small shopkeepers and clerks'. According to Foster, the latter formed a massive 'social tail' to the bourgeoisie of Northampton and Shields, yet, politically at least, identified with Oldham's working class.[38] Geoffrey Crossick, in contrast, defined the petty bourgeoisie as consisting of 'small producers' and 'shopkeepers'.[39] In the absence of better statistics, Cape Town's petty bourgeoisie and non-manual workers are not easily distinguished or quantified. Instead of accepting Foster's distinction between what he defined as the petty bourgeoisie and its social tail, one would wish to dub both as petty bourgeois and include in their ranks the likes of hotel keepers, minor professionals and commercial travellers. If we do so, then the occupations of over 3,000 Capetonians clearly fall into either the grand or petty bourgeoisie categories. Yet, this is, equally clearly, an underestimate of the total number. Several hundred more must have existed among those broadly classified as artisans.

The 'social tail' to our petty bourgeoisie could be said to come from those unidentifiable number of Capetonians who were self-employed workers. These included cab owner/drivers and independent craftsmen. There were also 1,000 Capetonians who lived solely 'by fish'. Although fishing may have provided residual employment for many artisans, there seems to have been a hard core of fishermen and their families who did nothing else but catch, cure and sell fish.

Lastly, there were the manual workers. This group ranged from skilled to residual occupations, from engineers through to shell gatherers. The vast majority were, as we have argued, part of a large casual labour force. Only the highly skilled, such as the engineers, could hope to escape such casualisation. Even a large number of railway workers at Salt River were not on the 'fixed establishment'.[40]

The class position of Capetonians, as outlined in my rather crude categorisation, did not translate in any simple or automatic way into class consciousness. Among the majority of workers this is hardly surprising, given the nature of the labour market and imprecise divisions of labour. There is little evidence of workers articulating or demonstrating even occupational group consciousness through organisation or strikes in the mid-1870s.[41] Only with increased economic activity, industrialisation and a more complex and rigid division of labour – all consequences of the Mineral Revolution – did these become a frequent part of Cape Town life.

One exception is provided by fishermen. But among them sense of occupational solidarity was informed by community.[42] Many fishermen and their families lived in the crowded lanes near Rogge Bay. We know the words of a couple of songs popular in the community. One, which speaks of the difficulties facing fishermen, began:

> There are few bokkoms [pieces of dried fish] left on the line
> The fish is scarce and Batoe Gila [a spirit]
> Haunts the waters of the Bay.
> What shall we do about this wind
> That keeps on blowing?[43]

Fishermen fought for the preservation of their way of life, and thereby for the preservation of their community, when fish-curing at Rogge Bay

2 Selling fish at Rogge Bay

was threatened by municipal and central government interference in the late 1870s. Leadership was provided by a literate and relatively wealthy fish-curer, Jongie Siers. The occupational solidarity of fishermen might also have been enhanced by ethnicity: the sense of common origins as emancipated slaves. Siers wrote in one petition to the town council in 1878:

We were alway under the impression that we were emancipated in the reign of our most Gracious Majesty Queen Victoria, and freed from tyranny, but it seems that we are mistaken.[44]

Another group of workers who would appear to have had occupational identity were washerwomen. Such identity was enhanced by the isolation of what had become their traditional workplace, Platteklip Gorge, above the city on the slopes of Table Mountain. Kennedy saw the women 'washing clothes, banging them on the rocks, and scrubbing them with husks of Indian corn' over a distance of a mile and a half up the stream. Again suggesting a shared sense of slave origin, on 1 December each year (the anniversary of emancipation), 'the washer-women of Platteklip made merry with song and dance under the trees'.[45]

Class position which interacted with ethnicity more certainly translated into class consciousness for most of Cape Town's bourgeoisie. The major divide in the racialised categories of the 1875 census was between 'White and European' and 'Other than White or European'. According to these categories the vast majority of Cape Town's bourgeoisie fell into the former. Cape Town's total population was divided into 25,567 'Europeans or Whites' and 19,236 'Other than Europeans or Whites'. Among the bourgeoisie, census enumerators counted 2,988 Whites and only 316 people deemed to be 'Other than White'. When looking more closely at the latter, the socially successful become even paler.

Two-thirds of this section of the bourgeoisie were retailers. Most of them retailed agricultural foodstuffs (including fish), and their businesses were likely to have been small. Among the other third only one was described simply as a merchant. Many of the rest fell into clearly petty-bourgeois occupations with the exception of twelve 'Malay clergymen' and twelve teachers. There was only one 'Other than White' doctor out of thirty in Cape Town.

Allowing for the few exceptions noted above, Cape Town's grand bourgeoisie, more or less completely, and her petty bourgeoisie overwhelmingly, were White. Moreover it was the lower ranks of this combined bourgeoisie that contained the vast majority of those classified as 'Other than White'. In addition Whites owned the vast majority of property in Cape Town.[46]

Political as well as economic power was a White prerogative. The Governor of the Cape Colony, as well as central and local government legislators in the city, were White. The upper echelons of the civil service, the imperial and colonial defence forces as well as the Cape Town police were also the monopoly of Whites, according to the census.

In Cape Town, as in the Cape Colony as a whole, economic or political power could be perceived to be associated with Whiteness by those who possessed both. White ethnicity, based on the presumption of shared European ancestry and cultural heritage, served to unite bourgeois Capetonians across potential divisions of language, Christian denomination or individual economic interest. The synonym of 'White' was 'European'. White or European ethnicity obscured actual differences of ancestry or geographical origin. In fact at least some people who came to be accepted as Europeans also had African or Asian origins, or had slave or KhoiKhoi antecedents. A Dutch-language newspaper in Cape Town, *Het Volksblad*, conceded in 1876 that 'many people slightly but still unmistakably off-coloured have made their way into the higher ranks of society and are freely admitted to respectable situations and intermarriage with respectable families'.[47] In doing so they 'passed' for White. As Fredrickson put it:

> The Coloreds [sic] who were most likely to 'make it as white' in the late nineteenth century were those who both came close to a not very exacting notion of European appearance and had some degree of wealth or education.[48]

Sitongo, a novel published in 1884, concerned a man descended from the 'mixed marriage' of an African chief to a 'White lady'. In Cape Town he passed himself off as a German music professor, a Herr von Lutz, to gain (successfully) access to 'the higher ranks of society'. The fact that the author, J. D. Ensor, felt Sitongo *could* do so says something about the indistinct nature of the colour line in Cape Town. The fact that Ensor felt Sitongo *had* to do so helps to confirm the opinion that White ethnicity was part of the consciousness of belonging to the city's dominant class in Cape Town.[49]

From the work that exists on Cape Town's social structure at the time of emancipation it would seem as though White ethnicity had been part of dominant-class consciousness then, and for the same reasons. By the 1870s the correlation of Whiteness with economic and political power could be seen by their possessors to be based on a 'traditional system' of ethnic relations in the city that had continued to support the possibility of such correlation in living memory.[50] But such traditions may have to be maintained in different historical circumstances by new as well as old methods. Increasingly important in the course of the nineteenth century was the segregation of social institutions in which Blacks might have challenged the 'traditional system'.[51]

The Dutch Reformed Church (DRC) had been one of the first places in which such segregation was practised. Blacks were confined to the back pews of DRC churches in Cape Town as early as the late eighteenth century. Fredrickson has rightly warned against seeing the 'purely racial implications' of this development: 'It was no violation of normal Protestant practice to give the lowest social class the worst pews.'[52]

After emancipation, the DRC, Wesleyan and Methodist Churches established separate mission churches for ex-slaves and KhoiKhoi in town and countryside. By 1857, and under pressure from rural congregations, the DRC Synod had officially sanctioned such segregation in all its churches. Ethnic rather than class solidarity may have been a more important factor in promoting segregation outside the major urban centres. However, evidence suggests that colour, as in Cape Town, was perceived to coincide with class position: Whiteness with ownership of land or its management, Blackness with working it.[53]

By the mid-1870s, separate services for Whites and Blacks also existed for Anglican congregations in country towns such as Malmesbury and Swellendam. In the cathedral in Cape Town there would appear to have been a system of social exclusiveness close to eighteenth-century DRC practice. Meanwhile St Paul's Mission had been established in 1859 to cater for the emancipated and their descendants.[54]

Another group of institutions that witnessed almost total White bourgeois exclusiveness, in the years between emancipation and 1875, were the government non-denominational schools, established by the British in 1822. Consequently, by the 1860s, evidence to a commission of enquiry into Cape education stated:

We have two great classes of schools in this Colony, the Public schools and the Mission schools, which have practically become separate schools for the whites and the blacks; so that the Government is obliged to admit that the education of white and black children together is not practicable – on the whole, that is the case.[55]

Non-denominational schools, which taught a wide range of subjects including mathematics and history, received a government subsidy of £200. Mission schools, which taught only reading, writing and scripture, received £75.[56] Black and lower-class White children had to rely on mission school education or remain out of school, which many did. Education was expensive if required above the level of instruction in reading and writing offered in the mission schools.[57]

Few pupils not perceived to be White challenged the *de facto* Whites-only status of Government non-denominational schools. Within Cape Town a few 'off-coloured' pupils were admitted into these superior schools. This was probably in most cases because they possessed relatively light skins, and could 'pass' for White.[58]

However, it may also have happened because many bourgeois Whites, notably the Superintendant of Cape Education, Langham Dale, believed in principle that people categorised as 'Other than White' could acquire the benefits of European culture. In other words Blacks could become like Whites who were, whether this was explicitly stated or not, thought to be currently superior because of their possession of that culture. This transformation would happen through 'civilising' agencies such as schools, Christianity and hard work.

This belief in the potential equality of Blacks had prevailed among British administrators at the Cape, such as Attorney-General William Porter, in the course of the early nineteenth century. They had advocated policies based on this belief. The most notable were the colour-blind franchises (in 1853 and 1872) and technical equality of all before the law (after 1838). Together these policies have been dubbed the 'great tradition' of Cape liberalism by Stanley Trapido. The 'small tradition' consisted of local political constituency alliances between Whites and Blacks based on perceived mutual interests.[59]

Cape liberalism of both traditions was based on highly pragmatic considerations. The 'great tradition' was thought by its creators to be the best way of maintaining peace in the Cape Colony and of uniting the inhabitants across ethnic divides. Porter preferred to 'meet the Hottentot at the hustings, voting for his representative, than in the wilds with his gun upon his shoulder'.[60] The British Colonial Secretary, the Duke of Newcastle, said that his government wished to 'unite all the queen's subjects at the Cape, without distinction of class or colour, by one bond of loyalty and a common interest ... the exercise of political rights enjoyed by all alike would prove one of the best methods of attaining that end'.[61] Neither thought that the Black vote would be big enough to threaten White mercantile or property interests, despite the low franchise. Because of their general poverty, too few Blacks qualified for it. However enough did in several constituencies, such as Cape Town, for some White parliamentary candidates in those constituencies to seek their votes.

Both traditions of Cape liberalism gained support from merchants, businessmen and professionals in the main towns. Advocates of the great tradition of Cape liberalism have been called Cape liberals by historians, whether or not they accepted Blacks as their equals in practice. Most Cape liberals were probably what Fredrickson has described as 'evolutionary' racists.[62] In other words they racialised the Cape's population and believed in the superiority of European civilisation. Without agreeing on the time-scale involved, they believed that Blacks could change and become like Whites, and that such change was necessary for the economic development of the Colony. Education, labour and conversion to Christianity were thought to be the major agencies of change.

The logic of liberal ideology was that if Blacks did become like Whites they deserved equal treatment. In the meantime the superior social position of Whites in Cape society was both logical and desirable. If Blacks were not yet their social equals, and there was a close correlation between Whiteness and economic dominance before the Mineral Revolution, exclusionary segregation that appeared simply to protect social position was equally acceptable. The ideological foundations of Cape liberalism would only be seriously tested when Blacks in considerable numbers came to demand equal treatment according to its principles, and when this endangered White political as well as social supremacy.

Many White colonists, particularly farmers from the Eastern Cape frontier regions and the Western Cape *platteland* had opposed, and continued to oppose, the granting of the franchise to Blacks.[63] Farmers such as Robert Godlonton did not want equal treatment for Blacks because they saw this as against their interests as employers of Black labour or potential occupiers of Black-owned land. Consequently they did not believe in even theoretical Black equality; they were 'teleological' racists, who thought that money spent on educating Blacks in the same way as Whites was wasted, if not potentially dangerous.[64]

With Responsible Government in 1872, the British gave control of the Cape to White bourgeois colonists. Teleological or evolutionary racists among them naturally advocated different administrative policies towards Blacks. Differences in ideology and policies loosely coincided with economic and social cleavages between farmers and merchants, rural and urban dwellers, Afrikaans/Dutch and English speakers (with the notable exceptions of most Eastern Cape farmers).[65]

Many Whites in Cape Town, including those politicians and administrators who lived there, continued to be Cape liberals in the 1870s. Occasionally they expressed disapproval of fellow Whites who did not judge Blacks on merit, although merit was, of course, assessed according to their own bourgeois White values. Langham Dale expressed such disapproval in 1869 in a poem called 'Prejudice against Colour':

> 'Ne credo colori', the poet erst sang,
> Appearances ever delude;

But white is the hue, that to us is genteel.
The black one of course, is tabooed.
Jan Wit-Schyn he ranks with the favoured race,
Though conscience by vice is long sear'd.
What matter? He's truly veneer'd.
Poor Zwart-Kleur's an honest and truly good fellow
Fears, honours and humbly obeys;
But still, 'mid the fold of the black sheep, he's spurned,
'Tis colour, not merit, that pays.[66]

Langham Dale was not suggesting that 'Zwart-Kleur' was as yet his social equal. Zwart-Kleur was someone who feared, honoured and humbly obeyed, was implicitly a social inferior. What Langham Dale was criticising was the ethnic particularism of fellow dominant-class Whites which could make them prefer one social inferior rather than another just because he was a 'Wit-Schyn' like themselves.

Dale's poem suggests that most Whites did not judge Blacks on merit, even if they were Cape liberals. However in 1875 segregation in Cape Town, where it existed in institutions or facilities, operated as a class system that protected and emphasised White bourgeois status rather than an ethnic system that separated all Whites from all Blacks throughout society. *De facto* and *ad hoc* segregation sufficed to maintain in social practice the close correlation between Whiteness and bourgeois class position. Segregation symbolically protected this correlation. If it also prevented some Black Capetonians from gaining access to a resource such as better education, exclusionary segregation protected class position in a more practical way.

When it did not, when exclusionary segregation was absent, this was because administrators of an institution believed it was not necessary or was unaffordable. Lack of necessity could be the view of administrators who thought that few bourgeois Whites were likely to use the institution, be it a gaol or pauper hospital. Lack of necessity could also be the view of those liberal administrators who believed that some Blacks had qualified for equal treatment.

Segregation was not yet deployed to separate Whites from Blacks among the lower classes. One reason was that White poverty had yet to become the 'poor White question', the target of segregatory state action in the 1890s.[67] Segregation was also limited in the 1870s because of the interplay of economic activity and social structure in Cape Town. The city's grand bourgeoisie consisted of merchants, professionals, members of government and the civil service. Few of this elite directly employed Black labour, or any labour, in large quantities. Indeed, for many, experience of Black labour was confined to their positions as employers of domestic servants.

The Table Bay Harbour Board used large numbers of convicts in maintenance and construction. Stevedoring and dock labour employment was divided among a number of agents. Employers in the building industry required a mobile, fluctuating and closely available labour supply.

Not surprisingly then, there were few signs in 1870s Cape Town of a powerful employer class pushing for state intervention to bring about segregated labour institutions, as happened in Kimberley and Johannesburg. Cape Town's artisans were Black as well as White, a legacy of the skills acquired in the era of slavery. This, together with the permeability of the colour line and the imprecise nature of the division of labour within many occupational categories, meant that even an ethnic division of labour was far from rigid.

These considerations begin to explain the uniqueness of Cape Town's ethnic relations mentioned by Welsh and Fredrickson. Residential patterns generally appear to have followed the broad contours of class rather than ethnicity. If members of Cape Town's White dominant class lived in splendid isolation in villas in the suburbs, or even the Gardens, much of the poorer areas of Cape Town, as with New Orleans, were residentially integrated.[68] It seems probable that, by the mid-1870s, considerable numbers of Whites had found their way into mission schools. Kennedy visited the Presbyterian mission school and saw scholars who were 'English, Scotch, Dutch and coloured'. He listened to 'Well may the Boatie Row' being sung by a 'Dutch girl and a Malay'. We know that by 1885 there were 9,235 Whites in mission schools, compared to 12,358 in non-denominational schools.[69] By the 1890s, a high degree of mixing still characterised these schools in the major urban centres, in contrast to the virtual segregation in operation in smaller towns.

The lunatic asylum at Robben Island witnessed exclusionary segregation, but Whites and Blacks were not separated among the paupers and lepers there, nor among inmates of either the Old or New Somerset hospitals. Juries were mixed and those they sentenced did not experience segregation if they ended up at the Breakwater convict station. The sentences themselves do not show obvious signs that the Resident Magistrate was discriminating according to colour or ethnicity among Cape Town's poor who formed the majority of those he tried.[70]

As we would expect, Cape Town's bourgeoisie sometimes saw those they considered socially beneath them in class terms, sometimes in ethnic; usually, but not always, in both. In giving evidence to a select committee on sanitation an Anglican minister, Canon Lightfoot, talked mostly of the 'the poor people' or the 'poorer classes' of Cape Town, although he also mentioned the particularly high mortality among

Table 2 *Whites and Coloureds in mission schools in various towns of the Cape Colony, 1891*

	White	Coloured	Total
Cape Town	2,955	4,283	7,238
Port Elizabeth	1,118	1,180	2,298
Grahamstown	710	377	1,087
Paarl	113	1,038	1,151
Stellenbosch	38	678	714
Worcester	33	668	701

Based on *CPP*, G9–1891, 'Education Commission', Appendix B, p. 213.

'natives'. Medical committee and hospital reports seldom made distinction between White and Black in the mid-1870s.[71] In contrast John Noble, the clerk of the House of Assembly, said (in David Kennedy vein) that in Cape Town there were

white and coloured races, with all their varieties of nationality and gradations of colour, from the fairest Saxon to darkest Nubian ... halfe-caste Negroes ... mixed Hottentots and Kaffirs ... half oriental Malays ... and the European artisan.[72]

The report of the census of 1875 elaborates on the ethnic labels which both the enumerators and Noble used: 'Malay' was normally used to describe Muslims, whatever their actual origins; the label 'Hottentot' was given to people who looked like KhoiKhoi, though the latter were believed to be 'virtually extinct as a race'. 'Kaffir' referred to 'all tribes South of Delagoa Bay, excluding the Fingo [Mfengu] and Bechuana [Tswana]'. Using these categories the census found 7,656 'Malays', 19 'Fingos', 221 'Kaffirs and Bechuanas' and 11,340 'Mixed and Other'.[73]

Frequently class and ethnic perceptions coincided; colour was perceived to coincide with class throughout society, despite the fact that census enumerators found Whites in almost every occupation. When writing about the 'Cape and its people' Langham Dale stated:

The mixed native population of all the towns and villages, which constitutes *our* [my emphasis] lower orders, and furnishes the ordinary labourers, artisans, coolies or porters, and domestic servants, embraces individuals of all hues and sizes ... the mixed offspring of white and coloured parentage, of Europeans, Mozambique Negroes rescued from slavers, and Hottentots, forms the majority of the dusky inhabitants of Cape Town.

The 'our' referred to by Langham Dale were dominant-class Whites such as himself. They were a mixture of 'Dutch, French, British, ... and German', who formed a 'community heterogeneous in its prime

elements, but sufficiently amalgamated for social and political purposes'.[74]

The most common White synonym for 'Other than Whites' in the
1870s was 'Coloured'. Explaining the census categories a few years
later, Noble said that the chief divide had been between White or
European and the 'coloured classes'.[75] The term 'Coloured' was often
used to refer to all Blacks, including Africans, in the nineteenth century.
But it would be incorrect to say that before the end of the century
'Coloured' *always* referred to all 'non-Whites'.[76] Thus a report in 1873
had the Civil Commissioner for East London distinguishing between
'natives' and 'coloured inhabitants of the Western Districts'.[77] The *Cape
Blue Book* for 1875 divided its returns into White, Black and Coloured.
A school history book of 1871, by A. Wilmot, distinguished between
'Kaffirs' and 'the coloured population, of mixed races, which forms a
large proportion of the labouring class in the west'.[78] Thus the Civil
Commissioner's or Wilmot's Coloureds would have included those
categorised in the 1875 census as 'Malays' or 'Mixed and Others', but
not 'Kaffirs' or 'Bechuanas'. So the term 'Coloured' was used, by at
least some of those who thought of themselves as White, to refer to the
descendants of mixed marriages or liaisons between Europeans,
KhoiKhoi and slaves.

Using the term in this sense, Coloured ownership of individual
properties in Cape Town was quite common according to the municipal
assessment rolls.[79] Most Coloureds, however, were locked into what one
can see as structural poverty. Consequently, in White minds, to be
Coloured was to be associated with a 'socially disadvantaged lower class
within the Western Cape'.[80] All the major economic activities in Cape
Town were characterised by their employment of a very high proportion
of casual and seasonal labour. In other words, the vast majority of
Coloured or Black workers, as well as some White, could not depend on
continuous or regular employment. Instead, their ability to earn could be
affected by the weather, the season, the number of ships in Table Bay and
so on. They were forced to live in overcrowded tenements, on inadequate
diets and subject to high mortality rates.[81]

Most were unable to afford to give their children more than a basic
education in reading and writing; many were unable to afford even that.
As it was, even acquiring basic literacy was apparently beyond the means
of most of Cape Town's poor who also happened not to be White. Of the
latter 69 per cent in the city itself who were over the age of fifteen could
neither read or write. The equivalent White statistic was 9 per cent. In the
five to fifteen age group the respective figures for 'Other than Whites' and
Whites were 88 per cent and 26 per cent.[82]

How many Capetonians saw themselves as Coloured, or in terms of any of the other ethnic labels assigned them by Whites, is uncertain for the 1870s. In 1873 there was a 'Petition of Coloured Persons, Inhabitants of Cape Town and Neighbourhood' against the Albany liquor licensing board in the Eastern Cape. The board intended to stop liquor being sold on a Sunday to people it considered to be Coloured. The petition was signed by A. C. Jackson, the one Black doctor in Cape Town, and 120 others whose names were not published.[83] Jackson would seem to have been reacting against, and rejecting, what has been described as a 'white-imposed categorisation'.[84] But the petitioners had used that categorisation to describe themselves, which begins to reveal how the process of racialisation influenced the emergence of specific ethnicities. Several petitions to central government officials from the 1850s onwards came from people living on mission stations who called themselves Coloured in this context. A correspondent to the *Cape Times* in 1877 also used this categorisation. He signed his letter as coming from 'A Coloured Attendant'. He said that he believed 'coloured folk' would not be welcome among White pew holders in the town's Anglican cathedral.[85]

Scouring court cases in the mid-1870s for evidence of how lower-class Capetonians viewed one another has only revealed a few instances in which the term 'Coloured' is used by Capetonians to refer to fellow citizens. Not once is it used to describe themselves. Daniel O'Brien, a watchman at the harbour, spoke of seeing 'four or five coloured boys and one white one' in a case of theft in 1875. In the same year Ellen Hall, the wife of a quarryman, referred in another trial to a 'coloured woman'. In 1873 John Thomas, a jockey, said that he had seen gravel thrown by a 'coloured boy'.[86]

The names of these witnesses suggest European origin. It is likely that they would have been seen to be White by the census enumerators of 1875. In some situations they undoubtedly saw themselves in this way. One such situation could presumably come while giving evidence in court, partially also in response to the perceptions of court officials. Another occasion may have come when confronted by a census enumerator asking them which 'race' they, family members or co-residents belonged to, or when filling in the form themselves.

Both occasions would have produced at least moments of lower-class ethnicity before the experience of ethnic mobilisation or extended segregation lent greater salience to such identity. Again it is clear that dominant-class racialisation of the city's population was an important part of the process through which specific ethnicities emerged, even if it was not responsible for all the distinctions on which such categorisation could be made. There was a dialectical relationship between racialisation and ethnicity.

Times of conflict at home, work or (a common setting for passions to flare) the canteen produced further occasions of lower-class ethnicity. During a neighbourly row in 1876 a woman called her next-door resident, Clara Proctor, a 'short-haired Hottentot'. Conrad Harvey called Joe Maker a 'Mozambique' in a pub dispute a year earlier.[87] These occasions must be weighed up against silences in the records which argue for good neighbourliness irrespective of ethnicity at a time when lower-class residential areas were 'mixed'. Incidents of intermarriage, as well as cohabitation, between lower-class Whites and Blacks were not un-common. This might imply that ethnicity, let alone racism, was not strongly developed among those individuals. Equally most benefit or friendly societies among Cape Town's lower classes did not exclude people on the basis of racialised distinctions, and this may have reflected the lack of precise correlation that workers could make between ethnicity and division of labour.

Yet divisions of labour or status within occupations, even at this stage, may have promoted ethnicity when such correlation was possible. Artisan occupations – remembering the census makes few distinctions between employer and employee – were fairly evenly divided between 1,500 Whites and 1,400 'Other than White'. On the other hand domestic service (1,200 to 2,700 respectively) and general labouring (290 to 1,340) saw a preponderance of 'other than White', while again, White labourers and domestic servants, according to official statistics, received, on average, higher wages. Finally, self-employed members of what Rudé would call the 'traditional' classes saw the smallest White representation of all. Only 62 out of 284 fishermen and less than 100 out of over 1,000 washerwomen were White, which may help to explain the group consciousness displayed by the vast majority in those occupations who were not.[88]

Even among artisans, evidence suggests that there may have been quite a close correlation between colour and degree of training or skill within categories of employment such as 'carpenter' or 'cabinet-maker'. The *Lantern* in 1884 talked about an English mason being more specialised than a Malay one. The *Cape Times* in the same year said that English artisans were discovering that to be a plumber in Cape Town was to be a gas-fitter or tinsmith. Most of the highly skilled crafts, those least liable to casualisation, were White dominated. Whites were twenty-four out of twenty-six watch/clock makers, fifty out of fifty-five mechanical engi-neers, twenty-eight out of thirty goldsmiths and provided all the gunsmsiths, according to the census. In addition, Edna Bradlow has pointed out that furniture-making, shipbuilding, printing and book-binding, tallow chandling and blacksmithing were 'almost totally' or 'predominantly' White. In at least some crafts, Whites may have received somewhat higher wages.[89]

White ethnicity was likely to have been strengthened among those workers in Cape Town whose perceptions of the different physical appearances, origins or culture of other Capetonians was under-scored by divisions of labour or occupational specialisation. Kennedy, the visiting professional singer, implicitly offered his own brief observation on occupation and ethnic-group membership: 'Mr Smith sells drapery; Dirk Niewenhuys does all kinds of house-painting; Abdol Jamsetjee deals in curios; Macnab is there with his groceries; Jaliza Japartee, good woman, is excellent at laundry-work.'[90] Similar considerations may have strengthened Malay ethnicity. Malays were seen by many Whites to be a kind of 'aristocracy' among Black Capetonians.[91] Malays were in a comparably advantageous position to migrants from rural areas as White artisans, recently arrived from Europe, were to them. This was a result of skills acquired by Malays in, and passed on from, the period of slavery. Indeed it is possible from the Cape Town evidence to agree with Beinart that 'the very unevenness of the process by which people from different areas came on to the labour market ... suggests an internal dynamic to changing forms of ethnicity'.[92]

The language and religious differences that existed among Capetonians held the potential for ethnic identification across class and colour lines. One might be allowed to assume that most 'Kaffirs' in Cape Town spoke Xhosa, but it is impossible to be precise about how many Capetonians spoke English, Dutch or Afrikaans. On the other hand, we do know that there were over 8,000 White and 2,500 'Other than White' members of the Dutch Reformed Church. It is likely that DRC members were predominantly Dutch or Afrikaans speaking, that here there was a high correlation between language and religious persuasion as indeed there was with the mainly Afrikaans-speaking Muslims. Similarly there were 8,000 White and just under 2,000 Black 'Episcopalians', most of whom were presumably English-speaking Anglicans. If we include Presbyterians, Wesleyans and Baptists in the category of those Capetonians who were likely to have been English speaking, then we must add a further 1,500 Whites and 300 'Other than Whites'. From these figures, we can tentatively conclude that, by 1875, the number of White English-speaking Capetonians had crept ahead of their Dutch- or Afrikaans-speaking counterparts, while the majority of Black Capetonians spoke Afrikaans. In terms of potential religious identity there was also a small Jewish community in Cape Town, numbering 169.[93]

Leaving aside, for lack of evidence, the self-perceptions of the still-small African population, there is the likelihood that a 'Malay' identity did exist, on occasion, among those so described. At some stage between emancipation and the Mineral Revolution Whites had begun referring to Muslims, whatever their actual ancestry, as Malays. 'Malay' became virtually a synonym for 'Muslim', in the mouths of Whites, by the 1850s.[94] In the 1870s, if not before, the term 'Malay' was adopted by numbers of people so categorised to describe themselves, at least in their dealings with Whites. Abdol Burns, a cab owner and a fairly prominent figure in Cape Town political circles, replied 'yes' in 1875 when asked by a member of a cemeteries committee whether he belonged to the 'Malay Community'.[95] In 1878 'a Moslem' wrote a letter hoping Samuel 'a Malay man', was innocent of forgery.[96] According to the census, there were almost 7,700 Malays in Cape Town and over 8,000 Muslims in 1875; 16 'Whites', 11 'Hottentots', 3 'Kaffirs' and 585 'Mixed and Other' Muslims counted by the census explains the discrepancy.

It is probable that the vast majority of Malays or Muslims were ex-slaves and their descendants. Most people brought to Cape Town from the Malay archipelago had been slaves. Islam would appear to have united the vast majority of 'Free Blacks', and thus freed slaves, in the early 1820s. Of the estimated 1,900 Free Blacks in Cape Town in 1822, about 1,600 were Muslims. Of a total slave population of about 7,000 at this date, close to 1,300 were also converts to Islam.

I have argued elsewhere that conversion to Islam aided the process of giving slaves or their descendants pyschological 'self-ownership'.[97] Conversion to Islam also provided material support for the poor and social status for the wealthier which may have been denied to them by bourgeois White exclusiveness. Islam, distinctive dress, education in Arabic, culinary and medical practices became part of Malay ethnicity by the 1870s. Indeed, dress made the Malays particularly visible to others, as it presumably did to themselves. The men wore

large broad-brimmed hats of basket-work, and many have coloured handkerchiefs tied round their heads. The women flaunt gay head-dresses, and when a wedding or a feast takes place, the streets are ablaze with colour.[98]

Such flamboyant dress arguably obscured phenotypical differences among Malays, and became a more important external signifier. Occupational ties underpinned Malay ethnicity, as we have suggested. So did membership of what amounted to an inner-city Muslim community concentrated in District One and nearby, on the slopes of Signal Hill, an area that some were already calling the Malay Quarter.[99] Apart from through those shared activities already mentioned, Malay ethnicity was

3 Malay women in the 1870s

further strengthened in the 1870s by the formation of choral street-bands, such as the Star of Independence Malay Club. This ethnicity came to particular prominence between 1875 and 1886, the year that a large proportion of the community was involved in the Cemetery riots.[100]

By 1875, then, Cape Town displayed many structural similarities with Stedman Jones's London. In both cities economic power lay with 'those whose income derived from rent, banking and commerce'.[101] Seasonality of production, types of casual occupations and a strong artisan sector characterised both labour markets. There was, in both places, a notable absence of one of Marx and Engels' 'fundamental' classes, the industrial proletariat. Instead, within a sea of casual labour, there was the strong presence of the semi-proletarianised, such as fishermen or tailors.[102]

The most important difference between London and Cape Town, apart from the enormous discrepancy in size, was the significance of ethnicity for social identity in the latter. This chapter has argued that, in 1875, White ethnicity united a dominant class potentially divided by language, origins and Christian denominational difference. Exclusionary segregation protected White bourgeois status. Belief in White superiority was part of White ethnicity for many, as it apparently was for their contemporary counterparts in Buenos Aires or Rio de Janeiro. This explains why equation was made between colour and class, why, perhaps, the terms 'race' and 'class' were virtually interchangeable in mid-Victorian Cape Town.[103]

Our analysis of Cape Town's social formation has shown how the latter was crucial in determining the nature, and limited extent, of segregation in the city in 1875. In the absence of the much sharper correlation of colour and divisions of labour in the countryside, and the presence in Cape Town of a permeable colour-line and imprecise divisions of labour, rigid ethnic ordering among the lower classes was unlikely to happen as the result of factors purely internal to the city's social formation. Nonetheless, social 'integration' would appear to have been very much a lower-class phenomenon, as it was in contemporary New Orleans.

This does not mean that Cape Town's lower classes necessarily evinced much working-class solidarity. It would have been surprising if they had done, given differences of physical appearance, language, religion, occupation and skill that often overlapped, and may have been mutually reinforcing. Moreover, the nature of Cape Town's labour market militated as yet against occupational, let alone class, consciousness. Important in this respect was the high quota of seasonal and casual employment, the blurred division of labour and the small units of production.

Gradually some of these obstacles were removed in the course of the late nineteenth century. This was largely because of growing industrialisation and the restructuring of employment patterns, consequences of the Mineral Revolution. But new obstacles, such as a reservoir of unemployed in times of depression, sprang up to take their place.

The Mineral Revolution was the major motive force behind economic and demographic change in Cape Town in the late nineteenth century. Such change brought a number of challenges to Cape Town's 'traditional system' of class and ethnic relations. More immediately, it confronted Cape Town's dominant class with the material problems caused by rapidly increasing urbanisation and the strains that this imposed on the town's resources.

English-speaking journalists and doctors, all of whom came from or were trained in Europe, as well as visitors from Britain such as Kennedy or Trollope, drew constantly on their 'Mother' country's experience of urbanisation to issue dire warnings and offer advice. They emphasised specifically the need to combat dangers to person and pocket posed by water shortage and abysmal sanitation which could lead to epidemics or the suspension of trade. The journalists in particular called on the 'intelligent' sector of Cape Town society to take up the cause and become involved in local politics.

This, together with the increasing number and proportion of English-speaking Capetonians, was the background to the emergence of a reforming 'Clean Party' in municipal politics in the early 1880s, similar to such parties in Britain. As with most British municipal contests it came as the result of a struggle within the city's bourgeoisie.[104] Clean Party victory signalled the importance of Englishness as an efficacious ethnicity in the late 1870s and early 1880s. During this period it helped, at least temporarily, to undermine the unifying bonds of White ethnicity among Cape Town's dominant class. The growth of Englishness interacted with the growth of Afrikaner ethnicity; they fed off each other. The next chapter explores these developments.

3 Problems of prosperity

Increased economic activity through the 1870s to 1882, a consequence of the discovery of diamonds at Kimberley in 1870, initiated a period of rapid demographic and social change in Cape Town and the Cape Colony as a whole. Both the rate and nature of this change came to be perceived as problems by a section of Cape Town's bourgeoisie. Perhaps the major difficulty they identified was how to cope, in material terms, with urbanisation and the strains it imposed on the existing limited resources of the city's town council. Their solution was, in part, to reform that institution.

The victory in local elections of a reformist Clean Party in 1882, consisting of merchants and businessmen, signalled the emergence of a dominant class in Cape Town that was not only White and bourgeois but also predominantly English. This victory was facilitated by the mobilisation of English ethnicity in the city, particularly by campaigning journalists. The Englishness they promoted could potentially assimilate all White English speakers, including the numerous Capetonians from Scotland, and even those Dutch speakers who had become sufficiently Anglicised. To be acceptably English all one had to do was to be White, English speaking, in favour of the Empire and, that ubiquitous Victorian virtue, respectable. Respectability implied acceptance of the values of the English elite: thrift, the sanctity of property, deference to superiors, belief in the moralising efficacy of hard work and cleanliness. To paraphrase Colls, Englishness in this colonial context was ultimately about white skins, English tongues and bourgeois values. It had the potential to unite all Whites in Cape Town who shared its values. The corollary was that those who did not share these values could be perceived as 'other' than English, the least adaptable as the most foreign.[1]

Englishness then, as with any ethnicity, involved relationships with others. For Cape Town's English speaking bourgeoisie this relationship was to be one of dominance. Thus the 'colonisation' of those 'others', the imposition of English values, became part and parcel of the achievement of English hegemony in the city, where English hegemony also meant, of course, bourgeois hegemony.[2]

Imperial intervention in southern Africa, and opposition to that intervention, undoubtedly encouraged the rise of a more assertive Englishness in the colony in general. In the mid-1870s the British government was involved in diplomatic initiatives aimed at bringing about a confederated South Africa under the British flag. After these attempts had failed, the Transvaal Republic was annexed by Britain in 1877. Two years later imperial armies won wars against Africans in Natal and the Eastern Cape. In 1880 Griqualand West, and with it Kimberley and the diamond fields, was annexed to the Cape. English hegemony was almost complete in the whole of southern Africa. The only trouble was that other ethnicities were strengthened, and given new content, at least partly in response to heightened Englishness, which led to an escalating cycle of ethnic mobilisation between 1875 and 1882.

Before 1872, under Representative Government, farmers and merchants, or men who were both, provided two-thirds of Cape parliamentarians. The remaining seats were filled by professionals and a few businessmen. Several predominantly rural seats were represented for much of the period by merchants or businessmen resident in the major towns. Central government was securely in the hands of politicians favourable to British mercantile interests. These were, after all, bound up particularly with the success of wine and wool farmers, whether they were English, Dutch or Afrikaans speaking. In the event there was little in the way of party organisation or ethnic particularism. The major recurrent political division would appear to have been regional, most notably between east and west, over such matters as state expenditure on infrastructure.[3] English parliamentary hegemony was marked by the fact that two-thirds of parliamentarians were of British origin. In part this was because all members had to speak English since this was the official language of parliament as it was, at least in theory, the official language of local political institutions, non-denominational schools, courts and the civil service.[4]

However, the advent of Responsible Government and the Mineral Revolution brought the beginnings of party political organisation along interconnected lines of economic interest and ethnicity. The Cape parliament was now directly in charge of greatly increased revenues and powers. It was struggle for control of these resources that became a crucial factor promoting the mobilisation of an Afrikaner ethnicity.

The initial mobilisers were clergymen and teachers such as the Du Toits, A. Pannevis and C. P. Hoogenhout. They founded the *Genootskap van Regte Afrikaners* (fellowship of true Afrikaners) at Paarl in 1875, to stand for 'our language, our nation and our country'. By 'our language' they meant creolised Dutch, or Afrikaans. By 'our nation' they meant people who spoke Afrikaans and were White. In 1876 members of the *Genootskap* brought out a newspaper, *Die Afrikaanse Patriot*, which attacked Britain's annexation of the Transvaal the following year and had 3,700 subscribers by 1882. This readership, according to the editors, was rural and *minderbevoorreg* or 'under-privileged'.

In 1877 S. J. Du Toit published the *Geskiedenis van ons Land in die Taal van ons Volk* (the history of our country in the language of our people). The *Geskiedenis* promoted the idea of Afrikaners as Whites of Dutch, French or German origin who had been bound together by common experience and the Afrikaans language since the late seventeenth century. Two years later Du Toit formed a political party, the *Afrikaner Bond*, which although theoretically open to people of English origin aimed at preventing 'the sacrifice of Africa's interests to England, or those of the Farmer to the Merchant' and attacked state expenditure on 'one section of the population, while another and larger part is totally neglected'. *Bond* branches were established not only in the Cape Colony but also in the Transvaal and Orange Free State, demonstrating the *Genootskappers'* pan-Afrikaner ideals.

Du Toit's Afrikaner mobilisation in the Cape was aimed at a petty-bourgeois audience who could and did respond to the view that economic 'under-privilege' was the result of English discrimination against them. This audience was predictably suspicious of Anglicised Afrikaners and could readily believe, and with some reason, that English capitalists were contributing to rural Afrikaner poverty. Du Toit's policies consequently included the establishment of Afrikaner banks, the boycotting of 'foreign' ones (too ready to call in credit) and greater state support for Afrikaner education.[5]

In the event the leadership of this Afrikaner ethnic mobilisation was hijacked and partly reshaped by wealthy commercial farmers, people who spoke a dialect closer to high Dutch and who had done well out of their ties with English merchants for much of the nineteenth century. These ties seemed less secure by the 1870s. Wheat farmers felt increasingly threatened by cheap imports of grain. In 1878 the wine merchants failed to oppose a government excise on brandy, one of the chief products of Western Cape wine farmers, and began to import foreign wine and spirits in increasingly large quantities.

Therefore commercial farmers began to form their own political organisations. Wheat farmers formed the Malmesbury Protection Committee in 1869, although it disintegrated after 1871, due to a recovery in the wheat price. Wine farmers formed a similar organisation in 1877 called the *Wijnbouwers Vereeniging*, or wine farmers' co-operative. They were given support by a Dutch-language newspaper in Cape Town, the *Zuid Afrikaan*, edited by J. H. Hofmeyr (the son of a wine farmer). The excise on brandy led the leaders of the *Wijnbouwers Vereeniging* to approach Hofmeyr for help in organising a broader *Boeren Beschermings Vereeniging (BBV)* (farmers' protection association) which won almost half the seats in the Legislative council and a quarter of those in the House of Assembly in the elections of 1878-9. After this electoral success the *BBV* threatened to go the way of the Malmesbury Protection Committee. The *BBV*'s continued existence and growth in the early 1880s occurred largely because its leaders began mobilising Afrikaner ethnicity, along the lines of Du Toit's *Bond*, while campaigning for political support. Their task was facilitated by the Transvaal's War of Independence, which was fought by people hailed as fellow Afrikaners against the British in 1881.

Amalgamation between the *Afrikaner Bond* and the *BBV* took place in 1883, under the former's name but *BBV* leadership. Hofmeyr's *Bond* did not attempt to build a pan-Afrikaner party across the Cape Colony's boundaries. The newspapers of Hofmeyr's *Bond*, such as *De Paarl, Onze Courant* or *Zuid-Afrikaan*, discarded the more militant republican, anti-English and anti-capitalist rhetoric of *Die Patriot*. The more moderate tone in this respect reflected the class concerns of the wealthy farmers who supplied most of its leaders. They campaigned for the institutional use of high Dutch, as more refined than the *kombuistaal* (kitchen language) or *hotnotstaal* (Hottentot language) Afrikaans. The policies they pursued did not challenge existing class relations and were concerned above all with change within the existing constitutional framework. The Cape parliament was seen as the means by which they could secure legislation or government intervention which promoted or protected their interests: protectionist tariffs, provision of markets and the supply and control of cheap labour.

The *BBV* could take over the leadership of Afrikaner mobilisation at this stage because they, not the *Genootskappers*, controlled links of paternalism and patronage in the countryside. Afrikaner ethnic mobilisation for its patrician leaders was about maintaining these links through promising, and sometimes delivering, legislative benefits to their supporters. This, together with wealth, enabled the *BBV* and then the new *Bond* to fight and win often expensive and corrupt elections before the introduction of a secret ballot in the 1890s.[6]

Afrikaner mobilisation in the late 1870s and early 1880s provoked an English response that culminated in the formation of the short-lived British Empire League in 1884.[7] Considerably increased immigration from Britain made political appeals to Englishness possible from the late 1870s. In the context of local politics in Cape Town, the need for such appeals coincided in the minds of professionals, merchants and businessmen with the need to address urban problems. As we have suggested, these were caused by the prosperity that came with the diamond bonanza.

Initially for Cape Town's merchants and businessmen the signs were entirely encouraging. Through the 1870s, Cape government revenue steadily escalated, quintupling from £660,000 in 1870 to £3,500,000 by the end of 1882.[8] Such expansion of revenue enabled government to improve the economic infrastructure of the Colony. This expenditure on infrastructure touched Cape Town directly, as well as indirectly via improved inland communications. Between 1879 and 1883 £450,000 was authorised by the state for the city's harbour. In November 1882 a graving dock was completed while the breakwater protecting the harbour continued to grow, reaching 2,500 feet by 1884.[9]

Imports through Cape Town, worth just under £1,000,000 in 1870, had doubled by 1875 and trebled by 1882. Moreover the inland growth of the railway brought the beginnings of a tourist trade to Cape Town by the early 1880s, even before Cape Town was linked to Kimberley in 1885. The summer months saw a seasonal migration of wives and children from the arduous heat of the diamond fields followed, for a month or so, by their menfolk. A special fast-train service no doubt helped this development and ensured that Cape Town, the first Cape port of call for ships from Europe, became the main port of entry to the interior.

After initial overspeculation, over-trading and a minor recession in 1876–7, Cape Town merchants were enjoying unprecedented prosperity by the end of the 1870s. This prosperity was enhanced by rising agricultural prices which increased the spending power of Western Cape farmers on imported products.[10] War on the eastern frontier also provided import opportunities. With swollen capital resources merchants more than doubled the number of joint stock companies in the town between 1875 and 1882. Besides banking, insurance and diamond shares, they put their money into transport and minor industrial projects such as glass manufacturing and a steam laundry company.[11] Investment in infrastructure and industry by both public and private sectors produced a demand on their part for an increased labour supply. Economic expansion also meant more employment opportunities at the Cape. Both factors furthered demographic growth in Cape Town, particularly in the second half of the 1870s, the nature and extent of which would influence the rise of Englishness.

The Cape government, at a cost of some £224,000, introduced more than 22,000 people from Europe and St Helena between 1873 and 1884, half of them between 1879 and 1883. The vast majority of these immigrants were British. Almost half of them had been brought for railway work, as recruits for the Cape Mounted Rifles or as agricultural settlers. The remainder were 'aided' immigrants, the cost of whose fares had been split between the government and their employers in the Colony. Most of the latter were artisans for the building industry and domestic servants, many of whom came to Cape Town.[12]

Government, largely in response to demands from Western Cape farmers, also brought 4,000 Africans to Cape Town from the eastern frontier between April 1878 and January 1879. Some were prisoners of war, others were starving loyalists. From a depot 'somewhere in the southern suburbs' these Africans were contracted to local employers in Cape Town and its hinterland.[13] Similarly, between 1879 and 1882, the government organised the arrival of over 2,700 indentured African labourers from Mozambique. Their numbers were added to the 400 who had been brought by freelance labour recruiters to farms in the Western Cape between 1876 and 1878. Several hundred of these 'Mozbiekers' were employed at the docks.[14] Between 1879 and 1882, a small number of Berg Damaras, from what became German South West Africa, were also brought to Cape Town. A large portion of these imported African labourers, men, women and children, remained in the Western Cape after their contracts expired.[15]

Many people made their own way to Cape Town in this period without government assistance. The vast majority of such arrivals were either (like the aided immigrants) from Britain, or came from Cape Town's agricultural hinterland. The population of the municipality *sans* suburbs increased from 33,000 to about 40,000 between 1875 and 1880. By 1891 the number of people in greater Cape Town had almost doubled since 1875 to 79,000, despite the severe depression of the 1880s.[16]

A growing population helped trade to expand as well as being the result of such expansion. All in all, the great importance of Cape Town as the centre of colonial government and leading client of the latter's patronage, as well as the benefit of some £300,000 per annum spent on defence by the imperial government, seemed finally to have secured the town's position as commercial capital by the early 1880s.[17] Yet economic and demographic growth required adequate material resources to support them. Only in this way could the town remain viable as a centre of commerce.

Contemporaries commented frequently on the growth of the town and the need for more houses.[18] More ships in Table Bay, let alone more people in the town, put greater strains on the existing water supply. A higher volume of trade would do the same to harbour facilities and thoroughfares between the docks, warehouses and railway station.

Improving these resources became a matter of growing concern to Cape Town's mercantile community between 1875 and 1882. Their concern was taken up and promoted by visitors from Britain as well as resident journalists and doctors of British origin who made unfavourable comparisons between Cape Town and cities they were acquainted with in Europe. A broad rhetoric urging urban reform developed, emphasising above all the need for a clean and well-watered city.

British visitors to Cape Town in the mid-1870s did not fail to criticise its physical condition. We have seen the comments of Kennedy and Trollope. A series of articles in the *Cape Monthly Magazine* for 1875, 'By an Old Traveller revisiting Cape Town', spoke of the necessity of street improvement and an increased water supply. The articles were liberally sprinkled with more favourable references to other places in the world with which the author was acquainted.[19] Trollope, who visited in 1877, suggested in typically succinct style that the 'officers of the municipality' were 'not alert'.[20]

English-speaking residents of Cape Town, who had experience or knowledge of British cities through direct contact or via literature, made similar criticisms. John Noble wrote of Cape Town in 1875:

Now there is a Mayor and town council in the modern corporate style – who are expected to keep pace with the requirements of these progressive times, and to make the city as presentable as it should be. A thorough system of drainage, the removal of 'stoeps', the construction of paved streets, and some abatement of the plague of dust during 'South-easters' have still to be accomplished before that will be obtained.[21]

Criticisms of the council were not new to the 1870s.[22] What was new was that between 1875 and 1882 a campaign to reform the town council and, in general, to improve the sanitation and infrastructure of the city, became part of the promotion of Englishness in Cape Town.

In other words, control of the parish pump became as important as control of Pretoria in the minds of many English Capetonians; perhaps even more so. Both were desirable. But by the early 1880s Afrikaner ethnicity, or its nationalist manifestation, seemed to make control of either more difficult, and began to threaten English hegemony in central politics at the Cape. In the process a common White ethnicity came under strain. In Cape Town this happened as conflict over local politics became increasingly bitter.

In 1875 the *Cape Argus*, at that time the only major English-language newspaper, urged the 'intelligent' sector of Cape Town society to get themselves elected to the council, to carry out a programme of reforms along the lines outlined by Noble. The *Argus* was fairly moderate in its tone. It criticised a 'fussy' party, obviously still in the minority, that wanted to 'turn the city upside down', and bring in European reforms. On the other hand, it also disapproved of the fact that the 'mass of householders' opposed all additional expenditure. The newspaper said that it believed in the 'middle way' – an appropriate position perhaps for the organ of Saul Solomon, a leading Cape liberal.[23] The *Argus* adhered to the tradition of promoting the idea of common purpose and conciliation among White colonists adopted by a predecessor, the *Commercial Advertiser*. This had also been the journal of a Cape liberal, John Fairbairn, which suggests that Cape liberalism was partly about such accommodation.[24]

Nevertheless from about 1876 the *Argus* did join two English-language newspapers, established in the late 1870s, in pressing for urban reform. These two publications were the *Cape Times*, a daily newspaper first issued in 1876, and the *Lantern*, a weekly, which started three years later. The editor and owner of the *Cape Times* was F. Y. St Leger. St Leger had arrived in the Colony in the late 1850s after graduating from Cambridge. He gave up his position as an Anglican clergyman in the Eastern Cape in 1871 to try and make his fortune in Kimberley, but without much success. He arrived in Cape Town in 1875 to pursue a new career in journalism.[25] We know much less about the editors of the *Lantern*. It was initially owned and edited by an E. Geary, but he was soon displaced in both roles by a young British immigrant, Thomas McCombie.

All these men became energetic ethnic mobilisers of Englishness between 1876 and 1882, devoting hundreds of editorials, cartoons and poems to this cause. Their advertisers were almost exclusively members of the English-speaking bourgeoisie. These newspapers were read by Capetonians who could mostly, and correctly, be assumed to be White and English speaking by the editors, thanks to the linguistic and literary divides in the city. Unfortunately there are no circulation figures for the *Lantern*, but the *Cape Times* claimed an average daily readership of over 4,000 in 1880.[26] If accurate, and according to our calculations in chapter 1, this must have meant the vast majority of adult White English speakers in Cape Town were among them.

St Leger, Geary and McCombie were well aware, as they demonstrated in editorial comment, of how urban problems had been defined and tackled in the Motherland. One problem that particularly worried them was sanitation. This focus is understandable given water shortages and the lack of drains in Cape Town, as well as the fact that the British sanitary revolution was very much a contemporary development. British-trained Cape doctors, for similar reasons, also began to urge the Cape Town council to adopt sanitary reforms.[27]

Seemingly sensible enough, the sanitation rhetoric of journalists and doctors echoed similar campaigns in England.[28] The reform campaigners wished to increase the powers and personnel of the council. In their minds the two were connected. Both require examination to make sense of the campaign and thereby the rise of Englishness. This exploration takes us into the murky world of nineteenth-century municipal politics.

The extent to which town councils involved themselves in the material development of Cape Town was at least partly a function of the motives of those who controlled the Town House. This was particularly true of Cape Town in the 1870s when municipal policy was firmly in the hands of the eighteen councillors themselves rather than being the product of interplay between executive and professional advisers. The only municipal officials of note were the 'secretary' to the council (not yet entitled town clerk), a treasurer and some sanitary inspectors. In 1876 they were joined by a city engineer, and in 1879 by a superintendent of public works. All major municipal work was in the hands of contractors. The city engineer did instigate the only major infrastructural project in the 1870s, the building of the Molteno Reservoir. But he resigned out of frustration with the councillors in 1880.

The extent to which the council could further the material development of the city, if it so wished, was also a product of its powers. A municipal board had been established as far back as 1840. The Board was supposed to provide adequate water for its citizens, ensure that the streets were clean and make provision for lighting them. The legislation that 're-established' a municipal board for the city in 1861 did not radically alter the powers of its predecessor, merely adding the right to license vehicles and make compulsory purchases for street improvements. In 1867 the board was turned into a council, and the city divided into six districts for electoral purposes, hence the names District Six or District One.

The council inherited the board's powers, but its use of them was severely limited by financial constraint until the 1880s. The maximum rate in Cape Town in the 1870s was fixed at a paltry 2d in the pound, the maximum loan at £20,000. In contrast the Port Elizabeth council was raising a rate of between 9d and 1s. To increase its borrowing powers Cape Town's council had either to get the consent of the 'householders' (owners and principal tenants) or to go to central government. As it was, municipal revenue in 1875 amounted to a mere £24,500, £16,000 of which came from the house rate and virtually all the rest from the sale of water, market dues and licences.[30]

In the 1870s most Cape Town councillors showed little inclination to increase revenue and thereby embark on major infrastructure projects. As a result they were initially called those who 'oppose all costs' or 'reactionaries' by the English-language press. They were given the sobriquet of 'Dirty Party' by 1878.[31] The first reactionaries to be identified were P. J. Leibbrandt, C. G. Prince and J. C. Hofmeyr. Hofmeyr appears to have been the leader, or at least the most active spokesman, of what was in reality an informal political alliance rather than a formal party. All members of this alliance were property owners living in the municipality itself, rather than the suburbs which were home to most Cleans. One Dirty Party member, describing supporters, said that they were 'the middle class landed proprietors, men who have got a little property, and live in a quiet way, out of the rent of their property'.[32]

Thus in Cape Town, as in London, opponents of sanitary reform included 'small' property owners.[33] Yet prominent members of Cape Town's Dirty Party were among the largest proprietors in the city. The Dirty Party was, then, a loosely knit interest group of property owners, from large to small, who derived some, or most, of their income from rent. Unlike many of their 'Clean' opponents, they lived in the municipality itself rather than the suburbs. They feared the implications of city 'improvements' for rates and additional expenditure on their property. Consequently they rejected the reform advice of the Cape Medical Board and journalists.[34]

But there was another dimension to the nature of the Dirty Party. In 1875 Hofmeyr applauded 'Africanders' for having 'come forward' at the recent municipal election, and described them as 'the most fit to rule'. He went further and told them to 'become a nation'.[35] Twelve years later a Dirty Party candidate was still addressing a group of supporters as 'my fellow Africanders'.[36]

"Africander' or 'Afrikaner' was a term of some ambivalence in the late nineteenth century. For S. J. Du Toit, 'Afrikaner' had described only people of Dutch, German or Huguenot descent who spoke Afrikaans. J. H. Hofmeyr, a relative of J. C. Hofmeyr, gave the term a broader definition. He used 'Afrikaner' to describe 'anyone who, having settled in this country, wishes to remain here to help to promote our common interests and to live with the inhabitants as members of one family'. When he wished to refer to Dutch or Afrikaans-speaking Whites he usually referred to *Hollandsche Afrikaanders*. Under J. H. Hofmeyr's guidance the *Bond* congress of 1883 defined an Afrikaner as 'everybody, of whatever origin, who aims at the welfare of South Africa'. Nevertheless the vast majority of his supporters were Dutch or Afrikaans speakers who would have taken the term 'Afrikaner' to refer to themselves as distinct from English speakers.[37]

Given J. C. Hofmeyr's use of English and Dutch (even if he used Afrikaans as well), his treasurership of the *BBV* and his later position on the Cape executive of the *Bond*, it is pretty certain that in his public utterances he was using the broader definition of 'Afrikaner'. After all, he was also seeking and getting support from property owners of British descent, such as Prince.[38] But it seems clear that the majority of those who thought of themselves as Afrikaners did so for the same reasons and in the same way as S. J. Du Toit, the way espoused by the *Geskiedenis* and *Die Patriot*.

For J. C. Hofmeyr seems to have been urging mostly, if by no means exclusively, Dutch- and Afrikaans-speaking Capetonians into a common identity *vis-à-vis* the attacks made on them by an English-language press that sought its inspiration and rationale in the urban experience of the Motherland. In Cape Town common class position as property owners underpinned Afrikaner ethnicity for many of its adherents. In rural areas, judging by the nature of the amalgamated *Bond*, ownership of farms was to have much the same effect.[39]

Dirty Party Afrikaner ethnicity manifested itself most obviously in opposition to imperial causes or interventionism. In 1877 J. C. Hofmeyr snubbed the Governor, Sir Bartle Frere, when he offered advice over the handling of municipal elections not long after the Transvaal annexation. In 1879 J. C. Hofmeyr, T. Hofmeyr and M. J. Louw, all Dirty Party members of the town council, opposed the idea of organising a municipal reception for a visiting British commander. In 1880 Louw and J. C. Hofmeyr objected to the city engineer being given any honorarium on his resignation because he had previously left his job 'to fight in the Queen's wars'. His opposition to the Englishness he saw in individual political opponents surfaced on these as well as more trivial occasions. In 1883, for instance, he criticised a mayor who said he wanted leave to go 'home' to England.[40] By the early 1880s, if not before, J. C. Hofmeyr was at the forefront of attempts to formally organise an Afrikaner political movement in Cape Town. In March 1882 it was reported that he had met with eighteen others to form the *Zuid-Afrikaansche Vereeniging van der Kaapstad*, or the Cape Town 'Afrikander' society, as the *Lantern* put it. J. C. Hofmeyr became its president. The first public meeting of the *Bond* in Cape Town came in 1884. The *Cape Times* reported that apart from J. H. Hofmeyr, the new *Bond* leader, J. C. Hofmeyr and another Dirty Party member, G. A. Ashley (presumably of some English ancestry), were present.[41]

Hofmeyr and other 'Dirty' town councillors, and their supporters, were criticised as obstructionist and reactionary by the new English-language journals of the 1870s which were, unlike the *Argus*, unashamedly jingoistic. St Leger denounced the *BBV* as a Fenian organisation almost as soon as it was formed in 1878.[42] Failure to rejoice in British imperial success by Dirty Party members produced vitriolic and personal attacks in the *Lantern* and *Cape Times*, as well as from reformist councillors. One suggestion was that J. C. Hofmeyr should 'be stuck before the country's enemies'. And these attacks brought results.[43] For instance in the mid-1880s, at 'one of the noisiest' political meetings in Cape Town, J. C. Hofmeyr struggled to deliver a speech against the backdrop of a rowdy rendition of 'Rule, Britannia'.[44]

Associating the Dirty Party with Malay support became part of the attack. As a result Malays were themselves stereotyped as 'Dirty' and obstructionist. In the process opponents of reform, Afrikaner and Malay alike were being perceived as un-English, be it for their rejection of British ideas on sanitation or British imperialism or both. In one of his earliest editorials on 'the dirty' opponents of sanitary reform, St Leger talked of 'Abdol' whose house 'is guiltless of the trace of the scrubbing brush'. Two years later he was attacking J. C. Hofmeyr and his 'Moslem friends'.[45] In 1882 an article in the *Lantern* epitomised this perception of otherness. It compared living conditions in Britain to those at the Cape and the plight facing a British woman who immigrated to Cape Town:

When her husband in desperation, and only at the point of compulsion, leases a miserable four-roomed cottage in a back slum, *reeking of Malays* and drains, for her at £60 or £70 per annum, she recalls the state and dignity such a rental would represent in England.[46] [emphasis added]

Sanitation rhetoric became inextricably mixed with the rhetoric of British imperialism. This fusion was taking place during a period of considerable resistance to both sets of ideas from Afrikaners, Malays and Africans alike. Most British visitors who criticised the streets and drains of Cape Town also sneered at it for having a part 'oriental', part Dutch appearance – for not being sufficiently English. Trollope thought that the municipality, rather than the suburbs, was not inhabited by 'White men'.[47]

Those who seemed to oppose Englishness, such as J. C. Hofmeyr and many of his colleagues, were naturally viewed with hostility. Removing the control of property owners over the town council thus went hand in hand, in the *Cape Times* or *Lantern*'s view, with ending foreign, un-English, if not anti-British, control. The Hofmeyrs, the 'reigning family of Cape Town' as the *Lantern* put it in 1879, had to be toppled from their throne.[48]

The problem was how to do this. The beginning of the end of Dirty Party control of municipal politics was foreshadowed by the results of elections to the Cape Legislative council and House of Assembly in November 1878 and May 1879 respectively. The success of English speaking mercantile candidates in these, and subsequent, elections showed the latter capable of coupling economic to political domination of Cape Town's social formation.

The council election was a four-way contest for three seats in the upper house. The constituency included Cape Town and its rural hinterland in the south-western cape. The four candidates were Ebden, Murison, Neethling and De Korte: two English mercantile candidates against two Afrikaner/Dutch ones, as one correspondent to the *Cape Times* perceived the contest.[49] Both Alfred Ebden and James Murison were members of Cape Town's grand bourgeoisie, with impeccable social links with other English-speaking members of this group, whose support they were given.[50] Such mercantile solidarity in Cape Town was similar to that evidenced in Melbourne.[51] Both had the further support of the *Cape Times*. St Leger, a fellow member of the City Club, actually served as a member of Ebden's election committee.[52] On the other hand, Marthinius Neethling was the candidate of J. H. Hofmeyr's *BBV*, and De Korte had local political links with J. C. Hofmeyr via ratepayer resistance to greater municipal expenditure. Alfred's brother, J. B. Ebden, attacked Neethling for his *BBV* membership and specifically appealed for support in his campaign from what he called the 'patriotic sector' of the community.[53]

The results showed that Ebden and Murison depended for their successful election on the votes they collected in Cape Town. Neethling was returned because of his overwhelming support in the 'country' and largely Afrikaans- or Dutch-speaking areas. The defeated candidate, De Korte, did best in Cape Town presumably because of his 'Dirty Party' connections.[54]

The Assembly election was a contest between five candidates for the four Cape Town seats. J. C. Hofmeyr stood alone against four merchants or businessmen, two of whom were to be Clean candidates in the 1880 municipal election.[55] The first of these, William Farmer, was a partner in the mercantile firm of W. Anderson & Co. He had extensive share holdings in a range of companies including the City Tramways Co. His own estimate of his wealth, in 1881, was £170,000.[56] The other future Clean was P. J. Stigant. He owned a furniture and undertaking business.[57]

The remaining two candidates were Thomas Fuller and Saul Solomon. Fuller was general manager of the Union Steamship Company and member of the Harbour Board. Solomon was owner of the *Cape Argus*, of which Fuller was a former editor. Yet again the connection between the English-language press and political interests was intimate.[58]

At the end of a very corrupt election, Hofmeyr came bottom of the poll with just over 2,000 votes. He received about half as many votes as Farmer, who had come top, and 600 less than Solomon, who was fourth. According to a newspaper that supported him, Farmer had done so well in the election because he had spent a great deal of money in securing votes. A secret ballot was only introduced in the 1890s. However, it was also reported that Farmer was the 'first choice' of Cape Town merchants.

J. C. Hofmeyr was unable to match the wealth of someone like Farmer, was unable to buy sufficient votes. On the other hand he was alleged to have threatened his mortgagees with the calling-up of their mortgages if they did not vote for him. Whether or not the allegation was true, J. C. Hofmeyr's failure to get elected as one of Cape Town's four representatives, despite the backing he received from J. H. Hofmeyr, demonstrated his inability to mobilise sufficient Afrikaner support in the city. The unique 'plumping' system that operated only in Cape Town Assembly elections allowed a voter to use all four of his votes for one candidate or to spread them between others. Hofmeyr had only needed 750 supporters casting all four of their votes for him to have been fairly sure of election. The 'English' vote would have to have been spread evenly over the other four candidates to keep him out.[59]

The Legislative council and Assembly elections not only demonstrated the effective hegemony of English mercantile and business interests in the town, it gave the latter the experience of organisation necessary to take Hofmeyr on at the local political level. In 1880 the *Cape Times* identified six reformers among the candidates for town councillors.[60] Bolus, Brown, McKenzie and Fleming were, like Farmer and Stigant, merchants and or businessmen. All of them could be said to have belonged to Cape Town's grand bourgeoisie. H. Bolus was a partner with his brother Walter in a stockbroking firm described as doing the 'chief' broking business in Cape Town.[61] J. L. Brown was a merchant and a director and chairman of the Equitable Fire Assurance and Trust Company.[62] A. R. McKenzie, although an extensive property owner, had vast investments in diamond and other shares in 1881, and a lucrative business as the chief landing agent at the docks.[63] Fleming was another successful merchant, as well as being the member of the Assembly for Graaff-Reinet.[64]

Their motives for standing for local government seem clear enough. All of these reformers possessed liquid capital. Most of them lived outside the municipality, in the southern suburbs between Mowbray and Wynberg, but had their stores or places of business in the centre of Cape Town. Trade was buoyant in 1880, the peak year of the first Cape Town boom of the Mineral Revolution. Yet the twin threats to trade of water shortage and disease, added to the third posed by the muddy, semi-impassable state of the streets in winter was not lost on the reformers. These men were able to draw on the British experience of urbanisation either because they were themselves British immigrants, or educated in Britain, or because of their close business ties, as merchants, with that country. There was also the fact that, as members of the 'worthy' and 'intelligent' English-speaking elite, they were targeted for action by the English-language press, which communicated the experiences of the Mother Country. Business experience itself might, as in England, help to explain why the raising of loans to finance reform would both seem necessary and, if large, would hold no terrors for them.[65] Moreover, they were not likely to be particularly hard hit by a relatively small extra charge on their property if rates had to be raised.

There may have been a more specific reason why reformers emerged to fight the municipal election of 1880. The election came at a time when merchants and businessmen were putting money into local infrastructure and industry, so that their attention was currently focused on local investment opportunities. Farmer and the Bolus brothers were principal investors in both the City Steam Laundry Company and the much more important City Tramways Company.[66] Both enterprises could benefit from a sympathetic town council. The Laundry Company, and any other industrial enterprise using steam, required an adequate water supply. A parliamentary report had suggested that Cape Town's was not.[67] The coming of tramways meant constant negotiation between council and companies on routes, road surfaces and so on. By the mid-1880s the *Lantern* was complaining that a Tramways ring now ran municipal affairs.[68]

Interest in local politics may have been enhanced for Fleming, Farmer and the editor of the *Lantern*, Mr Geary, when they became involved in establishing the Residency and Hotel Company in the city in 1879, the *Lantern*'s inaugural year. Fleming's firm also happened to be the agent for the Electric Light and Telephone Company, established in 1881, which began negotiations with the council in the same year. Zoutendyk, the Dirty Party member, suggested in 1880 that reformers only wanted to spend money on the central business area, not on the residential parts of the municipality.[69]

To dislodge the Dirty Party was made difficult for the Cleans by the nature of local elections. The eighteen members of the council, three for each district into which the municipality was divided, were elected by the votes of every adult property owner or occupier – provided their property was valued at more than £10, which all were by 1875. The same qualification applied to those standing for election. It is likely that the number of eligible voters was about four or five thousand.[70] But, as with central elections, there was as yet no secret ballot. This gave the landlords or their representatives the power to intimidate tenants as employers could intimidate workers. In the 1870s J. C. Hofmeyr apparently presided over polling, helpfully providing voters with a list of candidates they should vote for. There were also allegations that votes were bought.[71]

Manipulation of elections was possible in a number of other ways in the 1870s. First, it seems that the electoral lists, compiled on the orders of the council, were far from complete. The major deficiency lay in the absence of the names of most occupiers with only, on average, one name down for each house. Most of these houses should in theory have been able to supply many more eligible voters. The shifting nature of Cape Town's labouring classes must have contributed to the deficiency. There were also accusations that the council in this period deliberately failed to add new, possibly hostile, names to the list or even removed them.[72]

Another important method of manipulation was the ability of the council to fix the time when the poll took place. A poll between, say, 9 a.m. and 11 a.m. would effectively disenfranchise would-be voters unable to get permission from their employers to leave work. In practice both the timing and duration of council polls in the late 1870s were impressively anti-democratic. Always in working hours, many polls were succinct in the extreme. Between 1874 and 1876, for instance, a separate poll was held in each district and kept open for only half an hour. In 1877 one district had a poll lasting only ten minutes. The ease with which elections could be manipulated by the council helps to explain how property owners, once elected, could hang onto power. As the town council secretary put it in 1879: 'Ever since the the establishment of the municipality, as a rule the majority of the town councillors have always been landed proprietors.' The *fait accompli* nature of council elections in turn helps to explain the tiny polls that characterised the 1870s.[73]

Cape Town elections were never overtly party political in the nineteenth century, in the sense of national parties fighting elections. Fraser has shown that 'non-political' Manchester witnessed greater public apathy in local elections than any other city in Britain.[74] Only by the early 1880s did a clear choice emerge between Clean and Dirty

Parties, these loose associations of like-minded individuals and their supporters. When it did, in the elections of 1880 and 1882, interest in the election increased considerably.[75]

The limited powers of the municipality, before 1882, must also have aided apathy. For some such apathy presumably stemmed from the fact that they actually lived in the suburbs and saw municipal elections as irrelevant. They only had the municipal franchise because they were owners or occupiers of business premises.

The major problem for the reformers was to overcome all of this apathy. Merchants and businessmen were tied to the English-language press as the latter's advertisers and major source of income. In turn that press, and particularly the *Cape Times* and *Lantern*, served as willing proponents of their cause. One way of removing apathy and getting voters to support a Clean Party was through appeals to shared Englishness.

These appeals were seldom direct. Instead, the *Cape Times* and *Lantern* made implicit appeals to all White English-speaking Capetonians to give political support to a business and mercantile elite. These calls were coming at a time when the numbers of such Capetonians were swelling as immigration increased, presumably itself a reason why the town could support these new publications. Thus the *Lantern* asked in 1879 for a 'Colonial Dickens' to demonstrate 'how not to do it' in terms of municipal affairs. In the following poem of 1881 it referred to the town councillors as 'Bumbles':

> Waterless, rainless, sewerless and drainless,
> Surely our Bumbles are senseless and brainless!
> Thick through our streets the canteens abound
> But the devil the drop of good water is found.
> Stoeps all around us trip the unwary,
> Of dust and mud they are never chary;
> Of dead rats and cats, of crackers and noise,
> Of half drunken sailors and troublesome boys,
> Of *off-coloured* women and perfumes not sweet,
> Our councillors find us a plentiful treat;
> But of water they never find us a drop,
> For a cup of good tea or a stewed mutton chop.
> Of gas they have plenty –and cheap it would be,
> If they bottled their own for you and me;
> Of water committees and water rates too,
> I warrant they've plenty us all to undo;
> But of water they never will find us a sup,
> Unless these old Bumbles we haste to stir up! [my emphasis added][76]

The understanding of such references, in general the appreciation of such poems, necessitated a shared English culture, including a common perception of the admirable qualities of 'a cup of good tea'. Their use, by newspapers and magazines, suggests that a shared set of values, of symbols, were being used to unite and mobilise White English-speaking Capetonians. Mention of a different group, in this case 'off-coloured women', would strengthen self-identity. Comments on how cities such as Edinburgh had solved or were solving their sanitation problems could serve the same end.[77]

Englishness was undoubtedly informed by the Christian denominational difference of its adherents, be they Anglicans, Presbyterians or Methodists, compared to the DRC membership of most Afrikaners. Such differences could feed into the reform campaign. In 1880 a sermon in St George's Anglican Cathedral was on 'the Religion of Sanitation'.[78] The minister reminded the congregation that a municipal election was about to take place and urged them to vote for those 'pledged to sanitation'. P. J. Stigant, one of the Clean candidates in that election, was a cathedral churchwarden. The report of the sermon was in a newspaper owned and edited by an ex-Anglican minister and member of St George's congregation, St Leger.

With the combined efforts of journalists and ministers of religion, including those of the ex-minister turned journalist, the six reform candidates duly won seats in 1880. Presumably because of the watchful presence of the Cleans and their supporters, the poll was kept open until 3 p.m., 'much longer than usual'. More than twice as many people voted as on the previous highest occasion, 827 as opposed to 401. One tactic employed by the *Cape Times* was to spell out to suburbanites that they were not immune to the dangers of disease, even if they thought that they were remote from the filth and squalor of the town: 'The seed is sown in Waterkant [i.e. in town] and the harvest reaped in part on the breezy slopes of Wynberg.'[79]

The message was more easily conveyed when disease actually appeared. This happened in June 1882. Smallpox ravaged the town just weeks before the election of that year. Estimates of the number of victims have ranged from 800 to 4,000.[80] The *Cape Times* was able to berate the still insufficiently reformed council:

Now they hope in a week to accomplish the reforming work of years, and by a few buckets of whitewash or chloride of lime to compensate for the continuous stolid neglect of every sanitary precaution until the city is simply ripe for plague.[81]

The Lantern, something of a muck-raking journal, weighed in with renditions such as this:

THE TWO PLATFORMS.

4 The 'Clean' and 'Dirty' parties, *Lantern* magazine, 5 August 1882

Sing a song of smallpox
Hofmeyr gone askew;
Ashley, Louw and Zoutendyk,
In a pretty stew!
When the scare is over,
These rascals will begin
Their dirty tricks, to stop the bricks
Who would a Clean town win.

The same publications had dramatic cartoons depicting candidates as Clean or Dirty.[82] Attacks became highly personal. Readers were told that, for instance, Zoutendyk had 'unworthy' motives for seeking office and that Hofmeyr, Louw and Ashley had been insolvents. The Dirty Party as a whole were alleged to have promised no sanitary reform in return for Malay votes.[83]

Disease helped produce the desired result in this election, as it did for reformers in Leeds in the 1880s. It helped to overcome apathy and the possible reluctance of small businessmen and shopkeepers to vote for a party pledged to more expenditure, a higher rate. The result was Clean

Party victory. Thirteen of the successful eighteen candidates were identified as Cleans.[84]

The Dirty Party for their part had only been defended late in the day by J. H. Hofmeyr's Dutch-language *Zuid-Afrikaan*, which had attacked the Cleans as suburbanites, pointing out that only seven of their eighteen candidates actually lived in the municipality. The implication was that they were without a real interest or understanding of Cape Town's needs. The *Zuid-Afrikaan* singled out Hofmeyr and Louw as the most energetic individuals on the council in 1882. This and the English-language press's denigration of the couple as, at best, do-nothingers, strengthens the view that Clean versus Dirty incorporated an ethnic dimension.[85] That the *Zuid-Afrikaan* had not come to Dirty Party defence earlier was probably due to the fact that, as the mouthpiece of the *BBV*, it was more concerned with rural or Colony-wide issues and aimed primarily at a rural audience. This was a tendency among most Dutch-language newspapers in Cape Town throughout the late nineteenth century, as well as the Paarl-based and Afrikaans-language *Die Patriot*. In addition, although J. H. Hofmeyr had been personally against the Transvaal annexation, the *BBV* as a party only moved formally beyond farming issues in 1882 when members began to argue for the use of Dutch in parliament.

The division between Clean and Dirty over economic interests was made abundantly clear between 1880 and 1882. In September 1880, shortly after the election, a committee had been appointed by the town council consisting of councillors Fleming, Stigant, Brown, Farmer and Louw to decide what amendments, if any, were needed to existing legislation. This predominantly Clean committee reported in February 1881 that amendments were necessary. Aided by their three members of the House of Assembly, Fleming, Farmer and Stigant, the reformers proceeded to introduce a bill into parliament that contemplated a considerable increase in the financial powers of the council.

The bill proposed raising the borrowing powers of the council from £20,000 to £150,000, without the latter having to obtain the permission of the ratepayers. The bill allowed the council to increase the rate to at least 3d in the pound. They also wished to abandon the free supply of 25 to 50 gallons of water per day to every dwelling house (in reality to about half the dwelling houses). Instead, the council was to have the power to make property owners supply 100 gallons of water daily to each house, and the owners would have to pay for it.

The Dirty Party grudgingly accepted the very modest increase in the rate. They most definitely opposed the changes in the water regulations and the increase in borrowing powers. J. C. Hofmeyr was supported in his stand against the bill, when it came before a parliamentary select committee, by a petition sent in by seventy-one 'householders and ratepayers'. These included L. P. Cauvin who had property valued at over £10,000, Prince with nearly £4,000, R. H. Arderne with £7,500 and J. C. Wicht with £15,600. The Wicht family between them had owned 496 houses in 1875. Two members of the family became *Bond* members of the Cape parliament by the 1880s, which once again demonstrates the ethnic dimension of the Dirty Party.[86]

The bill was passed and became law in 1882, with only insignificant amendments.[87] But despite this and the 'Clean Party' victory of 1882, reforms in the 1880s were in practice limited, if not unimportant. The smallpox of 1882 made the establishment of a permanent quarantine hospital at Maitland a logical and immediate priority. Of most significance was the fact that a municipal officer of health, Dr G. H. Fisk, was appointed during the same emergency and his reports, published annually in the local press, continually highlighted the sanitary deficiencies of the town and suggested lines of action. They also suggested the additional powers that the council would require to make his plans a reality. But only some of these reports were acted upon, and usually after considerable delays.[88] Thus the council only succeeded in closing the cemeteries, near the centre of the city, in 1886. Thereafter they insisted on burial at Maitland or Mowbray. Municipal wash-houses, advocated in 1882, were eventually established on the slopes of Table Mountain, in 1888. The butchers' shambles, previously situated on the beachfront, was only demolished in 1889, and then moved outside municipal boundaries. Little was done to increase the water supply, except to repair and complete, by 1886, the Molteno Reservoir, whose dam had burst in 1882. A sanitary engineer was at last appointed, in 1887.[89] But the initiation of plans for a comprehensive drainage scheme in 1888 only came as the result of renewed pressure from reformers outside the council. The latter succeeded in getting parliament to appoint a select committee to investigate the city's sanitation. This committee recommended a comprehensive drainage scheme. The effective implementation of this scheme was to be a major achievement of the Clean council of the 1890s.[90]

Nothing was done before the 1890s to help relieve the housing shortage, increased by recent demographic growth, despite the fact that Fisk's brief had included dealing with overcrowding. Once again this mirrored developments in Britain where, as Briggs has shown, the strongest argument for sanitary reform was that it would save money in the long term. Attention to housing could not be justified in the same terms and was thus virtually neglected for the whole of the century.[91]

The relative lack of activity by the supposedly reformed council for a decade after 1882 can be explained by the fact that the Clean Party victory coincided with the beginnings of a deep depression. Smallpox had played a part in both. The consequence of the depression, and especially the contraction of the property market from the mid-1880s, was to slow the growth of municipal revenue, even allowing for the increased borrowing and rating powers of the council. Depressions aided the cause of parties of economy in England and the Dirty Party, Cape Town's equivalent, enjoyed a comeback in the late 1880s in a series of elections characterised by the small polls of the 1870s. Rates were levied lower than the new maximum of 3d in the pound. Minimal sums were raised in loans between 1882 and 1890.[92]

Dirty Party recovery was aided by the fact that some leading Cleans were themselves among those seriously embarrassed by the sudden economic downturn. McKenzie, with debts of £400,000, disappeared from municipal politics for more than a decade. Fleming's firm became 'virtually insolvent' and Fleming himself resigned from the mayoralty in 1883, just before the election of that year. It was not to be until the 1890s, until a period of renewed economic boom, that a reconstituted Clean Party presided over a really substantial package of reforms.[93]

In the intervening years the acquiescence of central government permitted the passing of municipal legislation which made political power at the local level more securely the preserve of Cape Town's bourgeoisie, and specifically its predominant White English-speaking component. Changes to the municipal franchise in the 1880s and 1890s were aimed at restricting the vote and thereby making the town council more safely the creature of 'better', i.e. bourgeois, White Capetonians. The *Cape Times*, in 1882, had expressed the hope that municipal politics would no longer be 'flooded with an overwhelming tide of ignorance and besotted obstinacy', which had allegedly been the case when every tenant had the vote.[94] Legislation in 1885 duly cut down the number of tenants able to vote, stipulating that the franchise should be confined to those who paid the tenants' rate under Act 44 of 1882. As the town clerk explained to the select committee responsible for approving this legislation:

For instance there is a house in St John's Street occupied by very common people, who each have a separate room and each one of those tenants would be entitled to be registered – that is why we now define what is the meaning of the word occupier.[95]

If the Hofmeyrs had been Cape Town's ruling family of the 1870s, then by the 1880s they had clearly been deposed, even if the new ruling elite experienced a kind of economic Fronde before taking firm control of the local state in the next decade. The Clean Party victory of 1882 confirmed the strength within the city's wider bourgeoisie of the section that was White and English speaking. It came after several years of economic growth and British immigration into Cape Town. The combined motivation for merchants and businessmen to participate in local politics stemmed from their desire to ensure the continued viability of Cape Town as a commercial centre. They were prompted, and supported, in their bids for local political office by English-language newspapers that preached the new gospel of Lord Beaconsfield: 'Sanitas, Sanitas, Omnia Sanitas.'[96]

Sanitation rhetoric was part and parcel of Englishness in the Cape Town context. Such Englishness demanded loyalty to the empire, respectability, deference and cleanliness from those it sought to colonise. In the course of the reform campaign, individuals, such as J. C. Hofmeyr, Zoutendyk or Louw, came under attack for implicitly un-English behaviour. The ethnic dimension to these attacks was influenced by the contemporary annexation of the Transvaal, the latter's rebellion in 1880 and the rise of the *Afrikaner Bond*.

Despite the efforts of the Hofmeyrs, Afrikaner ethnicity appears to have remained weak in Cape Town in the late nineteenth century. One reason was that there was no complete or enduring correlation between Dutch or British origin and economic activity that could sustain ethnic divisions within the town's bourgeoisie. There were merchants of Dutch descent and English property owners. By the 1890s Dutch speakers, such as D. P. Graaff and D. C. De Waal, had left their Dirty Party affiliations of the 1880s behind, carved out business fortunes and become leading figures in the Clean Party of that decade.

There must also have been a high rate of Anglicisation among bourgeois Capetonians of Dutch descent. During 1881 the *Cape Times* attacked Afrikaner republicanism, and accused J. H. Hofmeyr of stirring up sympathy for the Transvaal in Cape Town, while praising the loyalty of the 'old' Cape Dutch families.[97] These families would have been at least bilingual in English and Dutch, and some might have been wholly English speaking by the 1870s. English had become the language of commerce and public life in general by then. In 1889 services in the main Dutch Reformed Church in Cape Town alternated between English and Dutch. The medium of instruction in government schools in the town was English. This included the Normal Colleges, established to help produce teachers. Afrikaans had become the language of poorer Capetonians, be they White or Black, and only a small number of rural White Afrikaans speakers migrated to the city in the late nineteenth century to add to their numbers. The very divide, along class lines, of Dutch and Afrikaans speakers probably helped to weaken Afrikaner ethnicity in Cape Town.[98]

These factors, together with its focus on rural issues, may explain why *Bond* membership remained small in the city in the late nineteenth century. In 1884 the *Cape Times* described the *Bond*'s presence in Cape Town as 'feeble'. Almost ten years later the Argus was referring to the 'little known' branch of the *Bond* in the city.[99]

What was crucial was that White ethnicity continued to be a potentially uniting or reuniting identity for English and Afrikaners alike. The English may have been stereotyped in Afrikaans popular discourse as smooth and untrustworthy townsmen, the potential and actual seducers of Afrikaans women from their simple and honest rural roots.[100] References to Afrikaner political movements in Cape Town's English newspapers may have ridiculed them as unpatriotic. Afrikaners or 'the Dutch' were often stereotyped in English discourse as 'deliberate and slow' or 'inert', the English (or Anglo-Saxons) as bringing progress.[101] This was also the English perception of the divide between Dirty and Clean, and demonstrates how racism usually stems from or rationalises actual social relations and conflict.

But despite these racist utterances, both English and Afrikaner discourse continued to stress what the two 'races' had in common, rather than always emphasising their differences. Langham Dale, while believing that Afrikaners were indolent, graciously stated that 'the qualities that lie at the base of the greatness of the Anglo-Saxon race find their analogies in the Dutch character'.[102] Wilmot concluded his history by saying that his narrative had been about how 'colonists' had successfully struggled to hold their position against a 'savage race'.[103] Colonists were Whites of English and Dutch descent, and both were depicted as defending civilisation. In his history published in 1878, Noble sympathised with the *voortrekker* Piet Retief and his followers. They had been 'cruelly murdered' by the Zulu King Dingaan in 1838 and Noble applauded the fact that other *trekkers* had revenged themselves on this 'treacherous savage'.[104] J. A. Froude had been sent out by Disraeli's government to further South African confederation under the British flag in the mid-1870s. In a book published in 1881 he argued that such a development required conciliating 'the Dutch people there'.[105] For their part J. H. Hofmeyr and the leaders of the new *Bond* subdued much of the virulently anti-English rhetoric of early Afrikaner mobilisation. They retained a definition of Afrikaner that could incorporate English-speaking colonists.

White ethnicity had the potential to unite Afrikaner and English colonists. Continued stress on their mutual Whiteness by members of the Afrikaner and English elites, even at moments of conflict, kept open the door to reconciliation. When Neethling was expressing sympathy for the Transvaal cause in the Legislative council he talked about 'what the *white* inhabitants ... had suffered in their desire to be free from the rule of the British government' [my emphasis]. In 1877 St Leger, for all his English jingoism, argued in an editorial that Whites should take pride in their common heritage.[106]

The rhetoric of White supremacy more actively encouraged belief in the mutual economic and political interests of the Cape bourgeoisie – be they merchants, rentiers, farmers or mineowners – as it could between employers and workers. White supremacy, cries such as 'South Africa for the Anglo-Saxon and Teutonic races', made by Alfred Ebden at an immigration society meeting in 1881, promised primary access to state resources for those so defined.[107] When such mutuality of interest was perceived by its intended audience, and this possibility was further enhanced when rhetoric became social practice, it encouraged White ethnicity above English, Afrikaner or class identity.

We have seen that segregation already existed between White and Black, albeit in differing forms, in some churches, schools and medical institutions in 1875. In 1878 supremacist rhetoric preceded, and segregation followed, the introduction of legislation on the colonial defence force. The Cape Mounted Yeomanry Act confined membership of this semi-professional cavalry force to men of 'European extraction'. The Prime Minister and Colonial Secretary, J. G. Sprigg, had introduced the bill by saying that 'the ease with which the natives had been enabled to acquire arms, had led them to think they were in a position to cope with the European population'. He said that the government had been warned not to rely on the forces under its disposal, a warning which had proved correct. So now it intended to create 'a force we can rely on'. In similar manner, the Attorney-General, Thomas Upington, argued that the time had arrived for changes in the existing burgher force. He motivated the successful enactment of legislation which allowed for adult males in the colony to be listed 'according to race'. White inhabitants would thereafter be called up as burghers, 'others' as levies. Upington explained that such a measure was necessary because recently 'Hottentots, in a particular ward, outvoted the white men upon the election of officers'. They had chosen one of 'their own' to lead them. The Whites had then refused to serve under 'Hottentots' and complained to the government.

Dutch- and Afrikaans-speaking members of parliament, such as De Korte and the *BBV* member Neethling, supported the creation of a segregated defence force. Their main concern was that such a force might be used outside the borders of the Colony, implicitly against Whites in the recently annexed Transvaal. Therefore Sprigg gave specific assurances that the new force would not be used to put down disturbances anywhere in the 'European portions of South Africa'. The purpose of the force was obviously to maintain White supremacy which specifically meant, in 1878, controlling 'Natives' inside, or near, the colonial border.[108]

There were certainly differences among Whites over appropriate policies towards ruling Blacks. These differences would often directly reflect different material interests. But the belief that most Whites had in their (at least current) superiority over Blacks was predicated on the continued correlations that they could make between pigmentation and divisions of labour in the late nineteenth century. The corollary was that if such correlations were eroded the social basis of White supremacy, and therefore the ideology itself, would be undermined.

The Mineral Revolution, which radically increased economic activity in southern Africa, introduced new divisions of labour and threatened to destabilise old ones. The discovery of diamonds had, by the 1870s, rapidly improved the Cape government's finances, enabling and inspiring its newly Responsible ministers to embark on extensive railway building to the interior in that decade. A major problem they faced was the need to acquire sufficient and suitable labour as cheaply as possible.

In the early 1870s it was difficult for the Cape government to get an adequate labour supply, according to these criteria, from within the Colony or from African societies on its borders. The latter remained relatively prosperous and unravaged by wars and drought. When this situation began to change, in the late 1870s, the cost of acquiring African labour was cheapened. African labour, while still semi-proletarianised, could meet part of its own subsistence, something which was not true of White labour.[109]

To begin with though, large numbers of 'hardened' White navvies had to be imported from Europe to work on the railways. They supplemented local labour, for which the government was competing with private employers, notably farmers. Though the White navvies were paid considerably more than the available local Black labour, the railway authorities apparently calculated that they were cost effective for the particularly arduous work involved in taking the lines from the coastal plains on to the inland plateau, a task completed by 1878. Thereafter the search for a cheaper labour supply was intensified. This was the background to the importation of Africans, including prisoners of war, into the Western Cape from 1878 and the increasing utilisation of White labour in a reduced and supervisory capacity.[110]

By 1879 the government was faced with Western Cape farmers, now organised in the *BBV*, who complained of a shortage of labour, meaning a shortage of labour on the terms they required. The problem appears to have been that the government had paid higher wages to its Black railway employees, as well as the imported Whites, driving up labour costs for farmers. The farmers wanted state intervention to supplement and cheapen the cost of their labour.[111]

The Governor, Sir Bartle Frere, believed that the answer was to import more labourers from Europe, arguing that 'all' recognised the need to increase the White part of the Colony's population.[112] Implicitly such a policy would have increased the number of English speaking colonists, and thus have aided the continuation of English hegemony. In the event the majority of farmers thought that Black labour was preferable to White, if only because the latter was believed to be more independent, more likely to seek better positions. The evidence shows that part of the reason for this 'independence' of White labour was that the latter expected more than farmers could offer. The corollary was that Black labour was cheaper. Among potential Black labourers, those from Mozambique were generally held to be better than the other prime candidates, Africans from the Eastern Cape. This was largely because so many of the latter, brought to the Western Cape between 1878 and 1879, had deserted. Eastern Cape Africans would only be adequate, according to several witnesses, if they could be properly controlled and their services secured. Thus the Cape government in 1879 brought Mozambiquan labourers to the Western Cape. The lack of skilled labour was to be met by importing White artisans ready trained from Britain.[113]

Despite subsequent suggestions by government officials of the possibility of importing unskilled White labour, the experience gleaned from the late 1870s and early 1880s appears to have set the pattern for state employment: a division of labour between White skilled, supervisory or management and Black unskilled. As the Agent-General for the Cape Colony in London, Sir Charles Mills, put it in 1886: 'Unskilled native labour is plentiful, and European labour finds it difficult to compete with the natives who are able to subsist upon lower wages.'[114]

The pattern was confirmed by contemporary developments in the diamond industry of Kimberley, Griqualand West, which was annexed to the Cape in 1880. In the early 1870s White unskilled labour had been employed by claim owners 'when African labour was scarce and before the growth of the production unit required the employment of overseers'.

Before the 1880s it was not a *fait accompli* that unskilled labour would be Black. According to Sammy Marks, one of the major Kimberley mine owners who had experimented with imported Cornish labour, White labourers were too expensive and difficult to control. Because of these considerations, a White–Black division of labour came into being on the mines. White ex-diggers or share owners became supervisors of Black labour while, with increasingly sophisticated mechanisation, White engineers and other highly trained White labour had to be imported from Europe. Black labour was controlled through its segregation in closed compounds, the labour registration office and pass laws.[115]

The Table Bay Harbour Board also experimented with the employment of White labour in construction and maintenance work. Between March and December 1882 the Board, which consisted of leading merchants such as Murison (who had been elected to the Legislative council in 1878), brought about a hundred Irish labourers to Cape Town and housed the men in a 'coolie barracks' on the East Quay. But these White labourers also demonstrated independence. They deserted the Board for better employment or got drunk and had to be sacked. The experiment was therefore abandoned as a failure. The Board confined its importation of unskilled labour to men from Mozambique.[116]

So the diamond stage of the Mineral Revolution, and consequent employer experiments at the Cape with White unskilled labour, failed to break down the approximate correlation between lightness or darkness of pigmentation and divisions of labour in town and countryside. The maintenance of this correlation was not simply the result of inherited prejudice, on the part of employers, from the era of racial slavery or immediate post-emancipation rural social relations. The belief that White unskilled labour was more independent than Black, and that mixing the two would not work, seemed also to be supported by contemporary evidence. So the ideology of White supremacy and the consequent negative stereotyping of Blacks continued to be sustained in the consciousness of White Cape colonists, be they English or Afrikaner, by their experience of social relations in the early 1880s. Ironically this racist discourse was fed by the growth of English and Afrikaner ethnic mobilisation that still threatened to divide them.

Cape Colonists who thought of themselves in ethnic terms as White racialised the rest of the city's population while doing so. In other words, they categorised others according to real or imagined biological distinctions, which they believed to be heritable. Various qualities were then attributed to the groups of people in different categories.[1]

As early as 1875 the process of categorisation demonstrated a familiarity with the 'scientific' ideas about the division of humanity into 'races', and the relative qualities of these 'races', which had emerged in Britain from the late eighteenth century. Wilmot's history explained that 'Kafir ... as a family of the human race ... is classed as being of a modified Negro physical conformation'. Hottentots were believed to be 'virtually extinct as a race', according to the author of the 1875 census report, and none were found by the enumerators in Cape Town. This categorisation was not entirely random. It reflected the observation by Whites of a variety of differences in other peoples according to appearance or culture, or both, which those people themselves were likely to have felt when looking at Whites or each other.[2]

Racialisation by Whites was at least in part based on the apparent self-perceptions of those categorised, even if the labels were White inventions. Therefore 7,700 Capetonians could be called 'Malays', despite the fact that they were acknowledged to be of 'mixed race,' because they seemed to have their own cultural self-identity, part of which was adherence to Islam. In contrast more than 11,000 Capetonians were only labelled as 'Mixed and Other', because the census compilers had some difficulty, at this stage, in assigning them to a more specific category on the basis of easily perceivable phenotypical or cultural difference. The census enumerators were not the only ones to face this difficulty. Langham Dale talked of 'the mixed native population of the towns and villages'. Wilmot referred to the 'coloured population, of mixed race, which forms a large proportion of the labouring class in the west', assuming them to be of slave descent. Among rural White Afrikaans speakers they were commonly called 'Di bruin folk' or 'Di werk folk' (brown people or work people).[3]

The qualities that Whites attributed to people of other categories or 'races' in the course of the nineteenth century were not always racist, in the sense of being predominantly negative. Nor were they consistent over the years. Predominantly positive as well as negative qualities were observed as characterising different racialised groups at various times. Frequently this stereotyping suggested that both positive and negative traits were present in the same group. Stereotypes, wherever conferred and by whom, could survive or move beyond the historical situation that gave rise to them, be it Western Cape slavery, Eastern Cape wars or rural social relations in the nineteenth-century Transvaal. But they were reused or reinvented elsewhere, and shaped into 'coherent theories' in articles and books, because they continued to have meaning in similar or even somewhat different circumstances. Obviously the attributing to others of good or bad qualities depended on the value system of those doing the stereotyping.

The nature of their relationship with those they stereotyped often directly and demonstrably affected the qualities Whites perceived and how this consciousness translated into social practice in the nineteenth century. This is revealed in the evidence given by employers to a labour commission in 1879. Discussion, prompted by parliamentary questioners, revolved around the relative intelligence and suitability of the 'races' for particular labour or, more broadly, life roles. The replies were similar to those discussions that took place in the post-emancipation Caribbean. Witnesses attempted to classify racialised groups according to their labouring prowess. What they were doing was to attribute qualities to the whole group based on their experience of individual labourers held to belong to it, while ignoring the effect of material factors on that experience.

If generalisations about racialised groups of labourers contained some truth, then this was due to factors other than biologically inherited characteristics. Western Cape farmers had experienced labourers from Mozambique earlier in the nineteenth century as their slaves or as apprenticed Prize Negroes on extremely low wages. In either case, the cost of maintaining these labourers had been low, their 'independence' curtailed by legal sanction and the fact that desertion was a difficult option. In contrast Eastern Cape Africans, brought to the Western Cape between 1878 and 1879, had deserted home in large numbers.[4]

In the years immediately before the growth of a more assertive Englishness in the late 1870s, the stereotypes of non-English people in Cape Town in English-language newspapers and books were generally positive. Stereotypes seem to have been largely reserved for Black Capetonians, although the Dutch as we saw were sometimes described as 'slow' or 'unprogressive'. The racialised groups most commented on were Malays, with occasional remarks about those in the 'Mixed and Other' category of the 1875 census. Together, according to the census, they made up over 98 per cent of the city's Black population. The town's small Bantu-speaking African component provided the other 2 per cent. In the early 1870s, when their numbers were small, they received little descriptive attention.

Stereotypes of Malays are frequent in English descriptions of Cape Town from the 1830s onwards. By the middle of the nineteenth century opinions that were apparently widely held among White Capetonians were that Malays were either sober and hardworking or 'addicted to pilfering' and capable of evil magic, or perhaps both. In 1855 J. S. Mayson brought together mostly positive stereotypes in a book which helped establish 'Malay' as an enduring racialised category in White discourse. In *The Malays of Cape Town* he distinguished between what he called 'Malays proper' and 'Arabs, Mozambique prize-negroes, Hottentots, and Christian perverts' who, because they were also Muslims, formed part of Cape Town's Malay population. While stumbling through this rather difficult explanation of his categorisation, and admitting that the Malay 'complexion varies from a light brown to a deep olive shade', Mayson saw no contradiction in describing Malays as though they were all of a similar physical type, as though they were a single 'race'. He could then go on to describe what he took to be Cape Town Malay qualities and characteristics. Some of their virtues were honesty, sobriety, cleanliness, devotion to each other and fidelity to the government; their vices were cunning, deceit, petty thieving and vengefulness. He thought that at least some of the vices 'have been transmitted hereditarily'. Details of Malay characteristics included particular diet, distinct dress and occupations (he thought Malays were particularly good horsemen, artisans and domestic servants) and their Islamic practices.[5]

By the early 1870s the negative stereotyping of Malays still apparent in Mayson's book had all but disappeared. Langham Dale thought that the Malays 'brought the deftly-handed characteristics of the Asiatic amongst the duller souls of African mould'. Noble described Malays as 'very serviceable not only in household occupations, but in various mechanical employments'. The *Cape Argus*, in a leader in February 1876, said that they were 'orderly' and 'respectable' and followed 'public affairs'.[6]

The stereotypes of the 'Mixed and Others' were less frequent, presumably because of the rather vague nature of the category. But they were paternalistic rather than being predominantly negative. Noble said that the 'mixed native population' were the working labourers, 'contented with warm sunshine and a meal of rice, and always full of animal spirits, grinning with natural good humour, or ready to explode in fits of laughter'. Wilmot believed that 'the coloured population' had 'been trained to habits of decency and order'.[7]

These highly condescending comments reflected the interacting class and ethnic identities of their authors. Their dual and overlapping perspectives as English and bourgeois influenced how they viewed other Capetonians who appeared to be, and mostly were, neither. For Noble, like Mayson and many other bourgeois White observers, racialised categories conformed to divisions of labour in the city's social order. For Noble, Malays were artisans and domestic servants, 'mixed coloureds' were labourers or 'coolies'. What all bourgeois English commentators saw were large numbers of their social inferiors who were behaving satisfactorily, who were 'respectable' or 'orderly', who implicitly accepted the values of Englishness.

These perceptions are in sharp contrast to the decidedly negative stereotypes of Black Capetonians – Malays, Coloureds and Africans – that increasingly littered the pages of the English-language press in the late 1870s and 1880s. Their appearance closely paralleled, chronologically, the rising campaign for urban reform in Cape Town. Both climaxed in 1882 with the smallpox epidemic. Racism went in tandem with Englishness and the discovery of urban problems.

Before examining what this increased racism may have implied for changes in social practice in Cape Town, and how both ideology and practice were informed by developments outside the city, it is necessary to examine the particular content of Cape Town racist discourse in this period. This content was not random but stemmed, directly or indirectly, from existing social relations between adherents of Englishness and people in other racialised categories. It implicitly or explicitly suggested both the main defect of the group being targeted and possible 'solutions'.

This discourse found expression chiefly in those two new English journals of the late 1870s, the *Cape Times* and the *Lantern*. Their editors, St Leger, Geary and McCombie, were perhaps the prime ethnic mobilisers of Englishness in the city. The negative stereotyping of Malays would appear to have been part and parcel of their newspapers' campaign against the Dirty Party, since Malays were represented as the latter's allies and supporters.

This means that Malays fell victim to English ethnic mobilisation, which grew by distinguishing itself from the 'otherness' it perceived in the rest of Cape Town's population. In general the English section of Cape Town's bourgeoisie was attempting to assert its hegemony over the rest of the city's population. Cape Town's Malay community, 40 per cent of

Black Capetonians in 1875, could be seen as the largest and most cohesive obstacle to that achievement.

The journals behind the promotion of Englishness brought together different negative stereotypes. The *Cape Times* in 1876 had talked of 'Abdol' whose house 'is guiltless of the trace of the scrubbing brush', directly contradicting and reversing Mayson's stereotype of the clean Malay. In 1878 the same newspaper, while discussing the need for sanitary reform, described the horrified reactions of a visitor to the 'Moslem quarter' who nevertheless walked 'erect, with the manly bearing of an Englishman'.[8] The *Lantern* carried an article supporting European grocers who had to compete with their 'monopolistic' Malay counterparts in 1880. Hostility was focused on these Malays who 'amass fortunes' and 'ride out for holidays'.[9]

Economic interests fed the different negative elements in the resulting stereotypes that appeared between 1875 and 1882. Merchants did not want trade disrupted and denigrated Malays for supporting an (Afrikaner-led) Dirty Party unwilling to raise rates to improve roads and water supply during a period of rapid economic and demographic growth. English shopkeepers, threatened by cheaper prices, could potentially benefit from criticisms of Malay greengrocers, the created equation between dirt and Malays, which might drive custom in the desired direction. Employers resented Malay 'independence' and their alleged fondness for holidays because they made labour scarce or wages higher.

Negative stereotypes in the newspapers had the potential to promote or confirm 'knowledge' about Malays among Cape Town workers, particularly English-speaking artisans most likely to be readers of the journals. In 1880 'Ulster Irishman' wrote to the *Cape Times* saying skilled trades were 'divided between Malays and Europeans, but the former are too fond of holidays and airing their wives to be reliable workmen'.[10] In 1882 the *Lantern* carried an article attacking Malay sweated labour in the domestic tailoring industry: 'We have seen a sickly mass of drunkenness, pallor and dirt, stitching a dress suit destined to adorn the person of...our merchants and our husbands.' These unfavourable impressions can be compared with Trollope's comment a few years earlier that Malays were 'the most valuable race' as workers.[11]

By the early 1880s Malays were being accused of making Cape Town both an immoral and dangerous place for English habitation. *Lantern* editorials accused Malays of running the brothels and shebeens of the city. 'Civis' wrote to the *Cape Times* complaining about 'shouting and screaming' Malays who beat the police, suggesting that 500 of them should be sent to the front to fight against Africans: 'Cape Town could spare them.' The *Lantern*, not to be outdone, reported that Malay 'outrages' were getting 'fearfully common ... rowdy Malays haunt the streets in gangs ... the centre of the town itself ... [is] unsafe after dark'.[12]

The *Cape Monthly Magazine* offered one explanation of Malay 'independence': the younger generation were breaking with tradition. The writer of an article in 1875 regretted the fact that only 'old Moslems' now wore conical hats and wooden clogs. In contrast young Malay 'swells' were 'aping' Europeans.[13] A few years later a Christian evangelist summed up what was thought in some bourgeois English minds to be a recent lack of Malay deference or acceptance of place:

Formerly the Malays were the trusted servant class. There were bonds of affection between them and their White employers. They were much humbler and more accessible than at present ... Malays were spoken of as specially faithful, though humble citizens ... There is no longer the same intimacy of dependence ... The Malays are now rather exclusive, and independent.[14]

It would appear that by 1882 all the key elements of the negative stereotyping of Malays had been expressed in either the *Lantern* or *Cape Times*. Malays were independent, dirty, lazy, profligate, ignorant and unruly. A letter from 'Disgusted Citizen' to the *Cape Times* in March 1881 brought all of these elements together in a vicious verbal attack. Malays were 'a motley lot of blacks, half-breeds and Europeans'. They would only condescend to do four days work per week, never saved, monopolised 'certain' branches of industry, were ignorant, their votes could be bought, they dressed like 'peacocks' but lived at home like 'swine'.[15]

That these stereotypes of the Malays were widely accepted among the audience of the *Cape Times* and *Lantern* is suggested by the paucity of refutations by anyone other than one correspondent, 'Fair Play', two Anglican clergymen and Malays themselves.[16] Racist diatribes reflected, from a White perspective, social relations and conflicts with Malays which existed between 1875 and 1882. They also reflected the strength of Malay ethnicity, and its apparent and real opposition to English values and hegemony.

The fact was that Malays really had been more 'accessible' and 'dependent' earlier in the nineteenth century: before emancipation. Freedom for them had been very much about establishing as much independence as possible, both during the erosion of slavery and after formal emancipation itself. As fishermen, retailers, cab owners, self-employed artisans, or as washerwomen working above the city at Platteklip, ex-slaves could have some sense of self-ownership, of escape from master-class surveillance. So they could when choosing not to work a six-day week, and when to 'ride out on holiday', indeed by defining what day was a holiday, Saturday over Sunday. Islam as a choice over Christianity offered, before and after emancipation, a degree of spiritual independence. It also offered 'parallel' educational, medical and legal institutions and practices to those proferred by exclusionary White Christian authority. A popular phrase by the late nineteenth century was that ''Slam's Kerk is die Zwart Man's Kerk' (Islam's church is the black man's church). Islamic institutions, kinship and occupational ties, as well as shared slave heritage, commemorated in annual celebrations on 1 December (emancipation) and 1 January (the traditional slave holiday), and their version of the Afrikaans language served to give people who lived in close proximity to one another in the inner city a sense of community which underpinned Malay ethnicity. Equally, part of Malay otherness in English discourse was their apparent imperviousness to Christian evangelism. Indeed Islam appeared to be on the ascendant and even gaining converts among Whites in the 1870s and 1880s.[17]

Malays had struggled to become 'independent' and wished to remain so. As Abdol Soubeyan put it in 1882: 'Independence is the aim of everyone who is a little above grovelling in the mud.'[18] If Soubeyan had read the journal of Lady Duff Gordon, who visited Cape Town in 1860, he could have pointed out that she had seen Malay independence as a positive quality. On the other hand Duff Gordon reported that Dutch Capetonians hated the Malays, their former slaves, whose ' "insolent prosperity" annoys them'.[19] A previous Dutch, ex-master class, negative stereotype of Malays could well have survived in Dutch racist discourse and was now being borrowed by English, rather than being newly invented.

Urban reform, particularly the English discovery of the sanitation gospel, threatened Malay identity and independence as a community. Fish-curing on Rogge Bay beach might be seen as a 'nuisance' by English politicians and doctors; its prevention, and any threat to the viability of fishing as their livelihood, was seen as oppression by Malay fishermen. Jongie Siers and John Mahomet had referred to the days of slavery in their 1878 petition: 'We always thought that we were emancipated in the reign of our Gracious Majesty Queen Victoria, and freed from tyranny, but it seems that we are mistaken.'[20]

An even more alarming attack on the Malay community was seemingly posed in the early 1880s by English sanitary and medical practices that were perceived by Malays to threaten their religion: the impounding of potentially contaminated holy water from Mecca and the proposed removal of cemeteries outside the municipal boundaries. The latter would make it difficult to continue with the traditional practice of carrying the body in procession to the grave. During the 1882 smallpox epidemic, fumigation, inoculation, hospitalisation and quarantining were also seen to be interfering with Islamic practice or to be contrary to Islamic belief. Communal or ethnic perceptions of the threat posed by government actions in times of epidemic were not, as Elizabeth Van Heyningen has pointed out, unique to Muslims or the Cape. In Cape Town they led to a mixture of deferential and defiant responses by members of the Malay community. Ethnic mobilisation, and leadership during particular moments of opposition, was provided by imams and members of the wealthier elite, who had been educated in Christian schools as well as their own, such as Jongie Siers and Abdol Burns.

Burns was a cab owner and driver whose surname came from his Scottish father. But his mother was 'Coloured', and he had been brought up as a Muslim. As a fluent English speaker he represented Malay grievances to local and central government, as well as to the press.[21] During the smallpox epidemic he initially denied that the disease was contagious, claimed that fumigation and vaccination were against Islamic beliefs and, at a public meeting, threatened to shoot anyone who tried to take his children to the isolation hospital.[22]

Such defiance only appeared to confirm the stereotype of dirty and illogical Malay intransigence, in English minds. The Prime Minister of the Cape, Sir Thomas Scanlen, in a letter to a fellow member of the Legislative Assembly about Malay objections to the quarantining of holy water, railed venomously against 'accursed Abdol, and his filth', 'these brutes' and 'dirty Malays'.[23] In the course of the smallpox epidemic Malays, like Jews in medieval Europe, were singled out as scapegoats. Malay objections to quarantining and vaccination contributed to the panic and fury.

Towards the end of August it was reported in the English-language press that Malay washerwomen had been instrumental in spreading smallpox by deliberately putting the underclothes of Whites in contact with the infected bodies of the dead and dying. The fact that this was held to be their 'diabolical method of revenge' was perhaps a perverse admission of class guilt on the part of the White bourgeoisie. Certainly it suggests that the negative stereotyping of Malays had made the acceptance of such a rumour possible.

The fact that the Malays wanted to continue to bury their dead in the traditional manner was also seen as tantamount to wishing to infect Whites. These rumours seem to have been quite widely believed. At the end of September, the *Lantern* continued to fuel them by reporting that the spread of smallpox among Whites was still a matter to be investigated. The *Lantern* also mentioned that Whites were ignoring quarantine procedures, but did not, of course, suggest that their lapses demonstrated a prima facie desire to spread smallpox.[24] It is possible that some Malays, themselves tired of what they experienced as interference and prejudice, played on the latter: 'It was not an uncommon thing for a Malay woman, on meeting a European in the street, to throw out her hand ... as one did to me once ... and say, "There, take the small-pox".'[25] If this happened, it could only have increased English fear and fury. Whether it did or not, it seems that 'Malay' had become a term of abuse in the mouths of many 'other than Malay' Capetonians by the early 1880s.[26]

Racist diatribes against Malays went with suggested 'solutions' to the defects detected by editors and their correspondents. In 1879 Geary argued for an educational test as a franchise qualification to stop political representatives being elected who knew how to canvass the 'Malays and Blacks'. The following year he was saying that Malays should be made part of the colonial levies. In 1882, after the smallpox epidemic, McCombie railed against 'dirty, lazy, erratic and independent Malays' and declared that Chinese labour ought to replace them in the Western Cape. A week later he published a letter from 'Faugh-a-Ballogh' in favour of residential segregation of Malays.[27] A similar letter appeared in the *Cape Times* from 'Friend of the Free State'. This unpleasant missive argued that 'it is high time that the White people of the Metropolis built a town for themselves and left the present town for [a] location for the Malays, Mozambiques ... *et hoc genus omne* ... to breed fever'.[28]

Racist diatribes against Malays in the press may have affected donations to the relief committee set up to help victims of the smallpox epidemic and their families. When forced to provide a smallpox isolation hospital in 1882, the town council employed 'rigid segregation', between Malays, Coloureds, 'Mozambicans' and Whites. This segregation was not entirely White imposed. Apparently Malay 'priests', initially opposed to the removal of Muslim patients to hospital for religious reasons, changed their minds but demanded separate facilities.[29]

In the event few of the suggestions in the newspapers led to changes in social practice before 1882. The residential segregation of Malays and Whites would have been extremely expensive. It was not clear whether local or central government would have to implement it, and therefore who would have to pay. Only in the 1890s did leading politicians such as Cecil Rhodes, the Prime Minister, and J. H. Hofmeyr come out in support of such segregation, as we shall see. But they did so while debating the powers and responsibilities of the Cape Town council, implicitly suggesting that establishing locations should be one of them. But among members of Cape Town's dominant class there was little material motivation to separate the lower classes residentially. Residential exclusion had already been purchased in the Gardens or the suburbs; to paraphrase Trollope, this was the part of Cape Town in which 'White men' lived.

The municipal franchise was changed to reduce Malay influence in local politics, but not only their influence. Changes also reflected the class interests of the English-speaking bourgeoisie. St Leger said that one provision of the Municipal Act of 1882 was aimed at counteracting Dirty Party support from the Malay vote. When three councillors were elected for each of the six different municipal districts, the geographically concentrated Malay vote was more influential than if the entire municipal electorate voted in a single constituency. So the 1882 Act changed electoral arrangements accordingly. But after the Act was put into operation, and after the outbreak of smallpox, St Leger still thought that the municipal electorate was 'flooded with an overwhelming tide of ignorance and besotted obstinacy', because every tenant had the vote, irrespective of whether they paid taxes.[30] The Municipal Act of 1885 duly confined the franchise to principal tenants or 'occupiers', those who paid a tenants' rate.

Changes to the central franchise, or decisions on the composition of the colonial defence force, were matters for central government politicians and administrators. The matter of altering the franchise was raised by J. H. Hofmeyr in the Legislative Council in 1879, during a debate on a possible poll tax: 'The evils of the present franchise were generally admitted, but people hesitated to deal with it.'[31]

In fact there was no majority support in parliament for reducing the Black vote before the *Bond*'s electoral successes of 1884. This is demonstrated by the failure of petitions or motions to this effect, put forward by representatives of rural constituencies (largely in the Eastern Cape) in 1874, 1878 and 1882. That there were no changes in the franchise until 1887 was partly because some members were reluctant to confront the imperial government on an issue that needed the latter's consent so soon after the granting of Responsible Government.[32] But other members, such as Saul Solomon, who practised the 'small tradition' of Cape liberalism in their constituencies, did so while genuinely believing that the 'great tradition', the non-racial franchise and equality before the law, was both the morally correct and most effective way of governing Blacks.[33] J. X. Merriman, the Commissioner of Crown Lands for six years between 1875 and 1884, worried about all policies that produced 'a black race banded together and in secret or open hostility to a white race, who regard themselves as masters and nothing else'.[34]

The 'small tradition' of Cape liberalism existed in Cape Town and the south-western Cape in general. This tradition united, at election times, White political elites with the small numbers of Blacks who could vote. Within this tradition was the fact that Farmer had Malays on his election committee in 1879 and Neethling and Murison had Coloured supporters in their council campaigns of 1878. Such alliances continued in Cape Town into the 1880s despite increased racism.[35] This political alliance across the colour-line explains why Cape Town members were to consistently vote against alterations in the franchise before Union in 1910. Not to do so could have endangered their election chances. But it is difficult to see the small tradition as much more than political expediency. It would not appear to have undermined social exclusivity. For instance Neethling's Coloured supporters were present at his victory banquet in 1878. They were invited to dine at the same table as Whites, rather than having to dine separately. But significantly, they were asked to sit at the lower end of the table.[36]

Different positions on the franchise were part of the 'Native Question', the debate about how to govern Blacks who were racialised as Africans, which dominated so much English and Afrikaner discussion about the future of southern Africa well into the twentieth century. Existing social practice and experience influenced theoretical discussion. But the 'Native Question' was not just about ideological speculation on Black traits, or capacity for change, it was also about appropriate policies. New policies could change social practice and remould social experience.

The view that it would take Africans a long time to become like 'us' became an explicit part of the discourse of Englishness in Cape Town between 1875 and 1882. Journalists on the *Cape Times* and *Lantern* wrote numerous racist articles about African intelligence and the difficulty of inculcating 'civilised' (i.e. English) values. For instance the *Cape Times* carried an article in 1880 on the 'Native Problem' which spoke of Africans as just emerging from barbarism. It warned of the 'mistake' of endowing 'the native with feelings and sentiments exactly corresponding to those of an enlightened European' and went on to quote Walter Bagehot on the uneven development of the human race. The article concluded: 'We burden the native with the fine arts, the franchise, and a host of other ideas which his unformed intelligence cannot grasp.'[37] In 1881 St Leger was approvingly citing an article in the British *Contemporary Review* which argued that Africans and Whites would not, and should not, mix and that Whites were trying to interfere too much and uselessly with African customs. A couple of months later he returned to this theme when dismissing mission-school education for Africans as useless.[38]

Apart from arguments offered by metropolitan 'science', readers were also fed the negative stereotypes of 'experts' in other parts of the Cape. One such expert was the inspector of African locations in King William's Town. This intellectual luminary argued that Africans 'would rather steal than work to make an honest living'.[39]

One of the factors leading to a more assertive Englishness had been imperial intervention and wars against Africans in the late 1870s. The achievement of English hegemony in Cape Town could appear to be but a small part of the achievement of a wider hegemony throughout southern Africa. In 1879 the *Cape Times* and *Lantern* had leading articles that attacked the Zulu King, Cetshwayo, as 'only a big savage' or 'barbarous'. Both ridiculed any apparently hesitant or dissenting opinions, such as those aired in Saul Solomon's *Argus*, as 'negrophilist'. This ridicule may have encouraged Mr Smart, a leading builder, to organise a meeting in support of Sir Bartle Frere, the architect of the Zulu War. At the meeting he, and other speakers, attacked Solomon and his newspaper.[40]

The wars against Africans in the Eastern Cape and Natal between 1877 and 1879 had been the background to the *Cape Times* New Year's Day editorial of 1880 which talked of the struggle for 'supremacy of race', and of how Whites had demonstrated their intention of 'being the governing class'. Supremacist rhetoric in newspapers and parliament preceded the introduction of segregation in the colonial defence force and the implementation of the policy of disarming Africans, itself a cause of rebellion, in the late 1870s.[41] Resistance by Africans to English conquest, like apparent or actual Malay resistance to English urban reforms, produced racist outbursts in those newspapers actively promoting English ethnic pride. Such pride certainly had moments of enthusiastic public resonance in Cape Town by 1880. Spontaneous shouting and cheering, 'never before known', greeted Sir Bartle Frere when he visited the theatre in August. Equally the *Lantern* reported with some glee that an effigy of a 'negrophilist philanthropist' was burnt on Guy Fawkes Night, that very English festivity of 5 November.[42]

Racism justified the conquest or suppression of African peoples. The views of the *Cape Times* and *Lantern* may merely have given coherence to, or confirmed, the existing racist prejudices of many Cape Town English speakers. Capetonians who had little or no direct contact with Africans would have picked up negative stereotypes by word of mouth. Certainly Kennedy, who collected a large number of such unpleasantnesses in the Eastern Cape, was told by one anonymous informant in the capital that African prisoners would not set fire to the city because 'they're too lazy'.[43]

Racist discourse about Africans in Cape Town drew on a reservoir of pre-existing negative stereotypes of 'Kaffirs'. Many of these, such as the African as barbarian or dangerous savage, had been created in frontier conflicts fought by White settlers and imperial armies, and were available in the likes of Wilmot's *History* or Du Toit's *Geskiedenis* as well as, presumably, in oral tradition. Certainly *Ons Klyntji,* the *Reader's Digest* for rural Afrikaners in the 1890s and which published their stories, portrayed the African as 'nameless, cruel, credulous and superstitious, a brave fighter and a dangerous foe'. Other stereotypes, such as the African as lazy, libidinous or thieving (the latter also a stereotype of the Malays in the 1850s), more probably came from White employer discourse after conquest.[44]

From at least the 1840s, negative stereotypes of 'Kaffirs' were being assembled in 'coherent theories' for English-speaking Cape Colonists in such books as the Orwellian-titled *Impartial Analysis of the Kafir Character*. This decidedly partial and racist analysis by a Rev. Niven argued that 'Kafirs' were idle by nature and scarcely human.[45] Subsequent books such as Cole's *The Cape and the Kafirs*, written during the Eastern Cape war of 1852, took much the same line.[46] Their authors were undoubtedly drawing on contemporary 'scientific' ideas in Britain – themselves informed by stereotypes gleaned in the process of European exploration and conquest of other parts of the world – which unsurprisingly put Whites or Caucasians, and specifically Saxons, as the most intelligent and civilised of the 'races', and Blacks, and specifically Negroes, Hottentots and Australian Aboriginals, as the least. Cole for instance, writing two years after the publication of Robert Knox's *The Races of Men*, reflected this work's racial determinism when arguing that 'the fate of the Black man ... [will be that] his race is exterminated. The Kafir's time is well-nigh come'.[47] Wilmot's *History of the Cape Colony for use in Schools*, published in 1871, said that during the frontier war of 1834 'fighting against fearful odds, the white men proved their superiority'.[48]

The influence of 'scientific' ideas about 'race' continued to pervade bourgeois colonial discourse throughout the late nineteenth century and the considerable number of books by visitors to southern Africa. Cape Town newspapers evidence this influence. In 1875 a sub-leader in the *Cape Argus* wrote that Africans would serve well as 'labouring-machines', but the Cape should have an introduction of a 'higher class' of immigrant. A sub-leader in the *Cape Times* reported disparagingly on the performance of the Malay fire brigade in 1878. It referred snidely to

the Malays as members of an 'Asiatic race', the report going on to say
that 'happily energetic Europeans' were on the spot to help. Or in 1879 a
sub-leader in the *Cape Times* mentioned an attack on a 'dwarfed couple'
who looked like 'Bushmen' or 'Hottentots'. It went on to say that the
latter were almost 'extinct' which was 'no loss' as 'even the lovers of the
lower orders will admit'.[49] The influence of scientific racism is also
evident in the J. H. Hofmeyr's Dutch-language *Zuid-Afrikaan*. In 1884
an editorial argued that 'the lower people are in the scale of humanity,
the more will they be taught by working, obeying and submitting'.[50]

Comments on Africans in Cape Town newspapers increased between
1875 and 1882 not only because the 'Native Question' was a concern of
White bourgeois colonists in general in these years, but also because
of the increased African presence in the city itself. In 1875 the number
of Capetonians distinguished by the census as 'Kaffirs', 'Bechuanas' or
'Fingos' had been small, just over 200. As African numbers increased in
the late 1870s, so they, like the Malays, became the target for hostile and
fearful comments in the English press, which climaxed in the early 1880s.
Between April 1878 and January 1879 the Cape government had brought
4,000 prisoners of war and destitute loyalists to Cape Town. The
government had brought them to the Western Cape because their labour
was in demand from local employers, particularly farmers. They were
housed in appalling conditions, 'stored more like pigs than human
beings', in a 'depot' in the southern suburbs where, on average, one
inmate died every day.[51] The goverment's Secretary for Native Affairs,
W. Ayliff, arranged that many were soon hired out as contract labourers
in Cape Town's hinterland. From there, some escaped back to Cape
Town or to the Eastern Cape, most of the rest to the same destinations
after their contracts had expired. The almost three thousand Mozambiquan and Berg Damara labourers, also brought by the Cape government
to the Western Cape to provide cheap contract labour, came to Cape
Town between 1879 and 1882.[52]

The English stereotypes of Africans that emerged in Cape Town
between 1878 and 1882 took place against the mass arrival of these often
impoverished and apparently dramatically 'different' workers. As with
Malays, both class consciousness and ethnicity informed bourgeois
English perceptions of Africans. But stereotypes of Africans were also
more obviously informed by past and contemporary events elsewhere in
southern Africa, as well as by metropolitan ideas about 'race'.

Two strands in Cape Town English discourse about Africans would
seem to have had local and contemporary input between 1878 and 1882:
the African as 'immoral' or 'indecent', and the African as 'dangerous' or
'savage'. The first negative stereotype was fed by initial experience of

African 'nudity', perceived from an English moral viewpoint. Thus that future Clean candidate and St George's churchwarden, Mr Stigant, was reported in the *Cape Times* one month after the arrival of the Eastern Cape Africans complaining of 'almost naked Kaffirs' wandering about town and begging from the inhabitants. In his view they were trying to avoid work, revealing the close connection between morality and labour – discipline in the English value system.[53] Stigant feared that the 'lazy Kaffir' could become the immoral and dangerous one. A few days later a member of the House of Assembly, Mr Bam, was reported as saying that African women were producing reactions of 'annoyance and disgust' from Capetonians. Confirming this view, a letter to the *Cape Times* said that Africans should be made to wear blankets in public.[54]

In 1879 the government labour contractor, Mr Stevens, alarmed by an outbreak of fever among Africans living in Papendorp, proposed a Cape Town 'location' for Africans. The term 'location' was used in the nineteenth century to refer to both rural and urban sites set aside for Black settlement on private, central or local government land. Thus there were African locations on White-owned farms, on crown land and on the edges of towns in the Eastern Cape by the 1840s. Locations for 'Hottentots and emancipated slaves' had also appeared in both the Eastern and Western Cape. Cape urban locations by the late 1870s were the result either of the consolidation of squatter camps by central government or the deliberate allocation of sites by municipal authorities. In some locations, such as 'Fingo' Village in Grahamstown, inhabitants could own freehold land.[55] In others, such as the one in Worcester where the land remained under central government ownership, they could not.[56] But, unlike the Orange Free State, there was no legislation in the Cape that prevented Africans, or any other racialised group, from buying freehold land where Whites could do so. Equally, no legislation prevented Black Cape Colonists from renting accommodation from Whites or Blacks in towns. This would, after all, have been contrary to the 'great tradition' of Cape liberalism. Nor, and partly for the same reason, was there the idea that African urbanisation could be limited by decree, as was the view of the Transvaal *Volksraad* from 1844.[57] There was also no equivalent of Durban's (Natal) *togt* system, which controlled entry into the city by making Africans register as employed workers.[58]

The Cape government had brought Africans to the Western Cape because their labour was in demand from employers. The question for the government was how to satisfy that demand in Cape Town while responding to the fears of members of the city's dominant class. Without going into much detail, Stevens argued for a location which would deliver in both respects. He also thought that a location could provide a *cordon sanitaire*, implicitly to protect Whites: if disease broke out among residents it would not infect the rest of the population. Stevens concluded that location residence would teach Africans the futility of waging war against the Colony by enabling them to learn, by proximity, 'the superiority of the European race'.[59]

The upshot was that Mr Stevens was given permission by the government in 1879 to allow Africans to build their own huts on waste ground between Salt River railway station and the main road through to the southern suburbs. Significantly though, Africans in Cape Town were still able to live where they could afford to, or where landlords or landladies would accept them as tenants. This was now no longer the case in Kimberley, for which the Griqualand West government had just passed restrictive legislation in the form of a Native Locations Act.[60]

Stevens could not force Africans to live in his location. This was still the situation as the Mozambiquan and Berg Damara labourers started arriving in Cape Town in large numbers. On arrival they were, like the prisoners of war before them, housed in another depot, this time in Newmarket Street in District Six. By the early 1880s many were living further afield, including among Eastern Cape Africans in houses and yards in Salt River and Papendorp. Most avoided Stevens' location because, according to Stevens himself, they did not want to risk the possible 'constraints' that could go with such a decision – presumably both the regulations and being further from work in the city centre.[61]

But constraints were precisely what some Capetonians came to demand, and with growing vigour up to 1882. In 1880 St Leger described Africans squatting on the slopes of Table Mountain, who were being brought before the Resident Magistrate on vagrancy charges. Despite the fact that he thought that few landlords accepted Africans as tenants, he stated confidently that 'Kafirs prefer huts to houses', and wondered why the town council had not established a location.[62]

The growth of an African population in houses and shacks in Papendorp, Salt River and on the outskirts of the Cape Town municipality increased the volume of morally outraged and fearful articles and letters published in the *Cape Times* and *Lantern* in the early 1880s. 'Why must our ladies see them?' squealed one correspondent to the *Cape Times* in February 1881.[63] Reporting from Papendorp in September, a correspondent of the *Lantern* found 'ten, twelve, or even more, natives . . . in miserable, filthy, hovel homes and huts. Women half, and children wholly nude, tumble indiscriminately out and in, amidst an atmosphere reeking of profanity, drunkenness, and immorality'.[64]

The stereotype of the 'dangerous' African surfaced in reactions to the violent mugging of an English carpenter, John Anderson, in May 1880, which turned into a highly publicised court case in July 1881. The prosecutor was quoted as saying: 'Since Cape Town had been flooded with Kafirs there was no safety in walking out after dark.'[65] One month later, another 'White man' was attacked and killed, and fighting broke out between Africans and a mob of 'Whites and Coloureds', apparently a vigilante group. The latter set about the indiscriminate destruction of African property. The assault on the White man produced a flurry of letters to the press from inhabitants of Papendorp, drawing attention to what was called the 'Kaffir problem'. The subsequent fight gave rise to many more letters and concerned editorials which expanded on White bourgeois perceptions of this problem.[66]

The 'Kaffir problem' was chiefly a question of control: how to make Papendorp, and Cape Town in general, safe from the 'Kaffir' danger, from these 'savage' people. This danger was perceived to be both directly physical, fear of assault, but also to be related to the more indirect fear that African living places bred crime, disease, drunkenness, profanity and immorality – all, in their own way challenging English hegemonic values. 'Solutions' suggested by newspaper editors and their correspondents included the introduction of a curfew, the confiscation of knobkerries, the strengthening of the police and the carrying of passes. The latter had been a requirement for KhoiKhoi in the Colony between 1809 and 1828, and still applied to 'foreign' Africans entering the Colony under legislation of the 1850s and 1860s.[67] In a somewhat wry editorial that nonetheless threatened a further addition to the list, St Leger noted that 'Cape Town' did not force Africans to walk in the road, rather than on the pavement, implying that this already happened in other towns in southern Africa. But he wished Africans would not move about the town six abreast 'howling "I'm the monarch of the sea"'.[68] The most frequently mentioned 'solution' was compulsory residence in a location.

Why was this solution not adopted until 1901? Part of the answer was, as we have suggested, the nature of economic activity in the city. Many sectors of the economy called for a fluctuating and, in the case of building, mobile labour supply. Units of production were in any case small, allowing for close supervision of labour, and industrialisation was only in its early stages. As the case of Kimberley demonstrated, renters of property to Africans did not welcome their residential segregation and retailers did not lobby for the removal of customers from their vicinity.[69]

Significantly, the only identifiable employer who called for the segregation of African labourers was T. E. Fuller. Fuller, as a member of the Harbour Board and general manager of the Union Steamship Company, was a relatively large employer of labour. As such his opinion had been sought by the Select Committee on Labour of 1879. In his evidence to the Committee, Fuller said that one of the problems of importing African labour into Cape Town was not being able to keep them together in proper accommodation, 'owing to our difficulty in housing them they are as costly to us as ordinary dock coolies'.[70] It was perhaps with this problem in mind that Fuller reported on the state of housing in Cape Town at the time of the smallpox epidemic of 1882:

The houses thus tenanted [i.e. overcrowded], are not all in one quarter, but on the contrary *widely distributed*, and thus *scattered all abroad* the Coloured labourers will be found, here ten in a room, here a dozen, here perhaps fifteen, sleeping in their clothes at night, and emitting as they pass through the streets by day a distinctly characteristic aroma.[71] [my emphasis]

Fuller suggested that places should be considered for the housing of labourers working at the docks, housing the Harbour Board was now providing for Irish labourers imported from Britain since March. As labourers involved in dock work were also among the hardest hit by smallpox, Fuller was able to suggest that the possibility of contagion for the rest of Cape Town's population would be less if these particular labourers were to live in the docks. So Fuller's 'solution' for over-crowded living conditions was the segregation of an undisclosed percentage of Cape Town's casual labour pool who were Black and involved in dock work. Appealing to prevailing dominant-class concerns about health and sanitation, what Maynard Swanson has dubbed the 'Sanitation Syndrome', Fuller hoped to gain approval for the segregation of 'his' labour. This was to become a recurrent desire of employers of dock labour, climaxing in the establishment of the docks location in 1901.

The fact that Fuller was unsuccessful in 1882 was presumably due to the lack of interest that other members of the dominant class, and in particular other employers, had in promoting the segregation of part of Cape Town's labour force. The other obvious reason that there was no location in Cape Town before 1901 was that after 1882, and for fifteen years or so, the 'Kaffir problem' seemed less menacing to Cape Town's White bourgeoisie. First, a considerable number of Africans, perhaps half, returned to the Eastern Cape or Mozambique. Second, most of the Africans still resident in Papendorp appear to have moved to vacant ground on the fringes of District Six by the mid-1880s. There they came within the ambit of evangelising Anglicans, the Cowley Fathers, who proceeded to make a considerable number of converts to Christianity. Finally, the severe economic depression of the 1880s combined with African ability to resist proletarianisation so that their numbers did not again increase dramatically until the late 1890s.[72]

White racism was so ubiquitous at the Cape throughout the nineteenth century because it could 'explain' unequal social, political and economic relationships with Blacks after conquest, as well as conquest itself. The racist discourse in Cape Town newspapers between 1875 and 1882 continued to explain and justify the 'traditional' social order of White over Black in city and Colony alike. This discourse could also justify and explain divisions of labour and segregation that served to maintain that order.

We have seen that segregation already existed between White and Black, albeit in differing forms, in some churches, schools and medical institutions in 1875. One of the reasons exclusion increased thereafter has been suggested by Fredrickson: the number of public institutions and facilities, where exclusion might be deemed necessary, were also on the increase.[73] But exclusion also grew as economic prosperity increased the chances of social mobility for some Blacks.

Andrews, writing about Buenos Aires, has argued that a greater strain was put on 'race relations' in periods of economic expansion as the consequently enhanced social mobility of Blacks threatened the 'traditional system of race relations'.[74] Buenos Aires experienced an economic boom between 1870 and 1914. In 1879 and 1880 there was growing *de facto* segregation of Blacks from places of entertainment in the city. *La Broma*, a newspaper of the Black middle class according to Andrews, protested:

Today it is the theater that is closed to us, tomorrow it will be some other public place, and the day after it will be the church, where we all have the right to go to worship God, who is the kind father of all human beings, regardless of race or color.[75]

In Cape Town, as in South American cities such as Buenos Aires and Rio de Janeiro, the 'traditional system' had been one of White dominance and Black subordination which had its roots in slavery.[76] For four decades after emancipation at the Cape the growth of the economy was slow, as was, consequently, the demographic growth of Cape Town. The discovery of diamonds dramatically quickened the pace of both rates of growth between 1875 and 1882.

Potentially, the way was now open for more Black Cape Colonists than ever before to enjoy social mobility and 'claim admission into the upper caste' in a society with theoretical equality for all Colonists. In practice, as we saw in the last chapter, Black social mobility was restricted by considerable de facto White job reservation. In the case of the supervision of blasting, this job reservation was made *de jure* under pressure from White workers. The division of labour on farms, mines, the railways and the docks remained largely one between Whites in skilled, supervisory or management positions and Blacks providing the unskilled labour.

In Cape Town, and probably in the other port towns of the Cape, there was more chance for Black accumulation and social mobility. Certainly the number of Blacks in the 'Cape' census division (80 per cent of which consisted of greater Cape Town), in professional, commercial or industrial employment rose both proportionally and in absolute terms between 1875 and 1891. The figures were, respectively, 136, 515 and 3,203 in 1875; 338, 1,697 and 7,254 in 1891. Over the same period the total Black population of this area only rose from 26,589 to 48,739.[77]

This upward mobility helps to explain the greater incidence of exclusion from the late 1870s, as well as bourgeois Black objections to it. A privately owned roller-skating rink, opened in the city in 1879, excluded Blacks. Cape Town's only Black doctor, Andrew Jackson, who was probably a West Indian and had been educated in Edinburgh and London, wrote to the *Lantern* in words that uncannily echoed those of the *La Broma* editorial:

We, the excluded, may soon expect to hear churches refuse us admission, theatre doors closed against us, the very side walks in the streets we dare not tread. In train and tram-car we'll be refused, because we are inferior.[78]

In 1880 'wealthy Malays' were not allowed into Cape Town's agricultural show until after 12 p.m. when European 'loafers' and 'town girls' were admitted.[79] Exclusion of Blacks from 'first-class' hotels was common practice by the 1880s. The equation was made by hoteliers between respectability and Whiteness, colour and low class status.[80] By 1902 exclusion would have affected many more institutions and facilities.

Jackson's letter and the *La Broma* editorial remind us that 'horizontal' social segregation between White and Black, replacing the vertical relationship between master and slave, was a common development in American post-emancipation societies. This suggests at least some common explanations.[81] Economic expansion and consequently greater Black social mobility was one contributing factor. An increasingly negative stereotype of Blacks was another.[82] This racism, which could draw on 'scientific knowledge', reflected a more intensive class consciousness or fear of class conflict on the part of the British and American bourgeoisie, and promoted a 'less sympathetic view of the plight of the non White classes in multi-racial colonies'.[83] Events such as the Indian mutiny, Morant Bay uprising and continuing wars in Africa helped to undermine liberal arguments about the possibilty of Blacks changing to become like Whites.[84]

But the lessons that bourgeois colonists usually chose to learn from contemporary 'science' or external events interacted with their own experiences, hopes and fears. Therefore the eponymous hero of Cape Town's first popular novel in English, *Sitongo*, published in 1884 and written by a Capetonian, ultimately failed to assimilate to European society despite his ability to 'pass for white'. The story ends with Sitongo returning to being a 'native' in the remotest part of the Cape Colony: 'I was still a Kaffir at heart.'[85] Revelation had come to Sitongo when coming face to face with his White South African (former) master in London:

Before a man like Thompson, who so thoroughly understood my native race, and who knew me better than I did myself, I stood unpretentious and abased, feeling there was nothing like equality between us, and that he was in truth my superior.[86]

The moral of *Sitongo* was that mid-nineteenth-century ideas about the assimilability of Blacks to White culture, ideas which had prevailed among British administrators and previously informed Cape liberal ideology and the practice of the great tradition, should now be questioned.[87] Certainly the view that assimilation would not be easy was shared by the editors of the *Cape Times* and the *Lantern*, and was one that few Whites challenged in their correspondence columns. Almost the only exceptions were clergymen, specifically missionaries. The Cowley Evangelists, operating in District Six from 1884, retained the belief that Africans could be swiftly converted to English values. After all, success justified their presence: 'It is a great blessing that we are able to show ... by actual visible facts that the Cape Town Kaffir can be tamed, and trained and taught.'[88]

But increasing pessimism about African ability to change, or change in the foreseeable future, even affected the thinking of 'negrophilists' among the Cape liberals, the political supporters of the great tradition. This pessimism can be found in Saul Solomon's election manifesto of 1879 which he delivered to the Cape Town merchants and businessmen who signed his requisition. The manifesto demonstrates the key influence of the wars and annexations of the late 1870s in promoting a shift in Cape liberal ideology away from assimilation.

The questions which grow out of the contact of civilization and barbarism are under any circumstances complex, intricate and difficult of settlement; but those difficulties are much increased when the barbarism is fed from unfailing sources, and the uncivilised race – by the peace, security and other advantages thereby enjoyed – is attracted in increasing numbers to settle among, or near to, their civilised neighbours.[89]

Solomon was infamous in Cape Town society for not only talking about potential Black equality but actually treating Blacks as his equals. In a colony where most Black servants were called 'boy' whatever their age, when employers expected to be called 'master' or '*baas*', Solomon even went as far as allowing his Malay servant to call him Saul. But by 1881 he publicly opposed the importation of Mozambique labour because 'he was sure there were enough black and yellow faces here already'.[90]

Pessimism about assimilation and doubt about the Victorian civilising mission, among even the most liberal of the Cape liberals, combined with an earlier concern that there could be the wrong kind of contact between barbarians and the civilised. Europeans would not always provide a moralising and uplifting example. Dale, for instance, had argued in 1869 that 'habits of so-called civilised life, introduced by demoralised Europeans, traders and others' harmed Black Cape Colonists.[91]

One possibility was that even 'negrophilist' politicians would abandon the ideological baby of the civilising mission with the bathwater of assimilation. An alternative model of ruling Africans, through denial of rights backed up by force of arms, was close at hand in the Transvaal and the Orange Free State, a model that had plenty of advocates among White farmers in the Cape. But the great tradition of Cape liberalism had been about pragmatism as well as ideals, about making the conquered less likely to rebel. Simple repression could promote rebellion and expense, and in every way was thought to be economically retrogressive by liberals such as Solomon or John X. Merriman. In Merriman's words: 'The Dutch Republican mode of dealing with natives ... means absolute subjection, and results in driving them out of the country, and no labour, thus defeating its own ends.'[92]

A partial solution to this Cape liberal dilemma was provided by the report of the Native Laws and Customs Commission of 1883. This Commission was appointed by the Cape government precisely to recommend solutions to the question of how to rule large numbers of newly conquered Africans, while making their labour available to sustain state and private economic activity. The Commissioners turned to Sir Theophilus Shepstone, the Governor of Natal, for evidence on the policies employed in his Colony. The perceived wisdoms of Shepstone, combined with their own experience and investigations, informed a report abandoning assimilation in favour of, at least temporary, segregation. Significantly, the author of *Sitongo*, J. D. Ensor, was a shorthand writer for the Commission.

Hitherto Cape 'native' policy had been aimed at destroying 'tribalism', and refused to acknowledge African law. This Commission concluded that recently annexed Africans should retain a great deal of their own social and legal system, as well as their land, *sans* unacceptedly 'barbaric' practices and while incorporating the British jury system. Chiefs and headmen would continue to rule, under the control of the Resident Magistrates, the servants of the colonial state. Gradually the elements of British law, together with the work of Christian missionaries and exemplary behaviour of the Magistrates, was expected to 'remould' African 'nature and character' towards 'superior knowledge and higher hopes'.[93]

If and when that happened there would presumably be no need for a separate system of government. In the meantime vagrancy legislation and a *de facto* pass system regulated the desired movement of these Africans onto the Cape labour market and into regular work, the main aim of the civilising mission. This pass system was supposed to apply to Africans from beyond the colonial boundaries. But as a government report commented in 1886, 'an almost universal practice has prevailed in the eastern province, of requiring all natives to carry passes'; this must have included residents of existing locations outside the Transkei.[94]

Racism in the late nineteenth century, whether evolutionary or teleological, explained White supremacy. New occasions of segregation by members of the Cape's White bourgeoisie in town and countryside emerged in response to a variety of potential challenges to that supremacy. Different forms of segregation – such as social exclusivity, mine compounds or the territorial and administrative separation of newly conquered Africans – had their own particular histories and were accompanied and justified by specific racist discourses. What they had in common was that they all functioned in Cell's words 'as means and ends in one group's efforts to keep another (or others) in their place within a society that ... [was] becoming unified'.[95] But, as Shula Marks has written of segregation in South Africa in general, segregation in the Cape Colony was also 'directed at a conquered majority with their own traditions and geographical base, and also sustained a labour system and provided a foundation for economic development'.[96]

The uniting concern of Cape Town's White dominant class remained the maintenance of their own elite position. This concern prompted social exclusion, be it at the town's roller-skating rink or agricultural show. Such segregation was easily, and cheaply, achieved. On the other hand, integration among the lower classes was, at this stage, ignored. Employer interests did not dictate interference.

In general, Cape Town's dominant class derived its income from 'rent, banking and commerce' rather than from primary production. This being so, there was little pressure from within this class for new measures to control and regulate labour – the Masters and Servants Act of 1873 would suffice.[97] The exception was Fuller who, in his capacity as a member of the Harbour Board, employed several hundred labourers in construction and maintenance at the docks. Although the Harbour Board experimented with the importing and housing of Irish labourers in 1882, the experiment was not a success, the labourers proved to be too 'independent'. After 1882 the need for labour was reduced due to the severe economic depression, and the reorganising of labour at the docks postponed.

The Harbour Board was responsible for arranging that goods were moved by landing and dock agents. From 1879 the Board contracted this work to A. R. McKenzie, who then subcontracted to other agents. But there remained no strict division of labour between those employed by agents in the harbour and those they used to move goods to and from town. Equally there were still several different employers of dock labour.[98] Only when this situation began to change, in the boom years of the 1890s, were first some dock labourers and then most segregated, in a cross between Fuller's and the Kimberley model.

So residential integration remained a feature of lower-class areas such as District Six, paralleling the situation in the poorer, run-down areas of Kimberley. Across the Atlantic the same pattern existed in New Orleans and Kingston, Jamaica.[99] However racism towards Black Capetonians continued to justify social exclusion for many Whites and threatened to promote and justify further segregation. On an individual basis, racism meant that some Whites in the 1880s preferred to employ fellow Whites in intimate situations such as domestic service and to exclude Africans as tenants.[100] Particular negative stereotypes, such as that of the dangerous and immoral African, could be used by members of Cape Town's dominant class, if and when the need arose, to motivate particular forms of segregation.

During the depression of the 1880s the need for exclusionary segregation in Cape Town was reduced. But the depression years saw growing dominant-class concern about the mixing of White and Black among the lower classes. Class tension mounted in the course of the depression and, specifically, lower-class Black Capetonians came to be seen as threatening the social order. Coinciding with this development came the discovery of 'poor Whites' in town and countryside. By the 1890s dominant class ideology favoured state intervention on their behalf as well as the separation of all Blacks from all Whites.

5   The dangers of depression

The years of prosperity for Cape Town merchants climaxed in 1881. Such heady times did not return until virtually a decade later. In the ensuing period of intense or relative depression, English-speaking bourgeois dominance of the city was not translated into the material transformation promised by the Clean Party victory in 1882. Instead, this particular section of Cape Town's bourgeoisie, continually alert to the changing challenges of urbanisation, was forced by disease, crime and organisation by the lower classes to look more closely at the problems of poverty rather than dealing with those caused by their own prosperity: the need to expand the material resources of the city to meet rapid economic and demographic growth.

In looking at the question of poverty, Cape Town's dominant class expressed attitudes very similar to those of their contemporary counterparts in London. The major difference between the two was the role that colour played in moulding bourgeois attitudes to poverty in Cape Town.[1] Negative stereotypes of Black Capetonians were carried into the depression years of the 1880s. These stereotypes had been built up in the course of the campaign for urban reform and were influenced by developments beyond the confines of the city. During the 1880s the 'residuum' in Cape Town came to be explained by most of the city's dominant class not just by a theory of urban degeneracy, as was the case in London, but by one of urban Black degeneracy. Malays, Africans and Coloureds made up Cape Town's residuum.

Added to the existing belief in the need for White bourgeois exclusiveness, the racialisation of problems of poverty in Cape Town furthered the emergence there of a dominant-class ideology of social separation for the 'races'. This ideology promoted the view that exclusionary segregation alone was not enough to protect White bourgeois supremacy. The social separation of all Blacks from all Whites was required. The emergence of this ideology was connected with the *ad hoc* development of segregatory practices not just in Cape Town but in other parts of the Cape and beyond, especially with what was happening in Natal and the American South. For Cape Town's dominant class, the depression of the 1880s played a crucial role in this development.

By the end of the depression, Black weakness and tendency to corrupt, so dominant-class rationalisation went, made separate treatment of White and Black poor essential. Discriminatory social practice was necessary. It would help control Blacks while preventing the degeneration of poor Whites. State intervention, by the 1890s, was justified specifically on behalf of poor Whites, a departure from previous *laissez-faire* attitudes to poverty. Renewed prosperity in this decade made intervention possible.

In November 1881, after a year of unprecedented economic optimism, the general manager of the Standard Bank informed his head office in London that there was a sudden 'crisis' in Cape Town.[2] The reasons for this crisis were graphically described in the Bank's Inspection Report of 1883:

All wars in South Africa of any importance ceased with the treaty of peace signed with the Boers at Laings Nek. From a humanitarian point of view this is a matter for congratulation although hardly so from a commercial one. The sudden cessation of hostilities beside stopping the circulation of gold, left merchants with large supplies of goods specially ordered for field purposes and which thus became unsaleable. Following very soon upon this came the collapse of the Diamond Fields, the depreciation of ostriches and their feathers, and drought with its consequent bad harvests. Everything that was bad seemed to come down upon us at once.[3]

The problems facing Cape Town's trade were compounded by the smallpox epidemic that hit the town in the winter of 1882. Despite the continued property boom and a bumper harvest in 1883, the commercial depression deepened in the mid-1880s, with the problems facing British trade in the same period.[4] The situation was not much improved by the arrival in 1884 of the Warren expeditionary force *en route* to Bechuanaland.[5] The depression was extended by the devastation by phylloxera of Paarl wine production three years later.[6]

The crisis led to over 1,000 insolvencies in the Cape in 1883, almost 800 in 1884. It led to the financial failure or difficulties of many of the leading mercantile firms of Cape Town. This meant problems for the whole commercial network of the city. The Cape Commercial Bank and many shopkeepers became insolvent.[7] The building boom unsurprisingly halted amid the gloom, leaving a large number of stores and houses empty and a large number of building workers unemployed.[8]

The depression had the effect of reducing central and local government revenue and thus expenditure. Central government expenditure had risen from £2,000,000 in 1875 to a peak of well over £6,000,000 in 1882/3.

Thereafter it dropped steadily to half this amount by 1887/8, only moving back to above £6,000,000 in 1890/1.[9] Similarly Cape Town's town council expenditure rose from £13,000 in 1875, to £41,000 in 1884, before slowing down, or moving lower, until the 1890s.[10] Trade through Cape Town also decreased. Imports and exports both reached a peak of over £3,000,000 in 1882 before falling back to lows of around £1,500,000 in 1886. The £3,000,000 was only reached again in the the 1890s.[11]

Reduced trade through the town undoubtedly had the effect of reducing the demand for casual labour for the moving of commodities, though statistics for the latter are not available. We can reasonably deduce, however, that occupations such as stevedoring, dock labouring, cart driving and so on would have been affected. One estimate suggested that 9 per cent of adult males were completely unemployed by 1886.[12]

Prosperity for Cape Town merchants, largely a result of the Rand discoveries and their development, was not securely revisited until the early 1890s. After steady and then spectacular growth in the period between 1870 and the end of 1881, Cape Town was plunged into a depression severe and prolonged enough to shake even the most complacent member of the bourgeoisie's view of economic laws, and the belief that there was no such thing as able-bodied undeserving poverty. After all, many had themselves been victims of the depression.

The depression of the 1880s made the position of casual labourers and their families move from parlous to desperate. Worsening the effect of the depression was the fact that it came after eight years of artificial demographic growth, thanks to those Cape government immigration schemes that had brought considerable numbers of Africans and Europeans to Cape Town. This invasion had reached its peak in 1881, heightened by an influx of disbanded soldiers, on the very eve of the economic downturn.[13] Some Africans from the Eastern Cape made their way back to that area, in the belief that they would at least be able to subsist, while others remained in Cape Town. Perhaps half the Mozambiquans stayed behind.[14]

The casual labour pool grew rather than diminished in the depression years as people drifted into Cape Town from nearby farms looking for work. According to one observer, District Six was steadily filled by 'coolies' who 'come into the town by thousands seeking work'. An African, when asked why he and others had come to Cape Town during the depression, replied that 'we came down here to get food and money'.[15] Despite the smallpox epidemic and the depression, the population of the municipality of Cape Town grew to 51,000 in 1891. This was well above the 1875 figure of 33,000, or even the 1882 estimate of 42,000.[16]

With the coming of the depression many White artisans simply moved on to overseas destinations such as New Zealand.[17] The majority of workers were unable to display such mobility. Stedman Jones has outlined the reasons for the immobility of casual labour in London, reasons which almost certainly applied in Cape Town. A labourer 'known' in his neighbourhood was more likely to get credit there, in time of need, than somewhere else where he was unknown. Equally there was the family employment factor: a husband may have been unable to get work, say, at the docks, but his wife could still earn through 'home' work, or his daughter in a nearby jam or match factory.[18]

We know that sewing and washing were leading occupations of women in Cape Town, so 'home' work was presumably available to many wives and daughters. Women's employment in workshops and factories was a development of the 1870s. It began when a printing firm (Saul Solomon & Company) hired women to replace men as bookbinders and then as typesetters.[19] By the mid-1880s women were employed in workshops making matches, cigarettes and boots, as well as in the printing business.[20] By 1891, and presumably in the 1880s, when these industries commenced or expanded, they were also being employed in furniture and confectionery works. But in general these industries remained subject to the seasonal fluctuations in demand that had previously characterised production in Cape Town. Many of the jobs required little training. This, together with the availability of alternative labour, is one of the reasons why factory workers were mostly badly paid and poorly organised in the late nineteenth century. They demonstrated little ability to resist casualisation, let alone improve their conditions of employment.[21]

Another reason was that they, like other workers in Cape Town, were subject to punitive legislation if they were caught defying employers in almost any way. The Masters and Servants Act of 1873, one of the first legislative measures of the newly Responsible government, was heavily weighted in favour of the 'master'. Although it gave some right to the 'servant', such as the possibility of taking an employer to court for non-payment of wages, a wide range of behaviour on the part of the worker was defined as a misdemeanour. These definitions, adapted from the Cape Slave Codes, included 'careless work', 'bad language' or 'neglect', as well as 'absence'. They were sufficiently vague to allow Resident Magistrates to punish, with fines of between £1 and £5 or imprisonment up to three months, virtually any behaviour on the part of a 'servant' that threatened an employer's authority.[22]

Strike action was effectively illegal for all Cape workers until the 1890s. This was a lesson swiftly taught to migrants coming to Cape Town. For instance, British typesetters, who obviously had a knowledge

5　Washerwomen drying clothes at their homes

of trade unionism and strike action in Europe, were brought out to work for Saul Solomon & Company in the 1870s. They struck work in 1876 on what proved to be the correct rumour that women (i.e. cheaper labour) were going to be employed in their place, and tried to persuade compositors in other firms to do likewise. The British compositors fell foul of the Masters and Servants Act. They were fined and their contracts cancelled.[23] Cape Town's Resident Magistrate, John Campbell, made his actions quite clear:

It will never do for immigrants coming out here to establish the practice of what is called 'picketing', and intimidating or threatening others from working for their master. Any such system as that I will endeavour to put down, as it is a most dangerous thing, and I hope will never be introduced into this colony. At all events, I shall do my best to prevent it, so far as the punishment to be awarded permits.[24]

The most important reason for the immobility of young single members of the casual labour pool, and therefore their weak bargaining position with employers in the 1880s, may have been that they had nowhere else to go: or nowhere within reach of their limited or non-existent capital resources that could offer any better prospects of work than they already had. There was a temporary migration of workers outwards looking for work on farms during the harvest months of October through to February. But job opportunities there would have been affected by poor harvests and phylloxera, and the overall trend was most certainly inwards.

The weak position of labour meant wage reduction and redundancies for even highly skilled artisans in the depression years, though many of the latter were able to choose emigration over starvation. The plight of the majority of Cape Town's workers was undoubtedly desperate by the mid-1880s. It was made more so by the fact that the Harbour Board relied increasingly on cheap convict labour in these years: the proportion of convicts to free labourers rose from two-fifths in 1882 to three-quarters by 1887.[25] This, then, was the background to grinding poverty that marked this period, and to crime, disease, protest and riot that brought the poor forcibly to the attention of the bourgeoisie.

Before the depression, members of Cape Town's English-speaking dominant class seem to have had a fairly clear idea of who were poor and deserved their sympathy, and who were poor merely because of their own moral shortcomings. As with bourgeois perceptions of poverty in England, the 'deserving poor' were those who 'could not work' or be responsible for themselves because of age or infirmity.[26] They deserved their charity even if it was believed that there was not enough poverty in the Cape Colony to necessitate poor laws or workhouses. In their absence the 'deserving poor' were taken care of chiefly by church institutions and the Free Dispensary, founded in 1860 in the wake of a smallpox epidemic and supported entirely by private donations.[27]

Ethnicity did play some part in the perception of this kind of deserving poverty. Dale expressed his specific concern in 1869 for White children who were not being educated, when delivering a speech to the South African Teachers' Association in his capacity as Superintendent of Education. Ironically this was the year in which his poem against colour prejudice had been published. In his speech Dale hoped that 'this blot on our character as colonists and citizens' would be gradually erased. But he wanted the DRC to help them, and does not appear to have thought at this stage that it was the duty of the state to intervene especially on their behalf. Dale believed that schools benefited 'the children of our labouring poor' in general, not just White children, and his ideal seems to have been compulsory attendance for all within a single education system, when funds permitted the building of enough schools.[28]

Members of Cape Town's dominant class were generally unsympathetic to the plight of the mass of Cape Town's casual labourers and their families. It was acknowledged, at least by doctors, that overcrowding and squalor might be partly the result of bad sanitation and a shortage of houses, but even those gentlemen also blamed the 'dirty habits' and 'ignorance' of slum dwellers. The latter's lack of economic resources was considered as a crucial part of explaining slum conditions, but this poverty was not deserving because it supposedly resulted from laziness, improvidence and overindulgence in alcohol.[29]

The British bourgeoisie believed at this time that such undeserving poor could be morally improved, and thus educated out of their poverty.[30] Yet some at least of their counterparts in Cape Town were not absolutely sure that this solution would work in the colonial context. This doubt was well expressed by Dr Ross in his evidence to the Select Committee on Sanitation of 1877: 'I think the dirty, ignorant people might be made cleaner: in the old days of slavery they were higher in the scale of civilisation than their descendants are now.'[31]

Yet Ross was ultimately pessimistic about the capacity for self-improvement of this section of Cape Town's population. His pessimism was in the same vein as the negative stereotyping of Malays associated with the 'Clean' campaign for urban reform:

I do not see how you can prevent the mortality amongst the black people. They die from dirt and ignorance, and vice, and drink, and their habits and surroundings are so odious that they repel all sympathy. Unless you compel them like slaves they will never improve.[32]

But the fact of the matter was that outside the professional circles of some doctors and churchmen, knowledge, let alone concern, about the undeserving poor was at a low level in the years of prosperity between 1875 and 1882. Only because of the threat that their living conditions posed to the health of the bourgeoisie, and the fact that this was made a part of the 'reforming' campaign by the English-language press, were slum conditions kept in the minds of bourgeois suburbanites. As it was, these conditions were described in a very general way and with more emphasis on habitations than inhabitants. A sharper focus on the living conditions of the 'undeserving' poor occurred only when life and limb had actually suffered via disease or crime. It was high mortality from a variety of diseases early in 1877 that had prompted detailed investigation into Cape Town's slums by a parliamentary select committee, and the publication of its evidence in the press.[33] Violent crimes, specifically those perpetrated on Whites, produced periodic occasions when bourgeois attention was also focused on the living conditions of members of the lower classes.

One such occasion was the murder of a young White man in the vicinity of Rogge Bay, District One, in 1879. He had been in the company of a number of prostitutes, and their trial for his murder revealed something of the lives of this section of the town's population. Most importantly, it drew attention to the fact that there were, beyond the slum dwellers themselves, a group of homeless Capetonians. One correspondent to the *Cape Times* was mildly sympathetic:

True, the class of persons to be found there are mostly of the lowest – debased by drink and almost repulsive in their habits and appearance. Still, there is a duty devolving upon us as a Christian community we should not overlook – the disease is there, and our responsibility exists in applying the remedy. Boats, sheds ... logs of wood, shelter the loafers, many of whom claim the same nationality as ourselves, and who, I fear, are not removed in the scale of wretchedness from their coloured brethren.[34]

But the overwhelming reaction in the press was unsympathetic. Editorials emphasised that 'vagabonds', 'loafers', 'footpads' and 'loose women' constituted a public danger, and demanded the strengthening of the police. The message was driven home by references to the 'human vermin', 'loathsome set of wretches' and 'fearful-looking beings' who had to be driven from the city.[35] At least some correspondents saw the threat coming specifically from poor people who were Black. This was not altogether surprising given that the latter were the overwhelming majority of Cape Town's poor. 'Blood', while saying that the perpetrators of the crime should hang, drew this lesson from the tragedy: 'It seems that every encouragement is given to the black Negroes in this town to do whatever they like, but work.'[36]

This stereotype of Black Capetonians as particularly dangerous was enhanced by the incidents involving Africans in Papendorp in 1881. At almost exactly the same time, the *Lantern* proclaimed the frequency of 'Malay outrages', saying that 'rowdy Malays haunt the streets in gangs'.[37] In September the same journal warned of the danger posed both by Africans and Malays.[38]

Inextricably linked with their mobilisation of Englishness, the *Cape Times* and *Lantern* portrayed problems of social control as problems about controlling Blacks. Thus in complimenting the Resident Magistrate for 'moving against' adolescent street games, St Leger wrote that the 'European' population would be glad of such action. When the Magistrate was asked by a government commission in 1881 about the identity of seventy-two offenders under the age of sixteen that he had sentenced to flogging and imprisonment in a two-year period, he said that they were all 'coloured'. In fact, reformatory records show that some were classified as White. Clamping down on street activities, such as games of pitch-and-toss, usually meant the arrest, and often the imprisonment, of Black Capetonians by police who were White. Not surprisingly arrest was frequently resisted, and the police attacked, which furthered the idea of Black unruliness when these occasions were reported in the press.[39]

If occasions of violence gave bourgeois Capetonians some glimpses of poverty in their town then these occasions were few and far between. However, when they did occur the evidence suggests that bourgeois Capetonians took very much the same view of the poverty they revealed as did bourgeois London. Most homeless or slum dwellers were seen as 'undeserving' poor. But they were nonetheless seen as the victims of moral shortcomings, of drink, of vice, which might be educated out of them. For this purpose the mission schools existed and temperance lodges and benefit societies were formed.[40] The few specialist investigations into crime and sanitation did find that insufficient housing was a problem that could not be blamed on the undeserving poor. The implication here was that steps should be taken to rectify this problem.[41]

For Cape Town's White bourgeoisie poverty was only an occasional concern between 1875 and 1882. When they thought about the problem at all their response was to say that the undeserving poor in general needed moralising. If the tone was on occasion somewhat more pessimistic than that of middle-class London then the difference seems to have lain in the fact that bourgeois Capetonians could use the increasingly negative ethnic stereotypes of Blacks as an additional factor in explaining moral shortcomings. Colour was not something that could, like vice, be educated out of the poor. Instead, the 'Sebastopol' area, surrounding Rogge Bay and popular with Black vagrants, needed to be 'cleared of human vermin'.[42]

However, before the depression, no effort was made by bourgeois Capetonians to racialise the treatment of poverty. Nor did most newspaper references to the low social status of Black Capetonians explain it in racist terms. Moreover, the constitution of the Free Dispensary stipulated that help should be given to the sick poor of Cape Town, with no distinction of 'colour, class or creed'.[43]

But the very limited concern shown about poverty, the tiny contributions to charity, the lack of housing schemes in the manner of Octavia Hill self-help dwellings in London, all suggest that the bourgeoisie in general did not see poverty as a serious problem in the boom years.[44] Indeed a *Cape Times* editorial could state in 1880 that 'it is often said that there is no poverty in the Colony'.[45] Such complacency was severely rocked in the years after 1882 when the amelioration of poverty came to be seen as an immediate necessity largely because of the rapidly expanded numbers of those defined as deserving poor. In these changed circumstances, ethnicity began to play a crucial role in the definition of deserving and undeserving poor. The 'poor White problem' was about to be discovered.

The smallpox outbreak of 1882 hastened the economic downturn in Cape Town. It was also one of those occasions that forced the dominant class to look at the living conditions of the poor. Smallpox epidemics had periodically devastated the population of Cape Town in the eighteenth and nineteenth centuries. The most recent outbreak, that of 1858, had killed up to two thousand Capetonians at a time when the total population of the city was only about twenty-four thousand.[46] Thus, when reports of smallpox reached the town council in June 1882 it was not slow to respond, ordering street-keepers to report on the 'conditions of the lower classes and their habitations'.[47] The first suspected case had lived in a house inhabited by a total of seventeen men, women and children.[48]

In the course of the next few days the council received the required information and the press some graphic descriptions. For instance councillor Ashley reported on the conditions of District Six in the vicinity of the suspected case: the streets were not made up, they had no guttering, there were pools of black filth in 'every direction' and no dirt carts (to collect stercus) came that way. In respect of the actual house of the suspected victim, there was no lavatory, inside or out, and the resulting filth was piled up in the street against the walls of the house. Ashley also noted that the inmates had no change of clothing, that 'people of this class were always scantily provided with clothes'.[49]

Some were also scantily provided with houses, as the press soon revealed. The *Lantern* had several articles on the 'dig-out' population of Table Mountain, along the lines of Mayhew's work on the street folk of London. A reporter duly went to several 'burrows' and informed *Lantern* readers of the circumstances of their inhabitants in the same mixture of self-reproach and dread that characterised Mayhew's melodramatic prose. The article argued that the 'Burrow-Squatters of Table Mountain' were all immoral, drunkards and vagabonds. Although the writer only found about a hundred at the time of his visit, he warned darkly that there were often 'many more'.[50]

More responsible articles showed that crowded living conditions and squatting were not confined to those with moral shortcomings. There were the reports of the council's investigations. There was also Fuller's description of the labourers working at the docks, 'here ten in a room, here a dozen, here perhaps fifteen', and Fuller made it clear that some labourers were without formal housing. A settlement existed in the Dock Road 'extemporising shelter' by means of tin cases. There was a 'warren' towards Zonnebloem College and 'on the hillside near the [Roeland Street] gaol'.

Fuller still denied that poverty was a permanent problem. He maintained that people who lived in the open or in shacks were 'not poor'. They lived in these conditions purely because of a temporary shortage of housing.[51] The editor of the *Cape Times*, in the years of prosperity, had said that 'economic laws' would soon remedy this deficiency.[52] The existence and further threat of disease now suggested to the council, with its six Clean members elected in 1880, that those laws should be given a little help.

The attempt, which began in July, to provide additional low-cost housing ended in failure. The council planned to appropriate part of Green Point Common for the purpose. The position of the new houses would have been conveniently close to the docks, and thus have met with Fuller's approval and presumably that of merchants living in the far-off southern suburbs. But the plans did not have the approval of the predominantly bourgeois residents of Green Point, 760 of whom signed a petition against the council's housing scheme. In the course of their successful attempt to stop the council, the Green Pointers expressed their fears that 'the scum of Cape Town' would be put on the Common, 'whose habits are not moulded on the severest type of social discipline'. Residence in Green Point had enabled members of the bourgeoisie to achieve social distance from the poor; they did not want the gap they had opened up to be so traumatically narrowed.[53]

One section of Cape Town's bourgeoisie checked the remedial plans of another, the provision of additional housing stock. But a smallpox relief committee did come into existence in August. The Committee comprised a number of clergymen and 'humanitarians' and asked for donations in aid of the 'genuinely distressed'.[54] Immediately there was considerable dispute over who these were. The committee accepted that many breadwinners had died or were dying from smallpox, swelling the numbers of the deserving poor. They were divided over whether Malays qualified for inclusion in this category.

The view that Malays should not be helped had been promoted by the racist diatribes against them in the press before and after the epidemic had started. Mr Goldschmidt was against Malays getting relief because 'they did their best to communicate disease to Europeans' and therefore there was a 'strong feeling' against them. Mr Langlands said that 'people' did not subscribe to the funds because they thought that they might go to Malays. That the latter did qualify for some relief was thanks largely to the advocacy of Canon Lightfoot.[55]

Negative stereotypes of Black Capetonians justified for many members of the dominant class their existing reluctance to do anything for members of the lower classes, a reluctance rationalised by the dogma of 'pauperisation'. Significantly, the smallpox epidemic seems to have increased bourgeois doubt that, specifically, the Black poor could be moralised. St Leger wrote an editorial in September 1882 claiming that the 'town classes' in other countries could be 'reached by example, by instruction, by a certain infiltration of ideas through the strata above them'. But this was unlikely to happen in Cape Town because 'we do not have a homogeneous population'. Instead, 'there is a very large element ... that exists only to propogate dirt ... reeking yards [are a] mere reflection of the mental condition of those who create them'. The problem of poverty in Cape Town, from St Leger's perspective, was that Black Capetonians were not just dirty by 'habit and necessity', but by 'instinct'.[56]

Outbreaks of disease, such as the smallpox epidemic of 1882 which killed about four hundred people in Cape Town, fed the sanitation syndrome in late nineteenth-century colonial cities: the desire of bourgeois Whites to be protected from contamination by 'dirty' Blacks. Segregation was seen as a means of gaining that protection.[57] Although there had been plenty of previous negative stereotyping and ideas about what to do about Malays from bourgeois Whites, calls for their residential segregation came during, and because of, the smallpox epidemic. So did further calls for a location for Africans, including support from St Leger for Fuller's idea of segregating those working at the docks within the harbour itself.

The fact that these calls came to nothing, at this stage, had a great deal to do with the nature of Cape Town's social formation and the fact that African employment at the docks dropped rapidly after 1882, as we saw in the last chapter. There was also the unresolved question of who would have to pay for residential segregation: central or local government, or individual employers? In the case of segregating Malays, such expense would be massive at a time when the Colony was moving into recession. In addition, many of Cape Town's dominant class probably felt that they had already bought sufficient segregation, by living in suburban villas on the other side of Table Mountain.

The smallpox epidemic prompted further suggestions about where segregation might be needed from Whites who were probably not members of the dominant class but were treated sympathetically by some of the latter. 'Sufferer' wrote to the *Cape Times* wanting the Tramway Company to 'classify' its passengers. The writer complained of having to sit beside 'a perspiring malodorous African, or a dirty hussy ... carrying a bundle of foul linen'.[58] The choice of invectives conjured up the imagery of potential contamination. This letter preceded the rumours about Malay washerwomen deliberately waging biological warfare against Whites by infecting their underclothing. These rumours could only increase the apparent necessity for Whites to protect themselves. St Leger, in April 1883, wrote an editorial that stopped short of advocating tram segregation but which moaned about the 'ghastliness' of the Tramway Company and the 'indescribable emanations from ethnically unctuous humanity' on their vehicles.[59]

But if St Leger now sympathised with the complaints of Whites who wanted segregation on the trams, there remained the question of who would have to implement it, and whether they would wish to do so. Directors of the City Tramways Company included those wealthy Clean candidates in the 1880 election, Farmer and the Bolus brothers. They, like many other members of the Cape Town's dominant class, did not have to rely on trams to get around town; they owned private transport. Even if these directors were converts to sanitation syndrome ideology, personal need did not argue for segregation on their trams and cost probably argued against it.[60]

A White convict had written before the epidemic asking for segregation at the Breakwater prison. During the epidemic St Leger interviewed, and wrote an editorial sympathising with, an ex-convict who made the same plea. But a few days later St Leger published a letter from 'Observer' which said that part of the punishment for White criminals was to be imprisoned with 'coloureds'. Segregation in prisons, understandably, does not appear to have been a priority for Cape Town's dominant class, but now, due to the sanitation syndrome, they 'understood' why White criminals might want it. And by making demands on prison administrators, seemingly in the course of the smallpox outbreak, White criminals did get lavatory 'troughs' set aside for their own use.[61]

Some government administrators may still have adhered to those principles of Cape liberalism still evident in the 'Observer' letter. The writer had somewhat grudgingly admitted that there were 'some decent Blacks' and that it would be bad for them to be among their 'own low people'. There was also the problem, as 'Observer' pointed out, of deciding who was White or Black 'in face of the infinite gradations of colour in races so mixed as our population'. But, importantly, 'Observer' appeared to take it for granted that mixing with 'low' Blacks was punishment for all Whites.

More importantly, administrators, be they of prisons or hospitals, had to worry about expense. Classification that meant physical separation of different inmates in government facilities, such as prisons and hospitals, required building more cells or wards, which meant finding the money to do so. Therefore even if particular administrators came to the conclusion that all Whites, by definition, suffered by being with most Blacks, cost could restrain the extent of action. Separate lavatory troughs were one thing, separate cells would be much more expensive, and the recession sharply reduced government revenue.

So the rate and extent of segregation in government facilities was not just about politicians or administrators coming to believe it was desirable; although this was a precondition. It was also about cost, and therefore about expenditure priorities. This was true whether the desire was for exclusionary classification, as it had been before the 1880s, or separation of all Whites from most Blacks, which became the aim in the course of the decade. The same considerations apply in explaining segregation in local government or privately owned facilities.

Expenditure priorities and the smallpox epidemic determined that most medical institutions were more thoroughly segregated before most prisons in Cape Town. The segregation of prisons only came in the 1890s when Cape government revenues began to recover thanks to the discovery of gold in the Transvaal in 1886 which increased trade through Cape ports and railways. In 1888 White and Black prisoners still slept in the same barracks at the Breakwater convict station. The Resident Magistrate stated that there had hitherto been 'no distinction of colour' in the treatment of prisoners in Cape Town's Roeland Street gaol. In fact there were already some informal arrangements at both the Cape Town and Wynberg gaols, whereby the gaolers (on what appears to have been their own initiative) separated White and Black prisoners at night.[62]

The smallpox epidemic played a part in promoting the ideology of racial separation in 1880s Cape Town by appearing to lend substance in White minds to its sanitation syndrome component. The emergence of this component was closely connected to the growing importance and prestige of the medical profession in colonial society in the second half of the nineteenth century. Members of this profession propagated beliefs, such as the germ theory of disease, on which sanitation syndrome arguments for segregation were based. Before the 1890s, Andrew Jackson was the only doctor who was not White. Organised from 1830 under the Colonial Medical Committee, the ideological and administrative significance of doctors had grown as they took up positions in an expanding state bureaucracy in the course of the Mineral Revolution.[63]

If doctors were racist, like Ross, they actively promoted the sanitation syndrome in the arguments, publicised in the press, that they gave to government commissions concerned with public health. For instance, the problem with 'natives' in the mental asylum on Robben Island was that their 'ideas of cleanliness' were different from those of Whites, 'particularly in closet arrangements'. Such arguments gave 'scientific' backing to calls for segregation based on other concerns such as social control or social prestige. In evidence given to a commission of inquiry into the mental asylum on Robben Island in 1879, Dr Biccard stated that Whites were more likely to be cured than Blacks. According to another 'expert' witness, treatment was liable to be more effective if Whites were separated from Blacks, and Whites 'would almost certainly be injured by being mixed with them'. This was not only because some Whites 'were accustomed to refined society' but now also because other Whites who were not might have 'some tender susceptibility' against colour.[64]

Sanitation and psychological discourse turned into institutional practice after, and partly because of, the smallpox epidemic. When forced to provide a quarantine station and hospital, the town council and central government paid equal amounts towards the cost, and Whites were segregated from Blacks, who were divided into Coloureds, 'Mozambiquans' and Malays. Malays had apparently favoured their own separate facilities for religious reasons. Smallpox lymph was taken from White children only.[65]

Official reports on the Old and New Somerset Hospitals for 1882 made no mention of classification by colour.[66] By 1883 considerable reorganisation and 'reform' had taken place in colonial health administration. This included the publication of reports by District Surgeons and the passing of the first Public Health Act which made central government responsible for dealing with epidemics.[67] Government reforms in the wake of the epidemic would also seem to have included the provision of 'White and Coloured' wards in the New Somerset Hospital. In the Old Somerset Hospital Whites were separated from Blacks among the 'chronic sick', and by 1884 this separation had taken place among the 'lunatics'.[68]

In 1883 the Colonial Medical Committee advised the Colonial Secretary that the establishment of cottage hospitals was impossible unless there was separation between 'Europeans and Coloureds'.[69] Such segregation in new medical institutions would appear to have become government policy. Possibly the last to be separated in existing institutions, and perhaps because they were almost all likely to be lower class, were the lepers on Robben Island, accommodated in appalling conditions: 'I saw human beings kennelled worse than dogs ... here were black, halfe-caste and white, all mixed together in hideous confusion, but thank heaven! no females'.[70]

The smallpox epidemic had prompted segregated treatment of the 'deserving' poor, the sick, and this became part of government practice thereafter. What the epidemic and sanitation syndrome rhetoric had only begun to do was to redefine the understanding of who belonged to the deserving poor in bourgeois minds. There was some doubt as to whether Blacks might not have brought misfortune on themselves, or be inherently responsible for the dreadful conditions in which they lived, and not automatically deserving of sympathy. There was not, as yet, a rethinking of what constituted poverty among Whites.

As the immediate crisis caused by the smallpox epidemic died away, the recession in Cape Town deepened. The reality of retrenchment and insolvency, from which members of the dominant class were not immune, made some of the latter begin to acknowledge that there were a large number of Capetonians who 'will work' but were temporarily unable to, through no fault of their own. Thus the *Cape Times* had a sub-leader in August 1883:

The depression of trade in and around Cape Town results in a great amount of poverty and destitution, with which private charity is unable to cope. Numbers of men and women are absolutely homeless, by no fault of their own, but simply because employment is not to be had.[71]

In a similar vein a J. Spencer-Smith had written a month earlier saying that the distress was genuine, and that the churches and citizens should unite to help. In the past 'laziness, extravagance, waste, dirt and independence have characterised the bulk of the lower order of the working class'.[72] But there was now a real need, unemployment was genuine enough.

With their credentials established, the unemployed could feel happier about approaching the bourgeoisie for relief rather than just waiting for help from private charity, which was in any case insufficient. One did so in a somewhat menacing tone. 'B.' wrote at the end of August 1883 asking whether the unemployed were going to be allowed to become 'hungry, desperate and with a sense of grievance'.[73]

Under these circumstances a relief committee was again established. Significantly though, a distinction was made by the bourgeoisie between different members of the unemployed. A night refuge committee was set up specifically to deal with the problem of unemployed clerks and bookkeepers who, as we saw in chapter 2, were overwhelmingly White. Nonetheless they still had to undergo an unpleasant labour test, quarrying stone to prove their 'deserving' status.[74] Similarly, 'J. A.' wrote about the traumas of '*Europeans*' [my emphasis] being forced to work for farmers at 6d a day because of the depression: they would have to work side-by-side with the 'niggers', share their food, and sleep under the same roof. Of the 150 men who came to the relief committee to seek employment, 50 were interviewed, 'mostly Europeans', which suggests both a degree of selectivity on ethnic grounds as to who were deserving poor, and the fact that this was known among the latter.[75]

The initial concern of the bourgeoisie seems to have worn off in the summer months of 1883/4. However, one candidate for the Assembly election, T. J. O'Reilly, who described himself as the working man's candidate in his nomination speech, made the substitution of White labour for 'Delagoa Kaffirs' part of his platform in February 1884. Another candidate, J. L. M. Brown, also said that he was looking for what he called the working man's vote and did not want to be put into parliament by 'Kafir ... coolies who hardly [knew] their right hand from their left'. The speeches suggest that it had occurred to both O'Reilly and Brown to attempt some White ethnic mobilisation among Cape Town's lower classes, but neither was elected. Practising the small tradition of Cape liberalism was still required for electoral success, as was demonstrated by the different tactics employed by Fuller. Towards the end of 1883 he was helping Abdol Burns with representations to central goverment that Malay cemeteries be allowed to remain open. St Leger commented that the most hideous form of corruption would be 'a graveyard vote'.[76] Fuller also argued in a campaign speech that once 'natives' had proved themselves good citizens they should be treated like anyone else.[77]

The election took place as the depression deepened. Even workers in

jobs least liable to casualisation had their wages reduced or faced
redundancy in the mid-1880s. Perhaps because of the threat of the Masters
and Servants Act hanging over them, workers mostly confined their protest
to petitions and letters to the newspapers.[78] One exception was provided by
workers from the Salt River railway works. Led by British artisans,
including engineers who were among those least liable to casualisation,
they succeeded in getting their wages paid weekly instead of monthly in
March 1884, which apparently meant slightly increased pay. To press their
demands, five hundred marched four abreast to the city centre and stormed
the office of the general manager of the Cape Railways. He immediately
gave way to their demands. But by the beginning of August many of these
railway workers had also been retrenched.[79]

On the only other recorded occasion when a strike was attempted in
the mid-1880s, it ended in failure with more redundancies; but its nature,
like the behaviour of the Salt River workers, undoubtedly alarmed the
dominant class. In August 1884 the landing and dock agent, A. R.
McKenzie, reduced his employees' wages. About five hundred of his
workers then struck work under the leadership of John Titus, a West
Indian, Henry Yateman, an Englishman, a West African Frenchman
called Phillip Susa and another West Indian nicknamed 'Long Dick'.

The prominence of these immigrants in the strike, and the way the
latter was organised, suggests that they had experience of combination in
other parts of the world. Certainly Titus was literate and a regular reader
of newspapers, which, together with the fact that he was older, must have
increased his leadership ability and stature. Using a nearby pub as their
headquarters, the leaders organised a mass picket to keep out hundreds
of would-be strikebreakers eager to get employment. Presumably because
peaceful persuasion failed, the pickets used violence. Armed with knives,
revolvers, daggers and sticks they beat up some of the blacklegs. Titus
was alleged to have said that he did 'not care a damn for McKenzie or
the government or anyone'.

The arrest of the 'ringleaders', the size of the reserve pool of labour
and police protection of strikebreakers ensured that the strike was soon
over.[80] The *Cape Argus* had predicted this failure: 'As so many men were
out of employment in Cape Town at the present moment, there is certain
to be no difficulty in filling the void opened by the strikers.'[81]

But the Magistrate's fears in the late 1870s about immigrants bringing
new methods of worker organisation had been realised. The strikers had
also demonstrated the ability of desperate workers to organise across
potential ethnic divides, and the possible danger posed to bourgeois
Capetonians when they did so. A few days later St Leger wrote an
editorial appealing to the rich to look after their own health by looking

after the health of the poor. He probably had more than the smallpox epidemic in mind.[82]

The failure of the strike made many more workers redundant, as McKenzie brought in 'Zanzibaris', housed in stables, to replace them.[83] But far from relief efforts increasing in the winter of 1884, the main charity, the Free Dispensary, was running short of money. It therefore established a committee to see how to cut down on the numbers of people being helped. The committee decided to require anyone wanting relief to carry a card, certifying their genuine poverty, and signed by some 'respectable' person.[84]

It is not clear who qualified for relief under this system but members of the unemployed were unimpressed. Shortly after the end of the dock strike, a letter to the *Cape Times* in August, from 'One of the Many Sufferers', spoke of the fact that 'hundreds' were out of work, that many had no funds to pay the rent or for food, and that the Night Refuge made no provision for married men. It was, the writer affirmed, a question of 'Food or Death', otherwise there would be a meeting of 'all men regardless of creed or colour'.[85]

Two weeks later the meeting took place. Four hundred men attended. A reporter on the *Cape Times* stated that the gathering was not a good advertisement either for 'dire straits' or for the quality of men looking for work. On the platform were three or four 'respectable-looking' artisans, but there were also several 'Malays'. In the crowd there were 'all sorts' of men, including 'Moslems' and 'Blacks'. Most revealing was the paper's comment that throughout the city 'the cry had been about *European* [my emphasis] craftsmen and labourers'. Yet here was a meeting of 'all sorts'.[86] The implication was that this meeting challenged prevailing bourgeois attitudes as to who constituted the genuine unemployed, the new category of 'deserving poor', and that they had been thought to be Whites.

The meeting of the unemployed set up a committee of 'all sorts' which proceeded to put a notice in the newspaper addressed to 'Working Men Out of Employment', urging them to register their names at the Metropolitan Hall.[87] The reaction of bourgeois Cape Town to this alliance of Black and White unemployed, coming so soon after evidence of Black and White workers in violent combination at the docks, was swift and aimed at defusing the potential threat. The mayor opened their next meeting. The Commissioner of Crown Lands, the member of the government responsible for public works, was also present. In the next few days the central government, the Harbour Board and the town council all took steps to relieve the unemployment problem by finding work for those on the register.[88]

That help was given chiefly to Whites is suggested by the fact that, as Lightfoot pointed out, for 'obvious reasons' (the implication being that they were illiterate) the names of Coloureds or Africans did not appear on the register.[89] But little was done to rectify the problem, presumably because most dominant-class Whites, with notable exceptions such as Lightfoot, did not think that much, if any, Black poverty was 'deserving'. The government provided free passes on the railways for artisans, 'nearly all' of whom were White. The *Cape Argus* made its contribution by advertising for 'respectable European' boys to sell the newspaper.[90]

In 1886 another meeting of the unemployed was held on the city's Grand Parade, at what was probably the lowest point of the depression. Three hundred men attended, who represented 'different trades' and were, by implication, 'respectable'. They talked of 'oppression', and what would happen if employers were threatened with violence: 'then they would come forward and help us'.[91] Acting swiftly again to deffuse this possible threat, the town council agreed the following day to keep a register of the unemployed. But, under the leadership of a Mr Weytze and a Mr Raphael, the unemployed went ahead and, within a week, established their own register. Apparently half the names they collected belonged to Whites, half to 'coloureds'.

It seems that, faced with this new organisation among Black and White unemployed, town councillors provided the money for Raphael to rent a room to serve as a 'labour bureau', where simple meals were also provided. Shortly afterwards Weytze led a deputation to the Prime Minister, armed with 625 names from the labour bureau, demanding government intervention on their behalf. The result was that both central government and the town council employed about fifty men each on public works. A further seventy-seven men were given free rail passes to Kimberley and over a hundred and twenty given free soup and bread daily until the end of the winter.[92]

The organisation displayed by the unemployed in both 1884 and 1886, together with the clear threats that they expressed, forced both the Cape government and Cape Town's dominant class to include some of them in a new definition of deserving poverty. The *Cape Times* commented in August 1886 that 1,000 unemployed (the number now registered) put paid to arguments for '*laissez-faire*'. Economic recession, the paper acknowledged, had caused genuine distress.[93]

But for many members of Cape Town's dominant class, in this new definition of poverty, to be deserving you also had to be 'respectable'. Almost the first question that Upington asked the deputation in July 1886 was how he was to judge the respectability of those on their list. An article in the *Cape Times* four days earlier had distinguished between 'respectable artisans' and 'loafers'. A fortnight later the paper reported that the artisans 'were nearly all White men'.[94] In 1886, as in 1884, it can be presumed that these Whites were the chief beneficiaries of dominant-class concern and new kinds of local and central government help such as free rail passes and the provision of employment on public works.

It would seem that for many bourgeois Capetonians there was a very close correlation between the conferring of that ubiquitous Victorian virtue, respectability, and the Whiteness of the recipient. In their view if not all Whites were respectable, virtually all those deemed to be respectable were White. The inference was that most Blacks were not respectable, that Whites should be rescued from what was increasingly represented as a Black residuum. In this vein the *Lantern*, investigating 'Cape Town by Night' in 1885, verbally contrasted a description of a nine-year-old White girl and her sister, who kept their mother by begging, with racist remarks about 'the foulest daughters of the African Eve' squatting in a railway truck. In February 1886 the same journal focused specifically on the plight of the White unemployed in the city. In 1888, W. F. Taylor, manager of the English Church Mission Schools, wrote to the *Cape Times* complaining of the small government grant to mission schools and commented on the increasing number of 'White poor'. By the early 1890s new forms of government intervention were devised for their rescue.[95]

There is no hard evidence to suggest that White workers themselves appealed to White ethnic solidarity, as some were overtly to do in Cape Town in the 1890s and as White workers were already doing in Kimberley. It would appear to be significant, in this respect, that it was in Kimberley rather than Cape Town that a rigid ethnic division of labour had come into existence by the 1880s. In Cape Town White and Black workers alike were represented at meetings of the unemployed. Yet it would be dangerous to overemphasise non-racial solidarity among Cape Town's working class. O'Reilly had campaigned for jobs specifically for White workers in 1884. The fact that he was only narrowly beaten in that election may suggest that some of the latter identified with his stand.[96]

Severe recession and the threats used by the unemployed made Cape Town's dominant class redefine who should be included among the deserving poor. It did not make them relinquish the desire to distinguish between deserving and undeserving poverty. On the contrary, the evidence suggests that many members of the dominant class not only wished to make distinctions throughout the depth of the depression but were ethnocentric or overtly racist when doing so.

Sanitation had been defined as an urban problem in the discourse of dominant-class Capetonians before the depression. English ethnic mobilisation at the local political level was aimed at solving it. Consequently, if also connected to processes outside Cape Town, the stereotyping of Black Capetonians became increasingly negative in English discourse in the late 1870s. When crime, disease or organisation by the unemployed made members of Cape Town's dominant class look at the city's lower classes, most did so by the 1880s from a racist perspective.

A further reason why this happened can be attributed to the minor riots that followed the closure of the Muslim cemeteries on Signal Hill on 15 January 1886. The vast majority of Malays perceived the closure of the cemeteries – together with the selection of far away Maitland as an alternative burial ground – as a threat to their community. At risk was their practice of carrying the dead to the grave: the Maitland cemetery was seven miles away. The threat to this practice had ensured that thousands of Malays took part in protest meetings and demonstrations in 1885, as well as in the stone-throwing incidents that constituted the riots themselves.

Another probable element in the ideology of many Malays who participated in the riots was anti-authoritarianism.There had been frequent attacks by Malays on policemen in the course of the nineteenth century and, as we saw, several examples exist for the late 1870s. Such anti-authoritarianism could explain why one of the cries of the crowd in January 1886 was 'Kill the *Deeners*' [policemen].

Attacks on policemen should be seen within the context of police action against street activities, such as games of pitch-and-toss or 'screaming and shouting' which could lead to imprisonment in the Porter Reformatory or Roeland Street gaol.The police were English-speaking and White, could easily be identified as protecting the interests of the dominant class. In addition Malays had their own legal system for solving disputes within the community, just as they had their own medical practices as alternatives to British doctors and their advice.[97]

The riots took place in the depths of depression, when discontent born of poverty and hunger was at its most intense. The disturbances came shortly after an occasion which twentieth-century participants were to call the 'Coon Carnival': the parading of lower-class Black Capetonians through the city at New Year, the traditional slave holiday, in elaborate dress and to the accompaniment of musical instruments and popular songs. Both Gerald Stone and, more briefly, Don Pinnock have analysed the carnival as it was after the Second World War. Stone, from his own participant experience in these carnivals in the 1960s, says that

'Coloureds' played up to existing White stereotypes, rather than challenging them. But such occasions, whether in Cape Town or early modern Europe, were not without danger to the dominant class. As Peter Burke demonstrated, carnival under certain circumstances could easily turn to riot.[98] Pinnock has suggested a more assertive dimension to Cape Town's carnival because it

> entailed the annual symbolic storming of the city by the poor, an act which clearly unnerved both the city authorities and the police. Thousands of noisy street brothers were demanding freedom of the streets, lampooning 'respectable' citizens and actually being seen ... a mob on the wrong side of town. Troupe members got little out of the Carnival but a one-day sense of freedom and a hangover. But for this they waited a whole year, and they put everything into it.[99]

We may suspect that the anti-authoritarianism and communal solidarity displayed in the weeks leading up to and beyond New Years's Day, as well as anger stemming from particular hardship caused by the depression, fed into the subsequent incidents during the 'illegal' burial of a Muslim child on 17 January. Three thousand people took part in the burial, an act of defiance in itself. After the funeral part of the crowd attacked fifteen policemen who had followed the procession. Stones were thrown and several policemen were injured, one quite seriously. Two White onlookers were also hurt. The fighting stopped only when the Commissioner of Police assured the crowd that his men had not intended to prevent the burial.

Later in the day a crowd of Black Christians and Muslims broke into the DRC cemetery which had also been closed. Watched by the police this group of 'street urchins and hobbledehoys' buried the coffin of a small child. Having done so they showed their defiance by shouting with triumph. The following day a similar crowd, this time armed with knobkerries, again hurled abuse at the police.

The government's response to the events of 17 January was to arrest sixteen Muslims whose occupations ranged from cab-driver to coolie, and to call out the Volunteers. The latter camped on Green Point Common for several days in full view of the cemeteries. They patrolled the city at night, and their presence was clearly intended to intimidate would-be rioters. In as much as no further incidents occurred, this intention was obviously successful.[100]

Within a couple of days the Muslims were burying their dead outside the boundaries of the municipality. They were not doing so at Maitland but considerably closer, at Mowbray, indicating that Muslims had gained something from violent protest which non-violent protest had failed to deliver.[101] The riots gave rise to an outpouring of fear-induced racism in the English-language press. An editorial in the *Cape Argus* stated: 'There has been so much of organisation in the opposition of the Malays, and so much of half smothered Asiatic fanaticism on the one side, and of dangerous resentment on the other, that the situation is alarming.' The *Argus* concluded that the Malays were not free from their 'ancestral tendencies' to 'run a muck'. The *Cape Times* insisted that the rioters must not win, otherwise 'we allow the Colony again to become the country of the Hottentots'.[102]

If the riots themselves had been partly the result of ethnic mobilisation by Malays, as we shall see in chapter 8, then the rationalisations of their occurrence in dominant-class minds were mostly racist. Behind these rationalisations, as with so much negative stereotyping, lay fear. The fear articulated at the time of the riots was fear of violence and even of displacement, of revolution. One employer, who found his men unwilling to work on the Monday following the riots, reported that his workers had told him: 'We are to have our turn now, you have ruled over us long enough'.[103]

The crises caused by the Malay riots and the organisation by the unemployed passed away by 1887. Thereafter the discovery of gold on the Witwatersrand created employment opportunities for those Capetonians mobile enough to take them, and eventually fuelled economic recovery in the Western Cape. But the threat or reality of disease and crime continued to produce racist responses from the dominant class.

If the threat of disease was not entirely lost sight of after the end of the smallpox epidemic, this was largely due to the reports of Dr G. H. B. Fisk, the council's sanitary officer, appointed in 1883 as a result of the smallpox epidemic. The English-language press popularised these reports in continued pursuit of a Clean Cape Town, and with the specific purpose of getting the council to adopt a comprehensive drainage scheme. This meant that more 'expert knowledge' was disseminated in the form of sanitation syndrome rhetoric, suggesting an equation between Blacks and the residuum in the late 1880s.

Fisk blamed slum conditions on the 'domestic habits of [a] peculiarly dirty and reckless *coloured* population' [my emphasis] in his 1886 report. When giving evidence to a government commission on Cape Town's sanitation in 1888, he argued that the 'dirty habits of the coloured population' had increased the mortality rate of the town. In his report for the same year he wrote on the extent of 'coloured' drunkenness in Cape Town. The problem of drink was implicitly made insoluble for Fisk by the fact that those whom he called 'the denizens of Hanover street [i.e. District Six] ... lacked the kind of personal pride that typified the wine drinking peasants of Andalusia'. His reports of 1887 and 1889 both blamed 'coloureds' for the insanitary state of Cape Town.[104]

James Easton, a self-appointed specialist, shared the concern of Fisk and the English-language press. A series of lectures he gave to the Young Men's Christian Association were published in book form in 1888. The discourse of the first lecture focused on the need for sanitation, but in arguing his case Easton stressed that the inhabitants of the slums he had visited in his investigations were 'all coloured ... Kaffirs, West Coast men, Mozambiques and so-called Malays'. According to Easton none of them had any sense of decency and they were all half-drunk. Drink was responsible for their '*hopeless* filthiness' [my emphasis].[105]

The solution advocated by the Dean of Cape Town, in a sermon he delivered in the year Easton's book was published, was the residential segregation of Coloured Capetonians. The Dean's message was applauded by 'Ulysses', a correspondent to the *Cape Times*, who said that it was impossible to teach Coloured people cleanliness. Their houses should be demolished and Cape Town would then be able to attract 'the wealthy, the scientific, and the cultivated'.

The 'Ulysses' letter was a highly provocative, racist diatribe. It talked of 'Coloured' Capetonians as 'this hopelessly filthy and pestilent hydra', 'a nightmare and an incubus on the community'.[106] What was significant was that there were no immediate or obvious rebuttals to the sentiments expressed. The only letters published in the English press that sought to defend 'Coloureds' or 'Malays' from the latest round of negative stereotyping came from people so defined.

This image of a Black residuum, beyond any easy or immediate moralising by example and which threatened respectable White Cape Town, was promoted by the growth of 'slumming' journalism in the 1880s. This kind of journalism proved popular all over the English-speaking world in the late nineteenth century, from Hull to Melbourne. The establishment of this trend had gone hand-in-hand with the expansion of the industrial city and the growth of geographical distance, reflecting social distance, in residential patterns in this period.[107]

In Cape Town the *Lantern* was the main outlet for articles with such titles as 'A Night in a Threepenny Lodging', 'Seamy Cape Town', 'Loafer Town', 'Social Evils', or 'Round Dangerous Cape Town with a Detective', which explored with lurid delight the immorality, deprivation and dangers of Cape Town's residuum. Ethnic labelling or stereotyping characterised the latter. A typical Cape Town prostitute was described as a 'fearful looking stupid Black beast', prostitutes collectively as 'the foulest daughters of the African Eve'. The Malays were held to be White-slavers, the controllers of brothels and canteens.[108]

Tales of the 'dangerous classes' of Cape Town, new to the 1880s, were all the more titillating because the exoticism of a different class could be widened in the telling by the exoticism of the perception of ethnic difference. Cape Town's slums became 'King Malay's Territory'. After an outbreak of 'fever' in 1888, the *Lantern* published two articles in successive editions on 'Cape Town Slumdom'. The first article stated that slums were places where 'the Malays and Kaffirs prefer to locate themselves', and went on (implying a sense of danger) to state that Coloureds outnumbered Whites by ten to one in the municipality. The writer described a line that divided White Cape Town from Coloured and stated that the White 'middle-classes' had little or no experience of the Coloured parts of the city. His first article described

coloured women-folk, who appear to spend all their time basking their raggedness and filth in the sun and wind on the stoeps of their dwellings, yell and shout to one another with violent windmill-like waving of the arms and a vigorous use of the tongue, tipped with a vernacular unknown except to the Philosopher learned in barbaric tongues.

This part of the town would really give '"dear Dora" and "dear Frances" and their gallant dancing lawn-tennis playing, cigarette smoking, dandified acquaintances a distaste for Cape Town for the rest of their natural lives'. Continuing on this theme in his second article, the acquaintances of 'dear Dora' and 'dear Frances' were invited to view the 'al fresco residences' on the lower slopes of Devil's Peak (i.e. in District Six) to become truly sadder and wiser.[109]

The message of the *Lantern* was that the truly dangerous and unpleasant of the 'dangerous classes' were Black. In August 1887 an article on crime was illustrated by a cartoon which showed a 'Cape Coloured' criminal. Another cartoon, early the next year, showed a Black man being executed with the caption 'A Horrible Necessity'. An article in the same issue suggested that 'a half-dozen of these brute beasts strung up, in view of their fellows throughout different parts of the land as their crimes fall in would do much to remedy the insecurity of what is dearer to our wives and sisters than life'. In June 1889 another article was called 'Our Cape Town Heathen'. It said that 'We' tolerate them and are 'absolutely callous, blind, and indifferent to the terrible social evil, the festering sore on the body politic which pollutes the purity and healthfulness of our social existence'.[110]

In the course of the depression years of the 1880s, respectability and Whiteness had become closely linked in dominant-class consciousness. Such linkage was at least in part a result of the appropriation of bourgeois attitudes to poverty current in Britain. The Cape Town poor, like the poor of *Outcast London*, were divided by the bourgeoisie of both cities into two parts: the deserving and the residuum. The deserving poor were the respectable working class, poor through no inherent moral fault of their own, the victims of temporary economic depression. The residuum, on the other hand, consisted of generically poor, doomed to perpetual poverty.[111]

London's dominant class, in the course of the 1870s and 1880s, came to explain the existence of their residuum by means of the theory of urban degeneracy: degeneration, now innate or biological, which had resulted from exposure, over generations, to the debilitating urban environment. This theory had its counterpart in the United States and Australia. Davison has shown how Melbourne's bourgeoisie, from the safety of their hilltop and seaside homes, thought the poor in their slums inhabited a 'separate moral universe'.[112]

Members of Cape Town's dominant class appear to have had similar thoughts to those of their counterparts in Australia, America and Britain. In fact British ideas were certainly influencing Capetonians. The *Lantern* in 1884 used Mayhew's *London Labour and the London Poor* as a guide for classifying poverty. The *Excalibur* in 1889 talked of the 'bitter cry' of Robben Island lepers, a reference to Andrew Mearns' *Bitter Cry of Outcast London* written in 1883, and so influential in changing attitudes to poverty in the British metropolis.[113]

The British theory of urban degeneracy, as Lorimer has shown, fed on the mid-Victorian equation between class and 'race'. Bourgeois Victorians saw the division between the urban poor and respectable classes virtually in terms of inherent characteristics. Lorimer also argued that a strident racism emerged in Britain towards people of colour, when 'a clear identification occurred between race and class'. Such an identification already existed in Cape Town before the depression. But it would appear that it only gave rise to intensified racism as the promotion of Englishness, and English ideas, became part and parcel of the reform campaign and English ethnic mobilisation in the late 1870s. Consequently Cape Town's dominant class came, in the course of the 1880s depression, to see their residuum in racist terms, as the poor who were 'Other than White', whose degeneracy stemmed from racial inferiority. Some of these Capetonians were almost beyond the pale of humanity. The unquestionably deserving poor in this scenario were Whites; it was the latter who could and should be helped out of their temporary plight by the action of relief committees and the local and central state.[114]

What had happened by the late 1880s was that the metropolitan idea of urban degeneration had fused in the colonial context with 'knowledge' drawn from the new science of social Darwinism. This taught that 'races' could degenerate and that the degenerate 'race' could corrupt the superior one, rather than being improved by it.[115]

Importantly for Cape Town's dominant class, one of the lessons learnt was that people of 'mixed race', who formed the vast majority of the city's Black population, were particularly likely to succumb to degeneration. The application of social Darwinist ideas to the Cape context was made in a series of books published from the mid-1880s. William Gresswell, in a two-volume work published in 1885, wrote that 'the black corrupts his master'. J. J. Aubertyn, who published in the following year and had visited Cape Town in 1884, wrote that the 'black will bring down the white'. The Reverend James Mackinnon, in a book sympathetic to the ostracised plight of the only African admitted to the Stellenbosch DRC Seminary, saw the 'bastard Hottentots' of the Western Cape as examples of racial 'retrogression'. He ascribed this to the human tendency to 'absorb the bad and neglect the good'.[116]

By the 1890s a pessimistic discourse about the result of miscegenation was firmly established. J. Ewing Ritchie, in *Brighter South Africa*, published in 1892, thought that the 'half-breeds' in Cape Town were close to the 'missing link'. In *What I think of South Africa,* which came out in 1896, Stuart Cumberland thought least of people he called the 'Cape Boys': 'He has a little of everything and not much of anything ... he belongs to the dirty-coloured races ... he looks dirty and is dirty.'[117]

By the mid-1890s Cape Town's leading English-language newspapers had all succumbed to vicious invectives against Cape Town's 'half-breed' residuum. The *Cape Argus*, which had been less racist than the *Cape Times* and *Lantern* before the depression, now competed in this arena, with virulent diatribes talking of 'Cape Town's Curse', and the 'criminal and vicious tendencies of the human scum of this city, the offensive and aggressive half breeds'. This change was facilitated by change of ownership. Saul Solomon sold the paper to Francis Dormer in 1881. Dormer was given financial backing by the conservative mining magnate Cecil Rhodes. According to the *Argus* of the 1890s, Cape Town's problems were more serious than those revealed in the *Bitter Cry of Outcast London*. Large numbers of 'coloured' people were not poor but 'wasteful, indifferent, and, worst of all filthy'. In other words Cape Town's residuum was even more of a problem to this city's dominant class than was the case in London.[118]

Even Olive Schreiner, the novelist who became known for her socialist and anti-imperialist sympathies, succumbed to these arguments. She wrote, in 1896, that 'half-castes' filled the gaols and brothels of the Colony, that three-quarters of the women at the Lock hospital in Cape Town (i.e. prostitutes) were half-castes, that the latter 'unite the vices of

all races', that they hated their own blood, and that Africans looked
down on them. She added that they were particularly licentious.[119] That
Schreiner's view of Coloured people was widely held is given further
testimony by the work of Van Heyningen. She cites the comments of a
suffragette, Emily Conybeare, who visited Cape Town in the early 1890s,
and was concerned with the harsh treatment of prostitutes under the
Contagious Diseases Act. In this respect, Conybeare was particularly
concerned about Coloured women whom she herself perceived to have
no 'inherited instinct of respectability'. Conybeare wrote:

The general tone of contempt for the coloured people which I found pervaded the
whole population naturally reacts on both sides, it tends to prevent the coloured
people developing any self-respect, and the white population regard these half-
breeds and the Natives as almost beyond the pale of humanity.[120]

Appropriate policies for dealing with Cape Town's residuum were
suggested by members of the dominant class. The Dean of Cape Town had
wanted segregation. Other alternatives had been supplied by Easton, and
it was these that the *Lantern* advocated when it said in 1889 that 'we'
should either 'exterminate them' or 'raise them'. The first method was
recommended for the older generation, via the use of prisons, and reminds
us that segregation was not necessarily the worst way that racism could
translate into social practice. The second method was suggested for the
younger generation, through the compulsory learning of discipline in
schools. The 'raising' of the residuum did not mean producing the social
equals of Whites. In practice, prison, in the form of the Porter
Reformatory in Constantia, as well as direct apprenticeship of homeless
youths by Cape Town's Resident Magistrate, was used as a means of
inculcating work discipline among the many young Coloured children.[121]
Increasingly from the late 1870s local or central government intervention was sought by Cape Town's dominant class as a remedy for social
problems, be they questions of public health or poverty, mirroring a
similar development in Britain.[122] Crucially, by the 1890s, different kinds
of intervention were advocated for the Black and White poor. The
former should be controlled by segregation, police, prisons and
education that disciplined them. The latter by public works for adult men
in times of short-term distress and by education in the long term which
genuinely 'raised' their children and saved them from the residuum. This
was essential, according to editorials and articles in the early 1890s,
because poor Whites in towns were 'sinking, sinking, sinking into the
social conditions of the snuff-and-butter coloured population'. These
were people, such as respectable White artisans, who were 'compelled' to
live in the slums and were 'degenerating by reason of their surroundings'.

Equally their children could degenerate by mixing with Blacks in mission schools or in organisations such as the Anglican church's Boys Brigade.[123]

The answer was for the government to give the children of the White poor superior education to that of Blacks. This kind of government intervention on behalf of White children had been part of Afrikaner ethnic mobilisation. Political mobilisation of Afrikaners by S. J. Du Toit in the 1870s was partly about promising to tap the resources of the state for their benefit, including the benefit of poor Afrikaners. *BBV* pressure in parliament after 1879 led to a government investigation in 1882 which found that only about one-sixth of White children were receiving regular education. In response the Cape government introduced the one-teacher farm schools, already established by the Orange Free State government, in 1883. *Bond* politicians during the depression of the 1880s demanded that the state should extend its responsibilities beyond education because of rural White poverty. The party congress in 1884 discussed the difficulty facing 'poor whites' on the land. Subsequent congresses passed resolutions demanding government intervention in the form of loans, irrigation schemes and railway lines.

The *Bond*'s ability to deliver on these resolutions improved as both membership and, more significantly, the number of seats it won in parliament increased after 1883. In that year the party captured a majority of the seats in the Legislative council and, in the 1884 elections, about thirty-three of the seventy-four seats in the Legislative Assembly. In 1886, the central committee of the *Bond* made government assistance with education a priority because Afrikaners were 'falling behind against well-educated immigrants'.[124]

In the late 1880s Langham Dale, as Superintendant General of Education, listened to the pleas from town and countryside. Dale had been sympathetic to the children of the rural White poor back in 1869. His White ethnocentrism had been perilously close to the prejudice against giving equal treatment to respectable Black and White workers which he condemned. The contradiction inherent in early- to mid-nineteenth-century Cape liberalism was that while it advocated a non-racial class system it was based on the presumption of current White superiority. The presence of White poverty, or of White vice, challenged that presumption. In his 1869 essay on the 'Cape and its People', Dale had gone through something of an existential crisis when attempting to confront this contradiction:

Those who are favoured by nature with white skins hug themselves in the notion that it is their business to whitewash that moiety of humanity that is of darker hue. The notion would not be so much amiss if they had settled among themselves some standard of moral and religious whiteness.[125]

Dale's poem, also published in 1869, had been called, and was hostile to, 'Prejudice Against Colour'. But in twenty years his own prejudice in favour of Whites would appear to have grown. In a special report on Cape education, which he produced in 1889, Dale demonstrated that he no longer had any doubts about expressing colour prejudice.

The first duty of the government has been assumed to be to recognise the position of the European colonist as holding the paramount influence, social and political; and to see that the sons and daughters of the colonists should have at least such education as their peers in Europe enjoy, with such local modifications as will fit them to maintain their unquestioned superiority and supremacy in this land.[126]

Dale's thinking was no more logical in 1889 than in 1869. It was precisely because European superiority and supremacy were 'questioned' by the presence of poor Whites in towns and rural areas that government intervention on their behalf was necessary. Whether this meant changes to the existing education system was the investigative brief given to a government education commission in 1891. Its discussions and recommendations will be revealed in the next chapter.

But preserving White supremacy, in White bourgeois debate, was not just a matter of educating poor Whites. It came from the associated requirements of keeping wealthier Blacks in 'their place', and preventing any serious challenge to White political supremacy. The former had largely been achieved by exclusionary segregation in Cape Town. This kind of segregation continued in the 1880s, even if economic depression reduced the rate of its extension to new institutions. In a *Cape Times* leader, St Leger discussed the position of Blacks at the Cape on the fifty-fifth anniversary of emancipation, and summed up existing practice:

As a matter of experience black passengers are not commonly met with in the saloons of steamships, or in first-class railway carriages, or in the reserved seats of the theatres, or in the best pews in churches or chapels, or in bathing machines and bathing houses, or at hotel tables, or even in the rooms of the Young Men's Christian Association.[127]

St Leger went on to say that there was no need to mention particular instances when the above had been 'brought home severely to the Black man of European education travelling in this country'. The message was 'brought home' in different ways. For instance on government-run trains, by 1890, there were 'very few occasions' when Coloureds were allowed into first-class carriages with Whites, which suggests that railway officials helped implement exclusion even if this was without legal backing. Only British soldiers, who were forced to travel third class though 'forbidden' to speak to Black passengers, complained about train classification in the early 1890s.[128]

Between 1887 and 1890 *de facto* exclusion in hotels was given *de jure* support. In a court case, Omar *v.* Norman, the Cape Town Resident Magistrate upheld the right of a Sea Point hotelier to prevent 'a well dressed Coloured man' from using his bar. The Magistrate said that 'anyone' could refuse a Coloured person service in the main bar and send him round to the 'tap', in other words the bar for 'unrespectable' Blacks. Omar, who had made his money as a cab proprietor in Kimberley, attempted to sue the hotelier, Norman, for £10 damages for refusal of service. The case was dismissed with costs. The *Lantern*, reporting the incident, said that a 'Malay Masher', accompanied by a 'poor White' girl was

very properly sent by the proprietor of the Sea Point Hotel to the Tap when he had the effrontery to tender a £5 note at the European bar 'for a glass of port wine for my young lady', ... any hotel-keeper in Cape town [sic] might have had his decent customers drawn away by the intrusion of swell Hadjes and their female companions.[129]

Although the legal basis for this form of exclusion was overturned in a case involving a visiting Black American in 1890, Blacks continued to be ejected from 'respectable' White bars, sometimes with violence.[130]

There remained the problem of maintaining White political supremacy, particularly after the conquests and annexations of the late 1870s made half a million more Africans citizens of the Cape. The Native Laws and Customs Commission of 1883 had been very important in providing a solution. Before the 1880s the majority of the Cape's Native Affairs administrators had been in favour of integration rather than segregation. Although the establishment of rural locations may have been immediately expedient to ruling newly conquered Africans, the aim of administrators from the 1830s had been to destroy 'tribalism' as rapidly as possible. Africans were brought under direct colonial rule and subject to the same laws, rights and obligations as other colonial citizens. Native Affairs Administrators had not wanted territorial segregation for its own sake, favouring the idea that proximity to Whites, including urbanisation, would aid the civilising process.

The wars and annexations of the late 1870s had called for the development of new administrative policies and new theories to justify them. So the report of the Native Laws and Customs Commission, informed as we saw by the evidence of Shepstone, concluded that traditional African social practice might have to be allowed to continue for several generations. In the meantime these newly conquered peoples

would be ruled indirectly through 'Native councils'. These recommendations were enacted in 1886 in the Transkeian Code of Law and
Government. The movement of Transkeians in the rest of the Cape,
following the investigations of a select committee appointed for the
purpose in 1886, would be controlled but not discouraged by the
carrying of passes.

In 1887 the Transkeian Representation Bill allocated only two seats in
the House of Assembly to the new territories. With *Bond* support, the
Sprigg ministry had prepared the way by reinterpreting the Constitutional Ordinance to remove communal land tenure as a qualification for
the franchise. This left most Whites in the constituencies eligible to vote,
while disqualifying most Africans in the Transkei and many in colonial
rural locations.

The *Bond* supported this disenfranchisement. Its congresses had
wanted government intervention on behalf of Afrikaners on a whole
range of issues beyond education. To ensure that Black colonists could
not do the same, the *Bond*'s political platform in the 1880s demanded
changes in the franchise to restrict the Black vote. The party duly
supported the constitutional reinterpretation of 1887 as a step in the
right direction.[131]

The fact that the non-racial franchise survived owed a great deal to
continued divisions of interest between Afrikaner and English politicians:
the farmer versus the merchant, rural versus town dweller, remained a
factor in Cape elections up to Union. Most English-speaking White
politicians and journalists continued to want at least some Black voters
in the 1880s precisely because of growing Afrikaner political power.
Some English-speaking politicians who practised the small tradition of
Cape liberalism actually opposed the 1887 constitutional amendment.

Adherence to the great tradition of Cape liberalism continued to
coincide for some White politicians with self-interest. Therefore when
Bond proposals were held to threaten the non-racial franchise those
English-medium journalists who supported these politicians protested.
They interrupted their own racist outpourings just long enough to draw
genuinely indignant comparisons between 'Dutch' and 'English' positions on how to rule Blacks. They dramatised the differences by attacking
Bond proposals aimed at giving farmers greater, more brutal, and direct
control over their labourers. St Leger, Dormer, McCombie and their
readers wanted the police and legal system to do the disciplining of the
Black residuum for them. This disciplining may have infringed the non-
racial legal 'tradition' at magistrate's court level in the form of bias
against Black offenders in the 1880s. The judgment on whether there was
consistent bias in sentencing must at this stage be 'unproven'. But a

White man was sentenced to five years and twenty-five lashes for raping Dinah Jacobs aged ten, who from her name was probably a 'Coloured' child. Two months later an African was sentenced to ten years and thirty lashes for raping a White child aged nine.[132]

White dominant-class belief in European social superiority in Cape Town was nothing new. What was new by the 1890s was the articulation of an ideology that argued for the social separation of all Whites from all Blacks. St Leger argued for social separation at the end of 1889. But, as he made clear, 'social separation does not involve the political extinction of the weaker race'.[133]

The Native Laws and Customs Commission played an important part in St Leger's development towards the idea of social separation of the 'races'. He used the report not just to cast further doubt on the wisdom of the existing education system but to suggest that the solution lay in a separate one for Africans. Apart from a number of editorials to this effect, he published an article on 'Our Great Question' which argued for separate political and educational dispensations for Africans and Europeans. The writer was probably influenced by another of those pseudo-sciences of the nineteenth century, phrenology. The article argued for separate education systems because Africans had small brains. The writer suggested that 'one of the few classics to which the average native might be introduced would be the "Georgics", with its lessons of honest and reproductive toil'. St Leger, having quoted Bagehot on the difficulty of passing from savagery to civilisation, concluded by 1884 that the answer was for African education to be put under the Native Affairs Department.[134]

This showed bourgeois English opinion moving closer to its Afrikaner counterpart on the matter. Hofmeyr's *Zuid-Afrikaan*, in what would appear to have reflected rural Dutch master-class ideology, advocated the separation of all Whites and Blacks in schools even before the formation of the *BBV* in 1878. The demands of the new *Bond* after 1883 for greater government expenditure on Afrikaner education, and less on African, implied such separation.[135]

By the end of the 1880s 'expert' opinion favoured separation of 'barbarian' Blacks from 'civilised' Whites. This opinion, popularised by newspaper editors and novels such as *Sitongo*, could be added by members of Cape Town's dominant class to that of other experts: sanitation-syndrome doctors who wanted Whites protected from Black contamination. These wisdoms already informed dominant-class sympathy for poor Whites and fears of the Black residuum.

By the beginning of the 1890s, these ideas had merged into an ideology of social separation of the 'races' widely articulated by English-speaking journalists and politicians in Cape Town. The editors of both the *Cape Times* and the *Cape Argus* presented social separation as both desired by Blacks and in their best interests. Much was made of the view of the Black West Indian nationalist, Edward Blyden, that the Black 'races' should work out their own future.[136]

Dramatic economic growth and demographic change returned to the Cape and its capital in the 1890s. With increasing numbers of lower-class Whites and bourgeois Blacks, social separation was advocated by many members of Cape Town's dominant class as the panacea that was going to preserve White supremacy. Debate revolved largely around precisely what forms separation should take, seldom over the theory itself. In the event social practice was to fall well short of social theory.

6   Problems of prosperity revisited

During the 1890s economic prosperity, as it had done between 1875 and 1882, brought problems for the city's dominant class: her White, English-speaking bourgeoisie. These problems were similar to those that confronted Wiebe's 'middle-class' Americans during the same period: rapid urbanisation, immigration and industrialisation.[1] The question was how to maintain both material and social order under these circumstances.

Part of the answer, as in the 1870s, was found in the control and use of municipal government to increase Cape Town's material infrastructure. But economic growth meant that the 'traditional system of class and race relations' was once more challenged and endangered.[2] In Cape Town, as in Buenos Aires, the 'traditional system' had been one of White bourgeois dominance and Black subordination that had its roots in conquest and slavery. After emancipation at the Cape in the 1830s, exclusionary segregation was used to maintain this tradition. By the 1890s, exclusionary practices alone were seen as insufficient by most members of Cape Town's dominant class. Instead they advocated the social separation of all Whites from all Blacks.

Before the depression of the 1880s members of Cape Town's dominant class had expressed only fleeting concern about the social integration of lower-class Whites with Blacks. Their priority had been to maintain their class solidarity, albeit enhanced by White ethnicity, *vis-à-vis* the lower classes of whatever colour. By the early 1880s there were calls to put Malays or Africans into locations, or impose curfews on them, calls essentially concerned with controlling specific sections of the lower classes. But new to the early 1890s was the belief that 'poor Whiteism', a problem discovered in the depression of the 1880s, could be solved via segregation.

Part of the reason for the identification of a 'poor White problem' lay in the concern of the DRC and *Afrikaner Bond* politicians for their own position within White society. This concern specifically for poor Afrikaners was part and parcel of Afrikaner ethnic mobilisation. But another reason lay in changing attitudes to poverty in the urban context.

The problem of poverty had become racialised by the 1890s, with the new 'scientific' racism of the metropolis incorporated to help explain the dangers of White 'degeneration' or 'degradation'. The numbers of poor, or poorer, working-class Whites increased in the late nineteenth century not just because of increased rural poverty, but also because of large-scale immigration consequent on the Mineral Revolution. The latter was even identified as the culprit by some commentators. When complaining about 'indigent whites' having to travel with Coloureds on the railways, the *Cape Argus* stated that this had been a problem 'since the development of the diamond and gold industry'.[3]

Despite the 'discovery' of poor Whiteism, the intermingling of White and Black continued in Cape Town in the 1890s as a lower-class phenomenon. This was partly because ethnic divisions of labour, although becoming clearer due to changing methods and organisation of production, were not as clear cut in the city as elsewhere in the Cape Colony. Evidence to the Labour Commission of 1893 showed that at the docks, on building sites and in the homes of the White bourgeoisie, White and Black still worked in similar categories of labour. Moreover, evidence also suggests that the number of marriages across the colour-line was increasing in this decade.[4]

A Grahamstown journalist was quoted in the *Cape Argus* of 1895 as saying that 'a fusion of races is going on here, from which every other community in South Africa would shrink'. The journalist then explained that this 'fusion' involved 'predominately coloured' people and 'white artisans and labourers'.[5] Residential integration, combined with social intermingling, would appear to have characterised working-class areas such as Woodstock and Districts One and Six. It was in these areas that working-class children intermingled in the mission schools that looked after the education of the poor: 'The child of pure English blood sits side by side with the Kaffir as black as your hand, or the Malay of yellow-brown complexion and almond eyes.'[6]

But despite the existence of Blacks and Whites in similar job categories, Whites did provide the managers, overseers and more secure and highly paid of the skilled workers. One newspaper commented on White workers who were members of the Working Men's Institute. While overstating the case, the article nonetheless accurately reflected the *approximate* division of labour in Cape Town:

It is to be remembered that the class of men included in its [the Working Men's Institute] title is a more enterprising, more industrious and more successful specimen of humanity, reaching altogether to a higher grade, than the composer of like name at home. He is a cultivated worker whom the coloured labourer serves.[7]

A clearer ethnic division of labour had come into existence at the docks since the days of the Irish labourer. Following the Kimberley model, as well as the division of labour on the railways, employers of dock labour appointed Whites in supervisory capacities, a policy adopted by several employers in the city's growing industrial sector. White and Black dock labourers were also employed in separate gangs. In 1893 the White gangs worked the ballast on a piece-work rate, mirroring the situation of White railway navvies in the 1870s. White dock labourers earned as much as 7s 6d a day compared to about 4s 6d for local Black labour or 1s for an African migrant labourer.[8] The approximate ethnic division of labour in Cape Town, if far from being as rigid as in the diamond industry, would nonetheless have promoted rather than restrained the ideology of separation for most members of Cape Town's dominant class, even if employers of skilled Black labour sometimes argued and acted differently. The ideology of separation was more easily put into practice, and thereby given new material foundation, by the creation of new divisions of labour as production methods changed. As in the American South, this facilitated the introduction by employers of spatial segregation in newly established factories in the garment, tobacco and confectionery industries in Cape Town by the early 1900s.[9]

The difficulty for Cape Town's dominant class was turning an ideology of racial separation, itself the result of 'experience' as well as 'knowledge' drawn from social Darwinism, into new forms of social practice. Members of Cape Town's dominant class could not reach unanimity over what, in practice, social separation would mean, precisely what forms it should take. This was partly because many were not employers of much labour at all, had no direct stake in wishing to control large numbers of black labourers, unlike the mine owners of Kimberley or Johannesburg. Also, employers of different kinds of labour in Cape Town, whose influence was pretty evenly balanced in local politics in the 1890s as we shall see, had different labour requirements, different ideas about where and under what conditions their workers should live. There was also the matter of who would have to pay for expensive forms of segregation.

The complexity of the debate reflected the complexity of the city's social formation. It was also informed by a similar debate within the Colony as a whole in this period. White supremacy and social separation in a racially ordered society was the holy grail for virtually all the participants in the debate; but their quest for this elusive trophy took them along a number of different routes and with varying degrees of enthusiasm.

The discovery of gold on the Witwatersrand in 1886 brought renewed commercial prosperity to Cape Town by the 1890s. Part of the trouble was that a good deal of the town's capital was immediately expended in an orgy of speculation on gold shares, similar to the one on diamond shares that led to the scrip disaster of 1881.[10] Both the Cape of Good Hope and Union Banks failed in 1890. The local stock exchange followed two years later.[11] Western Cape wine farmers, already hit by the vine disease phylloxera, were not immune to similarly rash speculation and the Paarl Bank also collapsed in 1890. These misfortunes reduced their demand for Cape Town goods, thereby contributing to the city's commercial difficulties.[12] The position of wine farmers only recovered in the mid-1890s, helped from 1893 by the replanting of vineyards with phylloxera-proof American vines.[13]

Nevertheless Cape Town's mini-depression took place against a backdrop of rising Cape government revenues from increased imports and, for the first time, profits from its railways. The railway line northwards reached Bloemfontein in 1890 and, importantly, arrived in Johannesburg in 1892, three years ahead of its rival from Natal. The improved economic position of the Cape Colony was reflected in its government's ability to raise loans on the London market at a reasonable rate, which in turn enabled yet more money to be spent on infrastructural development. As had been the case during the previous, diamond-induced boom of the 1870s and early 1880s, much of this expenditure came Cape Town's way, spawning more jobs, the need for more labour, more money in circulation and thus increased opportunities for retail trade.[14]

Between 1891 and 1902 the Cape government spent almost £3,000,000 on improving Table Bay harbour and a further £200,000 on Cape Town's railway station. By 1893 the breakwater was completed and in 1895 the 'New Dock' was opened as the Victoria Basin. Improved facilities helped to attract trade via Cape Town rather than Port Elizabeth or East London. Imports through Cape Town rose from just over £3,000,000 in 1891 to £14,000,000 in 1902, making this a golden period for Cape Town merchants.[15]

The Boer war, far from diminishing Cape Town's prosperity, came just in time to lift a depression that had begun to dampen the colonial economy in 1898. Rinderpest, drought, yet more phylloxera and a drop in the price of brandy in 1897 had been followed the next year by stagnation of trade in the Transvaal which adversely affected Cape merchants. Initially Cape Town was not as badly hit as elsewhere in the Colony. But, by early 1899, even Cape Town had begun to suffer from the deteriorating political and economic situation in the Transvaal. When war came later in the year it brought temporary relief from recession. A torrent of imperial army pay bills, amounting to £51,000,000, were negotiated in the town. Local firms did brisk business supplying both the needs of the military and a civilian population whose numbers had been artificially swollen by refugees from the Rand. The major share of the Cape government money spent on Table Bay docks and the railway station was expended in these war years.[16]

The prospect of prosperity revisited and reality of government expenditure led Cape Town capitalists, her merchants and businessmen, to unleash a number of ventures, apart from the gold scrip fiascos, after 1887. New joint stock companies were floated, and old ones were revamped. Much capital was sunk in the hardy perennial, insurance, but considerable sums also in the city's transport system, on the expectation of a return to urban expansion. In 1892 the Metropolitan and Suburban Railway Company constructed a line to Sea Point. The old City Tramway Company was wound up and reborn in 1894 with ten times the capital, while rivals sprouted and grew in the town and suburbs. In 1896 the first electric tram trundled up Adderley Street, four years after a syndicate had been formed to supply electricity for another purpose, light. Electricity also meant the possibility of refrigeration, and lay behind the first serious attempt, in 1893, to export fruit to Europe from the Western Province.[17]

Industrial opportunities in the city and suburbs were not neglected. Capital investment in machinery and plant in the Cape census division, which included Cape Town, rose from £375,000 in 1891 to almost £850,000 in 1904. Over the same period the number of industrial institutions rose from 487, employing 5,612 persons, to 611, employing 11,747. Few entirely new industries emerged, apart from lobster canning and cold storage. Rather, existing industrial activity was expanded, small factories erected, machines imported and more workers employed.[18] Probably the most important area of capital investment in Cape Town between 1891 and 1902 was in building and construction. By 1894 Cape Town merchants had largely rebuilt the heart of the city with new premises or additions to their old stores. Thereafter their interests moved further afield and syndicates were formed to develop ground within and without the municipality. The total number of buildings in the municipality rose from 7,608 to 9,808 between the census dates 1891 and 1904. By the later date there were close to 25,500 buildings in greater Cape Town compared to approximately 15,000 in 1891.[19]

Increased economic activity again promoted demographic growth.
With the help of some 70,000 migrants, mostly from southern Africa and
Europe, the population of greater Cape Town grew from 79,000 to
170,000 between 1891 and 1904, making the city the largest in pre-Union
South Africa. Of the 70,000, 2,000 came from Australia and approximately 34,000 from Europe, mostly from Britain but including about
9,000 Jews from the western parts of the Russian empire. If the further
2,000 Afrikaners from rural areas are added to these numbers, then
about 40,000 migrants were White from the point of view of Cape
Town's dominant class.

Of the remaining 30,000 Black migrants, 2,000 came from India,
9,000 were Africans (mainly from the Eastern Cape or Transkei) and
around 21,000 would have been classified as Coloured by the 1904 census
enumerators. The vast majority of Coloured migrants were from Cape
Town's immediate hinterland, from within a line drawn from Malmesbury through Worcester to Swellendam. A few hundred were aided
immigrants from St Helena.[20]

These extra Capetonians helped to make Cape Town one of the most
cosmopolitan cities in southern Africa by 1904. They also helped to give
Cape Town a really substantial suburban population; only 12,000 in
1875, it rose to 28,000 by 1891 and 92,000 eleven years later, overtaking
the population of the city itself. The suburb closest to Cape Town,
Woodstock (the village of Papendorp back in the 1870s), contained
29,000 people by the beginning of the twentieth century. Within the city
itself, demographic growth may have been less spectacular but still
involved a 50 per cent increase, from 51,000 to 78,000. Almost 30,000 of
the latter lived in District Six which had extended its built-up area to the
boundary with Woodstock.[21] In the course of the 1880s, this area
(together with District One and the 'Malay Quarter') had begun to hold
the same connotations for Cape Town's dominant class that London's
East End had for hers.[22]

The nature of demographic growth became part of the problem for
those who advocated social separation. The extent of urbanisation was
more easily dealt with. The town council, as in the late 1870s, was
perceived as the means by which potential problems such as water
shortage or insufficient drains could be solved. Merchants and
businessmen continued from where previous Cleans had left off in 1882,
and pushed through a programme of 'urban reform'. In their pursuit of
what may be called material order, this particular section of Cape
Town's dominant class managed to ensure that the transformation they
achieved in the resources of the city enhanced their individual ability to
accumulate capital.

In 1891, with prosperity returning to Cape Town trade and immigrants and migrants flooding to the city, a new 'Clean Party' won a town council election even livelier than that which had been won by its predecessor in 1882. In 1891 the new Cleans were once more up against J. C. Hofmeyr and his reborn 'Dirty Party' of the day, the 'Ratepayers Protection Association'. But this time a Clean victory did mean the enactment of a package of urban reforms many of which had been promised, but not delivered, in the early 1880s. The building boom of the 1890s meant that municipal revenues increased steadily after Clean Party victory, from £43,500 in 1891 to £118,000 ten years later, while the rate the council collected was allowed to drop. Many of the streets of the city were made up and paved, water in adequate quantities laid on to the majority of houses and a major drainage scheme all but completed by 1902.[23]

This material transformation had not been possible in the 1880s. After the 'Clean Party' victory of 1882 depression had intervened and dissipated both the economic muscle of the town council and the 'Clean Party' itself. But the financial demise of men such as Farmer and Fleming, of firms such as Barry & Nephews, or Wilson & Glynn, was also partly a result of their inability to participate in a business revolution. This revolution was wrought by vastly improved communications represented by a burgeoning telegraph and railway network as well as more, larger and faster steamships. By the 1890s, mirroring a similar development that Davison has traced for Melbourne, their position of dominance within the city's political economy had been taken by a new generation of merchants who understood the changed conditions of trade. These men obtained short-term overdrafts to finance their cash payments for goods which, because of the communications revolution, could be obtained at short notice. The danger of overstocking, the undoing of so many of their predecessors, was consequently reduced.[24]

Many of this new generation of merchants had also perceived the growing opportunities for retail trade presented by the growth of Cape Town and were directly responsible for the impressive new shops that adorned the city centre. The emporiums of Garlick's, Stuttaford's and Cartwright's became the Harrods or Macey's of Cape Town. Their size and the Victorian style of their architecture were symbolic of the status and origins of their owners. They stood as visible promoters of the latter's position of authority within the community, and consequently as monuments to their values.

The nucleus of the new Clean Party of the 1890s was drawn from the ranks of those merchants who were important retailers. Their colleagues were local businessmen, including many builders, and the occasional professional. Apart from the presence of the retailers, the 'Clean Party' which held power in the early 1890s differed from its predecessor in one important respect. It accommodated two leading members of the *Afrikaner Bond*: D. P. Graaff and D. C. De Waal. Both had been identified by the English press in the 1880s as members of the 'Dirty Party'. But by 1891, aided no doubt by the *Bond*'s support for Rhodes' brand of imperialism between 1890 and 1895, Graaff and De Waal put class before Afrikaner ethnicity and identified themselves with 'Clean' interests and dominant class ideology. According to John X. Merriman they represented the new group of politically influential and economically ambitious town Afrikaners. They had started in business as a butcher and ironmonger respectively and successfully exploited their close ties with government to their own economic advantage. They and their fellow 'Cleans' used their position in local government in much the same way. Being a town councillor became a means by which opportunities for capital accumulation within Cape Town itself were not only maintained but enhanced.[25]

One way this worked was by lavishing council money chiefly on the centre of the town, precisely the location of the businesses, shops and stores of 'Clean Party' members. By 1897 the enthusiastic pursuit of such mutual self-interest had earned the 'Cleans' the label of the Adderley and St George's Street clique from ratepayers in other parts of the town.[26] But there were also examples of what amounted to individual enhancement or accumulation. For instance John Garlick, a prominent importer and retailer, became the leading figure in the Gardens Syndicate that purchased land in that part of the municipality in 1897. This property was being developed with assistance from the council by 1899. Graaf was on the finance and waste lands committee when the latter approved his firm's plans to reclaim land on the foreshore for cold-storage purposes. This project earned the firm, Combrinck & Company, a profit of some £200,000. On a more modest scale, Garlick, in a similar conciliar position, was able to preside over the demolition of the newly built display window of a rival's emporium on the grounds that it projected just a fraction too far into the street.[27]

One reason why the Clean Party remained in power in the 1890s, despite its corruption, was because it became significantly harder to defeat at the poll. Franchise changes from 1882 onwards had been aimed at reducing the popular vote. In 1890 the minimum property qualification for owners or occupiers was raised from £10 to £100, disenfranchising mostly fishermen, artisans and labourers living in cheaper houses. These houses had formed roughly one-fifth of the total in the municipality.[28] In 1893 the Cleans introduced the plural vote for municipal elections: one to an owner or occupier of property valued between £100 and £499, two when the property was between £500 and £999, and three if it was £1,000 or more. In addition each partner of a firm whose building was valued at £1,000 or more (and there were few that were not) would get three votes. So some individuals could qualify for as many as six votes in all. In 1897, the town clerk, C. J. Byworth, confirmed the motives behind the franchise legislation of 1893 and revealed a sharp awareness of contemporary British municipal politics while doing so:

> If you were to revert to the system of a single vote ... it would tend to bring about ... a condition of things which actually exists in some districts of England, where there is a great Socialist element – where there is a feeling that working men's dwellings, municipal workshops, and municipal soup kitchens should be established ... Assuming that such a condition of things with a thoroughly socialist town council existed in Cape Town, these socialist people would have the power ... of taxing the very people who find the money.[29]

Byworth's fears were not unreasonable. Cape Town had witnessed increasing, and successful, trade union activity in the 1890s. Cape Town's first socialist club was opened in September 1897, shortly after a letter to the *Cape Times* from 'A Socialist' had referred favourably to the efforts of the socialist-controlled municipality of West Ham in London. The writer demanded a municipal housing scheme for the working class.[30]

The other reason why merchants and businessmen were able to control the town council was that they retained the support of the English-language press. In these newspapers 'Clean' government was justified by the package of paving, street surfacing, drainage, lighting, parks and increased water supply that it undoubtedly delivered, while favouring the central business district. Indeed 'Clean Party' members achieved both a measure of contemporary fame and civic immortality by having their names affixed to some of these improvements in the material ambiance of the city – such as the Woodhead reservoir, the Graaff generator or the De Waal Park – thereby further popularising Clean achievements.

Clean control of the town council, and achievements thereby, were also symbolised by the progressive adoption in the course of the 1890s of British municipal paraphernalia: mayoral robes, chain and mace. The height of municipal Anglicisation was reached in the building of a new Town Hall, eventually completed in 1905. This structure, grandiloquently baroque and dominating the Parade, radiated the civic pride which Asa Briggs has evidenced for earlier equivalents in Leeds or Bradford, and would not have looked out of place in either town.[31]

Cape Town's City Hall, together with the objects of British municipal

CITY HALL, CAPE TOWN. 2475.

6   The new Town Hall, Grand Parade

ritual, were symbols of the hegemonic dominance that Englishness had achieved in Cape Town by the end of the nineteenth century. They were appealing to a shared sense of Englishness among British or even Australian Capetonians, were part and parcel of the ethnic mobilisation of the latter, as they were part of the Anglicisation of Afrikaners. The recognisably Victorian Town Hall replaced the tiny flat-roofed and classically proportioned building that had originally housed Dutch local governments. This, the old 'Town House' built in the eighteenth century, had blended well with the flat-roofed, two-storied residences of similar vintage that once surrounded it.

In 1892 *The Licensed Victualler's Review* had published but one of a long line of lamentations about the deficiencies of Cape Town's material culture.

Even its commercial and social architecture has no trace of Anglo-Saxon genius except in the solitary instance of the Standard Bank which from its summit to its base, both actual and abstract, is alone typical of that splendid audacity of national egotism that has been acknowledged to be one of the secrets of our mastery in British colonization. Were its example followed, in methods and enterprise, Cape Town would no longer be that somnolent repression of the vigour which is inherent in British immigration.[32]

By 1902 there was far less reason for such lamentations. The shops and offices in the central streets had been almost completely rebuilt and now suitably reflected the required 'splendid audacity of national egotism'. New residences, humble or palatial, boasted adornments of imported 'broekie lace' wrought-ironwork and other features of colonial Victorian architecture. Central Cape Town now gave visual confirmation to the reality of a dominant class that was predominantly British in origin. This dominant class had at last transformed a foreign town into a place identifiably like home, at least in terms of its material culture, which glorified that home and reflectively themselves. As a *Cape Argus* editorial put it, this 'new metropolis' was very much better than the old Cape Town's 'dirty white half-bred orientalism'. E. Lowndes, a visitor from Britain at the end of the 1890s, summed up the reason why. By the time of his visit there was 'something indescribably English in the atmosphere of Cape Town'.[33]

Restructuring the material culture of the city in the course of the 1890s and early 1900s was one means by which a White and English bourgeoisie could promote its own conception of how society should be ordered. Social separation of Whites and Blacks was another. In the pursuit of this ideal, members of Cape Town's dominant class were

7   Adderley Street, c. 1900

prompted and supported by members of the White petty bourgeoisie and some White workers, anxious to stake their own claims and justify their own position within the social hierarchy.

The ideology of separation emerged from segregationist practices and an approximate racial division of labour in town and countryside. The Cape government and employers of labour, from the 1870s, were faced with the twin problems, and ultimately linked solutions, of newly conquered (but 'still pulsating') African societies and the labour needs brought about by a rapidly expanding, and industrialising, economy.[34] Crucially, after exploring the possibility of employing White unskilled labour, and experimenting with the latter, a fairly rigid ethnic division of labour had come into existence by the mid-1880s on farms, on the railways and on the mines. This division of labour had Whites as skilled workers, supervisors, managers and employers, Blacks as unskilled labourers; it helped to fuel, rather than restrain, the increasingly 'scientific' racism of the 1880s. In Cape Town, racism was also inflamed by the racialisation of metropolitan attitudes to the lower classes and social problems in the minds of members of the city's dominant class.

The ideology and practice of racial separation in Cape Town was boosted, and given particular forms, by the nature of the Cape government in the early 1890s. The new Prime Minister in 1890 was Cecil Rhodes, the De Beers mining magnate. He appointed both *Bond* and Cape liberal members of parliament to his cabinet. Rhodes needed the *Bond*'s support in getting parliament to ratify the charter of his British South Africa Company (BSAC), established to conquer and exploit lands north of the Limpopo River. He gave liberals such as J. X. Merriman, J. Rose Innes and J. W. Sauer ministerial positions in order to defuse their potential opposition to his expansionist plans.[35]

These liberals actively promoted separationist policies not just because they believed in them but at least partly because they opposed some of the more brutal policies towards Blacks mooted by Rhodes and the *Bond*. In particular the *Bond* appeared to want to destroy Black land ownership entirely, and wanted farmers to have the personal right to flog Black workers. Merriman, influenced by his reading of Blyden's *Christianity and the Negro Race*, thought that both the social and political separation of Blacks in their 'own country' might be the best solution for them and for Whites. Sauer also believed in social separation, but believed this was compatible with political 'equality' in one country. Innes took the same line while advocating preventative legislation on the availability of liquor to Blacks for their benefit.[36]

Innes helped to extend separation beyond previous exclusionary practices in Cape Town. In his capacity as Attorney-General he presided over the more complete separation of White and Black prisoners. This was in keeping with the advice he was receiving from his administrators. In 1889 a Mr Roper had already reported in favour of a formal and thorough system of prison classification. This included the separation of 'Europeans' from 'natives'. The new government took this to mean separation of Whites from Blacks.[37]

In 1891 Innes revealed to the Legislative council that he had made arrangements for European convicts at the Breakwater prison to have separate quarters. By 1892 there was similar separation of Whites from Blacks in all penal institutions in Cape Town. At the Porter Reformatory for young offenders in Constantia this separation of offenders prevented the 'contamination' of 'innocents' by the 'sweepings of the street', in the perverse logic of one MLC; in other words White inmates were kept entirely apart from Black ones.[38]

The new Attorney-General also appears to have ensured that Cape Town juries became exclusively White in the early 1890s. Ten years earlier the Chief Justice had remarked that 'here in Cape Town it is the most ordinary occurrence at the criminal sessions to have mixed juries of both races'. From about 1894 this ceased to be the case. Innes brought in a property qualification for jurors, but whether Blacks qualified or not they were no longer called.[39]

Rhodes' alliance with the *Bond* helped to promote White ethnicity above Afrikaner or English. To symbolise this temporary *rapprochement* Rhodes paid for a statue of Jan Van Riebeeck, the first Dutch commander at the Cape, to be put at the foot of Adderley Street.[40] Solving what had become known as the 'Poor White question', primarily by greater government expenditure on White education, became Rhodes' *quid pro quo* for *Bond* support for his imperialist ambitions.

Rhodes had calculated that a polical alliance with the *Bond* would make Cape Afrikaners less likely to sympathise with those in the Transvaal, who had similar plans to his for territorial expansion. Leading members of the *Bond* were given shares in the BSAC, or were sold them at preferential rates. It is not clear whether J. H. Hofmeyr was among them, but he profited from Rhodes' patronage following a deal involving De Beers shares in 1895.[41]

Bond leaders were not brought into alliance with Rhodes simply by bribes. They undoubtedly saw the alliance as a means to deliver on party congress resolutions of the 1880s. These had included demands for more state money to be spent on Afrikaner education, less on African, and for alterations in the franchise to produce fewer Black voters. It seems probable that Rhodes committed himself to dealing with these two issues before he took office.[42]

Higher grants to farm-school teachers was an early action of the new government. In 1891 Rhodes went further and appointed an Education Commission to examine how to give further support to these schools. But in keeping with the emergent ideology of racial separation, the Commission also investigated the mixing of White and Black children in mission schools, which was chiefly an urban problem. Evidence to the Commission brought together the racist discourses of town and countryside in mutual argument for racial separation in schools. Rural masterclass racism, stemming from conquest and class conflict and surviving on the desire to emphasise status distinctions, complemented urban theories of racial degeneracy.

The Commission recommended that non-denominational public schools, of various categories, should be for Whites and mission schools for Coloureds. A new category of public schools was the idea of Langham Dale. Apart from expanding the provision of third-class schools (which replaced the farm-school category), fourth-class public schools were to be created to rescue White children currently in mission schools and to give them superior education. Dale had revealed that almost 3,000 Whites were being taught alongside 4,000 Blacks in mission schools in Cape Town alone.[43]

Reactions to the Education Commission and its recommendations demonstrated the strength of support for segregation of all Blacks from all Whites among members of Cape Town's dominant class. This support was offered in newspaper editorials and correspondence, as well as in the evidence that some gave to the Commission itself. Those who affirmed their belief in the need to separate the 'races' included St Leger and T. J. O'Reilly, the law agent who had stood for parliament advocating that Whites be employed ahead of Africans. J. W. Attwell, a merchant and miller, added that it would be a mistake to overeducate people of colour because 'they would aspire to be clerks and the like'. A further witness was Edmund Powell, the editor of the *Cape Argus*, who said he wanted separation in education despite the fact that his paper trained Coloured printers alongside Whites. Dale himself wanted separation because of what he saw as the danger from the residuum, specifically of White girls mixing with Coloured 'street arabs'. Dale was more equivocal about 'off-coloured' children who considered themselves White, but thought that complete separation of the 'races' was the ideal to strive for.[44]

The little, if weak, resistance to school separation did come from Capetonians. The one Cape Town employer who told the Labour Commission that he saw no 'social objection' to the mixing of White and Black in education was the builder G. Smart. Smart may have had some self-interest in taking this position. He was mainly concerned about what would happen in terms of technical training, and complained that 'at the moment builders in Cape Town have to send to England' because there was a shortage of skilled artisans.[45]

Witnesses to the Education Commission who put up some resistance to segregation in schools were three White Anglican clergymen and Abdol Burns. Their evidence helps to reveal factors that complicated or delayed complete social separation between White and Black in the city. The three Anglicans taught in 'mixed' schools. They rejected the assumption that such 'mixing' was detrimental to White children. They implicitly did not accept the racist theory that Whites would 'degenerate' through contact with Blacks. Their objections to segregation also focused on the difficulty of identifying who was, and who was not, White. Thus the 'notorious permeability of the colour line', the 'infinite gradations of colour in races so mixed as our populations', was part of the argument against segregated mission schools.

The colour-line argument, however, was about practicality, not born out of fervour for non-racialism *per se*. One of the Anglican clergymen, Rev. Lightfoot, did not object in his evidence to the concept of superior cheap schools for Whites, but he did object to the mission schools themselves having to make the distinction between White and Coloured. Another Anglican clergyman, Rev. Peters, warden of Zonnebloem College, while arguing that it was not a disadvantage to White children if they mixed with Coloureds, went on to say that it was contact between the two 'after school' that 'does the damage'. While rejecting the need for separation of White and Black in schools, he did not object in principle to mission schools that were only for Whites. These arguments against school separation were more about self-interest than principles. If Whites were removed it would hurt their schools. They would lose fee-paying students. A Blacks-only school would lose 'tone' or status, and they themselves would lose control over the religious instruction of part of their congregation.[46]

Abdol Burns was the only Black Capetonian interviewed. He was in favour of mixed schools. Presumably mindful of his audience, Burns told the Commissioners that he thought that Coloured children were made 'clean' by being with Whites. This bizarre adaptation of sanitation-syndrome doctrine was unlikely to have been much help in swaying the Commissioners' minds against segregation: rather the opposite. Burns spoilt his argument in favour of mixed schools by saying that educating Coloureds was more important than the question of separation.[47]

Burns was right in thinking that the case for Coloured education needed to be made. *Bond* members of parliament and farmers who gave evidence to the Education and Labour Commissions had shown hostility to any education provision for Coloureds. Farmers thought schools kept children out of their employment and that education made Blacks uppity. The prevailing opinion among Cape Town's dominant class, one advocated by the English-language newspapers, was that Black schooling was necessary to instil some discipline in their residuum, was a necessary form of social control.[48] According to Dale, mission schools in towns kept children 'tidy' and off the streets.[49] As an *Argus* editorial put it in 1896, when describing Coloured children 'wallowing and lurking in the gutters of Cape Town', 'gaol and the lash ... [could only] keep the evil down'. The only alternative to education, and one that was frequently mentioned, was 'extermination'.[50]

By 1894 government education policy was clearly defined by Dale's successor, Dr Muir (who took over in 1892), as being aimed at fitting Whites and Blacks for their 'future positions' in Cape society.[51] This meant restricting Black education to the reading, writing and arithmetic lessons they would get in the mission schools, where pupils were not allowed to go beyond Standard Four.[52]

In contrast non-denominational 'poor schools' were made available for Whites and attracted more than twice the subsidy of mission schools per pupil. Between 1893 and 1894 the number of 'European' schools of all 'classes' doubled, with the government spending, on average, more than five times as much money on White children as it did on Black.[53]

Improving secondary education for Whites was only part of the strategy of solving the Poor White question in the first half of the 1890s. Egged on by DRC and newspaper campaigns, including a series in the *Argus* called 'Unexplored Cape Town' which talked of poor Whites degenerating in the slums, two government reports in 1894 found in favour of providing Whites with technical training in industrial schools or by means of apprenticeship in government workshops. One of them was the Select Committee Report on the Destitute Childrens' Relief Bill; destitute children were defined as children with European parents 'on both sides'.

The government duly acted on their recommendations. Apprenticeship at its railway workshops in Salt River became a White preserve, and the government was helping only indigent White children with technical apprenticeships. Only Whites were allowed to attend the two 'industrial schools' established at Uitenhage and Cape Town.[54]

Despite government intentions, and dominant class demands, not all Cape Town schools were segregated in the 1890s. Government policy did not yet have the sanction of law, which was effectively admitted by Dr Muir in 1894 under pressure from White clergymen and members of the city's small Black elite.[55] Until 1905, when segregation in schools was given legal sanction by the School Board Act, admission would appear to have remained a matter of individual decision by school authorities. But most took government policy seriously, presumably because it accorded with their own prejudices. All first-class public schools were for Whites only from 1893, including the South African College School (SACS) which had previously admitted at least one 'off-coloured' pupil in the person of Abdullah Abdurahman. The teacher-training Normal College turned away 'coloured' children, as did the private Catholic Marist Brothers School which had previously admitted them. But there were still four 'coloured' students at the second-class West End public non-denominational school in the municipality in 1893, and two at Wood-stock. By 1905, both these schools were Whites-only institutions, as were the non-denominational public schools established in District Six, Tamboerskloof, Observatory, Maitland, Plumstead, Durbanville, Mui-zenberg, Bellville (near Parow) and Brooklyn (near Maitland), within greater Cape Town. Yet two public schools, at Mowbray and Parow, had one and five 'coloured' students enrolled respectively. Significantly, many mission or church schools, if by no means all, had become considerably less 'mixed' than in 1893. In some this had taken the form of a reduction in the proportion of Whites enrolled, or of Coloureds, or the fact that some, previously mixed, had opted to become all White (and were known as 'White mission schools') or all Coloured. Finally all the industrial schools and night schools, with the sole exception of the Anglican School of Industry, were for Whites only.[56]

If some 'mixing' continued in mission schools then this was probably because particular clergymen were not opposed, or actively favoured it. In the public schools lightness of pigmentation may have been a factor determining a child's admission. Apparently some schools asked whether a child was light or dark, accepting one sibling and rejecting another.[57]

Rhodes' split with the *Bond* after the Jameson Raid in 1895, as well as the colour-line 'problem', are probably the reasons why *de jure* segregation in Cape schools was not introduced until 1905. But before the alliance ended, Rhodes' government had further secured White supremacy by changing the existing non-racial franchise. Discussion about franchise changes in Cape Town, and by Cape politicians, showed that the ideology of social separation now threatened the maintenance of this part of the 'great tradition' of Cape liberalism. Several articles that appeared in Cape Town newspapers after 1889 talked of the merits of Black disenfranchisement, referred to its contemporary practice in the southern United States, and cited the problem posed for White rule by the beginnings of nationalism in India.[58]

The volume of articles increased when parliament began to debate franchise changes in 1891. J. H. Hofmeyr had introduced the debate, agreed to by the government, by asking in the House of Assembly whether legislation was required in this respect. This open-ended introduction of the matter left the way open for a number of potential legislative results, all of which were discussed within and outside parliament: a multiple voting system (along the lines later adopted by the Cape Town council); a differential or separate Black vote; or raising the existing franchise qualifications.[59]

During 1891 both the *Cape Times* and *Cape Argus* speculated on franchise changes, and their speculation revealed the fragility of dominant-class adherence to the non-racial vote at this time. St Leger, who had previously defended it, wrote a revealing leading article in August 1891. He said that the Black vote had always been thought of as harmless, but now 'there are so many of them'.[60] The *Argus* initially took a more definitively separatist line. Powell cited Merriman on the need for Blacks to work out their own future and to leave 'South Africa' for Whites. Powell thought that a growing desire to change the existing system was influenced by knowledge of what was happening in the American South and India, as well as by the fact that the Transvaal and Orange Free State excluded Blacks from the vote.

Eventually Powell dismissed the idea of a differential vote. This was possibly because he realised its implications for increasing Afrikaner, farmer and rural control of central government while diminishing English, business and urban influence.[61] The latter had partly been sustained by the 'small tradition' of White political alliances with Black voters at constituency level. In the event, T. E. Fuller, one of Cape Town's MLAs and unofficial leader of the English-speaking members of parliament not in government, did a secret deal with Hofmeyr over the nature of what became the Franchise and Ballot Act of 1892. The Act kept the non-racial principle, but raised the property qualification from £25 to £75 and required voters to be able to sign their names.[62]

The possibility of some form of separate political representation of Black and White colonists did not disappear after 1892. In June 1893 government instructions to electoral registration offices ordered them to take down the 'race' of prospective voters because, according to Rhodes, this was 'useful' information. The following year, African voters in the Glen Grey area of the Eastern Cape were disenfranchised. The government only granted them instead limited powers of local government.[63]

Rhodes' government made further inroads into the 'great tradition' in 1893 when they abolished Cape Town's 'plumping' system. This system had allowed each elector to have four votes. With a maximum of four

MLAs to elect, he could either spread his votes evenly or give as many as all four to one candidate. The new law meant that a Cape Town elector could give only one vote each to a maximum of four candidates.

The aim of this legislation was to prevent the election of a Black candidate, Achmat Effendi, whose decision to stand for parliament will be discussed in chapter 8. Effendi could well have been elected in 1894. In the elections of that year he was up against a 'ticket' of four, all of whom were returned. The least successful of them got 2,647 votes. Effendi only received 710, but under the plumping system he would have been elected, assuming he had been given four votes by all of the people who had voted for him.[64]

The debate over abolition revealed that three of the four Cape Town MLAs, Fuller, O'Reilly and Ohlsson, opposed the Bill. The fourth, Wiener, was in Chicago and consequently unable to vote. It is possible that the three who voted against the Bill did so because they not wish to alienate Black voters in the city on the eve of an election, rather than from any desire to defend Black rights. Although the Franchise and Ballot Act had halved the number of Black voters in the city, there were still about seven hundred, given the extent of Effendi's support in 1894. The position of Ohlsson and Fuller towards the abolition of plumping may therefore be explicable as quite in keeping with the 'small tradition'. Cape Town MLAs had voted against the Franchise and Ballot Act despite Fuller's dealings with Hofmeyr. Effendi had also served on Ohlsson's committee in 1884 and 1888.

Certainly two Cape liberals who voted against the Bill, Sauer and Merriman, stated bluntly in debate that they did not want a Black man in the House but thought that the timing of the legislation was inappropriate. The fact that both represented constituencies outside Cape Town may have allowed them to be more explicit about their voting behaviour than Fuller or Ohlsson. In contrast, O'Reilly openly said much the same as Merriman and Sauer. Judging from the election results of 1894, in which both he and Ohlsson lost their seats, O'Reilly may have voted against the Bill because he felt personally threatened by the abolition of plumping. Ohlsson might have thought along the same lines.[65]

That the erosion of Black political rights went no further than it did in the 1890s was probably a direct result of the Jameson Raid in December 1895. Rhodes' involvement in this ill-fated attempt to provoke a pro-British insurrection in the Transvaal ended his alliance with the *Bond*. The Raid produced dramatically increased tension between English and Afrikaner politicians and their constituencies at the Cape. Fuller's followers had formed a very loose and divided Progressive Party in 1893.

By the time of the first elections after the Raid, in 1898, Rhodes had become leader of a new and much more highly organised Progressive Party, supported by the pro-British South African League.

The League had been established shortly after the Raid as a pan-South African organisation to defend imperial ties. In the scramble for votes against the *Bond* the League, unlike its rival, was prepared to admit Black members, but only in separate 'B' branches. Although one 'B' branch did get Rhodes to alter his election dictum in 1898 from 'equal rights for all White men south of the Zambezi' to equal rights for all 'civilised' men, the principle of social separation was left intact.[66]

The policies of colonial government politicians and administrators had helped to turn principle into practice in institutions under their control by the mid-1890s. They had largely done so without having to resort to legislation. This might suggest that Fredrickson was right to argue that the great tradition of Cape liberalism had restrained the widespread *de jure* imposition of segregation. What seems more probable is that *de jure* segregation was seldom thought necessary. When it was, appropriate legislation was passed. This had first happened in 1878 when the Cape Yeomanry, in the forefront of the battle for supremacy of 'race', was confined to colonists of 'European extraction'. It happened in 1905 when *de jure* segregation between White and Black was brought about in Cape schools. In between there was plenty of legislation which made racialised distinctions between colonists, be it on who had to supervise blasting on Kimberley mines, which destitute children deserved government relief or who was allowed to vote in Glen Grey.

However, *de facto* segregation would appear to have been the more common method of achieving institutional segregation. This was probably because it not only made the task of drafting legislation unnecessary, but also because it gave administrators flexibility when deciding who was sufficiently pale to benefit from such segregation. They were dealing with a population in which exactly who was accepted as White was far from clear. Such acceptance had always been partly a matter of wealth and bourgeois values as well as perceived lightness of pigmentation, and deciding who was, or was not, White may have been particularly problematic for administrators fresh from Britain.

Cape Town's suburban railways, run by the government, remained a good example of *de facto* segregation before Union. Newspaper accounts suggest that railway officials decided who was White enough to be allowed into first-class carriages, and on rare occasions 'respectable' (most probably 'off-coloured') Blacks gained admittance to these compartments. Second-class carriages were a mixture of 'poor Whites' and 'better-class' Blacks. Third-class carriages were predominantly for Black passengers, as the letters of British soldiers who were forced to travel in them protested in the late 1880s and early 1890s. By 1894 the British army had allowed, perhaps enabled, even private soldiers to travel first class. By 1896 it seems as though both first- and second-class carriages were reserved for Whites, with 'some exceptions for coloureds and natives of a better class', and separation was therefore more complete if not absolute. This, together with financial considerations, may explain why Salt River railway workers who had previously been given passes to travel first class by the government could be issued with ones for second-class carriages in 1898. Only a few 'indigent Whites' travelled third class in the second half of the 1890s, which the *Cape Argus* still saw as a problem. The government was obviously not prepared to spend further money on extra coaches to solve this particular problem. The 'raising' of poor Whites, primarily through state expenditure on their education, was presumably thought sufficient to take care of this disorder in the near future.[67]

There remains the question of the extent to which ideology translated into social practice outside government institutions. The answer was that separation was extended into many aspects of lower-class social life in Cape Town from the 1890s, but remained far from complete. Most notably, although the majority of Africans were residentially segregated in locations in 1901, other Black Capetonians were not.

Cape Town's dominant class were themselves reluctant to spend much money on segregation. Instead, they tried to bring about separation as inexpensively as possible. One tactic they employed was pre-emptive. Acres of editorial and correspondence space, as well as public meetings, were devoted to preventing immigration of 'undesirable races', whose presence in Cape Town might further complicate or increase the existing search for order. As much effort was expended in favour of White immigration, although of a kind that would not endanger social order by increasing the poor White problem. The Cape government responded by keeping faith with the policies of the 1870s: aiding both male artisans and, as prospective partners to increase the White stock, female domestic servants from Britain. Between 1889 and 1902 some 2,000 people were brought to greater Cape Town in this way.[68]

The guiding principle behind which 'races' were deemed undesirable was that they threatened disorder in a world where southern African Blacks were supposed to be manual labourers and Whites to be everything else. Much of the newspaper invective, which echoed similar rhetoric in local and central political institutions, was directed at the 'Asian menace', particularly against Indian immigration which was seen to be imperilling the future of Natal and which was beginning to take place in Cape Town. Typical editorials on 'The Indian', acknowledged that 'he' was not a 'barbarian' and that some Indians were 'highly respectable'. But they concluded that he did 'not fit into our way', that we should 'control the composition of the community'.[69] More specific anatagonism towards Indians focused on their potential or actual rivalry with Whites as traders.[70] For similar reasons, racism was displayed towards the Chinese, the 'Yellow Peril', although there were only about a hundred and fifty Chinese in Cape Town at the beginning of the twentieth century.[71] Asiatics collectively were called 'parasitic hordes'.[72] The causes of anti-Semitism in the 1890s were similar. Its expression in newspapers and journals increased as Jewish immigration from eastern Europe grew in the course of the decade. Allowance was often made for the fact that wealthy Jews had helped 'build up' Cape Town and the Colony in general, had given generously to charity, had previously been accepted as White. But hostility was directed towards the new arrivals, the Polish 'paupers', the potential 'parasites' whose European credentials were doubted.[73]

This kind of racist discourse was equally pervasive among local and central government politicians and administrators in the 1890s and early 1900s. The Cape mayoral congress passed a resolution in favour of government legislation against Asiatic immigration in 1895. When parliament debated the issue the following year, Sprigg clearly stated that he saw Asiatic immigration as 'undesirable'.[74]

Restrictive legislation was delayed until 1902 because Asian immigration was slow before the 1900s, and because of the difficulty posed by the fact that Indians were British subjects. When the number of Indian and Jewish migrants increased during the Boer War, government administrators wanted legislative action. Within Cape Town pressure to restrict specifically Indian immigration came from the town council, a deputation of merchants and in the form of a mass meeting in Greenmarket Square.[75] The Cape government responded in 1902 with an Immigration Act that, without mentioning 'race', made knowledge of a 'European' language a requirement of entry to the Cape. Largely through the efforts of a Jewish lawyer, Morris Alexander, Yiddish was reluctantly accepted by the government as meeting this qualification.[76]

Immigration policy was one way of maintaining racial order. When dealing with the existing population, members of Cape Town's dominant class relied largely on incorporating lower-class Whites in social practices that excluded Blacks. Many of these Whites were doubtless only too happy to have higher social status offered to them. In addition there were individual initiatives to help poor Whites or to persuade the latter that it was wrong for them to associate with Blacks. Otherwise efforts chiefly consisted of continued appeals for local and central government intervention.

Exclusionary practices which included lower-class Whites grew outside, as well as inside, government institutions from the 1880s. By the early 1890s Blacks were kept to one side of the field at major rugby matches on Green Point Common: 'Seldom was there any trouble.'[77] In 1895 the Young Men's Christian Association, which had previously reserved seats at the back of meetings for 'coloureds', excluded them altogether. The President of the YMCA, J. B. Paterson, called a general meeting to announce this decision after some 'coloureds' had challenged the prevailing system by sitting in 'White' seats. Paterson asked, to applause, whether the YMCA should have to admit 'boys' as members.[78] By 1899, if not earlier, separation operated at the circus and theatre in Cape Town. During the war years, Blacks were excluded from the Town Guard.[79]

During the bubonic plague crisis of 1901 Whites and Blacks were inoculated at different times.[80] Africans were excluded from Sea Point municipality, unless they worked there, as well as from 'ordinary' trains and trams. The Tramway Company, under extreme pressure from White patrons and local authorities, had taken the decision to reduce the number of passengers in each tram and to exclude all 'dirty' ones. Fares were raised to recoup losses. White conductors appear to have judged dirtiness largely according to the colour of a prospective passenger, so many darker-skinned Coloureds were probably also excluded.[81] Meanwhile even some 'respectable coloureds' faced temporary problems at the hands of railway officials and were unable to board trains.[82] By 1903 Blacks in general were not allowed to go to the Tivoli Variety Theatre or, by 1904, to stay at any of the hotels in the Cape Peninsula. Cinemas came to Cape Town in the 1900s, and some of them also excluded Blacks.[83]

By the late 1880s many sporting activities were already informally segregated, and parallel White and Black organisations had come into existence. Yet in the early 1890s there were still instances of 'mixed' cricket matches.[84] Objections to mixed sport increased in the course of the decade. In 1894 a Coloured cricketer, T. Hendrickse, was initially selected to play for 'All Comers' against South Africa. Opposition to his playing came 'mainly' from the Western (Cape) Province. The *Cape Argus* came out clearly against mixed sport in 1894: 'The races are best socially apart, each good in their way, but a terribly bad mixture.' Three years later Hendrickse was prevented by the White-controlled Western Province Cricket Union from playing for his team, Woodstock, in the club championships. The *Cape Times* had a leader justifying the decision and stating that Coloureds were 'politically equal' but 'socially not so': 'both colours should ... pursue a policy of mutual exclusion'.[85] Similarly, in 1899 mixed boxing was condemned in the *Cape Argus*.[86]

The objections of some of the clergymen and of Smart to comprehensive segregation in education demonstrated the intimate relationship between ideology and self-interest. Equally the only White cricket administrator on record as defending Hendrickse's right to play in the 1897 cricket championships was Frank Robb. Robb was the secretary of Hendrickse's club, Woodstock.[87]

Separation in sport was advocated by newspapers and practised by most administrators by the end of the 1890s. But socialising, cohabitation and intermarriage between Whites and Blacks in working-class residential areas continued, despite dominant-class condemnation and the fact that some lower-class Whites probably did put social distance between themselves and Black neighbours. The Resident Magistrate might tell Whites who came in front of him that they should not associate with Blacks, but short of much greater state involvement in social engineering there was little that he could do to stop them.[88] The idea of 'raising' Whites was partly to make such mixing unlikely.

There is evidence of several private, rather than government, initiatives which served to promote separation by 'raising' Whites in the 1890s. In 1893, for example, Isaacs, a furniture company, took on twelve 'poor white boys'. The All Saints Sisterhood announced that they would train poor White shoemakers and carpenters in their new school in Kloof Road, because they wished to give preference to 'children of our own race'. Similarly a Mr Irving started a school in Buitenkant Street to train 'European' boys in book-keeping. Not surprisingly ministers of the Cape Town DRC were involved in a number of similar initiatives in the 1890s, including the establishment of a night school for poor Whites.[89]

Achieving rigid residential separation was far more problematic, largely because it would involve considerable expense, given the existing residential pattern of mixed lower-class areas that had existed from the beginning of the century. As Powell wrote regretfully in 1891: 'It is now too late to separate the white and coloured population [in respect to residence] as should have been done from the first.' As he wrote in a previous editorial, Powell saw this as a result of Cape Town's historical legacy: 'Places that have had a ... modern start ... [had the possibility] of separating the coloured population in locations.'[90] What Whites who could afford it were continuing to do in the 1890s was to buy their residential separation. By the end of the decade areas specifically for Whites only were being created and envisaged. They included Milnerton, Oranjezicht (to the south of the Gardens) and parts of Camps Bay, where separation would be protected more formally by clauses in the deeds of sale. In 1894 the *Cape Argus* hoped that all Europeans would move into areas like these, or into the southern suburbs. If they did, much of inner Cape Town could be left as 'virtual locations' for 'coloureds'. What Powell acknowledged that this would not solve was the problem of what to do with the poor White people who remained.[91]

Perhaps because of this realisation, Powell's newspaper ran a series of articles early in 1893 called 'Unexplored Cape Town'. These articles, albeit in the style of 1880s slummer journalism, stressed the plight of poor Whites in the slums. The implication was that additional intervention was needed on their behalf.

The first article described part of District One known as Waterside, informing the reader that 'poor white and filthy black live side by side'. In the sequel, which described parts of District Six and made mention of 'dangerous hovels tenanted by coloured folk', Cape Town's dominant class was also told that here was 'poverty to be sympathised with'. There were 'poorer white' families of labouring men living in Caledon Street, and the lanes that intersected it. These were the people who were 'compelled' rather than who chose to reside there and who were 'degenerating by reason of their surroundings'.

The town council, presumably to Powell's delight, discussed the articles and passed a motion in favour of launching an inquiry into building houses for the 'poor', making no mention of colour. There the matter might have rested. But the *Cape Argus* came out with yet another 'Unexplored Cape Town' feature under the heading 'Man's Inhumanity to Man'. This commented on the fact that the town council had received reports from its sanitary inspectors confirming the main thrusts of the first two articles, and then merely adopted the report without discussion. The *Argus* now pulled out all the stops to stir the council into further action.

Following on its earlier remarks about 'poorer White' families, it presented this kind of verbal vignette. 'Man's Inhumanity to Man' described a house in Coffee Lane. In one room lived eight people sharing one bed. In the next room was an old man, worn out by a 'long day's labour in the sweltering sun', and beside him on the bed lay his sick daughter. On a rag pile in the corner was a girl of fourteen or fifteen with nothing but a 'torn chemise that failed to cover her weary body'. The little sick girl stretched out her arm, 'she is dying of consumption'. The piece used virtually all the images of 'deserving poverty': the elderly, the innocent, the genuine worker and the hint of potential immorality in the description of the near-naked girl in the article gave the reader no respite, no room for easy rationalisations.

8   Coffee Lane, a 'Malay Quarter' backstreet

The result was that a special committee of the town council did investigate those slum areas that had been brought into the limelight.[92] But the extent of action that followed bordered on the farcical and revealed that sympathy for poor Whites (let alone the poor in general) was insufficiently grounded in immediate 'Clean' self-interest to overcome resistance to policies that might smack of municipal socialism. In April 1894 two pieces of council land in District Six were offered to the public on ninety-nine-year leasehold. Their sale was conditional on the purchaser building dwellings for 'labourers and artisans' within two years. They were sold to an E. Von Witt, who proceeded to do nothing with the land. The judgement of Garlick, who possibly had the requisite insight in this respect, was that selling off council land in this way would always attract unscrupulous speculators. Von Witt duly did nothing until forced to re-sell. Late in 1897 the Colonial Building Society built a dozen houses on the land. Appropriately perhaps, Von Witt, a Darling Street merchant, joined the council in 1899.[93]

Emphasising the plight of the White poor was one tactic employed by the newspapers to prod local or central government into action. Its complementary twin was to stress the threat of the residuum, 'Cape Town's Curse'. The possibility of such action was raised during the parliamentary debate over the Cape Town Municipal Bill of 1893. Rhodes suggested the appropriation of 'Malay' land and its redevelopment with 'proper buildings'. J. H. Hofmeyr compared Cape Town to Port Elizabeth where the 'rag, tag and bobtail' and the 'barbarians' had been 'removed' to a location. 'Where', he asked, 'were the locations of Cape Town?'[94]

The implication of Rhodes' and Hofmeyr's interventions in the debate were that the Cape Town council should take the initiative in establishing locations. The difficulty here was that although members of the Clean Party agreed about the potential dangers of 'contamination' from overcrowded housing conditions, they were not united in the solutions they offered. For many, the residential geography of the Cape Peninsula had already provided something of a *cordon sanitaire* between themselves and the residuum. In a situation analogous to Melbourne, Cape Town's prime residential areas were on the sylvan slopes of Table Mountain and by the sea, at Green Point and Sea Point. Priced beyond the reach of Cape Town's labouring poor, living on mountain slopes or behind the bulk of Signal Hill delivered a degree of topographical protection against Cape Town's dangerous classes.[95]

The fact that some 'Cleans' did display an interest in the matter of overcrowding by the mid-1890s may have been partly a result of pressure from journalists, from Dr E. B. Fuller (Dr Fisk's successor) or from electors who lived in the municipality.[96] Equally likely was that individual 'Clean' councillors once again saw self-interest potentially at stake. Certainly some members of what was effectively a Clean 'Ticket of Six' fighting the 1895 election singled out overcrowding as an issue. Two of them, Smart and McKenzie, were major employers of labour. Smart, one of the town's leading builders, had a business in the centre of the town. In his election speeches, he stated that overcrowding was caused by dock and town labourers. Many of them 'such as the Kaffirs' were unwilling to pay much rent and were 'quite content to live in the slums at a few pence a week'. Smart's remedy was for the council to build 'lodging-houses' for them within the Cape Town municipality.

Instead of pulling poor Whites out of the slums, or locating Blacks outside the town, Smart had provided another 'solution'. His argument was to isolate at least a portion of the residuum, but to do so while retaining an accessible labour pool.[97]

In contrast McKenzie favoured a location on the outskirts of the town for 'casual workers from the interior'. The fact of the matter was that he already had one, of sorts, by 1892. This he had established to house migrant Mfengu labourers. McKenzie had begun to experiment with the use of Black migrant labour as a response to the militancy of his Cape Town-based workers. After the violent strike of 1884, McKenzie had brought in several hundred 'Zanzibaris', whom he housed in stables that he owned in Hope Street. After the depression, McKenzie was temporarily forced to employ larger numbers of local workers and face their demands for increased wages. His need for a bigger workforce was aggravated by the fact that the Harbour Board gave him a monopoly in moving goods from shipload to store in one part of the harbour. After a massive strike in December 1891, McKenzie once again looked around for cheaper labour. Having looked at possibilities west of the Kei River, McKenzie through a recruitment agent brought down Mfengu labour from the Transkei.

Mckenzie's establishment of a tightly controlled, semi-compounded migrant labour system followed his achievement as a monopoly employer in 1890. This parallels a similar development on the Kimberley mines in the 1880s. McKenzie's Mfengu migrants were kept in the old 'coolie barracks' and were subject to a 9 p.m. curfew. As Smart had pointed out to the Labour Commission of 1893, this arrangement suited McKenzie very well. He had provided himself with an immobile pool of cheap contract labour over which he exercised a high degree of control.[98]

McKenzie and Smart made housing rural migrants part of their election platform when standing as candidates for the town council in the mid-1890s. That they did so seems to have stemmed more from their positions, and different needs, as employers of labour than from genuine concern about slum conditions. In his evidence to the Labour Commission in 1893 McKenzie had stated that the living conditions of the labouring classes in Cape Town were 'very good'. Nevertheless, Smart was the organising force behind a pro-migrant-housing 'ticket of six' in 1895, one of whom was St Leger. Having handed over the editorship of the *Cape Times* to Edmund Garrett, St Leger wanted to make the council a vehicle for intervention on behalf of poor Whites, and continually raised the housing question for altruistic, if ideological reasons.[99]

Once the ticket was returned, St Leger was responsible for successfully proposing another council investigation of slum housing. But the consequent committee was chaired by Smart and eventually found in favour of labourers' barracks 'as an experimental step'. The result was that the council funded one barracks with room for about two hundred single men, at the paltry cost of £8,000. When completed in 1897 the barracks was handed over to the Salvation Army to run. At first they tried to deal with the poor White problem and the residuum simultaneously. They advertised half the accommodation for Whites and the other half for 'Natives'. But by 1902 the whole building was given over to housing poor Whites and the problem of isolating the residuum remained.[100]

The problem remained partly because the council did not want to spend much money on working-class housing but also because employers of labour could not reach agreement on a question that had already been resolved by mining magnates in Kimberley and Johannesburg. McKenzie and men such as Smart in the building industry were among the largest employers of 'rural migrants' in Cape Town. But employers in the building industry required labour on a shifting basis in various parts of the town. Therefore McKenzie's 'solution' to his labour problem, a solution similar to that adopted by the mining industry, did not suit them. They favoured a rather different plan, at least by 1895: large lodging-houses spread throughout the municipality. Businessmen and merchants who employed African migrants in the centre of the town by the end of the decade tended to favour either this or the status quo, and were concerned that a location outside the town might mean diminished accessibility to their labour.

It seemed in the mid-1890s that Cape Town would adopt a policy to African migrants similar to Durban's *togt* system: housed in a mixture of municipal and private buildings. The difference might have been that Durban's proximity to rural reserves had prompted a degree of 'influx' control. Migrants had to pay a registration fee to enter the workforce, and this was raised sharply in 1903. Cape Town's distance from the Eastern Cape made measures that might restrict labour supply, when there was growing demand, less likely. Yet despite the relative lack of action by the Clean Party in general, Cape Town had two major locations by 1901.[101]

Rural migrants in general had been identified by Smart and McKenzie as aggravating overcrowding and slum conditions. White bourgeois pressure on the council to do something about specifically African migrants mounted in the second half of the 1890s, as their presence in Cape Town increased. Rinderpest outbreaks had helped to push peasants off the land and into the towns.[102] This pressure became intertwined with growing criticism of the Cleans as a central-business-district clique, as a group not interested in the problems and conditions of other parts of the municipality.

This criticism came especially from the White petty-bourgeois rate-payers of Districts Five and Six, residents of that part of the municipality east of the Grand Parade. In April 1898 a small group of these ratepayers came together to fight a by-election for four council vacancies. They included an old Dirty Party associate, Mr Kinsley. He and his colleagues wanted the Cleans to stop beautifying only the centre of the town while the rest of the municipality was 'reeking in filth and vice'. They wanted the council to establish two locations, one for the recent 'great influx of Natives', the other for the 'unfortunates', the 'poor Whites', until industrial expansion (and government education) improved their position.[103]

Kinsley's demand for an African location was taken up in the course of 1898 by an organisation calling itself the South African Working Men's Progressive Union (SAWMPU). The Union was the small political vehicle of three non-workers: T. Harris, J. Carver and I. Purcell, who themselves represented a petty-bourgeois grouping of small trade and property ownership. They claimed, with little evidence, to represent the interests of the British working man in Cape Town, by whom they meant White workers. The *South African News* did suggest in 1899 that they had 'several hundred' artisans as supporters. But this may have been deliberate inflation on the part of a newspaper that supported the *Bond* and was antipathetical towards the English clique on the town council. Another newspaper, also in 1899, put support for this 'worker's' party at sixteen. Undaunted, the SAWMPU petitioned the town council for a location on the grounds that members suffered from the 'nuisance' of the 'Natives'.[104]

After the failure of Kinsley and his colleagues in the by-election, ratepayers from Districts Five and Six also petitioned the council for a location. They said that these areas were 'being rendered unfit for the habitation of respectable working classes' [sic]. They argued that poorly clothed Africans posed a threat to European women and that property would be devalued. These petitions came at a time when the council's new Medical Officer of Health, E. B. Fuller, had already been giving the subject of 'Kaffir lodging-houses' his attention. In 1898 he gave the council details of various tenements let to Africans to illustrate their appalling condition.[105]

The result of the pressure from within and without the council was that the latter, yet again, set up a committee to investigate slum conditions. But this time its members were asked to look specifically at the question of African housing. The 'Kaffir' problem was being equated with the slum problem along the lines suggested by McKenzie and Smart. The committee duly came to the speedy decision in its first session that additional housing for Africans was necessary, in the form of a location. The site they chose was the municipal quarry at the top of Strand Street, which would have housed African labour conveniently close to the central business area – and cheaply. The committee thought that the 'old caretaker's buildings', could be used for the purpose. It would seem as though the Clean council was bent on solving the 'Kaffir' and slum problems on its own terms: as cheaply as possible and to the best advantage of its combined membership.

The council's scheme was not much more than a grander version of the labourers' barracks. As it was, the plans met with virulent opposition from property owners in the vicinity of Strand Street, who duly received the backing of the SAWMPU. This organisation proposed that instead of pursuing the Strand Street quarry idea, the council should approach the Cape government about the possibility of getting land outside the municipality for a location.[106]

This proposal sparked off over two years of negotiations between the council and central government. One observer of these wranglings, an Anglican evangelist in District Six, believed that there was strong opposition within the council to spending any money on African housing. He implied that the council was hoping that the government would foot the bill. Certainly the council showed little sense of urgency in resolving the issue once central government had promised little but sympathy.[107]

Eventually it was the Woodstock council that reopened negotiations with the Cape government. Woodstock was that fast-growing lower-class residential area similar in many ways to District Six which it bordered. Its councillors, who asked central government to provide a location in June 1899, spoke the same language as Kinsley or the SAWMPU: the

African 'invasion' meant falling property prices, lack of security and a threat to health.[108]

They were using arguments with which the government was sympathetic. Government concern, as Swanson has argued, was:

how to organise society to provide for the mutual access of black labourers and white employers in the coming industrial age without having to pay the heavy social costs of urbanization or losing the dominance of white over black.[109]

The reason for continued delay was that employers of labour in Cape Town had not yet given their clear answer to this question. Their differential labour needs help to explain the diffident response of the municipality. Moreover, the government of the day, in 1899, was W. P. Schreiner and the *Bond*, who had narrowly beaten Rhodes' Progressives in the Assembly election of the previous year. This probably explains why the 1899 Natives Location Act put the location ball, and subsequent expenses, back into the court of industrial employers and municipalities. This legislation allowed rather than compelled them to establish their own locations.[110]

Only a series of highly publicised 'Kaffir outrages' made the Cape town council decide, in January 1900, that they might establish a location near Maitland. Typically, councillors took the decision to wait and see what effect winter rains would have on the site. The period of delay conveniently coincided with the return of a Progressive ministry which, in July 1900, appointed a special Native Location Commission to investigate the situation in Cape Town.[111] The composition of the Commission made it eminently qualified within the logic of sanitation rhetoric to report on the nature and possible solutions to the problem posed by the 'Kaffir Invasion'. Two out of its four members were medical men: E. B. Fuller and Dr Gregory, the Colonial Medical Officer of Health. The other two were Mr Stanford, of the Native Affairs Department, and Captain Jenner, Cape Town's chief of police.

The Commission interviewed a cross-section of Cape Town's dominant class: doctors, employers of labour, property owners and representatives of local authorities. They agreed that one or more locations were desirable to alleviate overcrowding, to improve the social 'surroundings' of 'thrifty Europeans' and 'respectable artisans and clerks', and to protect property prices. In general, they wanted to get the 'raw Kaffirs' under control and make them less of a threat to dominant-class values and their conception of social order.

The Commission also interviewed two Africans, William Sipika and Rev. Elijah Mdolomba, who were in favour of a location because they thought that it would mean better housing and living conditions.

Mdolomba had already written to newspapers to this effect. This, together with the fact that no African was interviewed who was against a location, suggests that the Commission was doing little more than obtaining token African approval. An anonymous correspondent to the *South African News*, who seems from the content of the letter to have been an African, wanted to know who had said that 'Natives' were in favour of a location. This correspondent went on to point out the unpleasantness of East London's location.

Sipika and Mdolomba's optimism was no doubt sustained by doctors and clergymen who argued that segregation would be good for Africans as well as the rest of the population. One of the perceived benefits to clergymen was that Africans would be more susceptible to evangelical work. In a logical continuation of the theory of urban degeneracy, it became a commonplace in the arguments of White bourgeois professionals that contact with the evils of the city was debilitating for the 'Noble Savage'.

Only a few discordant notes were heard in the segregationist tune which ran throughout the course of the evidence. These were provided by employers of labour, including Smart and another builder, who were still worried about the implications of locations for their labour supply. This concern was belatedly shared by city merchants and businessmen in a Chamber of Commerce resolution.

But the views of these employers of labour were more than counter-balanced by the highly significant evidence given by the representative of the Harbour Board, Robert Hammersley-Heenan. His evidence revealed that the Harbour Board, in effect the government, was 'early next year' going to take over the whole operation of the docks – landing and loading of cargo as well as construction and maintenance – from dock agents such as McKenzie. The Board intended to erect a 'Kaffir barrack' in the vicinity of the docks. Hammersley-Heenan agreed, when asked, that the Board also needed to control the supply of African labour, which had increased from 200 to 2,000 men since 1892. Thus the government would effectively become by far the most important employer of African labour in Cape Town. Hammersley-Heenan was effectively telling his political masters, by means of the Commission, how best to regulate the supply of such labour at the docks. He had McKenzie's model, itself undoubtedly influenced by the Kimberley compounds, to work from. McKenzie himself told the Commission: 'We are bound sooner or later to have a compound in the docks.'[112]

The Commission's preliminary report was a victory for Hammersley-Heenan as well as sanitation-syndrome rhetoric. Brought out towards the end of 1900, it favoured two locations: one at the docks and one near

Maitland. The presentation of a final report was rendered redundant by the arrival of bubonic plague at the Cape Town docks in February 1901. Under the amended Public Health Act of 1897, the Cape government, in the person of the Colonial Secretary, was still responsible for containing an epidemic, and had been given additional powers to do so. Using these powers the Colonial Secretary's office in consultation with the Native Affairs Department enforced the residential segregation of Africans in the manner envisaged by the Commission. Central government financing of locations, combined with the racist hysteria generated by the plague, helped to overcome any lingering objections among representatives of local authorities. The fact that some of the early victims were Africans, hardly surprising given the locality of the outbreak, was grist to the mill of sanitation-syndrome rhetoric. After considerable African resistance to their removal, the government passed the Native Reserve Locations Act in 1902. With a few exceptions, such as those on the parliamentary voters' roll and domestic servants who could stay on their employers' premises, Africans were now 'legally' forced to live in locations in Cape Town.[113]

Just two months later the government, as Hammersley-Heennan had said they would, took over the landing and loading of cargo at the docks. They also inherited, and refined, McKenzie's migrant labour supply, controlling the rate of African urbanisation by means of a pass system. Cape Town's dominant class now had a controlled 'Kaffir invasion'. Employers of labour had a difficult time in 1901, when Africans were understandably uneasy both about the plague and the location, and stayed away from the city. Employers were aided by the fact that Africans already in Cape Town were effectively imprisoned by a plague regulation that forced them to obtain a pass, signed by the Colonial Secretary or his deputy, if they wished to leave the city. By 1902 the government was helping private employers to recruit their own migrant labour supply from the Eastern Cape.[114]

Economic and demographic change, associated with the Mineral Revolution, had given rise to a new sense of urgency on the part of the White ruling class in town and countryside who wanted to maintain White supremacy. Within Cape Town, the pursuit of this ideal was prompted and supported by petty-bourgeois Whites, as well as some White workers and soldiers, who saw the chance to improve their own position within the social hierarchy.

White supremacy was challenged in Cape Town by Black social mobility, 'Poor Whiteism' and the Black residuum. If there was agreement on the need for racial separation, there was disagreement about what this meant in terms of residential segregation. The

9 First forced removal of Africans to a location in Cape Town, the *Graphic*, 13 April 1901

complexity of this debate reflected the complexity of the city's social formation. Of crucial importance was the fact that most members of Cape Town's elite dominant class were not themselves major employers of labour. Consequently they had no direct stake in implementing the institutions of a segregated labour force that characterised the mining industry in Kimberley or Johannesburg.

Thus the 'special tradition of multiracialism' continued to survive in Cape Town, if in truncated form by the 1900s, as a lower-class phenomenon. As a result Fredrickson can quote Maurice Evans visiting that cinema in 1911 to imply that this tradition permeated the whole of Cape Town society. We could quote the existence of Whites-only cinemas in 1910 in an opposite argument to Fredrickson's. Cape Town did have more social mixing than Natal, the Transvaal or the Orange Free State. Its 'fusion of races' could startle a visitor from Grahamstown. But a visitor from outside southern Africa, a reporter from the Scottish *Dundee Advertiser*, had seen the city's 'special tradition' from another perspective in 1894. He wrote that although 'coloureds' were equal in the eyes of the law there was a 'line' between them and Europeans that was 'almost as rigidly drawn as if they were a lower range of beings'.[115]

The point is that 'multi-racialism' existed by the time of Evans' visit only in some social activities, areas of employment and residence. It was allowed to do so by Cape Town's dominant class, most of whom believed it was wrong in theory, because they realised that further intervention was either going to be enormously expensive or could endanger individual self-interest. But it also continued to exist because at least some Whites, and Blacks, did not believe that it was wrong. Numbers of White artisans did marry Black Capetonians, to the fury of most dominant-class observers. But among the latter there were also dissenters. Missionaries remained standard-bearers of a 'civilising mission' in the old Cape liberal tradition. Some, such as Dr Jane Waterston, kept alive the non-racial tradition of the Free Dispensary.[116] Others, such as the Anglicans Lightfoot and Osborne or the Methodist W. B. Shaw, protested jointly with Cape Town's Black elite when it became clear that separate meant unequal in Cape education. Shaw went further in 1895 and helped to establish the (albeit small) South African Christian Political Association in an attempt to solidify this alliance against 'class' legislation. W. A. Day, a lawyer who frequently defended Blacks in court, was another of the founder members.[117]

If missionaries provided the bulk of vocal separationist dissenters, a small band of socialists became of some significance in the late 1890s, particularly after they had formed the Socialist Club in 1897. Forsyth Bancombe fulminated against racism in letters that were published, if only to be attacked, in the *Cape Times*. Bancombe wanted Whites to join hands with Black comrades 'to declare to the world the truth that Englishmen really believe in equality of freedom, man and right'.[118]

If few bourgeois Whites would have welcomed this call, how many of the White working class put any of the ideas behind Bancombe's prose into practice, or to what extent were they, or Black workers, racist at the workplace? In the absence of evidence directly produced by lower-class Capetonians themselves, one way that we can begin to answer this question is by examining occasions when workers forced their way into the records of the dominant class. They had done so in the 1880s, when both employed and unemployed workers organised to protect or improve their positions. They did so more frequently in the 1890s, both because economic growth improved the chance of successful combination and because changes in the nature of production made this more likely.

7 Ethnicity and organisation among Cape Town's workers

Cape Town workers were undoubtedly made aware of dominant class racialisation and racism in the late nineteenth century. Even if they were unable to read the diatribes in the newspapers, dealings with census officials, magistrates and employers would have conveyed a great deal. So, more certainly, did the growth of separative and discriminatory practices which increasingly affected their lives outside the workplace from the 1880s.

But ethnicity and racialised opinions on the part of lower-class Capetonians were not simply imposed. Equally, social distance between workers, when it existed away from the workplace, was not just a one-way process promoted by White workers. For instance Malay ethnicity, for all that the name itself was probably a White-imposed label, was based on the desire of ex-slaves in Cape Town to assert an identity that expressed their achievement of freedom. Its durability into the late nineteenth century was partly a result of the persistence of kinship or occupational ties, sometimes both, but also of institutions and practices that conferred, together with residential proximity, a sense of community for its adherents.

Particularly in the first part of the nineteenth century, some Black and White migrants to Cape Town 'turned' Malay, and gained a new identity and communal support. Others, in part through dominant-class intervention to prevent the spread of Islam in the city after emancipation, built communities around Christian missions in the municipality such as the DRC's St Stephen's, the Anglican St Paul's, St Philip's or St Mark's, or Moravian Hill. A sense of community was conferred by attendance at church, of family members at day or night schools, or membership of benefit societies associated with the missions. For many members of these congregations, for virtually the whole congregation before the increase of long-distance migrancy in the last decades of the century, communal identity was further reinforced by their sense of shared heritage as slave descendants demonstrated in ceremonies that commemorated the anniversary of emancipation.[1]

Community membership for some members of the city's lower classes may have cut across potential ethnic divides. For others, community membership may have strengthened a sense of ethnicity, and vice versa. The evidence 'from below' is patchy and ambivalent for the late nineteenth century, particularly before the 1890s. What we do know is that by 1880 at least two benevolent societies, which consisted of 'mostly working men and tradesmen', constitutionally excluded 'coloured' members or 'any man who is supposed to have coloured blood in his veins'. One of these societies even rejected members whose wives were 'coloured ... to keep it as select as possible'. Such racialised discrimination accorded well with the racist discourse of Englishness in the late 1870s. We also know that members of the 'coloured classes' formed three or four such societies of their own. But there were another twenty-seven or so benevolent societies that were mixed. Equally, Black and White workers had jointly organised the unemployed in the mid-1880s.[2]

Ethnicity could be weakened by workplace experience. We have seen how this happened among dock workers in the mid-1880s. But ethnicity could also be strengthened by that experience, and by the timing of arrival of existing 'ethnically distinct peoples into distinct kinds of jobs' as Frederick Cooper has argued for Mombasa and as we argued in chapter 2.[3] Looking at moments of protest or more enduring forms of organisation by workers is an attempt to see how their collective consciousness as workers, expressed by group action, interacted with or cut across ethnicity.[4] But doing so also reveals something of the way that workers attempted to improve their lives through these methods. The focus will be on artisans and dock workers because, for reasons we will seek to explain, they were most involved in group protest and organisation.

Examples of worker protest and organisation in Cape Town increased in the last quarter of the century as the methods and scale of production changed, as did the way labour was organised at the workplace. These changes went hand-in-hand with the recruitment and arrival of migrants, notably from the city's immediate hinterland, from Mozambique, the Eastern Cape and Europe. The Mineral Revolution was behind these developments, which included the growth of factory production in the late nineteenth century. But there were only occasional signs of protest or organisation by Cape Town's emerging industrial proletariat before the twentieth century because of the nature as well as the scale of Cape Town's industrialisation. By the early 1880s the new factories clustered in the centre of the municipality and producing goods for local consumption had employed only a few hundred people. Mechanisation was speeded up in the late 1880s and into the 1890s, and factories spread through District Six into Woodstock and Observatory. But units of production remained, on average, fairly small. The number of mechanised works in the Cape Division, which included Cape Town, increased from just under 500, employing 5,500 people, to just over 600 employing almost 12,000 between 1891 and 1904. Therefore the average number of people employed in each factory rose from 11 to 19, and was seldom more than 100, enabling employers to retain close supervision and surveillance over their workforces. Most of the latter were unskilled or semi-skilled and, with industrial production still subject to seasonal fluctuations in demand, highly vulnerable to casualisation. Moreover, much manufacturing of clothing was still undertaken by the putting-out system.[5]

An exceptional place in terms of scale and nature of production, but one which requires further research, was the Salt River railway works. After the dramatic strike of 1884 which had united employees across divisions of labour, and because of the depression, their numbers had been severely reduced in the 1880s. They increased again with gold-induced recovery in the 1890s, reaching well over a thousand, but industrial action or trade union activity among the men was negligible. The branch of the British Amalgamated Society of Engineers, formed in the 1880s, appears to have been in abeyance until 1903. What may explain the quiescence of Salt River workers in the intervening years was that divisions of labour within the works now coincided more emphatically than ever with colour, after the government's decision in 1894 to restrict artisanal apprenticeship to Whites. Furthering a sense of White ethnicity among the skilled workers, and perhaps a deliberate strategy on the part of government, was the fact that they had been issued with passes to travel first class on the suburban railway. This might have made them feel not just aristocrats of labour but considerable ethnic affinity with employers. Certainly these artisans displayed no solidarity when unskilled labourers from the works attempted to strike for an increase of 6d per day in 1896. Rhodes was probably well advised to make his promise of 'equal rights to all *white* men south of the Zambezi' in 1897 to an audience on his Groote Schuur estate which included 800 skilled workers from the Salt River workshop.[6]

Other workers present on this occasion included members of the Typographical Union, the Amalgamated Society of Carpenters and Joiners, the Operative Masons, the painters' and the plumbers' unions. Nevertheless, the verdict as to whether all, or most, White artisans were racist must be 'unproven'. What is clear is that the emergence of craft unionism in Cape Town was a product of White migrancy. But the fact that unions succeeded in establishing themselves among the city's workforce in the last quarter of the nineteenth century, given the nature of the labour market that had existed in the 1870s, has a great deal to do with changing methods of production. Successful unionism, in the sense of winning improved conditions of employment, was largely a result of the organisational tactics of the workers themselves. These included how White English-speaking artisans decided to relate to other skilled workers who spoke different languages and differed in appearance, who could be perceived as Malay, Coloured, African or Black.

As Atkinson has shown for Bristol, the existence of seasonal and mobile labour, quite apart from cyclical depression, retards trade union development. When the latter first appears it is likely to do so among the better-paid artisans.[7] The flow of British building artisans into Cape Town in the 1875 to 1882 period had resulted in the establishment of at least one craft union by the later date: the Amalgamated Society of Carpenters and Joiners. But this union seems to have been moribund until the end of the decade. It would also seem likely that there was a typographical or compositors' union functioning in the late 1870s, or early 1880s but this also disappeared or fell into dormancy during the depression.[8]

It was only in the 1890s that trade unionism was more firmly established. A meeting under the auspices of a reborn Amalgamated Society of Carpenters and Joiners was held in March 1890. It discussed shorter working hours and overtime, and attracted an audience of 100.[9] By June 1890, and possibly as a result of the March meeting, a trades council had been formed, primarily to organise an eight-hour movement. Nothing more is heard of the trades council until 1897. Represented on the council in 1890 were plumbers, bricklayers, painters, engineers and plasterers, as well as carpenters. But this does not mean that all of these trades had formed individual unions by this date, or that unions previously formed were still in existence.[10]

The relative mobility of single artisans from Britain, as well as the fact that it took time for divisions of labour in Cape Town to become somewhat more rigid, may help to account for the stuttering beginnings of trade unionism in the city. Compositors had only definitely re-established a typographical society by 1896. Stonemasons and tailors both formed unions in 1897, plumbers in the same year and plasterers by 1898.

Bricklayers and painters both had false starts, in 1893 and 1897 respectively, before re-establishing unions in 1903 and again in 1905. But the reason for the false starts was connected to the particular insecurities facing unionists in those crafts.[11]

Craft unions in the 1890s were established by migrants from Britain or

Australia, who arrived in growing numbers between 1889 and 1902. Often fairly large groups of, say, carpenters or stonemasons, 'ordered' by the same employer, would travel to the Cape on the same boats, giving them an early chance to gain a sense of group identity. These immigrants brought with them the craft unionism they had learnt overseas. Membership entailed paying entrance fees and periodic (often weekly) contributions thereafter. Benefits included payments during unemployment and sickness. Members would normally have served several years of apprenticeship in their trade.

With this unionism came the consciousness among members of craft pride and the desire to protect privilege.[12] In using withdrawal of labour as part of protecting or improving their pay, they forced Cape Town's Resident Magistrate in the late 1880s and early 1890s to redefine who was a 'servant' under the Masters and Servants Act. They gained exemption not only for themselves but, in the process, for local Black artisans as well. The fact that they could do so was perhaps a result not only of greater dominant-class sympathy for lower-class Whites compared to the 1870s, but also of the heavy demand for skilled labour at the time.[13]

Although members of various unions may have had equal quantities of craft pride, they did not all have equal ability to protect a privileged position in Cape Town's labour market. After all, they had to compete within their respective trades with local artisans. Protecting privilege thus meant preventing undercutting and, if possible, casualisation.

The chronology of union formation begins to suggest a differential rate of success among immigrant artisans in this respect. This becomes more apparent when comparing the highest rates of pay that unionists, or would-be unionists, were receiving in Cape Town. Plumbers received £5 for a forty-eight-hour week as early as 1895. At the other end of the scale tailors were earning an average of £1 10s in 1897 for the same number of hours. Only if they worked about twice as long could they hope to make close to £4 a week, the rate that plasterers were receiving by 1899. Printers and painters were struggling to earn £3 a week as late as 1903, by which time carpenters had managed to raise their wages to £4 a week, plasterers to £5 and plumbers to at least £5 10s.[14]

Three possible factors – level of skill, supply and demand for their labour, and strategy towards other workers in their trade – determined the relative success of immigrant trade unionists in this respect, and the subsequent nature of their workplace relationship with local artisans. The nature of this relationship would be important in promoting or eroding ethnic and racialised distinctions between them.

The first of the factors, skill, can be defined as 'the capacity to perform technically difficult tasks'.[15] With this definition it is possible to argue that plumbers, say, were more successful in unionising and improving wages than painters or bricklayers because the former were more skilled: tasks within their craft – due to changing methods of production or construction – were more difficult, required greater training and commanded higher wages. Painters and bricklayers in Cape Town, like their counterparts in London, were only semi-skilled. Consequently they were much more vulnerable to casualisation, were worse paid and found successful protest and organisation to improve their situation more difficult.

We used differences of skill as an explanation of why White artisans, on average, received higher wages than their Black counterparts in the 1870s and early 1880s. Immigrant British masons in that period were described as more 'specialised', local plumbers as mere gas-fitters or tinsmiths. In turn, different remunerations between, and divisions of labour within, crafts might have promoted White or Malay ethnicity.

But Harrison and Zeitlin have argued that although the possession of skill was undoubtedly important, there was no 'simple one to one relationship' between level of skill and the power of artisans to organise and extract higher rates of pay. Other, interrelated, factors were significant. They included the ability of workers to understand the extent of demand for their labour and, if necessary, to form alliances with the lesser skilled within their trade.[16]

Pieter Van Duin has suggested a further factor. He has argued that White employers of labour paid more to White artisans than to Black out of 'sentiment' or ethnic solidarity. In pursuing this argument for the early twentieth century, Van Duin has said that differences of skill within the building trades were 'somewhat artificial'. Prejudice on the part of employers for White artisans may have played a role in determining that the latter got higher wages.[17] Belief that this was the case might explain why some White painters and bricklayers in 1903 formed Whites-only unions. They were attempting what Stanley Greenberg has called a kind of 'bounded' relationship with their employers. But these unions were short lived, their members' strategy changed in favour of non-racialised organisation by 1906. A White bricklayer had complained in 1897 that employers preferred to use 'coloured' artisans. What was probably the case, as other sectors of the economy and events in the American South demonstrated, was that employers would usually opt for Black workers if they were cheaper.[18]

If sentiment did work at times in favour of the employment of Whites, it was liable to do so only if all other considerations were equal. If White and Black skilled workers were thought to be doing the same jobs there is evidence that some received the same rate of pay.[19] The difficulty for many immigrants was that after they had been recruited at higher rates of pay than Cape Town workers, they could not protect those wage rates. Local Black artisans were often prepared to accept lower wages, perhaps at times to overcome employer prejudice. Therefore Fred Davies, a White painter, had emphasised the need to organise 'coloured' painters in 1897, because they provided effective competition.[20]

Supply and demand seems a more probable reason why White immigrant artisans initially received higher wages than local workers. Thereafter they formed unions to protect or improve their position, but some found this easier to do than others. Artisans were imported to southern Africa at times of skilled-labour shortages. Their wages had, at least initially, to match in real terms those in their country of origin. Certainly contemporary comments support the contention that the importation of British artisans was often thought essential. Trying to limit subsequent supply of workers in their trade, and being constantly aware of demand, was crucial to the success or failure of unionists' attempts to protect or increase their rates of pay.[21]

The final factor, strategy towards other workers, is intimately related to the first two. Strategy could take the form of exclusion, combination or alliance with local artisans. The successful adoption of a strategy of exclusion would appear to have been facilitated more by changes taking place within the building industry in the late nineteenth century than by prejudice on the part of White employers.

Throughout the 1890s and 1900s there are constant references in Select Committee Reports, as well as newspapers articles and advertisements for labour, to the difference between 'competent' and 'rough' work in the building trades. There were similar and genuine distinctions in Melbourne's building industry in this period. They had come about as a result of changes in building techniques.[22] There is considerable evidence to suggest that this is precisely what was happening in Cape Town during the latter's transformation from the Dutch to the Victorian city, a transformation which accelerated in the 1890s. As one immigration official put it in 1902: 'The introduction of modern methods ... has created a demand for skilled labour for which the set of workers is insufficient.' He went on to say that this had been the reason for the continual rise of wages and the Trades and Labour Council's attempt to prevent the further immigration of this new kind of skilled labour. Other comments testify to the fact that certain skills in late Victorian Cape Town were new and necessitated at least the initial importation of British artisans to perform them.[23]

From what we know of the changes in the building and construction industries in late nineteenth-century Cape Town, these comments were accurate. The introduction of 'modern methods' would have included the introduction of 'standardised measurement in building' which threatened the position of poorly educated Black artisans in the American South at this time.[24] The centre of Cape Town in particular was the scene of major infrastructural developments by local and central government. They, as well as individual merchants and businessmen, commissioned architect-designed structures which demanded new and exacting standards and expertise from builders and their artisans.

One of the most notable changes was in the growing use of finely cut stone, rather than brick covered with plaster, as both a prestigious and durable building material.[25] The introduction of 'modern' drainage had produced the need for plumbers who were not just 'gas-fitters and tinsmiths'. Victorian architecture could also require elaborate work from carpenters and plasterers. Thus the *Cape Times* reported that a British carpenter was paid more than other carpenters because of his 'expertise with stairs'. Presumably for similar reasons, White plasterers monopolised the quality work required in the construction of the new post office and the luxury Mount Nelson Hotel.[26]

Certainly local artisans could, in time, have become trained in the necessary new 'dexterities'; they undoubtedly had their own with which British artisans would not have been familiar. But some innovative techniques would have been more difficult to learn than others, and changes in methods of production could make old skills increasingly redundant. As Laidler has written, if with some exaggeration, 'between 1886 and 1897 furniture making ceased to be craftsmanship and became factory mass production, as did waggon and cart building, confectionery, jam making, bacon curing and soap making'.[27] There was also the question of who would teach the new skills when government industrial institutions in the Western Cape were barring Blacks and education at the mission schools was limited. Although there were places such as the Anglican industrial school that admitted Blacks, and some techniques could perhaps be learnt from observation, it would take time for many local artisans to learn the more difficult new skills. Immigrant artisans, keen to limit the supply of those who possessed them, do not appear to have been keen to take on apprentices. The government had also restricted apprenticeship at the Salt River works to Whites.[28]

Before Black artisans could learn the new techniques there would appear to have been practical reasons, other than the mere prejudice of the employers, why some unionists took the 'cream of the work' and with it the highest pay. This is what an immigration official, Mr Cousins, thought in 1907 when comparing the 'rawness' of all 'colonial' artisans with British ones. Once in a privileged position in the labour market there would be good reason for unionists to protect their position by themselves helping to decide and control who was, or was not, a 'competent' workman and thus eligible to join their union. The chairman of the Cape Town and District Trades and Labour Council, Mr Thomas Maginess, was asked how he measured competency as a means of admission to unions in 1908. He replied that 'when a member is proposed he must have a proposer and a seconder and men to support him, men who have worked with him and who know his ability, and if that man turns out to be a failure the union fines the men for proposing him'.[29]

By 1901 the masons', plasterers' and carpenters' unions had opted for exclusivity that left them solely for Whites. This may not have been simply ethnic prejudice on the part of these workers, although some Black artisans complained that it was. There is no evidence that Blacks were constitutionally barred from entry to any of the unions, at a time when White racism and exclusivity were entirely respectable. The carpenters' union was overtly open to 'any Africander or any competent man of any nationality'. Union leaders always talked the language of craft, rather than colour, exclusivity – although this may have been from awareness of the potential need for alliance or co-operation with Black artisans. But the Plasterers' Union did have a 'coloured' member in 1899, and a representative said that his union was not against 'coloureds' *per se*, but because they were 'labourers' who 'were permitted to do a rough class of work in a style not permitted in any other country where trades were advanced'.[30]

Changes in building methods had led to the introduction of large numbers of British stonemasons in the 1890s. Their expertise with a product newly in demand enabled them to maintain fairly convincingly (unlike other unionists) that there were no 'coloured' stonemasons in 1899. The lack of danger from undercutting explains why the Operative Masons not only had 120 out of 126 White stonemasons as members by then but also why they, like stonemasons in Melbourne, could successfully practise exclusivity.[31]

In Cape Town it seems probable that ethnicity reinforced craft consciousness and vice versa, thanks to the close correlation between level of skill and colour as new techniques were introduced to the building industry in the late nineteenth century. Thus when White plasterers refused to work on the same scaffolding as Black plasterers in 1901, ethnic and craft consciousness presumably converged. For plasterers, the strategy of White exclusivity made feasible by new demands for their particular dexterities went hand-in-hand with an awareness that plastering was more open to undercutting than stonemasonry, if less so than painting or bricklaying. The successful pursuit of exclusivity required White plasterers to keep more keenly informed of the level of demand for their skills. Thus they chose to go on (a successful) strike in 1903, when the local press was reporting a shortage of skilled labour. Reading the market in this way was obviously facilitated by literacy in English, a further skill in the possession of British artisans. As it was, some employers had managed to continue work with 'Malay and Indian' plasterers, underlining the relative vulnerability of immigrants in this craft compared to stonemasonry and the limits of White employer 'sentiment' for White workers.[32]

Like the Amalgamated Society of Carpenters and Joiners in Melbourne, the Cape Town Society practised an exclusivity that left many White, as well as Black, carpenters outside the union. They can only have been able to do so successfully because of the specific skills they possessed in, say, the production of Victorian staircases or cabinet-making. Unionised carpenters also adopted the strategy of seeking alliances with non-union, and lower paid, White carpenters in their strike actions of 1893, 1901 and 1903.

In the space of ten years the wages of 'competent' carpenters rose accordingly from 9s 6d to 14s per day. Carpenters showed as keen an awareness as the plasterers of the ebbs and flows in demand for their skills. In May 1890 they contemplated a strike, but decided that they were 'insufficiently prepared', possibly because of the relatively low level of demand in the mini-depression of that year. When carpenters did strike, in 1893, it was during the first phase of the building boom. They won an extra 6d a day. Strikes during the Boer War and shortly afterwards were when a new building boom was at its height.[33]

In the absence of state intervention on their behalf, those White artisans most vulnerable to undercutting had to opt for a different strategy to the overlapping craft and colour exclusivity of the masons, carpenters and plasterers. Bricklayers and painters would appear to have benefited less than other artisans from changes in the building industry. Some bricklayers and painters may have attempted to become the elite of their trade simply by refusing to take on 'rough' or 'plain' work, by defining their own work as particularly skilled and even appealing to employer 'sentiment'. But their relative poverty compared to, say, plasterers underlines the difficulty they faced in pursuing exclusivity. One reason may have been the lack of demand for quality work in their trade. Certainly in 1897 a painter talked of the 'low standard' of work passed by architects, a bricklayer of the 'slop and jerry' work he had come across in the Colony. Four years earlier another bricklayer had complained of the shortage of 'better brickwork'. But in the case of bricklayers and painters, skill would appear to have been more of a 'social aspiration' than a genuine capability to perform technically difficult tasks that others would find hard to learn, such as stonemasonry. Employers' 'sentiment' was obviously insufficient protection for these aspirations.[34]

The bricklayer of 1897 complained of a 'set of wasters' working for 3s or 5s a day who 'obtain the preference over the *Whites*' [my emphasis].[35] The fact that he saw the threat of undercutting coming from Black artisans was his individual expression of White ethnicity and racism in that situation. But during the attempt to organise a bricklayers' union in 1893, Black bricklayers were present and there had been no talk of exclusion. Equally, White painters apparently tried in 1897 and again in 1903 to recruit Blacks to their union. A strategy of White exclusivity, fleetingly adopted overtly by the painters in 1903, had little chance of success.[36] In 1906 both bricklayers and painters became members of non-racial unions within the umbrella General Workers' Union (GWU) set up by socialist skilled workers of the Social Democratic Federation (SDF). The GWU's constitution denounced colour prejudice and stated that 'membership would be open to every wage-earner, male or female'.[37]

Outside the building industry, British immigrant tailors and composi-tors were also highly vulnerable to undercutting, which helps explain the strategies of alliance and non-racial recruitment that they attempted. The establishment of a tailors' union coincided with the gradual move towards workshop production in this trade, away from out-work. But the latter continued well into the 1900s, and possibly beyond. The problems facing unionist tailors were compounded by the ethnic divisions of labour within workshops and the fact that Malays and Yiddish-speaking Jewish tailors were involved in the out-work. Malays were apparently engaged as trouser hands, White tailors as coat and vest hands. Members of the tailors' union, in the course of 1897, complained about the 'sweating' in their trade, the fact that work was taken home or produced outside a workshop, rather than low standards or differences of skill. They felt threatened by 'Malays' who 'live cheaper' and by 'Polish Jews' who were prepared to work long hours for little money. The tailors' union, moribund for a few years, was re-established in 1901 to push for higher wages. In the process the union tried to form an alliance with Malay tailors, who did pledge their support in a meeting organised for this purpose. However, they reneged on their pledge and the strike was confined to 'European' tailors. With the Malays still working within workshops, and the 'sweated' trade without, the 200 tailors who did strike only received a derisory seventh of what they had asked for.[38]

In 1897 members of the Typographical Union, seemingly hitherto White, embarked on a strategy not only of alliance with, but also inclusion of, Coloured and local White workers but exclusion of Africans and women. Such a strategy was advisable for artisans whose craft privilege was threatened by increased mechanisation in the industry. Lower pay to new recruits could be justified by employers on racist or sexist grounds. Coloureds were encouraged to join the union, although only twenty had done so by 1899. However, in the strike that the union embarked on in 1897, it received the support of non-union White and Coloured printers, as well as that of printers brought in to break the strike and the compositors won pay rises of from 5 per cent to 15 per cent. The union leader, Mr Farrell, made it clear that he wanted a standardisation of all compositors' wages irrespective of colour. When asked during the strike by the mayor of Cape Town whether Coloured compositors were as good as Whites he replied, 'Of course they are'.

The timing of the strike, just after a local firm had won the government printing contract, shows an awareness of the need to read the level of demand for their labour. Successfully persuading the Cape government, in 1895, to commit itself to keeping these contracts within the Colony shows a similar awareness. It may also have been an early indication of the greater political power of White workers. Finally, those compositors working on newspapers may have been helped in the 1897 strike by the 'perishable' nature of this product. The *Cape Times* immediately settled with its workers for 15 per cent and the *Cape Argus* offered 11 per cent only a day after the strike began. In contrast, those printers working for the firm that handled the government contract had to settle for 5 per cent.[39]

The relationship between ethnicity and craft or occupational consciousness was complicated in the various artisanal trades in Cape Town. Where craft unionism coincided with colour it doubtless increased the White ethnicity of its members, particularly when most Whites in the trade were unionists as in the case of stonemasons. If only some Whites were members but no Blacks, as with the carpenters, then it is possible that craft unionism promoted Englishness above a wider White ethnicity that elsewhere incorporated Afrikaners trained in government industrial schools. White exclusivity by unions, whether from craft or ethnic prejudice, and its practice by the likes of White plasterers on building sites, increased the colour consciousness of Black artisans. So would new divisions of labour correlating with colour within various trades, such as tailoring, whether unions were present or not. Inclusion of Coloureds but not Africans by the Typographical Union promoted ethnic divisions along these lines among Black Capetonians.[40]

In the Cape Town of 1891 to 1902, dominant-class discourse distinguished between Black and White among the lower classes.

Increasingly, segregation reached beyond previous forms of exclusion to separate White from Black throughout society. Together with considerable correlation between divisions of labour (particularly in terms of supervisory positions) and colour, it is probable that many immigrant artisans saw themselves as White as well as English, and felt and expressed racism towards Black or un-English Capetonians. Yet it is still surprising not only how little racism comes through in the rhetoric of craft unionists, but also how few appeals they, or indeed other White workers, made in newspapers to White ethnic solidarity across class lines. We can suggest that it was the lack of rigid divisions of labour, in many of the craft trades that employed Whites and Blacks, that promoted the need for potential or actual co-operation at the workplace and held such racism in check.

In only two instances (that I found) when a White artisan identifying his occupation complained to the press in the 1890s about Black workers in his craft, the White worker in question was a mason. The fact that stonemasons could successively opt for exclusion might have meant that they not only felt superior to Black masons but could afford to be racist. Another occasion when a compositor, Mr Scoggins, wrote to the newspaper to demand action against Black Capetonians he was wanting a location for Africans, in keeping with his union's specific exclusion of them.[41]

Both White and Black artisans resided in large numbers in close proximity in working-class areas such as District Six and Woodstock, and did not always maintain the 'social distance' that Van Duin argued normally existed between them. When the Governor of the Cape wrote to Joseph Chamberlain about the problems facing the authorities dealing with the plague he mentioned that one problem was 'the presence of a mixed population closely intermingled in their *domestic relations*, comprising Europeans, low class Jews, Malays, coloured persons, Chinese, Indians and Aboriginal Natives' [my emphasis].[42] A leader in the *South African News* at much the same time, commenting on British artisans in Cape Town, said:

We have been astonished, and from the standpoint of our social prospects disheartened, to find how surprisingly large is the percentage of such settlers who marry coloured women. Let the Imperial Government take a census on this point in, say, District Six of Cape Town, and the result will astonish them.[43]

Those bars or cinemas that were not segregated tended to be in lower-class neighbourhoods. Two of the three cricket teams that had Coloured members in 1897 were the Docks and Woodstock, working-class areas in inner Cape Town. The other was Simon's Town, a place which employed

White and Black artisans in its dockyard. The mixed boxing matches, so disapproved of by the dominant-class press, took place in District Six in front of mixed audiences.

What is probable is that most immigrant artisans distinguished between different degrees of Blackness and un-Englishness among local artisans. Many might have been prejudiced against Africans who largely were, and it was hoped would remain, unskilled labourers and some White immigrants possibly did join the SAWMPU. But the 'infinite gradations of colour' in Cape Town's population, perhaps particularly among her partly slave-descended artisanate, appears to have combined with imprecise divisions of labour in some trades to undermine immigrant racism at least towards the 'slightly coloured' workers in the same trade.[44]

The support of White artisans for Cecil Rhodes, which they demonstrated in the rally at Groote Schuur in 1897, was first and foremost a demonstration of support for his attack on Afrikaners in the Transvaal. The renewed friction between English and Afrikaner politicians at the Cape after the Jameson Raid forced Rhodes to change his cry of 'votes for all Whites' at the rally to 'votes for all civilised men south of the Zambezi' in the 1898 election campaign. We can perhaps conclude that some White artisans would not have distinguished between the terms 'White' and 'civilised'. Among them may have been the members of exclusive unions, and those artisans at the Salt River works who were sealed within a work situation where the government had intervened to promote a correlation between colour and division of labour. The works themselves could have provided something close to a communal focal point. But some White artisans had both the same status and physical proximity to Black artisans at the workplace, and in the building industry that workplace was constantly changing. Community networks which these White artisans built up could include at least 'off-coloured' fellow artisans, neighbours, or, through marriage, families. What was left of Cape Town's 'special tradition' still afforded them the social space in which this could happen, even though the growth of separation steadily encroached.

We know far less about the attitudes, let alone the practices, of unskilled White workers in the 1890s. But many of the comments about artisans would doubtless apply. Particularly where employers separated Whites from Blacks, workplace experience promoted ethnic rather than occupational solidarities. Such separation existed in many of the large shops and in some factories by the 1900s. Perhaps this explains why one shop assistant, writing to the *Cape Times* in 1897 supporting a half-holiday movement, said that they should 'stand up for their rights as

White men and women'.[45] The fact that participants were White might have helped their success.

Ethnic solidarities would also have been promoted where divisions of labour largely correlated with colour. It is likely that this was usually, if not always, the case in domestic service. The cost of importing British women, and their initial salary, made them more expensive than local labour, and may also have made their employment at the top of a chain of servants something of a status symbol to their employer. As we saw in chapter 4, there may also have been prejudice by some employers against Blacks working in the intimate circumstances of domestic service. Particularly when alternative employment was possible, White servants could afford to remind employers of the normal domestic colour hierarchy. On one occasion, recorded because the case came to court, a 'European' refused to work under a Black cook.[46]

Divisions of labour corresponding with ethnicity, workplace and residential separation affected dock workers. This happened as employers changed the way they organised labour to deal with new tasks, new demands of scale, to reduce its cost and, sometimes, in response to worker protest. In the process the kind of occupational solidarity across potential ethnic divides that dock workers had displayed in the 1884 strike, reinforced by strength of numbers, evaporated in the course of the 1890s. By then Whites had been appointed to supervisory or skilled positions. Both McKenzie and the Harbour Board increasingly relied on African migrants as unskilled labour into the 1900s.

Clearly they did so because they hoped to get cheaper and more easily controllable labour. Both in 1884 and 1892 McKenzie brought in migrant labour as the consequence of strikes and housed them in a form of barracks location. The background to his introduction of Mfengu labourers in 1892 was renewed labour unrest. McKenzie had taken on local labour to meet increasing workloads as the discovery of gold was beginning to lift the depression, and before the economic setbacks of 1890. In 1889 the dock workers had apparently demanded, and received, an increase in pay.[47] Almost three years later this advance was confirmed when between 200 and 300 dock workers struck again for increased pay, this time setting out their demands to McKenzie in 'a lengthy document'.

It seems as though the workers concerned were 'Cape Boys' employed in what was one of the heaviest and most unpleasant tasks at the docks: carrying coal to steamships. They had chosen their moment well, striking when there was an 'unusual' number of ships in Cape Town harbour. They succeeded in winning a rise in pay from 3s 6d to 4s 6d. But it was this success that prompted McKenzie to turn to migrant Mfengu labourers, whom he paid from only 30s to 50s a month.[48]

Table 3 *Wages of lowest-paid labourers at the Cape Town docks, 1860–1902*

1860–1867	2s 6d per day
1867–1889	3s per day
1889–1891	3s 6d per day
1891–1892	4s 6d per day
1892–1896	30s per month
1896–1902	4s 6d per day

Based on *South African Native Affairs Commission,* (Transvaal Colony), 1903–5, vol. 5, Annexure 4, pp. 10–11; *Cape Times,* 8 January 1889 and *Cape Argus,* 21 December 1891 show how strikes altered the rates of pay, changes not apparent from the *SANAC* evidence which is not alto-gether reliable.

McKenzie's Mfengu labourers came from the Willowvale and Ketani areas of the Transkei. They were apparently 'not well off', which presumably explains why they had been forced to become coal carriers at those wages.[49] But they were far less easy to control than McKenzie had perhaps imagined. Shared migrancy from the Transkei and employ-ment as coal carriers strengthened the interaction between ethnicity and occupational consciousness among Mfengu dock workers. Similarly, so did the fact that they were forced to live in barracks. Confining labourers in barracks, compounds or locations may have made them easier to supervise but could increase their sense of solidarity. The Harbour Board had used an old coal store in 1879 to house the first batch of Mozambique labourers and they had refused to work in April 1880, complaining of ill health, possibly a tactic to try and avoid the rigours of the Masters and Servants Act. But after cursory medical examination, they were made to start working again by the Resident Magistrate, under threat of imprisonment. Between 1881 and 1882 Mozambique migrants were put in the convict station's wood store. In July 1881 they successfully combined to resist the withdrawal of a twice-weekly meat ration from a diet that otherwise consisted entirely of mealies (maize).[50]

The Mfengu labourers were housed in the 'Coolie Barracks' on the east quay, built ten years earlier for the Irish labourers. McKenzie liked the site because, as he put it in his rambling and inarticulate prose, it was

situated close to the water side, and very secluded from passengers and others visiting that part of the Docks, and being inside the Dock gates, and continually under the direct supervision of the police, which is a preventative to many evils, which otherwise would undoubtedly be practised by the Natives.[51]

The new occupants, who numbered 500 by 1896, were subject to a 9 p.m. curfew, unless issued with a pass to be out later. No alcohol or women were allowed in their barracks, and many had to sleep on the floor. But such confinement bred solidarity, expressed not only in songs that talked of rural life but also in protest.[52]

Some of this protest took the form common to early industrialisation in Africa of workers attempting to desert in small groups from what were unpleasant living and working conditions. In March 1892, less than a month after they arrived, several tried to escape into hoped-for obscurity in Cape Town because carrying coal was 'too hard work'. Many further attempts were made in the next few years.[53] Another form of early industrial group protest was 'sloppy' work. In May 1892 a number of Mfengu workers were in court for throwing the bags into bunkers with the coal instead of pouring the coal in separately and saving the bags.[54]

But the Mfengu workers soon went beyond these forms of protest and attempted strike action. In 1892, when only seventy were working at the docks, fifty-eight refused to work because 'whenever they worked during the night they would not work the next day'. Still subject to the Masters and Servants Act, they were given the option of fourteen days hard labour or a £1 fine by the magistrate. In 1893 some forty-seven refused to work, saying that they had only signed six-month contracts. Although McKenzie denied this, and took them to court saying that they had signed for twelve months, the dock workers won their case and were free to leave. Later in the year 200 stopped working when McKenzie failed to pay them on the right day and only went back to work when he had.[55] In 1896, in another dispute over the length of contract, forty-five attempted to leave for the Transkei. Arrested, and after another court case, eight were initially sentenced to two months hard labour. But eighteen others won their case following corroboration of their argument by a magistrate in the Transkei. Their acquittal presumably cleared all the accused.[56]

There is no record of collective action by dock workers between 1897 and 1901. This may have been precisely because the migrant labour and barrack system set up by McKenzie fell away during these years following the court battles of 1896. At some stage during that year McKenzie certainly went back to paying all labourers at the rate of 4s 6d per day.[57]

It was only during the bubonic plague that African dock workers, then mostly living in District Six, next went on strike. They did so in February 1901 when made to file one by one through the Dock gates so that Harbour Board officials could register their names and addresses. These dock workers feared that they were about to be compounded in the severely restricted fashion of Black workers on the Kimberley mines.

After assurances from McKenzie to the contrary, they went back to work.

Less than a month later it became clear to Africans in Cape Town that residential segregation was imminent. Despite a further strike by African dock workers and two public meetings, including one on the Grand Parade which was broken up by the police, the majority of Africans were evicted from their homes and forced, at bayonet point, to move to locations. In the case of 1,500 dock workers this meant twenty-seven sheds near the convict barracks enclosed by a substantial fence and under the authority of a location superintendant appointed by the Harbour Board. There was a cookhouse, recreation room, and a small hospital. Sanitary arrangements consisted of an open trough flushed three times a day. Residence in this location was subject to the predictable regulations about alcohol and visitors, with the curfew set at 8 p.m.[58]

In the course of the next few months the Harbour Board took over all stevedoring work, as well as cartage to and from the docks. Apart from running the location, the Board established separate departments to handle the recruitment and employment of a labour force that was estimated to range in numbers from 1,500 to 3,000 Africans. Working through the Cape Native Affairs Department, migrants recruited in the next few years were largely Gaiakas and Gcalekas from the Transkei.[59]

The new migrants demonstrated similar solidarity to their predecessors. With limited alternative possibilities in the way of entertainment, they occasionally locked their huts from the inside and indulged in music-making and dancing. Some of their songs by 1903 talked not just of rural life, as they had ten years earlier, but also of life in the docks and the hard lot of Africans in Cape Town. One described the 'ringing of the six o'clock bell calling to work at the 'docksin' [Docks Location] and...the hard life of the native in Cape Town, banished from home and comfort, and compelled to eat calves' heads and such poor food'.[60]

Many of the disputes that migrant dock workers now had with the Harbour Board were about the conditions in the location. Some, such as the right to turn lights on or off in their huts throughout the night, they did manage to win. But solidarity bred in part precisely through mutual confinement spread into workplace conflicts, such as successful refusal to work in dreadful weather. From the middle of the year they challenged the Board's decision to deduct the cost of bringing them to the Western Cape from their pay.[61]

What was new about dock-worker protests in 1901 was their frequency and the forms that some of them took. In particular there were written protests from headmen. They had brought down batches of migrants

10   Alfred Mangena

from the Transkei and thereafter acted as serangs or gang leaders over the same men at the docks. The headmen, who wrote some letters of protest of their own, appointed a young man from Natal, Alfred Mangena, as their 'Senior Secretary' or chief negotiator with the Board during the passage money dispute. Mangena had arrived in Cape Town in 1898 to try and make enough money to get to London and train as a barrister. By 1901 he was staying in an Anglican parsonage and helping to run one of their night schools for Africans. After the establishment of the docks location, he visited the dock workers in their huts in the company of an Anglican evangelist, Father Bull. Both Mangena in his position as their secretary, and Bull in his capacity as their priest, wrote letters to the Harbour Board about the passage money dispute and conditions in the location. The cost was eventually borne jointly by the Board and the Cape Government Railways, which was another major employer of African migrant labour in Cape Town.[62]

The position of African dock workers was weakened by the fact that, until at least April 1902, they had to apply for 'Plague Passes' to leave the city. After April they were still subject to enforced segregation. The only legal alternative to the docks location was the one at Uitvlugt, soon renamed Ndabeni, several miles away from their place of employment. Yet African dock workers were successful in many of their protests in 1901 partly because their labour was still very much in demand, as labour was generally during the Boer War. In particular, the imperial army competed with the Board to employ African labour at its military camp on Green Point Common, almost next door to the docks location. The high demand for labour, combined with the scale of migrant worker protests in the 1900s, may explain why the Harbour Board ceased to use the Masters and Servants Act to prosecute strikers when it took over McKenzie's work.[63]

Dock workers successfully resisted an attempt by the Board to reduce their wages in November 1901. The presence of banners at an earlier strike, over which day of the week the Harbour Board should pay them, was significant. It demonstrated that the technology of literacy, employed in the correspondence of Mangena and the headmen with the Board, was becoming a weapon employed by African workers in moments of large-scale group protest.[64]

Group protest was not confined to dock workers or artisans. There were rare, recorded occasions when unskilled workers in other occupations demonstrated similar solidarity. When they did so, many of the factors that help to explain the extent of protest among dock workers were also present, particularly shared migrancy and isolated or confined living quarters. A group of five women were 'imported' from St Helena in July 1896 on a three-year contract to live and work at a boarding house in Sea Point. After two weeks they refused to go on working because their employer, a Mr King, was allegedly giving them too little to eat. They were duly hauled before the Resident Magistrate and forced back to work. In November they all attempted to desert King's service and, when unsuccessful, the 'ringleader' was fined £1 or about a month's wages. Sarah Samuels tried again in February 1897, and this time managed a successful defence when caught, on the grounds that all of their contracts were invalid: some of the women were under age and three-year contracts were anyway illegal at the Cape, a point of law strangely overlooked by the magistrate in 1896.[65]

Less successful were 100 Africans employed in building a reservoir. They were living and working on the top of Table Mountain when they went on strike for higher pay in May 1901. The fact that they were unsuccessful may have been because, at 3,500 feet above any place for buying food, they were rather too isolated.[66]

Forms of protest were not confined, of course, to group action. Notably, domestic service often involved a relationship between an individual worker and her or his employer. The expansion of employment opportunities for women from the 1880s onwards gave some domestic workers the chance to choose jobs as shop assistants or factory workers. This was one of the reasons why female domestic labour was imported from Britain and St Helena in the 1890s.

The fact that many women preferred factory or shop work to domestic service was probably the lack of freedom it involved.[67] Certainly many of the conflicts between 'Madams' and 'Maids' in the course of this decade involved the latter trying to increase her freedom: staying out late, sometimes overnight or smuggling in male visitors.[68] A rare letter to a newspaper from a domestic servant complained that domestics were often not given any day off on a regular basis. They had to ask if they wanted one and the frequent reply was that 'it was not respectable to go out in the evening'.[69] Domestic work usually involved lack of privacy, loneliness, long hours and low pay. There were also complaints of unfair demands or bad treatment by employers. The contracts that have survived for British aided immigrants demonstrate that even the better-paid domestic servants were subject to severe restrictions. The servant was required

to receive no visitors without special permission from her Master or Mistress ... to be within the house every day after sunset except by special permission from her Master or Mistress ... to inform her Master or Mistress forthwith of any act of drunkenness, theft or immorality on the part of a fellow servant of which she may become aware.

Under this contract the servant was allowed to attend church, but only every alternate Sunday. She was given leave of absence from 2 p.m. to 5 p.m. once every month.[70]

Such conditions were the background to recurrent cases of work done reluctantly, theft or desertion on the part of women in domestic service.[71] But even restricted as they were, a network of sorts existed that could lead to the boycott by local workers of particular employers. As one complained, if employers dismissed a servant, 'her version' would be told to acquaintances. A new servant would be obtained only with the 'greatest difficulty'.[72]

To avoid prosecution under the Masters and Servants Act, many workers pleaded sickness or unfair treatment when deserting in favour of better employment. In a period of economic expansion it was actions such as these, as well as the realisation by employers that they faced competition in the labour market, that raised the level of wages of unskilled workers unable to organise general strikes. One correspondent to the *Cape Times* wrote in 1901 that the 'Natives'' first question was 'Work, Boss?'. Their second was 'How much?'. He said that Africans understood the laws of supply and demand only too well.[73]

There are numerous examples of workers legally leaving service to seek better employment, one of the few legitimate weapons at the disposal of workers employed on a daily basis in Cape Town's labour market. For instance, in 1889 street-cleaners left the town council's employment to seek work at the docks after the strike of that year raised wages. In 1892 100 non-migrant dock workers gained higher wages by working for the Cape government on the Guano Islands.[74]

Both individually and collectively workers demonstrated the desire and often the capacity to improve the conditions and financial rewards of their labour. Collective action became far more frequent by the 1890s. It had been facilitated by changes in methods of production and by employers reorganising their labour often, somewhat ironically, in an attempt to make it more easily controllable. Those changes meant that divisions of labour not only accorded more closely with ethnicity, they promoted greater ethnic awareness among Cape Town's working class. Particular ethnicities often promoted occupational solidarity on the part of particular groups of workers. Equally, their ethnicity was given added salience to its adherents precisely through group action and organisation.

The arrival of African migrants in large numbers into specific occupations came at a time when some artisans were expressing craft exclusivity that was also White exclusivity. The dominant class was busy separating White from Black in many institutions and facilities, and then Africans from other Blacks. These developments promoted the emergence of a Coloured ethnicity in Cape Town.

8   A darker shade than pale?

The practice and ideology of segregation was the response of Cape Town's dominant class, as well as the Cape government, to the economic and demographic change that threatened White hegemony. Segregation and increased racism helped to shape the form of Black ethnicities and political responses, while being shaped by them. In the course of the 1890s the political initiatives of a Malay elite merged into a broader Black political identity which culminated in the establishment of the African Political Organisation (APO) in 1902. This happened largely because many Muslim and Christian Black Capetonians wished to distinguish themselves from 'Natives', people such as the Mfengus, Gaikas and Gcalekas who were mostly confined to locations in 1901. The African Political Organisation became, in fact, the political vehicle of people who called themselves Coloureds.

Black ethnicities were not the simple products of dominant-class racialisations and discrimination. But nor were they the mere creations of elite ethnic mobilisers. Labels, such as 'Native' or 'Coloured', may have been imposed by Whites and used by Black elites to challenge state policies or to demand resources in the late nineteenth century. But the labels had to make sense to those they wished to mobilise. The latter were not *tabula rasa*, and the content of ethnicities could not be purely imagined by elites, whose experiences anyway were not always far removed from those of lower-class members of the group. Equally, ethnic mobilisation for political purposes had to take some account of the needs of lower-class adherents, and thus did not solely reflect elite demands.

The term 'Coloured', as we saw in chapter 2, was used by Whites in the middle of the nineteenth century in two ways: either to describe all Blacks or, more narrowly, just those who were not Bantu-speaking Africans. In the course of the nineteenth century some people defined as 'Coloured' used the term to describe themselves. The fact that they did so was the result of a dialectical relationship between racialisation by Whites and self-definition.

186

Communities consisting predominantly of ex-slaves and Khoisan were formed during the period of slavery, and continued to be formed or re-formed thereafter. Some of these communities were in the countryside – on mission stations, in village locations and in the form of rare rural settlements such as those at Kat River. Other communities, for example that of Cape Town's Malays, were urban. Kinship and occupational ties, as well as cultural forms, helped forge community identities in these places. Cultural forms, such as stories about the past and Emancipation Day celebrations, served to remind members of their shared heritage of oppression and bondage. So did continued White domination of power and resources, the continued perceivable correlation between darker pigmentation and deprivation.

We still know very little about connections between communities, but some were undoubtedly provided by the labour mobility, migration and service in colonial levies of community members.[1] Creole-Dutch, or proto-Afrikaans, became the linguistic medium of communication. This language was not just a product of slave and Khoisan acculturation to colonial culture, the culture of their 'masters'. It was forged through social interaction and mutual linguistic influence.[2]

One occasion that brought members of Malay and Black Christian communities together in Cape Town was the New Year carnival. The form and content of carnival suggests how many Black Capetonians celebrated a shared heritage of bondage that cut across religious divides. There were three kinds of street paraders who participated: 'Malay Choirs' or *Nagtroepe* (night bands), 'Christmas Choirs' (who demanded alms for their churches) and 'Coon' troupes. Costumes were made by families engaged in tailoring and paid for on the set-aside system during the year.

The New Year celebrations were the climax of a festival period that started at the beginning of December, with a commemoration of Emancipation Day, and carried on to the 'big days' of Christmas and New Year, the traditional slave holiday. Street processions accompanied by music occurred as early as 1823. By the 1870s many paraders, influenced by visiting American minstrel groups, were organised into singing and sporting clubs distinguished by different costumes.[3] That Scottish singer David Kennedy, perhaps because of his own profession, had noticed Malay street singers on his visit in March 1879:

In the beautiful starry evenings you hear their part-songs, some of the fellows singing at their open windows; and now and again a string of them extending across the broad street and shouting ballads to the accompaniment of guitar and concertina ... the latest success of the concert-room is reproduced immediately in the streets of the Malay quarter.[4]

Celebrations on the streets of Cape Town closely paralleled their counterparts in Luanda, analysed by David Birmingham. Both sets of celebrations involved the 'taming' of peoples and cultures from 'all over the world'. Cape Town's celebrations incorporated the folk musical traditions of Malay slaves, Khoisan, Europeans and Americans. Both Cape Town and Luanda's carnivals would appear to have been occasions of conspicuous consumption, celebrating a counter-culture of 'hedonism and ostentation' that was the source of such adverse comment from members of Cape Town's dominant class.[5] As the *Cape Times* reported in January 1886, large and 'frivolous' groups of Coloured people 'dressed most fantastically, carrying guys, and headed by blowers of wind and players of stringed instruments' paraded through Cape Town. The songs they performed included variations on Rule, Britannnia! and the Old Hundredth.[6]

What we know of the form and content of Cape Town's festivities suggests the usual ambivalences of carnival. Most participants were motivated first and foremost by the desire to have fun. Many of the older 'street songs' or 'drum songs' (*ghoemaliedjies*) and their newer adaptations performed at New Year told of amorous adventures or misadventures, were in a sense 'frivolous'. But even some of these love songs contained satirical allusions to the dominant class which the performers and their families would understand. As such they were part of an alternative and potentially oppositional culture. Occasionally songs were overtly political. One variation of Rule, Britannia! that we know of, and that may not have been understood by English-speaking journalists, included the lines:

> *Kom Brittanje, jy beskaaf,*
> *Maak die nasies tot jou slaaf ...*
> *Jou dwinglandy sal gou verneer*
> *Die wat hulle land eige noem.*

> [Come Britannia, the civilising one,
> Make the nations into slaves ...
> You tyranny will soon humble
> Those that call this land their own.][7]

When not overtly political, *ghoemaliedjies* could still express satirical hostility to a post-emancipation society that retained similarities with social relations in the era of slavery, and that appeared to leave political and legal power in the hands of others:

> Here I am again ...
> In front of the door ...
> In front of the Judge ...

And the Magistrate, . . .
Oe la, my master,
What did I do?
Then they give me nine months
In Roeland Street [i.e. in gaol].[8]

Cape Town's carnival was a celebration of freedom like its counterpart in Luanda. Both were festivals 'in which people rejoiced . . . [celebrations of] . . . an identity with neighbours and kinsfolk . . . of defiance before the uncomprehending bourgeoisie'.[9] As such all the 'big day' festivities held the potential to promote a broader community consciousness among slave descendants which could comprehend Muslim and Christian alike. At least some of the lyrics of *ghoemaliedjies* overtly expressed, and furthered, this consciousness:

> Listen to what the people are saying,
> The people of Canal Town ['Kanal Dorp', another name for District Six in the late nineteenth century][10]

A number of factors helped to give this broader communal consciousness an ethnic dimension that could subsume Malayness. Christian evangelism and rural migration to Cape Town gathered pace in the late nineteenth century, and the percentage of Muslims among non-Bantu-speaking Black Capetonians dwindled from 40 per cent in 1875 to 22 per cent in 1904. At the same time industrialisation and new methods of production were eroding the juxtaposition of Malayness with remunerative skills in artisanal crafts and 'traditional' occupations. Fewer Malays were being apprenticed, and White exclusivity, whether imposed by government in its training institutions or by White artisans in their craft unions, aided this process of displacement.[11]

In the 1880s the opening of a municipal wash-house and the establishment of a steam laundry – 'better than Malays . . . bashing clothes against stones' – threatened the position of Malay washerwomen at Platteklip.[12] In the 1890s bigger fishing boats, manned by Italian immigrants, and trawlers undermined the position of Malay fishermen, as trams and (in the 1900s) cars undermined the position of horse-drawn cab-drivers.[13] Growing separation of all Blacks from all Whites in government institutions from the 1880s, as well as White social and workplace exclusivity, helped determine that an ethnicity based on darkness of pigmentation would become increasingly likely among Cape Town's lower classes. So did the experience of White racism.

The question was whether this ethnicity would include all Black Capetonians and what label it would be given. In 1884 a *Lantern* reporter travelling 'Round Dangerous Cape Town with a detective' was barred entrance to the Caledonian Dance Hall, situated in a working-class area above the castle. He was told that this hall was for 'brown' people only. In 1893 an *Argus* reporter visited a doss-house near the docks and was told that Whites would not be welcome. As one inmate told him, 'you tink a black man a —— loafer'.[14]

At the workplace, in canteens and during neighbourly rows Black Capetonians often had to suffer insults from Whites, were called 'Hottentot' or 'Nigger'. In 1889 some suffered more than mere insults – a hundred 'White boys' attacked about the same number of 'Negroes' with 'sticks, knobkerries and other paraphernalia'. At less impassioned times Blacks would have to hear themselves referred to by Whites as 'Cape Boys' or 'Girls', Browns, Coloureds, Malays, 'Coolies' or 'Kaffirs'.[15]

To what extent they accepted each or any of these appellations, or gave themselves others, is hard to ascertain. If many Muslims did think of themselves at times as Malays, such an identity would hardly have been an option for the majority of Black Christians. If people referred to themselves as Cape Boys or Girls, as some did on occasion, they may well have done so only in deference to White susceptibilities.

What is clear is that the large-scale migration of Africans in the 1880s and 1890s approximately accorded with divisions of labour. Arriving with a different sense of shared origins to most local Blacks, and with their own cultural practices including a Bantu dialect, many of these migrants were also residentially separated by their employers from other Black Capetonians. Combined with the Cape government's differential treatment of such Africans from the late 1890s, this helped to prevent the development of a strong and inclusive Black ethnicity among Cape Town's lower classes. Instead, the majority of Black Capetonians could and did distinguish themselves from Africans.

Labourers from Mozambique had arrived in large numbers between 1878 and 1882, and many stayed. 'Mozambiquan' became a term in the 1880s applied to strangers whether they were from that part of the world or not, a term that had connotations of colour (degree of blackness) and foreignness rather than being an accurate description of geographical origin; thus the incident in which Adriaan Levindaal, a 'dock coolie' who worked for McKenzie, was assaulted in a canteen by James Williams in 1884. The assault came after Levindaal had referred to Williams as a 'Mozambiquer ... you are not master of the canteen', and had gone on to say that he would kick this Mozambiquan to death. Williams was, in fact, from Sierra Leone. Similarly, in 1886, a fourteen-year-old girl, Abida, referred to a man called Frederick Punter as 'a Mozambiquan man'. Punter was actually from the West Indies.[16]

African labourers from the Eastern Cape in the 1890s became known among many other working-class Capetonians as 'Kaffirs' or 'Natives'. Thus, describing a fracas between a foreman and African labourers at the docks in 1892, Africa George said: 'I was working at the coal and was called and a lot of Kaffirs had the last witness down'. In 1897 a 'coolie' was asked by a White visitor to Cape Town whether he was a 'native' of the Colony. He replied that he was not, that he was English. Pointing to people the reporter described as 'coal-carrying Kaffirs', he said that they were the natives.[17]

The arrival of Eastern Cape Africans as migrant workers at the docks led to numerous fights between them and local Black labourers in the 1890s. Such conflict was not just the result of one ethnic group perceiving and disliking another due to differences in appearance, language or culture, although these factors helped to make distinction possible. Rather, conflict came because local dock workers were being replaced by cheap African labour – also a reason why the term 'Mozambiquan' may have been used as one of opprobrium by Levendaal – and because in some instances 'Cape Boys' were put in supervisory situations over Africans.[18]

Legislation or *de facto* practice that discriminated specifically against Africans helped to stifle an inclusive Black ethnicity. Thus the 1898 Liquor Law banned the sale of alcohol to 'aboriginal Natives'. The enforcement of this law meant that White liqour sellers and magistrates had to distinguish between 'Natives' and other Blacks and act on those distinctions. The difficulty that some had in doing so led to a deputation to the government in 1901 by liqour wholesalers and retailers. One complained that he had been fined for selling to 'Cape Boys' who turned out not to be Cape Boys, as well as for not selling to genuine Cape Boys. Another said that he employed a man 'conversant with native dialect ... to question each Cape boy or native' before he entered his premises. The Attorney-General, Sir James Rose Innes, told the deputation that they should decide 'by appearance, hair, colour, and other signs, whether a man was a Cape boy or whether he had the characteristic hair and features of the Bantu tribes'.[19]

It followed that Black Capetonians wishing to escape the provisions of the law would be encouraged to define themselves as not belonging to the 'Bantu tribes'. One instance of this took place in 1902 when Rosie Coetzee was convicted by the Simon's Town Resident Magistrate because he thought that she was illegally buying liquor. The case came on appeal to Cape Town's Supreme Court where the accused 'denied she was an aboriginal native, and said that her father was a White man'. The judge convicted Rosie Coetzee on the grounds that there 'seemed to be no doubt that this woman was of the Bantu race'.[20]

Two other pieces of legislation made similar distinctions between Black Cape citizens, promoted potentially similar self-definitions by those who did not wish to be prosecuted as a result. In 1902 'natives' were forbidden by the Morality Act from having sexual intercourse with White prostitutes. Much more importantly, in 1901 most Africans in Cape Town were forced into locations. This action was 'legalised' in 1902 by the Native Reserve Location Act.[21]

By 1902 some Black Capetonians, who wished to distinguish themselves from Africans, were calling themselves Coloured. From the 1830s 'Coloured' was just one of a variety of ethnic labels used by members of communities of the ex-bonded to describe themselves when outlining their demands, needs or fears to Whites. At Kat River from the 1830s to the 1850s this label seems to have been 'Hottentot'. A meeting at Philipton in 1834 was called to protest the possibility of vagrancy legislation. The people present described themselves as 'a small part of the remnant of the Hottentot nation, ... who were reduced to a state of want, servitude ... in some respects worse than slavery itself'.[22] Sixteen years later, this time under threat from a proposed squatter ordinance, many peasants at Kat River rebelled under the leadership of Uithaalder, who wrote 'we the oppressed Hottentot race' when appealing to the leader of another rural community, Adam Kok, to join the rebellion.[23]

Another label, 'Coloured', was used by petitioners from a number of mission stations across the Cape in the early 1850s who were worried about their fate under imminent Representative Government. There was a further petition in 1871, on the eve of Representative Government, from 'coloured persons engaged as general labourers' at Genadendal mission station near Caledon. These petitioners were responding to a government select committee on the Masters and Servants Act and complained of prejudice against 'colour, race and class'.[24] In 1873 Dr Andrew Jackson and his 120 fellow petitioners from Cape Town had also called themselves 'coloured' when protesting about possible discriminatory liquor legislation; the correspondent commenting on seating arrangements at St George's Cathedral in 1877 referred to himself and other 'coloured folk' as those on the receiving end of White exclusivity.

'Coloured' endured as a label into the late nineteenth century not just because it was a response to continued White racialisation and discrimination, although this was crucial. Like 'White' as a label for Afrikaners and English, 'Coloured' as a self-description stressed the fact that shade of pigmentation closely correlated with historical and contemporary experience at the Cape for Hottentots, Malays or people called 'Bastards' alike.[25] The label could have this meaning for members of different communities, whether community consciousness was partly the result of Islamic or different Christian denominational practices. And mission communities, such as the DRC St Stephen's and the Anglican St Paul's or St Philip's, had come into being in Cape Town as evangelisation gathered pace after emancipation.

Therefore, when a Malay elite made common political cause with its Black Christian counterpart in Cape Town and the Cape Colony at large in the 1890s, it made sense that they did so as Coloureds. This political mobilisation became part of the process that aided the emergence of a Coloured, rather than a Brown or (more obviously unacceptable) Cape Boy, ethnicity among members of Cape Town's lower classes. To understand how this happened it is necessary to begin by revisiting the Malay community and its conflicts with local and central government before the 1890s. Dominant-class antipathy to Malays between 1875 and 1882 had been heightened by the fact that the latter were part of an established, un-English and, in the early 1880s, increasingly assertive ethnic community. Malays were bound together by practices and beliefs that included Islam. Islam was thus a critical component of the community's 'inherent' ideology.[26]

The Malay elite, like other Black elites, consisted of the relatively small number of Western-educated, largely petty-bourgeois individuals who could qualify for the vote. Among them were 'small shopkeepers, fruit vendors, tradesmen, coachmen' as well as fishermen, artisans and the handful of professionals. The political ideology of this elite had at its core a belief in the legitimacy of the non-racial Cape constitution and the reality of equality before the law achieved by emancipation. Even when justice seemed scarce, belief in the 'fundamental morality of political institutions' continued, and not always without reason.[27]

As it was there were few obvious alternatives to taking the Cape constitution at its non-racial face value in a world where Whites had a virtual monopoly of arms. Unarmed resistance to colonial authority, or the use of stones in the case of the cemetery riots, led to swift and effective suppression. Black elites also had their own relatively privileged position within Cape society to consider. As Gavin Lewis has put it: 'Revolution and anarchy were not just unattainable, but also undesirable.'[28]

And participation in constitutional politics could bring small but meaningful victories, not always defeats. Thus fishermen had successfully petitioned the Cape parliament and Governor when trying to stop a ban on fish-curing at Rogge Bay in the late 1870s. Albeit with an evident degree of apprehension, Jongie Siers, John Mahomet, Jacobus Bruin and Andries Forster had written:

We were always under the impression that we were emancipated in the reign of our most Gracious Majesty Queen Victoria, and freed from tyranny, but it seems that we are mistaken, as our rulers (perhaps without intention) are depressing us [sic]; surely it is without the proper knowledge of the extent of our misfortunes.[29]

Petitions could be successful; with the 'proper knowledge' rulers did sometimes listen and reverse their policies. Together with the lack of obvious alternatives, this was presumably the reason why members of the Malay elite, such as Siers and Abdol Burns, lent support to the small tradition of Cape liberalism from the 1860s to the 1880s. They backed English-speaking mercantile or business candidates for central political office. In the process they helped to deliver the Malay vote. But they did not do so unconditionally. Burns, a supporter of Saul Solomon in the Assembly elections of 1879, supported Murison in the Legislative council elections of 1878. Significantly, in an election address Burns hoped that Murison would not discriminate according to 'colour, creed, or nation'.[30] Jongie Siers, who supported Ebden in the same election, said that 'we would that our children will never fail to support the name of Ebden'. But he went on to quote lines from Herbert, commending them to Ebden's attention: 'Find our men's wants and will.' Ebden replied glibly that he would do his best to be impartial 'to all classes'.[31]

The background to the partial disillusionment of Cape Town's Malay elite with White politicians, which ultimately led to their decision to field their own candidate in an Assembly election, can be traced to their letters in the English press from the late 1870s.[32] Initially, correspondents defended Malays from the racist attacks in letters and editorials made by bourgeois Whites. A recurring theme was that the whole community, a term they used, should not be judged by the actions of a few. Several Malay correspondents also complained about White exclusionary practices. For instance Abdol Kadier, replying to an attack on Malays by the anonymous 'Civis', wrote: 'The privileges which we enjoy are rather restricted, seeing that "Civis" and his white brethren have drawn a line over which we cannot step.'[33]

By the last quarter of 1882, after the vitriolic attacks on Malays in the course of the smallpox epidemic, there was a more defiant note in their correspondence. Abdol Soubeyan defended what Whites had seen as a negative stereotype by writing: 'Independence is the aim of everyone who is a little above grovelling in the mud.' He went on to suggest that if McCombie, the editor of the *Lantern*, read the *Illustrated Police News* he would stop stereotyping Malays. Soubeyan pointed out that in Britain there were 'vile abominations, foul murders, assassinations, cruelty, bloodshed, bestiality, and rapine', yet, he implied, this had obviously not led to the negative stereotyping of the British by themselves.[34] Mogarh-

Naheer, replying to the rumours about Malay washerwomen deliberately spreading smallpox, said that Malays stood to lose jobs as a consequence. He added that they were no longer interested in the press.[35]

From 1882 there were signs that Malays, faced with the increasing hostility of Englishness, were reluctant to give their support to White candidates at local and central political levels. Malays boycotted the 1882 town council and 1883 Legislative council elections.[36] The problem with boycotting as a political tactic was that its effectiveness was diminished if Malay voters only constituted a small percentage of eligible voters. Moreover, the intention of the Malay elite was to gain acceptance by the dominant class, not to bring the whole legitimacy of the Cape constitutional dispensation into question.

The frustrations they faced over the cemetery issue, coming on top of increasing English hostility and the experience of social exclusion, finally led to the decision by key members of the Malay elite to put forward their own parliamentary candidate in the late 1880s. Letters by Malays to the English-language press between 1882 and 1885 had been almost solely concerned with the cemetery issue. Members of the elite obviously hoped to obtain their wishes by agitating in a 'just and constitutional manner', in the words of Abdol Burns.[37]

This approach appeared to have been rewarded in November 1885. In that month a deputation, which included Burns, had been told by the Colonial Secretary, J. Tudhope, that he would grant a delay of twelve months in closing the cemeteries. In return, members of the deputation had to find a suitable alternative site before the end of January 1886. Thinking they had won, the deputation led 2,000 supporters up the Government Avenue alongside parliament 'as a sort of display' in honour of Tudhope.[38] Unfortunately Tudhope's decision was undermined by town council officials who turned down all the alternative sites. The result was the closure of the cemeteries and the subsequent riots.

Burns was a prominent member of the crowd at the burial on 17 June and was sentenced to two months hard labour for incitement. Other identifiable members of the elite who took part in the ultimately unsuccessful campaign against closure included Siers and younger men such as Achmat Effendi and H. O. Ally.[39] Both were to play leading roles in Black political mobilisation in the early 1890s.

This mobilisation broke with the previous 'small tradition' practice of Black support for White parliamentary candidates. In 1889 the *Lantern* reported that 'the Mahomedans [sic] of Cape Town are labouring under a violent political awakening'. Mahomet Dollie, 'a most intelligent irrepressible Hadje', had told McCombie that 'it is his down-trodden

Malay brethren's firm determination to return one of themselves at the next general election'.[40]

The next election to the Cape House of Assembly did not occur until 1894. In the meantime the raising of the franchise qualifications and government moves to introduce segregation in education, as well as the experience of exclusion in other social spheres, ensured that Christian descendants of slaves would begin to seek common political cause with their Muslim counterparts. In the process the latter's Malay ethnicity was subsumed within a broader Coloured ethnicity, just as Afrikaner and English ethnicities could be subsumed by White ethnicity.

In August 1892 a large meeting was held in Cape Town to protest against the passing of the Franchise and Ballot Act and to drum up support for a petition against it.[41] The leading figure in the drive to collect the eventual 10,341 signatures sent to the British Colonial Office was H. O. Ally. Ally, now resident in Kimberley, had helped form the Coloured People's Association (CPA) to oppose the Act.[42] The supporters of Ally and the Association in Cape Town were, according to a White reporter, 'essentially Moslem'. But at least two Christian Coloureds, James Curry and J. M. Wilson, were present.[43]

Black opposition to franchise changes in Cape Town would appear to have had some American input. In 1891 a 'coloured' house meeting on the franchise issue had been addressed by an 'American Negro ... educated at a well-known college for Negroes in the South States of America'. The *Lantern* concluded that there were 'agitators abroad'.[44]

The meeting in August 1892 was attended by 600 people. Abdol Burns was one of the speakers. He said that he respected Whites and expected respect from them in return. In a possible reference to the additional dangers to Blacks posed by the recently published Education Commission report, Burns said that he was attending because he wished to 'protect his children'. In his speech Ally stated that he wanted compulsory education for all, not just for Whites as mooted in the education report. Turning to the franchise issue, he told the audience that the supposedly liberal Merriman had said in parliament that the presence of 'Abdol' was an objectionable feature in any Cape Town election. Ally concluded by saying that he had no faith in sending petitions to the Cape parliament. Curry said that 'we coloured people have never rebelled', and asked whether 'our children' were to be slaves to the 'white man'.[45]

What we know of those who attended the August meeting, as well as Curry's words, suggests that the CPA was primarily aimed at mobilising communities of the ex-bonded. After all, Africans had rebelled in the recent past. 'Coloured' was being used as a label for those for whom the threat of slavery was almost as poignant in the 1890s as it had been in the 1830s or 1850s.

A few weeks later, Curry presided over another meeting against the Franchise Bill. Once again he also raised the matter of discrimination in education. He predicted that Coloured children would soon be taken away from school at the age of eight, that Coloureds would be unable to trade in their own names and that eventually they would not be able to own property.[46] These were all prophecies calculated to alarm Muslim and Christian Coloured elites alike.

Early in 1893 the *Cape Argus* confirmed that Achmat Effendi was going to stand as a candidate for the 1894 Assembly elections, and attributed this to the agitation over the Franchise and Ballot Act.[47] The *Lantern*'s report of 1889 suggests that such a candidature would have come with or without the Act. But both franchise and education changes in the early 1890s guaranteed such a move. The hardening of Malay opinion was revealed in January 1893 when Effendi addressed a meeting of 600 in a mosque at the top of Shortmarket Street. In his speech Imam Hamza said that 'in the past' Muslims had been paid to work for White candidates, but that this time he would not accept £1,000 for such work. At another meeting of Muslims, Imam Talip reminded his audience of previous occasions when they had stood together. 'In one body' they had refrained from voting in the town council elections of 1882, and the whole community had united over the cemetery issue.[48]

In the first half of 1893 Effendi's chances of getting elected looked promising. Because of Cape Town's cumulative voting system newspapers calculated that if all Muslim voters supported him, let alone some Christian Coloured ones, he was bound to be elected. Effendi got financial support from Kimberley, presumably courtesy of Ally and the CPA. The abolition of the cumulative vote in mid-year was the Cape government's response to this threat.[49]

Nevertheless Effendi went ahead with his campaign, overtly appealing for support beyond the Malay community. He emphasised in January 1894 that if elected he would look after all his constituents irrespective of religion. Equally he made compulsory education for all part of his election platform at a time when members of the Christian Coloured elite were continuing to hold protest meetings against government educational policy. This policy was now separating even 'off-coloured' children from White ones, and was apparently determining that school authorities would be more sensitive than hitherto to shades of pigmentation. That very month the private Catholic Marist Brothers School turned away a Coloured child.[50]

Although Effendi was defeated in 1894, he gained over 700 votes and, predictably, did best in Districts Two (which included the Malay Quarter) and Six.[51] Apart from standing on issues calculated to appeal to the small Coloured bourgeoisie, Effendi had looked for votes from those Coloured workers who still qualified for the franchise. Therefore he had demanded an end to the government practice of hiring convict labour to private employers, a practice designed to reduce the cost of labour and thereby to reduce the wages of Coloured workers in Cape Town.

Coloured political mobilisation continued after Effendi's defeat both within and outside Cape Town. A gathering of 'Coloured Political Associations' took place in the Eastern Cape in 1894. This conference had been organised by the CPA. There were delegates from a number of rural communities such as those at Graaff-Reinet and Rietvlei, as well as Somerset East itself. The conference resolved to strengthen Coloureds 'as a People', to establish branches of the CPA and to hold annual conferences. But there is no subsequent record of the CPA or any conferences it may have attempted to organise.[52]

A truly national Coloured political organisation did not reappear until the early 1900s. One reason why Coloured political mobilisation faltered in Cape Town was that members of the Christian Coloured elite were given a chance in 1895 to join a non-racial political party on equal terms with White members. Acknowledgement of their respectability, that they deserved to be accepted as equals by Whites, was the aim of Coloured elites. Political mobilisation that was also Coloured ethnic mobilisation was the reluctant alternative.

J. Wilson and a Mr 'W.' Currey, possibly James Curry, joined the Wesleyan W. B. Shaw's South African Christian Political Association (SACPA) in August 1895. At the inaugural meeting Shaw argued that 'negrophilists' had always worked in a patronising way, but he intended to work *with* Coloureds. Wilson spoke of the 'abominable' tendency towards 'class' (i.e. colour) legislation and predicted that if South Africa was united 'the coloured people would have to be sacrificed'. But the Christian Political Association seems to have been a somewhat spurious organisation, despite the credentials of its president. Shaw had defended African dock workers accused of desertion and lent his support to Coloureds fighting education segregation in 1894. He had even suggested that a test case should be made over the latter and taken to the Supreme Court if necessary. Shaw claimed that 'no man' had suffered what he had done as a result of his 'taking up the cause' of 'coloured people'. But the brevity and timing of this Association's existence casts doubt over the level of commitment of most of its probably few White supporters.

The SACPA came into existence shortly before the town council election of 1895 and folded shortly after it was over. The second and final meeting under its auspices overtly aimed at gaining Black support for one of its White members, W. A. Day. A. R. McKenzie, an opponent in the election, was condemned as the 'enemy of the coloured people'. Having failed to elect Day, the Association is heard of no more.[53]

Perhaps more important in restraining independent Coloured political mobilisation was the effects of the Jameson Raid. Stemming from the failure of the Raid came increasing imperial government intervention in southern African affairs in the late 1890s. This intervention, which culminated in the war of 1899 to 1902, was partly justified by British officials after 1897 in terms of the Transvaal Afrikaners' (or Boers') harsh treatment of Blacks, including pass laws that applied to Coloureds as well as Africans. Such rhetoric, which increased during the war itself, held out the hope of equal treatment for all British citizens to educated Coloureds. As Bill Nasson has superbly demonstrated, most Blacks in the Cape Colony threw their support behind Britain not out of mindless patriotism but because they believed that they could help turn rhetoric into reality.[54]

The Raid also polarised White politics at the Cape and breathed new life into the small tradition of Cape liberalism, appearing to convert White supremacist politicians into paragons of political, if not social, non-racialism. In 1896 the pro-British South African League launched its Coloured 'B' branches. At the 1898 elections, under pressure from the Kimberley 'B' branch, Rhodes changed his election platform from equal rights for all Whites to equal rights for all civilised men south of the Zambezi. In addition, in his speech in Cape Town on the eve of the election, Rhodes complimented the performance of the Coloured Corps (recruited from Cape Town's rural hinterland) in quelling African rebellion in Rhodesia.[55]

One of the Progressive Party candidates for Cape Town, T. J. Anderson, sensibly made education a central theme in two addresses to Coloured voters in August 1898. The first meeting was chaired by J. Wilson. Although stopping short of promising equal, let alone integrated, education, Anderson did say that he believed in 'proper' education for Coloureds, and that the government should pay for the education of those too poor to pay for themselves. He attacked the *Bond* for supporting a Transvaal government which subjected Coloureds to pass laws and the wearing of badges.

At both meetings Anderson camouflaged his vagueness on the education issue with compliments to his audience and further thinly veiled attacks on the *Bond*. He described Coloureds as 'one of the most intelligent sections of the population'. He attacked wine farmers, mostly supporters of the *Bond*, over the 'tot' system, whereby they paid their

Coloured employees partly in drink. Aware of the strength of the Temperance Movement among the Coloured elite – who believed that negative stereotyping of unrespectable Coloureds affected their chances of social acceptance by Whites – Anderson argued that employers should be forced to pay their labourers only in money. Rhodes also came out against the tot system in his last election speech. The joint efforts of Anderson and Rhodes ensured substantial Coloured support for the victorious Progressive Party in the Cape Town elections.[56]

The late 1890s did not witness the complete absence of independent Coloured political inititiatives. In April 1897 a meeting of 'Cape Coloured men' was held to protest against their inclusion under the Transvaal pass laws. W. A. Roberts, a future founder member of the APO, presided. J. Wilson, F. Gow, James Curry and the Rev R. A. Jackson were on the platform. Jackson read some poetry he had written about Coloureds that stressed their kinship with Afrikaners as well as Africans:

> For be it known by rich and poor,
> That they are akin to the black and Boer.[57]

In November 1897 a letter to the *Cape Times*, on the question of Coloured education, was written by N. R. Veldsman of the 'South African Coloured Protection Association'. Veldsman's letter came after the DRC's Rev. A. A. Weich had proposed the motion that mission education was not suited to the 'needs and wants of the coloured man' at a meeting of White mission school teachers. The motion was carried. Veldsman wanted to know whether this meant that the teachers thought that Coloureds were currently over-educated. Obviously any suspicion of further plans for inferior or different, as well as separate, education for Coloureds attracted the attention of members of the Coloured elite.[58]

In 1898 Mr De Jager, a butcher living in District Six, became the first Coloured person to stand for the town council. In an election speech, to a mostly Coloured audience, De Jager promised that he would 'fight for the coloured class'. Supported by Veldsman, De Jager went on to say that he stood for better lighting for District Six, for workmen's dwellings and against the 'capitalists' and 'speculators' already in the council. He said that he was also against the tramway companies because they took trade away from the cab drivers, most of whom were Coloured.

De Jager's candidature was partly a response to increased African migration. His speeches demonstrated a desire to distance himself and other Coloureds from 'Kaffirs', and thereby closer to Whites. He argued that African migrant labour was unnecessary, and equally that Africans worked 'for low rates' and subsequently threw 'others' (implicitly Coloureds) out of work.

De Jager's candidature was not successful. He came bottom of the poll, collecting only 355 votes. The lowest of the six successful candidates drew 1,132. De Jager was undoubtedly hampered by the plural voting system and the likelihood that few Whites voted for him. But some members of the Coloured bourgeoisie might not have supported him either. A letter to the press from 'a Coloured Voter' said that De Jager was not the right person to represent Coloureds. This was because he was 'far from fit', had 'no education, no experience and no property' and was unknown to a third of the Coloured population. De Jager was advised not 'to attempt to mix with those who are not your class'. In other words De Jager was not sufficiently respectable. De Jager might confirm White stereotypes of Coloureds, rather than eroding them, and consequently endanger the position of other, bourgeois Coloureds who had a better chance of being socially acceptable to members of the White dominant class.[59]

In the course of the 1890s 'Coloured', or 'Cape Coloured', was increasingly adopted as a self-descriptive ethnic label by people who were not accepted as White and who did not think of themselves as Natives or Africans. James Curry made the latter very clear when addressing an open-air meeting against bread and meat duties in 1897. He said that the Coloured people of Cape Town suffered as a result of them and that Coloureds 'were not like the natives of the interior who lived on mealie meal'.[60] Like De Jager, Curry was defining Coloured identity in contradistinction to 'native'.

Although there had been Black parallel organisations in the form of benefit and temperance societies or sporting clubs before the 1890s, it was in the course of this decade that both social and political organisations were established that included 'Coloured' in their title. A Coloured YMCA was formed in 1895 after the likes of James Curry had been insulted and told that they were unwelcome at the White one. W. A. Roberts, soon to be a founder member of the APO, was vice-president of the CYMCA.[61] By 1901 there was a Coloured Baptist Church. In 1898 the Western Province Coloured Rugby Football Federation included teams from Caledon, Stellenbosch, Paarl and Wellington as well as Cape Town. On 4 July 1902 the inaugural meeting of the Western Province Coloured Athletics Association and Cycling Union took place on Green Point Common. On 5 July there was a Western Province Coloured Union sports day at the same venue, which included Coloured rugby and cricket associations. Among the referees and sports officials were J. Wilson and J. Tobin, like Roberts a founder member of the APO.[62]

Through these associations and occasions, members of rural and urban communities – largely Afrikaans-speaking descendants of the ex-bonded with an educated English-speaking elite – were forging links through social activities as Coloureds. These new institutions and activities, coming on top of existing clubs and societies, helped to complete the process of forging ties and a greater sense of identity among the Coloured elite.

There is evidence that at least some Black parallel organisations, dominated by people who would appear to have thought of themselves as Coloured, accepted one or two Africans. In other words, they excluded them from the 'native' categorisation. For instance the first Black lodge of Freemasons in South Africa, launched in Cape Town, included two African clergymen as well as the likes of F. Gow and W. Collins, yet another founder of the APO. It is likely that the American African Methodist Episcopalian church (AME), which established a branch in District Six by 1902, followed a similar policy. Collins was one of its preachers.[63]

Most people who saw themselves and were seen by others as Coloureds by the early 1900s were members of those communities within and outside Cape Town dominated by descendants of the ex-bonded, even if, as in the case of the Malays, their communities were not closed to the absorption of others. It was members of these communities who joined the Coloured 'B' branches of the South African League. It was men in places as far apart as Uitenhage, Bredasdorp, Tulbagh, Swellendam and Caledon who attended meetings in October 1899 proclaiming their loyalty to Britain and calling for the formation of a Coloured Corps to fight the Boers. In the course of the war they formed Coloured town guards. If they joined the imperial forces, either as armed auxiliaries or in support capacities such as muleteers, they were likely to have their Coloured consciousness confirmed by being separated from Africans as well as Whites. As one folk song began:

> We Cape men of the farms
> Stand with the khakis and their arms
> We are spies ...
> We are scouts, we are dogs,
> We bark for Boer blood.[64]

Because communities were still being formed in Cape Town in the late nineteenth century – around places such as Moravian Hill, St Philip's or the AME – and because of the permeability of the colour-line, they probably remained more open than in the countryside. Nonetheless, members of these communities were likely by the time of the Boer War to have seen themselves, and been accepted by others, as Coloured rather than African. They were not all descended from the Cape's ex-bonded, but most were. This was partly because of the *de facto* segregation of African migrants at the docks in the 1880s and 1890s and the *de jure* residential segregation of most Africans in the early 1900s. African migration that accorded with divisions of labour at places such as the docks, as well as White exclusivity, increased the potential salience of an ethnicity that went with a sense of intermediary status.

The formation of Coloured parallel social institutions by members of the Coloured elite helped to promote Coloured ethnicity. They had doubtless formed these organisations reluctantly. But scientific racism fed into the dominant-class ideology of separation to exclude all but the very pale from inclusion in White institutions. In previous decades, the 'off-coloured' might have passed for White.

After something of a lull between 1894 and 1899, Coloured ethnic mobilisation through political organisation and journalistic endeavour gathered speed during the Boer War. To organise support for the war effort, Coloured vigilance or defence committees were established by the 'propertied' in rural communities and in Cape Town. They did so to gain from grateful imperial and colonial authorities the acceptance of Coloureds as 'civilised men', men who deserved the equal rights promised by Rhodes. When confronted with a deputation of 'Coloured men from the Western Province', the Governor of the Cape, Lord Milner, renewed this promise in January 1901.[65]

In at least one rural community, Mamre, as well as in Cape Town, Coloured political associations were formed for much the same underlying reason as the vigilance committees.[66] The guiding spirit behind both vigilance and political associations in Cape Town was F. Z. S. Peregrino, a British-educated Ghanaian. Peregrino had spent the ten years before his arrival in Cape Town in 1900 living in the United States.

In January 1901 Peregrino launched the *South African Spectator*. Peregrino used this newspaper to promote Coloured 'race' pride. His first edition was prefaced by the words 'This is for you', and went on to state that Whites had done everything to 'build up their race ... Coloured people! take a lesson from him' [sic]. His paper preached the gospel of self-help and respectability as the way to remove White prejudice. Peregrino savagely attacked those Coloureds, such as prostitutes, who fell short of the required standards.

Not unnaturally, given his own background, Peregrino sometimes defined 'Coloured' as 'all those not known as White'. At other times he distinguished in his columns between Coloureds and Natives. On these occasions his use of 'Coloured' reflected developing local usage. His appeals to Coloured 'race' pride could be read in this way both by Whites and Blacks.[67]

The political organisation Peregrino formed was the Coloured Men's Political Protection Association. W. A. Roberts became its secretary. In 1901 Peregrino also helped John Tobin establish regular open-air meetings every Sunday at the Stone, in District Six. The Stone was a large boulder in a piece of open ground at the top of Caledon Street. The meetings were intended 'for the political education of the masses'.[68]

If the promises of Rhodes and Milner had given the Coloured elite renewed hope of gaining equal rights with Whites, increased racism during and after the bubonic plague, particularly in the form of experiencing exclusion from trams and trains, partly disillusioned them. Peregrino himself was hit by a ticket-collector when he tried to board a suburban train at Newlands. In March 1901 Peregrino headed a deputation to the government to protest at this kind of treatment. The deputation included Roberts, Gow and Tobin. They were told by the minister in charge of railways that, in future, personal cleanliness would be the only criterion for deciding who could travel on trains.[69]

The Treaty of Vereeniging, which ended the war, was a more bitter blow delivered as it was by the imperial government. The treaty allowed the White settlers in the defeated republics the right to decide whether Blacks should be included in the franchise after self-government had been regained. In effect equal rights would not be extended to all civilised men south of the Zambezi. Promises given by White leaders had been broken, Coloured patriotism betrayed.[70]

Even before the war there had been Black scepticism about the likelihood of a new dispensation. In 1898 'Ishmael' had written to the Cape Times saying that Coloured people should not accept White leadership. Ishmael had attended a talk given by a Black American, Bishop Turner of the AME. Turner had stressed the equality of Black and White, and his speech was the inspiration for Ishmael's letter. But, according to Ishmael, no Whites led Blacks for the good of the latter and he thus urged Coloured leaders once again to take up their own cause.[71]

It was Tobin, Roberts and Collins, together with three other members of the Coloured elite, who answered this call in September 1902. They formed the African Political Organisation. The name conveyed their desire to 'promote unity between the coloured races'. But the APO became primarily a vehicle for defending specifically the 'Coloured People's social, political and civil rights', as stated in the party's constitution. This was a popular message with Coloured communities in the Colony as a whole. Soon after its formation the APO had branches at Genadendal and Caledon as well as two branches in Cape Town. By 1904 the APO had 2,000 members in 33 branches spread across the colony.[72]

The APO promoted Coloured ethnicity as a group identity that could unite communities of the ex-bonded. Contact between members of these communities had increased during the war when they served together as auxiliaries or in transport units, or when they visited new communities in these capacities. Contacts were also made as some Coloureds shared the experience of being refugees.

Abdullah Abdurahman, a British-educated doctor and Achmat Effendi's brother-in-law, became the APO's president in 1905, a position he held until his death in 1940. Given his prominence in Coloured musical and debating societies, Abdurahman's appointment was symbolic of the fusion of interests between Muslim and Christian elites by the 1900s. Ethnic mobilisation through the APO became the means by which those elites tried to organise Coloureds to fight politically for equal rights. Their efforts informed dominant-class racialisation. The compilers of the 1904 census divided the Cape's population into Europeans, Coloureds and Africans. As the introduction to the census put it, there were now three 'clearly defined race groups in this colony: White, Bantu and Coloured ... [who consisted of] all intermediate shades between the first two'.[73]

As part of the process of ethnic mobilisation, the APO became involved in defending the economic interests of Coloured workers in Cape Town, be they artisans, fishermen or town council street-cleaners against Whites and Africans alike. Prominent leaders, such as Abdurahman presided over sports meetings and, after 1906, at prize-givings for Coon Carnival performances repeated on Green Point Common after the frenzy of New Year itself. APO leaders were trying to save all Coloureds, including themselves, from the potentially worse fate of suffering discrimination aimed specifically at 'natives'.[74]

Africans in Cape Town also fought for their rights. They did not accept discriminatory legislation meekly. But their initial resistance to enforced residential segregation in 1901 was broken by force of White arms. Their meeting on the Grand Parade in 1901 was ended by a contingent of mounted police. Troops forced them out of their houses and into the locations.[75]

But in forcing Africans into either the docks location or Ndabeni the government was helping to create communities. Community consciousness, as so often in South African history, was welded by 'outside forces' and 'external acts of hostility'. The fence that delineated these locations was their all-too-obvious 'spatial boundary'.[76]

The 6,000 Africans moved to Ndabeni were forced to live in appalling conditions. To make matters worse, after three months the government decided to charge them rent to cover the cost of accommodation and the

11   Ndabeni location in 1901

train fares to and from central Cape Town where most worked. This made it quite clear to residents that their exile was not just a temporary measure brought about by the plague.

Ethnic identity as 'natives' interacted with communal consciousness and informed subsequent resistance by residents of Ndabeni to their predicament. Native, or what became African, ethnicity pre-dated 1901. This ethnicity was promoted by divisions of labour: Bantu-speaking migrants filled the least desirable jobs in Cape Town. They were also subject to prohibition under the Liquor Law of 1898 and subject to racist taunts by Whites and Coloureds alike. As one resident of Ndabeni put it: 'It is hard to live in Cape Town. It is Kafir, here, Kafir there, and Kafir everywhere. Poor Kafir!'[77]

The experience of forced removal, and having to come to terms with who was being singled out among Black Capetonians for this treatment, undoubtedly enhanced African ethnicity. As 'Disgusted Native' wrote to the *South African News* in 1901:

We are sent out, but foreigners are invited to come and take possession ... we deserve better treatment from a government that boasts of equal rights for all men, irrespective of creed or colour. Our homes are being broken up, furniture soiled and spoiled, and in many cases destroyed.[78]

The shared sense of wrong, of oppression, was crucial in producing a communal response to government actions in the form of highly effective rent boycotts in the course of 1901 and 1902. By January 1902, between £12,000 and £13,000 was due in rent, but only £700 had been collected. When the government separated the payment of train fares from rent, to try and cut their losses, residents boycotted the trains.[79]

Successful action was also facilitated by leadership. Here again, as was the case with African workers in the docks location, Alfred Mangena was prominent. Mangena, like members of the Coloured elite and 'Disgusted Native', had become disillusioned with promises of equal rights. In 1899 he had chaired a meeting of 'leading' Africans in the city held to demonstrate their support for the British cause. Among the resolutions forwarded to the British government was one that expressed gratitude that 'the Chief Minister of the Queen has mentioned the welfare of the Native peoples as one of the things he is bearing in mind'.[80]

When the removals took place Mangena, who had been allowed to remain living in a rectory in the city centre, wrote to the *Cape Times* complaining that there was 'one law for black, one for white'. He asked whether Blacks would be exempted from equal taxation and warned that the more Africans were rejected, the more the gulf would increase between them and Whites.[81] Mangena began to represent the interests of

12 The open-trucked train carrying location residents between Ndabeni and Cape Town

the Ndabeni residents more directly in August 1901, at much the same time as he began writing to the Harbour Board on behalf of the dock workers. Initially he protested about the accommodation at Ndabeni, where residents had to sleep on wet sand. By December he was arguing that the location was actually illegal.[82]

In 1902 Mangena was supported in his argument by a member of the British and Cape Bars, Advocate Wilkinson, and a 'law-agent', Mr Karie. Several clergymen, including the Anglican Owen Davis, were sympathetic to Mangena's argument and sided with the residents of Ndabeni, much to the horror of colonial officials. Dr Gregory, the Medical Officer of Health, wrote to the Colonial Secretary: 'This gentleman has not been many years in the Colony and looks upon the Native as an equal and a brother and practically treats as an equal the natives in his household.'[83] Another sympathiser was a District Six doctor and would-be 'working-man's' member of the Legislative Assembly, Alfred Sellar.[84]

It was the 'derived' knowledge that all these men provided, combined with the inherent sense of oppression of the residents themselves, that explains the effectiveness of communal action in 1901 and 1902. A further factor may have been the derived ideology of Ethiopianism: Black self-reliance as preached by evangelists of the Ethiopian Church in the location in 1902.[85]

One of the outcomes of communal resistance, resistance which has been vividly described by Christopher Saunders, was that the government was forced to 'legalise' the location by means of the Native Reserve Location Act of 1902. By the time the Act was passed, Mangena had left for England to start his legal studies. Resistance thereafter became more disparate, less obviously organised. Individuals left without paying their rent; the regulations banning the consumption of liquor in the location were ignored; large numbers of Africans went back to living illegally in Cape Town or squatting outside the boundaries of the municipality.

However, the nature of the communal resistance of Africans in Ndabeni foreshadowed similar tactics by location residents in South Africa in subsequent decades. And although Mangena left for England and duly qualified as a barrister, he returned to practise in South Africa. In 1912 he was one of the founders of the South African Native National Congress, the forerunner of the ANC.[86]

9   Conclusion

Between 1875 and 1902 the Mineral Revolution had fuelled changes in Cape Town's economic activity and demographic composition. Of crucial importance was the growth of new divisions of labour and their close correlation with ethnicity. The correlation stemmed from the particular and changing demands for labour in Cape Town – be they a result of changes in employment practices at the docks or changes within the building or tailoring industries – and how these demands were met from within and beyond Cape society.

Such correlation was not merely the inevitable, perhaps irrational, result of 'traditional' dominant-class ideology. After all, Cape Town's dominant class had made little distinction between Black and White among the lower classes in the mid-1870s. In the early 1880s the Table Bay Harbour Board had experimented, if unsuccessfully, with White unskilled labour. Thereafter White domestic labour was still imported to work alongside Black. Rather, the gradual emergence of a three-tier social hierarchy of White, Coloured and African – still by no means complete in 1902 – was the result of struggles and the 'ideologies available to protagonists in those struggles', which characterised proletarianisation in late nineteenth-century Cape Town.[1]

Part of this 'result' was the growth of segregation between 1875 and 1902. Segregation, initially confined largely to the social exclusivity of the dominant class, gradually reached down into Cape Town's lower classes and separated Africans, Coloureds and Whites. Africans were forced into locations at the docks and at Ndabeni, Coloureds were not. But Coloureds and Whites were subject to increasing instances of separation, of which the most important was the segregation of mission schools in the course of the later 1890s and early 1900s. Such separation had also affected the city's hospitals, prisons and asylums by 1902. As recreation became more organised, a process itself associated with industrialisation, segregation affected sport. Coloured and White athletes, cricket and football players learnt (save in the few mission schools that were still mixed) and practised

210

their sports in separate schools and thereafter under the auspices of separate organisations.

Exclusionary practices extended in scope after 1875 largely, as Fredrickson suggested, because the number of 'facilities' in Cape Town increased.[2] But the city's social formation, shaped by the dominance of merchant rather than mining capital, determined that Cape Town's White bourgeoisie had no immediate interest in separating members of the lower classes.

Responsible Government saw White bourgeois colonists gain control of the state and begin to use that control in the 1880s to reproduce the social order of Kimberley, as well as the countryside, in institutions under their control. Simultaneously the majority of Cape Town's dominant class, assertively 'English' and imbued with the class consciousness of their counterparts in Britain, came to see the question of controlling and explaining the city's lower classes in ethnic and racist terms. They sympathised with poor Whites while blaming Black poverty on Black inferiority. They therefore welcomed the segregation of government institutions in Cape Town.

In particular, members of Cape Town's dominant class supported the government's efforts to solve the 'Poor White problem' in the 1890s through separate and superior education. They had come to believe that the separation of Whites from Blacks at all levels of society was an ideal worth pursuing. They were encouraged in this belief by some White workers and members of the petty bourgeoisie anxious to stake their own claims within the social hierarchy. But if there was agreement among most members of Cape Town's dominant class on the theoretical ideal of segregation, there was no such unanimity as to what extent the latter should be actively pursued or enforced.

The complexity of the debate, and the resultant extent and limitations of segregation, reflected the complexity of the city's social formation. Notably the residential segregation in a location of the vast majority of Africans in Cape Town was advocated by employers of dock labour, doctors and some clergymen. Cape Town's merchant princes and at least two of her largest employers of building labour were much less enthusiastic, or actively opposed, because of the specific implications for their labour supply. The intervention of the Cape government in favour of a location proved to be decisive. The government, in the form of the Table Bay Harbour Board, was in the process of becoming the major employer of migrant African labour in the city. In contrast there was no such employer interest in the residential segregation of more permanently urbanised Coloured labourers, who continued to be employed extensively on a casual basis throughout central and suburban Cape Town.

What neither Cape Town's dominant class nor the Cape government had predicted was that their prejudices, practices and the precise pattern of proletarianisation would give rise to ethnic and community mobilisation that could, like White ethnicity, cut across class cleavages. Malay resistance in 1886, the Effendi candidature of 1894, the Ndabeni rent and train boycotts of 1901, and the founding of the APO in 1902 were all shaped, indeed provoked, by the racism and segregation practised by bourgeois Whites.

So was incipient Pan-Africanism. A sub-leader of the *Cape Times* demanded an enquiry into the African Methodist Episcopalian Church in 1902. This was because the AME journal had said that the Boers and British should be 'whipped' back to their country of origin, like the 'Afro-Haytians whipped the French'. The *Cape Times*, perhaps prescient for once, feared that these views were being 'fed' to young Africans.[3]

Anthony Trollope had visited Cape Town in the late 1870s and been disappointed with its physical appearance. If Trollope had revisited Cape Town in 1902 he would doubtless have approved of the visible changes. The city centre had been transformed by a town council that was now suitably alert to the need for sanitation, decent roads and pavements. The Dutch character of the town centre had been overwhelmed by Victorian architecture. Buildings of stone, broekie-lace ironwork, elaborate use of plaster and skilfully built staircases stood as monuments to Victorian dexterity and aggressive Englishness.

Trollope would have been less pleased with some of the continuities. Notably, large parts of central Cape Town were still not inhabited entirely by 'white men'.[4] In District Six and other predominantly working-class areas, Whites, Coloureds and Africans ('illegally') lived in the same streets, the same houses and with one another.

Here, at least, Cape Town's 'special tradition of multi-racialism' still survived in 1902, albeit threatened and partially eroded by racism and extended segregation. Such erosion ensured that in terms of 'race' relations the similarities between Cape Town and the rest of South Africa outweighed the differences at the time of Union in 1910. As much as the Eastern Cape, Natal, Kimberley or Johannesburg, Cape Town contributed to the emergence of the ideology and practice of segregation in South Africa. If Jim Crow in particular was a 'city slicker', he was as much a Capetonian as a citizen of any other town in South Africa or the American South.[5]

But differences were important. Cape Town's 'special tradition' was not confined entirely to murky backstreets and slums. It marked some facilities, institutions and social practices in more affluent parts of the city, parts that Maurice Evans would have visited. This enabled him to testify to its continued presence in 1911 'in the streets, on the tramcars, in the railway stations, public offices and in places of entertainment'.[6] But Evans ignored the segregation that made Cape Town much less of an 'exceptional place' in southern Africa before Apartheid than previous academic opinion or popular myth allow.

This monograph has attempted to explain the limits, as much as the extent, of segregation and racial stratification in late colonial Cape Town. Precisely what happened after 1902 can only be revealed by similarly detailed studies. The nature of social conflicts and co-operations within and beyond the confines of the city were far from static. For instance Clean control of the city council waned in the midst of the depression that struck South Africa in the mid-1900s, as it had similarly faltered in the depression of the 1880s. But in the later decade an anti-Clean alliance that cut across potential ethnic divides emerged among ratepayers and voters in District Six.

It was because of the support that he received from the District Six Ratepayers' Association that Abdullah Abdurahman became a town councillor in 1904. This organisation also helped to elect the lawyer and defender of Jewish civil rights, Morris Alexander. Abdurahman and Alexander[7] worked together in the early twentieth century to keep 'public institutions' under municipal control or influence open or available for Blacks: be they town hall concerts or the South African College, the predecessor of the University of Cape Town. And many of these institutions remained 'open', if often subject to restrictions, into the Apartheid era.

Inter- or non-ethnic political alliances, at the central or local levels, were made possible by the nature of the Cape franchise. This franchise was retained, in what became the Cape Province, by the constitution of the Union of South Africa in 1910. But it was not extended to the rest of the country and only Whites could stand for the Union parliament. At a mass meeting in 1909, Abdurahman spoke with prescience and vigour against the constitution:

It is founded upon injustice, ignorance, and prejudice; it does not embrace human rights; it lacks all ethical considerations; it will make the Coloured people discontented; and finally it contains in itself the germs of decay. And if it should be the foundation upon which a South African Union should be built, it can never expect to last, and the sooner ... it fails, the better.[8]

Disappointment with this constitution prompted delegates at the APO annual conference in 1910 to pass a resolution that 'all non-Europeans should stand together'.[9] Yet at the same time the APO, and later

Coloured political parties, frequently championed Coloured rights ahead of those of Africans, and sometimes at the latter's expense. This occurred within both local and national contexts which until the 1990s appeared to promise some material gains for such strategies. Predictably there was often a thin line between the promotion of Coloured ethnic pride and the overt or latent encouragement of Coloured racial prejudice.

One early example at the local level: during the depths of the economic depression that hit South Africa in the mid-1900s the executive of the APO asked both the town council and the Harbour Board to employ Coloured labourers in preference to Africans. They argued that Coloureds were 'natives' of the city.[10] In the case of the town council the request was successful. This was probably because Abdurahman could put their case, but also because other councillors would have been aware that Coloureds were a much more important part of the municipal electorate than Africans.

Because of the possibility of a special deal for Coloureds, the APO's opposition to segregation became more muted at the national level from the mid-1920s. The Prime Minister, General Hertzog, tabled legislation in 1926 aimed at extending Coloured political rights in the Cape to the rest of the Union, while removing Africans entirely from the common voters' roll. Although the first part of this package never materialised, Coloured political leaders could still hope until the 1950s that it might, and with some justification: only Africans were removed from the Cape's common voters' roll in 1936.[11]

The coming of Apartheid after the National Party victory in 1948 destroyed this hope. Coloureds were removed from the common roll in 1956. In addition comprehensive residential segregation brought about by the Group Areas Act hit Coloured Capetonians, and notably the political elite, particularly hard. Hundreds of thousands were forced to leave their homes in the city and southern suburbs and move to violent townships on the windswept Cape Flats, far from places of employment. The demolition of District Six, 'Cape Town's Hiroshima' in the words of novelist Richard Rive, was only the most infamous among many demolitions and evictions.[12]

Yet this series of disasters did not mean that a Coloured ethnicity was readily abandoned by many in favour of a broader Black ethnicity. Apartheid planning, which strengthened rather than undermined differences of Black cultural practice and positions in the labour market, made this unlikely. But Black ethnic mobilisation has certainly been attempted by politicians throughout the twentieth century. The likes of the National Liberation League (led by Abdurahman's daughter, Cissie Gool) in the 1930s, the Non-European Unity Movement in the 1940s and

1950s, the Black People's Convention in the 1970s and the National Forum in the 1980s tried but failed to attract more than limited popular support beyond teachers, students and professionals.

Perhaps the greatest popular success was achieved by the United Democratic Front (UDF), an ANC-aligned organisation, in the 1980s. The UDF was formed specifically to oppose P. W. Botha's new constitution of 1983. This constitution established a parliament with separate, and unequal, chambers for Whites, Coloureds and Indians, but not for Africans. The UDF drew considerable support from Coloureds as well as Africans in the Western Cape, embarking on populist political strategies such as the 'million signatures' campaign against the Tricameral Parliament.[13]

But the success of the UDF in drawing together trade union, church and community organisations under its leadership did not mean that it had effectively overcome popular ethnic particularism. After its unbanning in February 1990 the ANC inherited this problem. The ANC could count on the support of the majority of Africans in Cape Town. But many Coloured Capetonians – with echoes here of the 1890s and 1900s – were fearful of losing jobs or even homes to the 'newcomers' whose numbers could be seen to have increased very rapidly since the relaxation and final abandonment of African 'influx' control by P. W. Botha's government in the mid-1980s. This helps to explain why the majority of Coloured electors in the Western Cape voted for the National Party in April 1994.

Any new central, regional or local government will struggle to break down the racial prejudice that has accompanied such fear and the structural division of South Africa's peoples. These divisions, albeit with much earlier origins as we have seen, were solidified by Apartheid. Notably, from 1950 to 1991 all South Africans, and therefore Capetonians, were officially registered as belonging to different population groups such as White, Coloured, Indian or African (i.e. 'Bantu' or 'Native'). Membership of different groups meant different life experiences. The material position of most Africans in Cape Town continued to be worse than that of most Coloureds, which was worse than most Whites. The Group Areas Act may have been repealed in 1991, but this has yet to result in much residential integration.

Black disunity was enhanced by central government ideology that until the 1980s not only earmarked the Western Cape as a 'Coloured Labour Preference' area but also attempted to reduce or more strictly control the African urban 'influx'. The pass laws were tightened up in the late 1950s and few new houses built in the townships of Langa, Nyanga and Guguletu–Ndabeni was demolished in the 1920s to make way for factories. Consequently most Africans coming to Cape Town since the

Second World War have been male migrant labourers housed in overcowded barracks or 'illegal' families forced to live in shacks, many as squatters. In the early 1990s most Capetonians continue to have a sense of community that interacts with ethnicity.

The myth of an ethnically harmonious pre-Apartheid Cape Town originated as an ideological response by Whites and Coloureds, not noticeably Africans, to National Party policies after 1948. The apparent triumph of the S. J. Du Toit rather than J. H. Hofmeyr brand of Afrikaner nationalism was symbolised by the abandonment of Crown and Commonwealth and the establishment of a republic in 1961. English-speaking White Capetonians were witnessing the seemingly irreversible destruction of English hegemony in South Africa as a whole. Most of them exercised their dislike of Afrikanerdom by voting for 'liberal' opposition parties such as the United Party, and later the Progressive Party and its successor the Progressive Federal Party. These parties promised more equitable treatment for Black South Africans. Their supporters in Cape Town, most of whom continued to believe in White supremacy, railed against Afrikaner nationalists in the not entirely invalid belief that Englishness of the more *laissez-faire* Clean tradition had produced greater social justice. Certainly it had produced less overtly racist legislation. From the perspective of those English speakers involved in commerce and business, necessarily sensitive to foreign opinion, such legislation was responsible for international outrage as well as internal strife, although arguably the former had more to do with changes in the outside world than in South Africa itself.

Coloured Capetonians had their intermediary status in the city's racial hierarchy adversely affected by Apartheid legislation. The Group Areas Act forced thousands of Coloured families to move from their inner-city or southern-suburbs homes into Coloured townships, just as the vast majority of Africans had been made to move into 'Native' locations at the beginning of the century. The Separate Amenities Act (1953) not only destroyed most of what had been left of the 'special tradition' after 1902, it meant that in the newly segregated facilities Coloureds were categorised as 'non-Whites' alongside Africans. The Population Registration Act and consequent identity documents made 'passing' for White more difficult. The Prohibition of Mixed Marriages Act (1949) and the Immorality Act (1950) extended to Coloureds the prohibition from sexual relations with Whites that already applied to Africans. And Coloured–White unions undoubtedly constituted the majority of existing 'mixed' marriages or cohabitations.

Before 1956 it made considerable strategic sense to the majority of those Coloured Capetonians who had the vote to support the predominantly English-speaking United Party candidates in national elections. And after they had lost the central franchise, alliances with anti-National Party Whites could still take place at the municipal level until the 1970s.

It seems probable, then, that the myth of a pre-Apartheid golden age in Cape Town's history was forged in part at the hustings. It was developed over the years in newspaper articles, novels, musicals and plays, and in the post-destruction nostalgia by Whites and Coloureds alike for District Six. But it was also shaped by the Coloured experience of forced removals as well as Apartheid legislation which had destroyed the remnants of the 'special tradition'. Believers in the myth have not fallen prey purely to fantasy or nostalgia. But they have tended to airbrush out the less palatable parts of Cape Town's past.

Notes

1 INTRODUCTION

1 G. M. Fredrickson, *White Supremacy* (New York, Oxford University Press, 1981), pp. 258, 260, 267; H. N. Rabinowitz, *Race Relations in the Urban South 1865–1890* (New York, Oxford University Press, 1978), p. xiv.

2 D. Welsh, 'The Growth of Towns', p. 174.

3 M. S. Evans, *Black and White in South East Africa* (London, Longman's Green & Co., 1916), pp. 296–7.

4 A. D. King, 'Colonial Cities: "Global Pivots of Change"', in Ross and Telkamp (eds.), *Colonial Cities*, p. 21.

5 One occasion was a sub–leader in the *Cape Times*, 19 April 1883, which referred to 'ethnically unctuous humanity'.

6 There is now an enormous literature on ethnicity and race. Here are three works which perhaps most directly influenced my thinking about ethnicity: J. Rex and D. Mason (eds.), *Theories of Race and Ethnic Relations* (Cambridge, Cambridge University Press, 1989); J. Rex, *Race and Ethnicity* (Milton Keynes, Open University Press, 1986); E. Ellis Cashmore, *Dictionary of Race and Ethnic Relations* (London, Routledge & Kegan Paul, 1992).

7 B. Bozzoli, 'Class, Community and Ideology in the Evolution of South African Society', in Bozzoli (ed.), *Class, Community and Conflict*, pp. 1–43. See also B. Anderson, *Imagined Communities: Reflections on the Origin and Spread of Nationalism* (London, Verso, 1983); A. P. Cohen, *The Symbolic Construction of Community* (London, Routledge & Kegan Paul, 1992).

8 R. Miles, *Racism* (London, Routledge & Kegan Paul, 1989) has directly informed my definitions of racialisation and racism. See also N. Stepan, *The Idea of Race in Science* (London, Macmillan, 1982).

9 S. G. Checkland, 'An Urban History Horoscope', in Fraser and Sutcliffe (eds.), *Urban History*, p. 449.

10 Fredrickson, *White Supremacy*, pp. 257–268.

11 P. Maylam, 'The Rise and Decline of Urban Apartheid in South Africa', *African Affairs*, 89, 354 (1990), 57–84.

12 J. W. Cell, *The Highest Stage of White Supremacy* (Cambridge, Cambridge University Press, 1982), p. 134.

13 H. Wright, *The Burden of the Present: Liberal–Radical Controversy over Southern African History* (Cape Town, David Philip, 1977).

14 See, for instance, Fredrickson, *White Supremacy*, pp. xx–xxi, 188–9, 199–212, 288–9, 234; S. Marks and R. Rathbone, 'Introduction', in S. Marks and R.

218

Rathbone (eds.), *Industrialisation and Social Change in South Africa* (Harlow, Longman, 1982), p. 5.

15 Cell, *White Supremacy*, esp. chap. 3; Fredrickson, *White Supremacy*, pp. 199–212.

16 R. V. Turrell, *Capital and Labour*; Worger, *Workers and Monopoly Capitalism*.

17 S. Marks, ' "White Supremacy": A Review Article', *Comparative Studies in Society and History*, 29, 2 (1987), 385–97. The quotation is from p. 396. See also David Welsh, *The Roots of Segregation: Native Policy in Colonial Natal, 1845–1910* (Cape Town, Oxford University Press, 1971).

18 P. Harries, 'Plantations, Passes and Proletarians: Labour and the Colonial State in Nineteenth Century Natal', *JSAS*, 13, 3 (1987), 372–99.

19 Marks, ' "White Supremacy" ', p. 396.

20 C. C. Crais, *White Supremacy and Black Resistance in Pre–industrial South Africa* (Cambridge, Cambridge University Press, 1992).

21 S. Dubow, *Racial Segregation and the Origins of Apartheid in South Africa, 1919–1936* (London, Macmillan, 1989), pp. 20–3.

22 Cell, *White Supremacy*, p. 134.

23 R. H. Wiebe, *The Search for Order* (London, Macmillan, 1967).

24 G. R. Andrews, *The Afro-Argentines of Buenos Aires 1800–1900* (Madison, University of Wisconsin Press, 1980), pp. 204–5. Apart from showing that this happened in Buenos Aires, Andrews cites cities in the United States of America, as well as the case of Sao Paulo, to prove his contention.

25 Van Onselen, *'New Babylon'* and *'New Nineveh'*.

26 G. Lewis, *Between the Wire and the Wall: A History of South African 'Coloured' Politics* (Cape Town, David Philip, 1987), p. 20.

2   THE WORLD THAT COMMERCE MADE

1 *CPP*, G42–1876, 'Cape Census for 1875'.

2 The term 'Khoisan' follows R. Elphick, 'The Khoisan to c1770', in R. Elphick and H. Giliomee (eds.), *The Shaping of South African Society*, 2nd edn (Cape Town, Longman, 1989), p. 4. Khoisan is an amalgam, coined by scholars, of names for the two groups into which Khoisan are conventionally divided: KhoiKhoi, who kept sheep and cattle, and San who were hunter–gatherers. Europeans called the former 'Hottentots' and the latter 'Bushmen'.

3 Elphick, 'The Khoisan'; T. R. H. Davenport, *South Africa: A Modern History*, 4th edn (Johannesburg, Macmillan, 1991), pp. 3–8, 19–31; and S. Marks, 'Khoisan Resistance to the Dutch in the 17th and 18th centuries', *JAH*, 13, 1 (1972), 55–80.

4 For the little information we have on the development of Cape Town before the nineteenth centry, see Ross 'Synthesis'. Also R. Ross, *Cape of Torments* (London, Routledge & Kegan Paul, 1983), pp. 17–22; and N. Worden, *Slavery in Dutch South Africa* (Cambridge, Cambridge University Press, 1985). For a detailed account of the Cape economy in the eighteenth century which challenges the traditional orthodoxy of economic backwardness in this period, see P. C. Van Duin and R. Ross (eds.), *The Economy of the Cape*

Colony in the Eighteenth Century (Leiden, Centre for the History of European Expansion, 1987).

5 S. Newton-King, 'The Labour Market of the Cape Colony', in S. Marks and A. Atmore (eds.), *Economy and Society in Pre-industrial South Africa* (London, Longman, 1980), pp. 171–207; T. R. H. Davenport, 'The Consolidation of a New Society: The Cape Colony', in M. Wilson and L. Thompson (eds.) *The Oxford History of South Africa* (Oxford, Oxford University Press, 1969), vol. I, p. 288.

6 T. Kirk, 'The Cape Economy and the Expropriation of the Kat River Settlement, 1846–1853', in Marks and Atmore (eds.), *Economy and Society*, pp. 226–46; Davenport, 'Consolidation', pp. 290–1.

7 Ross, 'Synthesis', p. 115; A. S. Mabin, 'The Making of Colonial Capitalism: Intensification and Expansion in the Economic Geography of the Cape Colony, South Africa, 1854–1899' (Ph.D. thesis, Wits University, 1977, revised 1984), pp. 75–6.

8 Mabin, 'Colonial Capitalism', pp. 65, 71–2, 86–7, 98–100, 125–73. Davenport, *Modern History*, pp. 79–80. See also A. S. Purkis, 'The Politics, Capital and Labour of Railway Building in the Cape Colony, 1870–1885' (Ph.D. thesis, Oxford University, 1978).

9 Records of the Standard Bank in the possession of James Henry, Cape Town, hereafter Henry Archives (HA): General Manager (GM) to London Office (LO), 16 January 1869; 16 January 1870.

10 HA: GM to LO, 3 July 1876, 2 February 1877, 10 December 1880, 14 January 1882. *CBB*, 1906, p. xxii.

11 Ross, 'Synthesis', p. 107; Laidler, *Growth and Government*, esp. pp. 372–408; W. Bird, *The State of the Cape of Good Hope in 1822* (Cape Town, Struik, 1966), p. 354.

12 Ross, 'Synthesis', pp. 107–9; L. Guelke, 'Freehold farmers and frontier settlers, 1652–1780', in Elphick and Giliomee (eds.), *Shaping*, pp. 66–9.

13 Ross, 'Synthesis', pp. 108–9; Judges, 'Poverty', pp. 85–99; H. P. Barnett-Clarke, *The Life and Times of Thomas Fothergill Lightfoot, BD Archdeacon of Cape Town* (Cape Town, Darter, 1908), esp. pp. 140–2, p. 184. Particularly severe epidemics occurred in 1840, 1858 and 1867.

14 Marshall, 'Growth and Development', p. 59; A. F. Hattersley, *An Illustrated Social History of South Africa* (Cape Town, Balkema, 1969), pp. 98, 186–8; C. Saunders, 'Africans in Cape Town in the Nineteenth Century: An Outline', *Studies*, II (1980), pp. 15–23; Newton–King, 'Labour Market', pp. 180, 183–91; Judges, 'Poverty', pp. 18–19; Mabin, 'Colonial Capitalism', pp. 94–5; Laidler, *Growth and Government*, p. 309.

15 For a good overview of the physical geography of Cape Town in 1875 see Bradlow, 'Labouring Poor'.

16 For contemporary descriptions of Cape Town in the mid–1870s, see especially: J. Noble, *Descriptive Handbook of the Cape Colony: Its Conditions and Resources* (Cape Town, Juta, 1875), pp. 31–46; A. Trollope, *South Africa* (London, Chapman & Hall, 1879), pp. 2–4; R. M. Ballantyne, *Six Months at the Cape of Good Hope* (London, Nisbet, 1878), pp. 201–220; *Cape Monthly Magazine* (*CMM*) vol. 10, no. 60, and vol. 11, no. 61 (1875), articles titled 'Cape Town Revisited'; J. Rose Innes, *Sir James Rose Innes 1855–1942* (Cape

Town, Oxford University Press, 1949), p. 21. David Kennedy's book, *At the Cape*, pp. 8–18 is particularly lively.

17 Hattersley, *Illustrated History*, p. 208; Marshall, 'Growth and Development', p. 70. J. D. Linnegar, 'From Village to Municipality: A History of Wynberg to 1903' (Honours thesis, UCT, 1975), p. 35.

18 Rose Innes, *Sir James*, p. 21. See also Trollope, *South Africa*, p. 2 and Kennedy, *At the Cape*, p. 9.

19 Ballantyne, *Six Months*, p. 204.

20 *Cape Argus*, 8 January 1876; *CPP*, A19–1877, 'Select Committee Report (SCR) on Sanitary Arrangments of Municipalities', p. 7; *CPP*, A4–1878, 'SCR on Rogge Bay Nuisance'; *CPP*, G42–1876, p. 9; CA, 3CT 7/2/1/5, 'List of Registered Householders for 1872' gives names of householders, occupation and number of inhabitants.

21 See *CPP*, A19–1877, p. 7 and *CPP*, G42–1876, p. 1.

22 *CPP*, G42–1876. Subsequent statistics in this chapter all come from this source, the census for 1875, unless specified. Because of the likelihood of at least minor inaccuracies in the returns, I have usually treated the figures as estimates, rounding up or down the numbers given in the census. For more details of the census categories used in my calculations, and exact figures given by the enumerators, see V. Bickford-Smith, 'Commerce, Class and Ethnicity in Cape Town, 1875–1902' (Ph.D. Thesis, Cambridge University, 1989), chap. 2.

23 G. J. Davison, *The Rise and Fall of Marvellous Melbourne* (Melbourne, Melbourne University Press, 1978); J. H. Henry, *The First Hundred Years of the Standard Bank* (Oxford, Oxford University Press, 1963), p. 15; Standard Bank Archives (SBA) 1/1/24 Inspection Report (IR) Cape Town Branch (CT) for 1871 and 1874; SBA 1/1/25 IR CT, 1880; *CPP*, A3–1883, 'SCR on Colonial Agriculture and Industries'; Immelman, *Men of Good Hope*.

24 CA, Limited Company Registers (LC) 101, 'Colonial Bank'; LC 85, 'Cape Commercial Bank'; LC 45, 'South African Bank'; LC 32, 'Union Bank'; LC 11, 'Cape of Good Hope Bank'; CA, 3CT 7/1/2/1/31–3 'Town Council Assessment Rolls 1873–1875': the Wichts owned 495 of the 4,132 houses listed.

25 CA, Cape Harbour Board (CHB) 10, 'Minutes of the Table Bay Dock and Breakwater Management Commission', 18 January 1875 to 28 December 1877.

26 *CPP*, A3–1883; *CBB*, 1875, pp. FF 2–3; Whittingdale, 'Industries', pp. 9, 88–90; *CPP*, C1–1891, 'SCR on Colonial Industries'; Mabin, 'Colonial Capitalism', pp. 198–307; *Cape Times*, 19 November 1889.

27 *Clothes*: *Cape Times*, 26 September 1906, letter from Fred Burt, shows that a 'putting-out' system went back to the 1860s and presumably earlier; *South African News*, 4 April 1901 'Labour Movement' gives details of the system as it operated in that year; *Cape Times*, 15 September 1906, the first two clothing factories apparently opened in 1906. *Boot and shoe making*: *CPP*, A3–1883, pp. 56–7. In 1883 only the Western Tanning Company, located fittingly at Wellington, appears to have been producing boots for sale in Cape Town. *Excalibur*, 25 June 1886 provides the first description of a boot factory in the town itself, when Garlick's was employing forty men. Garlick himself had been behind the manufacture of boots since at least 1882.

28 *CPP*, G37–1892, 'Report of the Fisheries Committee', p. xv. No distinction is made in many categories of the 1875 census between employers, self-employed and employees, so 'fisherman' is a vague label in this respect. See also D. Grant, 'Bokkoms, Boycott and the Bo Kaap: The Decline of the Rogge Bay Fishing Industry between 1890 and 1920' (MA thesis, UCT, 1991).

29 *CPP*, A4–1878, Appendix G, p. viii.

30 *CPP*, G50–1876, 'Report of the Table Bay Dock and Breakwater Management Commission for 1875', p. 2. *CPP*, A7–1880, 'SCR on the Table Bay Harbour Board'.

31 E. B. Van Heyningen, 'Poverty, Self-help and Community: The Survival of the Poor in Cape Town, 1880–1910,' *SAHJ*, 24 (1991), 128–143; P. Van Der Spuy, 'Slave Women and the Family in Nineteenth-century Cape Town', *SAHJ*, 27 (1992), 50–74, gives useful analysis of the gender division of labour in the 1830s which helps to explain its manifestations in the 1870s.

32 G. Stedman Jones, *Outcast London* (Harmondsworth, Penguin, 1976), chaps. 2–5, has obviously informed my analysis here and in the next paragraph; *CPP*, C1–1891, p. 116 and *CPP*, G39–1893, 'Labour Commission', p. 27, evidence of G. Smart (builder) and A. R. McKenzie (dock agent and builder). See also *CPP*, A26–1879, 'SCR on Labour', p. 21 and *CPP*, A12–1890 'SCR on Labour', p. 37.

33 *Fruit season*: *CPP*, A6–1906, 'SCR on the Factory Act', p. 58. *Baking*: *Cape Times* 18 May 1907, 'Labour Market'.

34 Van Heyningen, 'Public Health', pp. 365–72 shows that there were 213 registered prostitutes in 1868, while the Colonial Medical Committee talked of 400 'public prostitutes' in the town in 1886. *Lantern*, 3 September 1881, mentioned that thirty-one houses of 'ill-fame' were 'known to the police'. Resident Magistrates' records and newspapers are full of brothel and illegal liquor-selling cases. See also Van Heyningen, 'Poverty', p. 142. V. Bickford-Smith, 'Meanings of Freedom: Social Position and Identity among Ex-slaves and Their Descendants in Cape Town, 1875–1910', in C. Crais and N. Worden (eds.), *Breaking the Chains* (Johannesburg, Wits University Press, forthcoming) discusses the cost of licence fees.

35 J. Foster, *Class Struggle and the Industrial Revolution* (London, Weidenfeld & Nicolson, 1974).

36 J. Foster, 'Nineteenth Century Towns: A Class Dimension', in H. J. Dyos (ed.), *The Study of Urban History* (London, Edward Arnold, 1968), p. 283.

37 SBA, Johannesburg, 1/1/24–6 IR CT, 1871, 1874, 1875, 1878, 1880, 1881. Information on capital and income is given under names of mercantile companies – such as W. Anderson & Co – and individuals such as H. M. Arderne (solicitor), M. J. Louw (tanner) or J. Silberbauer (retired miller).

38 Foster, *Class Struggle*, pp. 161–6.

39 G. Crossick, 'Urban Society and the Petty Bourgeoisie in Nineteenth Century Britain', in Fraser and Sutcliffe (eds.), *Urban History*, p. 307.

40 See Stedman Jones, *Outcast London*, chap. 4. The census listed fifty mechanical engineers in Cape Town. CA, Cape Government Railways (CGR) 20/1/3, 'Staff Register, Salt River Works 1879–1910'.

41 J. Iliffe, 'The Creation of Group Consciousness: A History of the Dock-workers of Dar es Salaam', in R. Sandbrook and R. Cohen (eds.), *The Development of an African Working Class* (London, Longman, 1975), pp. 49–72; his argument informs my own: organisation and occupational group consciousness were created 'by the workers themselves'. Consciousness is intensified by successful action, *vis-à-vis* an employer. In the course of 'the struggle', such workers become united with other workers and the latter constitute themselves as a class 'for itself'.

42 Bickford-Smith, 'Meanings of Freedom'.

43 Cited in Grant, 'Bokkoms', p. 28. Grant gives a good account of the struggles waged by this community in the late nineteenth century. See also C. Winberg, 'The "Ghoemaliedjies" of the Cape Muslims: Remnants of a Slave Culture', (unpublished English Department seminar paper, UCT, 1991), p. 26.

44 *CPP*, A4–1878, Appendix G, p. ix.

45 *Cape Times* 6 November 1971, 'District Six Wash-house Closes its Door for the Last Time'. Kennedy, *At the Cape*, pp. 17–18.

46 CA, 3CT 7/1/2/1/32–3, 'Town Council Assessment Rolls 1873–5'.

47 Cited in Fredrickson, *White Supremacy*, p. 133. Lewis, *Between the Wire and the Wall*, p. 9 suggests that 'passing' for White 'siphoned off many of the natural leaders of Coloureds'. For a broader discussion of 'passing' which focuses on Cape Town a century later, see G. Watson, *Passing for White* (London, Tavistock, 1970).

48 Fredrickson, *White Supremacy*, p. 133.

49 J. D. Ensor, *Sitongo* (Cape Town, A. Richards & Sons, 1884).

50 Andrews, *Buenos Aires* uses this expression. For discussion of Cape Town's traditional system at the time of emancipation see Judges, 'Poverty' and Bradlow, 'Emancipation'.

51 Crais and Worden (eds.), *Breaking the Chains* explores the reasons why.

52 Fredrickson, *White Supremacy*, pp. 257–8.

53 Bradlow, 'Emancipation', pp. 26–7; G. Cuthbertson, 'The Impact of the Emancipation of Slaves on St Andrews Scottish Church, Cape Town, 1838–1878', *Studies*, III, (1984), 49–63; *Cape Times*, 1 February 1988, 'Methodists Celebrate Unity'; P. Le Feuvre, 'Cultural and Theological Factors Affecting Relationships between the Nederduitse-Gereformeede Kerk and the Anglican Church in the Cape Colony 1806–1910' (Ph.D. thesis, UCT, 1980).

54 Le Feuvre, 'Theological Factors' refers to Black and White Anglicans worshipping together in the Cape Peninsula, but the *Cape Times* 21 November 1877, letter from 'A Coloured Attendant' reveals how they were separated in the Anglican cathedral. The census provides the statistical details.

55 *CPP*, G24–1863, 'Report of a Commission of Enquiry into the Government Education System', pp. 152–3.

56 *Ibid.*, pp. lxiv, 125, 145, 233, 235 and 242.

57 Bradlow, 'Labouring Poor', pp. 26–8.

58 E. Rosenthal, *Fishorns and Hansom Cabs: Life in Victorian Cape Town* (Cape Town, AD. Donker, 1977), pp. 101–4 refers to a 'fair number of SACS' (South African College School) scholars who were Coloured; J. and R. Simons, *Class and Colour in South Africa 1850–1950* (London, International Defence and

Aid Fund, 1983), p. 117. Certainly one of the only identified members of the Coloured elite who attended a 'White' school, SACS, was the light-skinned Dr Abdullah Abdurahman, later to become leader of the APO. There is a photograph of him in Lewis, *Between the Wire and the Wall*, photograph no. 6.

59 S. Trapido, '"The Friends of the Natives": Merchants, Peasants and the Political and Ideological Structure of Liberalism in the Cape, 1854–1910', in Marks and Atmore (eds.), *Economy and Society*, pp. 247–74.

60 J. L. McCracken, *The Cape Parliament 1854–1910* (Oxford, Clarendon Press, 1967), pp. 68–9.

61 *Ibid.*, pp. 69–70.

62 Fredrickson, *White Supremacy*, pp. 188–90, 195–6.

63 McCracken, *Cape Parliament*, p. 67.

64 Fredrickson, *White Supremacy*, pp. 189–90, 194.

65 Trapido, '"Friends of the Natives"', convincingly argues for the interrelationship of economic interests and ideological positions. For the argument that Cape liberalism was an ideological palliative divorced from economic interests, see P. Lewsen, 'The Cape Liberal Tradition – Myth or Reality?', *Institute of Commonwealth Studies Collected Seminar Papers*, 1, 1969–1970 (London, Institute of Commonwealth Studies, 1970), pp. 72–88. See also, Fredrickson, *White Supremacy*, pp. 184–5.

66 L. Dale, 'Prejudice Against Colour', in J. Noble (ed.), *The Cape and its People and Other Essays* (Cape Town, J. C. Juta, 1869), p. 104.

67 C. Bundy, '"Vagabond Hollanders and Runaway Englishmen": White Poverty in the Cape Before Poor Whiteism', in W. Beinart, P. Delius and S. Trapido (eds.), *Putting a Plough to the Ground: Accumulation and Dispossession in Rural South Africa 1850–1930* (Johannesburg, Ravan, 1986), pp. 101–28.

68 J. J. Jackson, *New Orleans in the Gilded Age: Politics and Urban Progress 1880–1896* (Baton Rouge, Louisiana State University Press, 1969), p. 22. Bradlow, 'Labouring Poor', 23–4; E. Bradlow, 'Cape Town 100 Years Ago: A "Somewhat Ragged" Place', in *Cape Times* Centenary Supplement 27 March 1976; Judges, 'Poverty', p. 134; Lady Duff Gordon, *Letters from the Cape* (Cape Town, Maskew Miller, 1925), p. 33 refers to marriages between Whites and Malays.

69 Kennedy, *At the Cape*, pp. 13–14; Fredrickson, *White Supremacy*, p. 265.

70 *Juries: Lantern* 12 April 1884, 8 November 1879. *Hospitals*: see this volume chap. 5, note 66 and J. Iliffe, *The African Poor* (Cambridge, Cambridge University Press, 1987), p. 103.

71 *CPP*, A19–1877, pp. 32–9. The quotation is from p. 36.

72 Noble, *Descriptive Handbook*, pp. 44–5.

73 *CPP*, G42–1876, 'Report', p. 3.

74 Langham Dale, 'The Cape and its People', in Noble (ed.), *The Cape and its People*, pp. 3–4.

75 J. Noble, *The Cape and South Africa* (Cape Town, J. C. Juta, 1878), pp. 131–3.

76 I. Goldin, *Making Race; The Politics and Economics of Coloured Identity in South Africa* (Cape Town, Maskew Miller Longman, 1987), p. xxvi suggests

that the term Coloured in official documents before the end of the nineteenth century always referred to 'non-Whites'.

77 *CPP*, G27–1874, 'Blue Book on Native Affairs for 1873', evidence of A. Orpen.

78 A. Wilmot, *History of the Cape Colony for use in Schools* (Cape Town, J. C. Juta, 1871), p. 120.

79 CA, 3CT 7/1/2/1/32–3, if names such as Abdol Saliel or S. Achmat can be presumed to belong to Black property owners.

80 Fredrickson, *White Supremacy*, p. 131.

81 Van Heyningen, 'Poverty' and her 'Public Health', esp. pp. 456–68 for discussion of mortality rates.

82 *CPP*, G42–1876, 'Education', pp. 75–6.

83 *CPP*, A13–1873, 'Petition of Coloured Persons, Inhabitants of Cape Town and Neighbourhood'.

84 Lewis, *Between the Wire and the Wall*, p. 4.

85 *Cape Times*, 21 November 1877.

86 CA, 1CT 6/74–9 'Criminal Cases in Court of Resident Magistrate, 1875', John Thomas v. Abdol Kabur, 24 April 1873 (so wrongly bound with 1875 cases); see case dated 29 July 1875 for Daniel O'Brien's evidence: CA, 1CT 6/80–91, 1876–7, M. A. Hall *v.* C. E. Holm (Case No. 1081).

87 CA, 1CT 6/74–9, case of Joe Maker, June 1875. Bradlow, 'Labouring Poor', p. 25.

88 G. Rudé, *Ideology and Popular Protest* (London, Pantheon Books, 1980).

89 *Cape Blue Books*, 1870–1875, 'Wages'. *Lantern*, 13 September 1884 and *Cape Times*, 3 August 1884.

90 Kennedy, *At the Cape*, p. 11.

91 Noble, *Descriptive Handbook*, pp. 44–5; R. Shell, 'Rites and Rebellion: Islamic Conversion at the Cape, 1808 to 1915', *Studies*, V, (1983), 3–4.

92 W. Beinart, 'Worker Consciousness, Ethnic Particularism and Nationalism: The Experience of a South African Migrant', in S. Marks and S. Trapido (eds.), *The Politics of Race, Class and Nationalism in Twentieth Century South Africa* (London, Longman, 1987), p. 306.

93 *CPP*, G42–1876, 'Religions of the People', pp. 349–52. Shell, 'Rites and Rebellion', pp. 24–5.

94 Duff Gordon, *Letters from the Cape*, p. 33; J. S. Mayson, *The Malays of Cape Town* (Manchester, Cave & Sever, 1855).

95 *CPP*, A2–1875, 'SCR on the Cemeteries Bill', p. 183.

96 *Cape Times*, 14 September 1878.

97 Bickford-Smith, 'Meanings of Freedom'. See also Andrew Bank, 'The Erosion of Slavery at the Cape, 1806–1834', in Crais and Worden (eds.), *Breaking the Chains*.

98 Kennedy, *At the Cape*, p. 11. See also Shell, 'Rites and Rebellion'; A. Davids, 'Politics and the Muslims of Cape Town: A Historical Survey', *Studies*, IV (1981), 174–220; M. A. Bradlow, 'Islam, the Colonial State and South African History: The 1886 Cemetery Uprising' (Honours thesis, UCT, 1984). Also Rosenthal, *Fishorns*, pp. 100–1.

99 Kennedy, *At the Cape*, p. 15; I. D. Du Plessis, *The Malay Quarter and its People* (Cape Town, Balkema, 1953).

100 For a discussion of the origins of such clubs, see Bickford-Smith, 'Meanings of Freedom'. Kennedy, *At the Cape*, p. 15 gives a description of Malay street singers.

101 Stedman Jones, *Outcast London*, p. 239.

102 Rudé, *Ideology and Popular Protest*, p. 8. For a stimulating account of a similar semi-proletarianised presence on the late nineteenth-century Witwatersrand, see Van Onselen, '*New Nineveh*', chaps. 2 and 3.

103 See Andrews, *Buenos Aires*, p. 60 and M. Karasch, 'Rio de Janeiro: From Colonial Town to Imperial Capital (1808–1850)', in Ross and Telkamp (eds.), *Colonial Cities*, pp. 142–7. D. A. Lorimer, *Colour, Class and the Victorians* (Leicester, Leicester University Press, 1978), p. 100 says that the terms were also interchangeable in Victorian Britain. See Noble, *Descriptive Handbook*, pp. 44–5, or the *Cape Monthly Magazine*, vol. 11 (1875), for Cape Town examples.

104 D. Fraser, *Urban Politics in Victorian England* (Leicester, Leicester University Press, 1976), p. 115. See also, for information on British Clean or Reform parties, A. Briggs, *Victorian Cities* (New York, Pelican, 1963), pp. 70–1, 205–24 and E. P. Hennock, 'The Social Composition of Borough Councils in the Large Cities, 1834–1914', in Dyos (ed.), *Urban History*, pp. 333–9.

3 PROBLEMS OF PROSPERITY

1 R. Colls, 'Englishness and the Political Culture', in R. Colls and P. Dodd (eds.), *Englishness: Politics and Culture 1880–1920* (Beckenham, Croom Helm, 1986), p. 45.

2 P. Dodd, 'Englishness and the National Culture', in Colls and Dodd (eds.), *Englishness*, pp. 1–28.

3 McCracken, *The Cape Parliament*.

4 T. R. H. Davenport, *The Afrikaner Bond 1880–1911* (Cape Town, Oxford University Press, 1966), pp. 2–3.

5 Davenport, *Afrikaner Bond*, chap. 3. Quotations are from pp. 28 and 35 respectively.

6 Davenport, *Afrikaner Bond*, chap. 2 and p. 309. H. Giliomee, 'Aspects of the Rise of Afrikaner Capital and Afrikaner Nationalism in the Western Cape, 1870–1915', in James and Simons (eds.), *The Angry Divide*, pp. 63–79.

7 P. Lewsen, *John X. Merriman* (New Haven, Yale University Press, 1982), p. 124.

8 *CBB*, 1906, p. xx.

9 See *CPP* Acts 27 of 1879, 5 and 17 of 1880; CA 4/2, 'Table Bay Harbour Board Records', pp. 1–9 gives a good description of the development of Table Bay harbour. *Cape Times*, 3 April 1883; Immelman, *Men of Good Hope*, p. 253.

10 *CBB*, 1870, 1875 and 1882; SBA, IR CT, 1881; HA, GM to LO, 14 January 1882.

11 HA, GM to LO, 19 August 1881; CA, LC 10, 'Steam Laundry Co'; CA, LC 172, 'SA Glass Co.'; CA, LC 3, 32, 45, 85 for investment in banking; and CA, LC 8, 9, 44 for investment in insurance companies.

12 J. Stone, *Colonist or Uitlander? A Study of the British Immigrant in South Africa* (Oxford, Clarendon Press, 1973), p. 114. CA, Public Works Department (PWD) 1693, 'Lists of Immigrants per Various Ships'; *CPP*, G58–1884, 'Immigration Report'.

13 Saunders, 'Africans in Cape Town', pp. 24–7.

14 P. Harries, 'Mozbiekers: The Immigration of an African Community to the Western Cape, 1876–1882', *Studies*, I, (1979), 153–64; *CPP*, A26–1879, pp. 60–1; CA, CHB 12 and 13, 'Minutes of the Table Bay Dock and Breakwater Management Committee', 3 August 1879–25 March 1881 and 1 April 1881–2 September 1881 respectively.

15 *CPP*, G58–1884, pp. 5–6.

16 SBA 1/1/26 IR CT, 1881; HA, GM to LO, 8 October 1881; *Lantern* 12 January 1884.

17 HA, GM to LO, 15 August 1879, 10 December 1880, 23 September 1881.

18 See for instance *Cape Times*, 26 February or 13 October 1880.

19 *Cape Monthly Magazine* (1875), pp. 44–8, 373–5.

20 Trollope, *South Africa*, p. 2.

21 Noble, *Descriptive Handbook*, p. 41.

22 See Picard, *Grand Parade*, pp. 70–4 for earlier criticisms.

23 *Cape Argus*, 14 August 1875. W. E. G. Solomon, *Saul Solomon* (Cape Town, Oxford University Press, 1948).

24 J. L. Meltzer, 'The Growth of Cape Town Commerce and the Role of John Fairbairn's *Advertiser* (1835–1859)', (MA thesis, UCT, 1989).

25 G. Shaw, *Some Beginnings: The Cape Times (1876–1910)* (Cape Town, Oxford University Press, 1975), pp. 1–8.

26 *Cape Times*, 29 June 1880.

27 Picard, *Grand Parade*, p. 77; the *Cape Times*, 25 September 1877, quoted from *Sanitary Record*, London, when referring to the inadequacy of water supply of Cape Town, for docks, labour market and railways; 1 March 1878, applauded the establishment of a Sanitary Association in Edinburgh; 12 August 1878, leader, quoted Lord Beaconsfield's dictum on domestic policy, 'Sanitas, Sanitas, Omnia Sanitas'; Van Heyningen, 'Public Health'.

28 See, e.g., R. Newton, *Victorian Exeter 1837–1914* (Leicester, Leicester University Press, 1968), pp. 252–4; E. Gillet and K. A. MacMahon, *A History of Hull* (Oxford, Oxford University Press, 1980), p. 329; Fraser, *Urban Politics*, chap. 7; Briggs, *Victorian Cities*, esp. pp. 70–1, 156, 211.

29 *Cape Argus*, 17 August 1876; *Cape Times*, 1 March 1877, 1 March 1879, 13 April 1906; Picard, *Grand Parade*, pp. 70–92; *CPP*s A1–1860, A7–1865, A10–1879, A13–1881, which were all select committee reports on municipal bills, or amendment bills; Van Heyningen, 'Public Health', pp. 259–61.

30 *Cape Times*, 13 April 1906, 'The Progress of the City'; *Cape Command Papers (CCP)*, Ordinance 1, 1839, 'For the Creation of a Municipal Board for Cape Town and the Vicinity thereof'; *CCP*, Ordinance 1, 1840, 'Act for Establishing a Municipal Board for Cape Town'; *CPP*, A1–1861, 'Act to Re-establish a Municipal Board for Cape Town', *CPP*, A1–1867, 'The Cape Town Municipality Amendment Act'; *CBB*, 1875, 'Municipalities'.

31 *Cape Argus*, 14, 19 August 1875; *Cape Times*, 10 June 1878.

32 For biographical details of J. C. Hofmeyr see *Dictionary of South African*

Biography (DSAB), vol. II (Cape Town, Tafelberg-Uitgewers, 1972), pp. 308–9; *CPP*, A13–1881, 'SCR on Cape Town Municipal Bill'. *Cape Times*, 4 February 1880.

33 Stedman Jones, *Outcast London*, p. 210.

34 *Cape Argus*, 18 February 1875, 19 October 1875; *Cape Times*, 19, 20, 29 March 1877, 14 April 1877, 21 February 1878.

35 *Cape Argus*, 19 October 1875.

36 *Cape Times*, 9 August 1887.

37 H. Giliomee, 'The Growth of Afrikaner Identity', in H. Adam and H. Giliomee (eds.), *The Rise and Crisis of Afrikaner Power* (Cape Town, David Philip, 1979), pp. 101–3; Davenport, *Afrikaner Bond*, pp. 326–7.

38 *Cape Times* 13 August 1878, 29 October 1884; *Lantern* 22 February, 1 March, 16 August 1879; *DSAB* vol. II, p. 308; *CPP*, A13–1881.

39 Giliomee, *Afrikaner Capital*; Davenport, *Afrikaner Bond*.

40 *Cape Times*, 23 August 1877, 11 December 1879, 25 November 1880, 17 May 1883.

41 *Lantern*, 4 March 1882; *Cape Times*, 4 April 1884, 10 July 1884.

42 Shaw, *Some Beginnings*, p. 16.

43 *Cape Times*, 25 November 1880. *Lantern*, 14 August 1880 nicknamed J. C. Hofmeyr 'Nosey', referring to his physical appearance. *Lantern*, 8 February 1879, said that people should not vote for J. C. Hofmeyr because he had been in court in 1866 over being a usurer while serving his articles. *Lantern*, 11 March 1882, talked of M. J. Louw's insolvent son 'escaping' to Buenos Aires. *Lantern*, 29 July 1882, repeats Louw's insolvency connection and said that Zoutendyk was seeking office from 'directly personal and unworthy' motives.

44 *Cape Times*, 18 December 1885.

45 *Cape Times*, 29 September 1876, 9 September 1878. See also 1 March 1878, 10 August 1881. For a visual variation on the same theme, see the *Lantern*, 14 August 1880 which had a cartoon showing Malays in favour of J. C. Hofmeyr and the Dirty Party.

46 *Lantern*, 27 May 1882.

47 Trollope, *South Africa*, p. 3. Kennedy, *At the Cape*, p. 9 used both adjectives to describe the town. Van Heyningen, 'Public Health', p. 107 cites Bertram Mitford, a visitor in 1882, who wrote that 'all is ugly, Dutch and squat'.

48 *Lantern*, 15 March 1879.

49 *Cape Times*, 28 October 1878.

50 *Cape Times*, 2 November 1878. Alfred Ebden, 1819–1908, lived in Rondebosch. He was a manager of the Cape of Good Hope Savings Bank and director of several companies. Ebden made most of his money from owning the Veroudzight Estate, which constituted much of the Kimberley mine: *DSAB* vol. III (Cape Town, Tafelberg–Uitgewers, 1977), p. 262. James Murison, 1816–85, lived in Sea Point. He was a member of the Harbour Board, director of the Cape of Good Hope Bank and a partner of W. G. Anderson. His firm acted as agents of the Castle Packet Co. He was a member of the Legislative Council until 1885: *DSAB* vol. III, pp. 643–4; Obituary, *Cape Times*, 28 September 1885.

51 Davison, *Marvellous Melbourne*, p. 19.

52 Shaw, *Some Beginnings*, p. 134; *Cape Times*, 2 November 1878. A. I. Little,

History of the City Club (Cape Town, *Cape Times*, 1938), pp. 11–16 shows that W. Fleming, W. M. Farmer, T. E. Fuller and W. G. Anderson all served as committee members. In 1879 they laid on a special dinner for St Leger.

53 *Cape Times*, 2 November 1878; also 20 March 1877, 4 December 1878.

54 *Cape Times*, 23, 25, 26 November 1878.

55 *Cape Times*, 19 May 1879, 9 August 1880; *Lantern*, 8, 22 February 1879, 1 March 1879, 24 May 1879.

56 SBA 1/1/26 IR CT, 1881; IR CT, 1883, W. M. Farmer's liabilities. CA, LC 44, 'SA Fire Assurance Co. Ltd'; LC 43, 'Baxter's Gully Diamond Mining Company Ltd'; LC 32, 'Union Bank Ltd'; LC 11, 'Cape of Good Hope Bank Ltd'; LC 3, 'Bank of Africa Ltd'; LC 10, 'City Tramways Co. Ltd'.

57 *Cape Argus*, 5 October 1891, obituary.

58 T. E. Fuller, 1831–1910: *DSAB* vol. I (Johannesburg, Nasionale Boekhandel Beperk, 1968), pp. 304–5; Saul Solomon, 1817–92: *DSAB* vol. I, pp. 759–61 and W. E. G. Solomon, *Saul Solomon*.

59 *Cape Times*, 23 November 1878, 25 January 1879, 19 May 1879; *Lantern*, 16 August 1879.

60 *Cape Times*, 9, 10 August 1880.

61 SBA 1/1/26 IR CT, 1883, liabilities section, under 'Bolus Brothers'; *DSAB*, vol. III, pp. 88–91, for details on H. Bolus.

62 *South African News*, 6 November 1903, obituary.

63 A. R. McKenzie's list of securities are in SBA 1/1/26 IR CT, 1881, in a separate folder; *CPP*, G39–1893, p. 16.

64 *Lantern*, 4 October 1879.

65 Hennock, 'Social Compositions', pp. 333–9; Briggs, *Victorian Cities*, pp. 206–14.

66 CA, LC 10, 'Steam Laundry'; LC 5, 'City Tramways'.

67 *CPP*, A15–1879, 'SCR on the Oranjezicht Purchase Bill', Appendix M, p. xix.

68 *Lantern*, 12 June 1886.

69 *Lantern*, 12 July 1879; *Cape Times*, 5 August 1880, 19 August 1881, 8 September 1881.

70 CA, 3CT 7/1/2/1/31–3, 'Street Assessment Rolls, 1873–1875'; *CPP*, A1–1867 and *CPP*, A1–1861; *Cape Times*, 15 February 1887, put the figure at 5,400 voters in 1887.

71 *Cape Times*, 13 August 1878, 14 August 1880, letter from 'Scrutineer'; *Lantern*, 4 October 1879; *CPP*, A13–1881, pp. 3 and 54.

72 *CPP*, A13–1881, p. 57: 'Many of the Coloured classes are continually moving'. *Cape Times*, 18 October 1877. An editorial in the *Cape Times*, 28 July 1882, complained that many merchants were not on the voting list but that 'Japie, Salie, Joe, Jack', 'coolies' living in miserable hovels, were.

73 **Duration of polls:** *Cape Argus*, 28 September 1875, by-election: poll 9.00–10.30 a.m.; *Cape Argus*, 15 August 1876, municipal election: poll 9.00–11.30 a.m.; *Cape Times*, 18 August 1877: ten minute poll; 23 August 1877 'Scandalous Elections'; 25 September 1877: short duration of poll; *CPP*, A13–1881; *CPP*, A10–1879, p. 10. **Size of polls:** *Cape Argus*, 19 August 1875, 15 August 1876; *Cape Times*, 14 August 1877, 13 August 1878, 12 August 1879, 10 August 1880, 10 August 1881.

74 Fraser, *Urban Politics*, pp. 143–5.

75 *CPP*, A9–1885, 'SCR on the Cape Town Municipal Act Amendment Bill', p. 25.
76 Quoted in Picard, *Grand Parade*, pp. 77–8.
77 *Cape Times*, 1 March 1878.
78 *Cape Times*, 4 August 1880.
79 *Cape Times*, 26 February 1880. See also *Cape Times*, 9, 10 August 1880.
80 Swanson, 'Sanitation Syndrome', p. 343; A. Lombaard, 'The Smallpox Epidemic of 1882 in Cape Town with Some Reference to the Neighbouring Suburbs' (Honours thesis, UCT, 1981), p. 128; *Cape Times*, 13 April 1906.
81 *Cape Times*, 27 June 1882.
82 The quotation is from *Lantern*, 1 July 1882; cartoons were in this edition and 5, 12 August 1882.
83 *Lantern*, 29 July 1882, 12 August 1882.
84 Hennock, 'Borough Councils', pp. 333–4; *Cape Times*, 15 August 1882.
85 *Zuid-Afrikaan*, 27 July 1882.
86 *CCP*, A13–1881; CA, 3CT 7/1/2/1/33, 'Street Assessment Rolls'; *Lantern*, 15 September 1888, obituary of J. C. Wicht.
87 *CPP*, A44–1882, 'Cape Town Municipality Act'.
88 Lombaard, 'Smallpox', pp. 52–3, 105; *Cape Times*, 14 July 1882, 3 May 1883, 7 February 1884, 15 January 1886, 18 February 1887, 13 January 1888; Van Heyningen, 'Public Health', pp. 127–39.
89 *Cape Times*, 5 July 1882, 3 May 1883, 19, 20, 21 January 1886, 8, 16 May 1888, 13 April 1906. Picard, *Grand Parade*, p. 87.
90 *Cape Times*, 18, 22 February 1888, 10, 17, 23 March 1888. *CPP*, A9–1888, 'SCR on Cape Town Sanitation and Water Supply'.
91 Briggs, *Victorian Cities*, pp. 21–2.
92 *CBB*s 1882–91, 'Municipalities'; Briggs, *Victorian Cities*, pp. 205, 211; *Lantern*, 14 July 1883; *Cape Times*, 12 August 1884, 18 November 1884, 15 February 1887, 3, 9 August 1887, 14 August 1888, 13 August 1889.
93 HA, GM to LO, 26 November 1881. SBA 1/1/26 IR CT, 1883, 'Liabilities Section'; *Cape Times*, 9 August 1883, 10 September 1895.
94 *Cape Times*, 12 August 1882.
95 *CPP*, A9–1885, 'SCR on the Cape Town Municipal Act Amendment Bill', p. 2. *CPP*, A28–1885, 'Cape Town Municipality Act'.
96 Quoted by St Leger in an editorial, *Cape Times*, 12 August 1878.
97 *Cape Times*, 25 January 1881, 21 March 1881, 1 April 1881, 30 July 1881.
98 Davenport, *Afrikaner Bond*, esp. pp. 1–7. Giliomee, 'Afrikaner Identity', p. 99; Ross, 'Synthesis', p. 115; *Lantern*, 17 January 1890. *CPP*, G9–1891, 'Education Commission', p. 88.
99 *Cape Times*, 12 February 1884. *Cape Argus*, 6 December 1893.
100 A. Walker, ' "Boer" and "Boesman", "Folk" and "Fyand": Attitudes to Race in *Ons Klyntji*, 1896–1906' (Honours thesis, UCT, 1990), pp. 18–25.
101 E.g. Dale, 'The Cape and its People', pp. 14, 18–19; J. A. Froude, *Oceana: Or England and her Colonies* (London, Longman's Green & Co., 1881), p. 34.
102 Dale, 'The Cape and its People', pp. 18–19.
103 Wilmot, *History*, p. 120.
104 Noble, *The Cape and South Africa*, p. 24.

105 Froude, *Oceana*, p. 51.
106 *Cape of Good Hope Legislative Council Debates 1879* (Cape Town, Saul Solomon, 1880), p. 33; *Cape Times*, 1 June 1877.
107 *Cape Times*, 21 October 1881.
108 *Cape of Good Hope Legislative Council Debates 1878* (Cape Town, Saul Solomon, 1878), pp. 87–100, 116–25. The quotations are from pp. 87, 116–18, 95–6 respectively; *CPP*, A5–1878, 'Act for the Establishment of a Colonial Yeomanry Force'.
109 Purkis, 'Railway Building', chap. 9.
110 *Ibid.*, pp. 322–412.
111 *CPP*, A26–1879, pp. 3, 18, 21, 24, 28, 30, 35.
112 *Legislative Council Debates 1879*, p. 5.
113 *CPP*, A26–1879; Harries, 'Mozbiekers'. *CPP*, A39–1879, 'Immigration Act', see schedule attached to this Act.
114 CA, PWD 2/8/20, 'Memo on the Subject of Emigration to the Colony of the Cape of Good Hope', Mills to Commissioner of Crown Lands and Public Works, 25 March 1886.
115 Worger, *City of Diamonds*, pp. 105–7, 110–11, 120, 148–61 – the quotation is from p. 133; Turrell, *Capital and Labour*, pp. 51, 87, 126, 128–54.
116 *Cape Times*, 17, 31 March 1882, 8 April 1882, 21 September 1882, 3, 6, 10, 24 October 1882, 3 November 1882, 15 December 1882.

4 WHITE ETHNICITY, RACISM AND SOCIAL PRACTICE

1 Miles, *Racism*, pp. 73–7.
2 Stepan, *The Idea of Race*; Wilmot, *History*, p. 58; *CPP*, G42–1876, p. 3.
3 Dale, 'The Cape and its People', p. 4. Wilmot, *History*, p. 120; Walker, '*Ons Klyntji*', p. 33.
4 *CPP*, A26–1879; R. T. Smith, 'Race and Class in the post–emancipation Caribbean', in Ross (ed.), *Racism and Colonialism*, pp. 101, 112–4.
5 Mayson, *The Malays of Cape Town*; F. Krauss, 'A Description of Cape Town and its Way of Life, 1838–1840', *Quarterly Bulletin of the South African Library*, vol. 21 (1966–7), 2–12, 39–49; Duff Gordon, *Letters*.
6 Dale, 'The Cape and its People', p. 4; Noble, *Descriptive Handbook*, pp. 44–5. *Cape Argus*, 8 February 1876.
7 Noble, *Descriptive Handbook*, pp. 44–5. Wilmot, *History*, p. 120.
8 *Cape Times*, 29 September 1876, 1 March 1878.
9 *Lantern*, 31 January 1880.
10 *Cape Times*, 26 July 1880.
11 *Lantern*, 12 August 1882.
12 *Cape Times*, 11 March 1881; *Lantern*, 20 August 1881.
13 *CMM*, 9, (1875), 49.
14 Father P. N. Waggett, 'The Malays of Cape Town', *Cowley Evangelist*, (August 1899).
15 *Cape Times*, 11 March 1881.
16 *Cape Times*, 12, 19, 25, 26, 28 March 1881; *Lantern*, 23 September 1882.
17 Bickford-Smith, 'Meanings of Freedom'; Rt Reverend A. G. S. Gibson,

Sketches of Church Work and Life in the Diocese of Cape Town (Cape Town, South African 'Electric' Printing and Publishing Co., 1900), pp. 29–44; Bank, 'Slavery in Cape Town'.

18 *Lantern*, 23 September 1882.

19 Duff Gordon, *Letters*, p. 43.

20 *CPP*, A4–1878, Appendix G, p. ix.

21 M. A. Bradlow, 'Cemetery Uprising'; A. Davids, ' "The Revolt of the Malays": A Case Study of the Reaction of the Cape Muslims to the Smallpox Epidemics of Nineteenth Century Cape Town', *Studies*, V, (1983), 46–78. Shell, 'Rites and Rebellion'; Van Heyningen, 'Public Health', pp. 151–63, 183.

22 Van Heyningen, 'Public Health', pp. 158–59 suggests that Burns threatened to shoot his own children if they were removed to the hospital; but the *Cape Times*, 2 August 1882, gave this other version of what he said at the meeting.

23 Cited in Van Heyningen, 'Public Health', pp. 167–8.

24 *Lantern*, 23, 30 September 1882. *Cape Times*, 18, 28 August 1882, 4, 19 September 1882, 4 October 1882.

25 V. Simpson, *My Reminiscences* (London, Longman's Green & Co., 1926), p. 7.

26 *Cape Times*, 18 January 1884: the Resident Magistrate fined a man £1 for insulting another by calling him a Malay.

27 *Lantern*, 4 October 1879, 2 November 1880, 16, 23 September 1882.

28 *Cape Times*, 31 August 1882.

29 Lombaard, 'Smallpox', p. 100; *Cape Times*, 4, 12 October 1882.

30 *Cape Times*, 12 August 1882.

31 *Legislative Council Debates 1879*, pp. 45–6.

32 McCracken, *Cape Parliament*, chap. 7.

33 Solomon, *Saul Solomon*; McCracken, *Cape Parliament*, p. 87.

34 J. X. Merriman to Bishop N. J. Merriman, 26 February 1879, in P. Lewsen (ed.), *Selections from the Correspondence of J. X. Merriman 1870–1890* (Cape Town, The Van Riebeeck Society, 1960), pp. 70–1.

35 Trapido, 'Friends of the Natives', pp. 259–68; *Cape Times*, 15 November 1878, 4 December 1878, 25 January 1879, 27, 28, 29 August 1883; M. Ryan, 'Anders Ohlsson, Brewer and Politician, 1881–1894' (Honours thesis, UCT, 1976), p. 100: Ohlsson was an MLA for Cape Town.

36 *Cape Times*, 4 December 1878.

37 *Cape Times*, 2 November 1880.

38 *Cape Times*, 30 April 1881, 6 July 1881. See also 22 April 1880, 8 December 1880, 5 September 1881, 7 October 1881; *Lantern*, 9 July 1881.

39 *Cape Times*, 14 October 1880.

40 *Lantern*, 6 September 1879, 25 October 1879; *Cape Times*, 3 March 1879, 15 September 1879, 14 August 1880.

41 Lewsen, *John X. Merriman*, pp. 84–7.

42 *Cape Times*, 20 August 1880; *Lantern*, 9 November 1880.

43 Kennedy, *At the Cape*, pp. 13, 42.

44 Walker, '*Ons Klyntji*', pp. 63–9. Crais, *White Supremacy*, pp. 128–9.

45 Cited in Crais, *White Supremacy*, p. 132.

46 A. Cole, *The Cape and the Kafirs* (London, Richard Bentley, 1852).

47 Cole, *The Cape*, p. 196; Knox is cited in Stepan, *The Idea of Race*, pp. 41, 42.

48 Wilmot, *History*, p. 75.
49 *Cape Argus*, 27 February 1875; *Cape Times*, 23 January 1879, 2 November 1880.
50 *Zuid-Afrikaan*, 7 June 1884.
51 *Cape Times*, 16, 17 May 1878.
52 Saunders, 'Africans'; Harries, 'Mozbiekers'.
53 *Cape Times*, 16 May 1878.
54 *Cape Times*, 22 May 1878, 12 June 1878.
55 T. R. H. Davenport, 'The Beginnings of Urban Segregation in South Africa: The Native (Urban Areas) Act of 1923 and its Background', *Occasional Paper No. 15* (Grahamstown, Institute of Economic Research, 1971); Crais, *White Supremacy*, pp. 74, 151, 77–80, 117. Welsh, 'Towns', p. 179.
56 T. Vienings, 'Stratification and Proletarianisation: The Rural Political Economy of the Worcester District, 1875–1910' (Honours thesis, UCT, 1985), p. 45.
57 Welsh, 'Towns', pp. 186–7.
58 Maylam, 'Urban Apartheid', 62.
59 Saunders, 'Africans', pp. 26–7.
60 Turrell, *Capital and Labour*, pp. 99–100.
61 Saunders, 'Africans', pp. 27–29.
62 *Cape Times*, 7 August 1880.
63 *Cape Times*, 24 February 1881.
64 *Lantern*, 3 September 1881.
65 *Cape Times*, 20 July 1881.
66 *Cape Times*, 29 August 1881, 3, 5 September 1881; *Lantern*, 3 September 1881; Saunders, 'Africans', pp. 30–1.
67 Crais, *White Supremacy*, pp. 59, 60, 114, 194.
68 *Cape Times*, 17 August 1880. Welsh, 'Towns'.
69 Turrell, *Capital and Labour*, pp. 100–3.
70 *CPP*, A26–1879, p. 61.
71 *Cape Times*, 6 July 1882.
72 *Cowley St John Parish Magazine* (from 1891 the *Cowley Evangelist*), February 1885, March 1886, May 1886, September 1886, March 1887; Saunders, 'Africans', pp. 30–3.
73 Fredrickson, *White Supremacy*, pp. 259–60.
74 Andrews, *Buenos Aires*, pp. 204–5.
75 *Ibid.*, p. 197. See also pp. 196, 204–5.
76 Karasch, 'Rio de Janeiro', p. 142.
77 *CPP*, G42–1876, pp. 277–81; *CPP*, G6–1892, 'Cape Census for 1891', pp. 380–1.
78 *Lantern*, 23 August 1879. See also 19 July 1879, 23 August 1879; Van Heyningen, 'Public Health', p. 78.
79 *Cape Times*, 28 August 1879, letter from 'Ismael'.
80 *CPP*, A21–1892, 'SCR on the Liquor Act', pp. 22, 40, 49.
81 Cell, *White Supremacy*.
82 For this development in Kingston, Jamaica see C. G. Clarke, 'A Caribbean Creole Capital: Kingston, Jamaica (1692–1938)', in Ross and Telkamp (eds.), *Colonial Cities*, p. 165.
83 Fredrickson, *White Supremacy*, pp. 188–9.

84 C. Bolt, *Victorian Attitudes to Race* (London, Routledge & Kegan Paul, 1971), esp. pp. 75–108; Lorimer, *Colour, Class and the Victorians*.

85 Ensor, *Sitongo*, p. 166. See also the preface and p. 171 for details on sales of the book and Ensor himself.

86 *Ibid.*, p. 157.

87 D. M. Schreuder, 'The Cultural Factor in Victorian Imperialism: A Case Study of the British "Civilising Mission"', *Journal of Imperial and Commonwealth History*, 4, 3 (1976), 283–317.

88 Father F. W. Puller, 'Letter from Cape Town', *Cowley St John Parish Magazine*, March 1886.

89 Solomon, *Saul Solomon*, p. 232.

90 *Cape Times*, 4 November 1881; *Cape Argus*, 17 October 1892.

91 Dale, 'The Cape and its People', p. 13.

92 J. X. Merriman to J. B. Currey, 25 February 1876, in Lewsen, *Correspondence of J. X. Merriman*.

93 *CPP*, G4–1883, 'Report and Proceedings on Native Laws and Customs'. The quotation is from p. 52. Shepstone's evidence takes up seventy-eight pages of the proceedings; Schreuder, 'Victorian Imperialism'.

94 *CPP*, A11–1886, 'SCR on the Pass Laws', p. iii; *CPP*, A26–1883, 'SCR on the Native Locations Act'; *CPP*, A23–1879, 'Vagrancy Act'.

95 Cell, *White Supremacy*, pp. 13–14.

96 Marks, ' "White Supremacy" ', p. 396.

97 *CPP*, A18–1873, 'Masters and Servants Act'.

98 *Cape Times*, 10 October 1882.

99 Jackson, *New Orleans*, p. 22; Clarke, 'Kingston', p. 162; Turrell, *Capital and Labour*, pp. 100–3.

100 *Cape Times*, 19 July 1880, advert for general servant, 'White preferred' or 15 November 1887, advert for cook, 'European preferred'; *Cape Times*, 9 August 1880, St Leger says that most landlords are prejudiced against Africans.

5 THE DANGERS OF DEPRESSION

1 Stedman Jones, *Outcast London*. Racialised perceptions did play a part in the attitudes of bourgeois Londoners as Williams has shown *vis-à-vis* the Irish poor in the city: K. Williams, *From Pauperism to Poverty: The Poor Law 1870–1914* (London, Routledge & Kegan Paul, 1981), p. 265.

2 HA, GM to LO, 26 November 1881.

3 SBA 1/1/26, IR for 1883.

4 SBA 1/126, IR for 1883; HA, GM to LO, half-yearly reports: 6 February 1884, 6 February 1885, 8 August 1885, 8 February 1886, 9 February 1887; SBA 1/1/27 IRs for 1884 and 1885; SBA 1/1/27, IR for 1887.

5 HA, GM to LO, 6 February 1885 (half-yearly report).

6 HA, GM to LO, 16 February 1887.

7 HA, GM to LO, 23 September 1882. Immelman, *Men of Good Hope*, p. 248.

8 *Lantern*, 20 March 1886.

9 *CBB*, 1906, p. xx.

10 *CBB*, 1875, 1884–90, 'Municipal Revenue'.

11 *CBB*, 1882–93, 'Imports and Exports via Cape Town'.

12 *Cape Times*, 29 July 1886.

13 *Lantern*, 24 September 1881.

14 Saunders, 'Africans', pp. 26, 28.

15 *Cape Times*, 29 January 1883; *Cowley St John's Parish Magazine*, September 1887.

16 *CPP*, G6–1892, pp. 32–5.

17 HA, GM to LO, 16 September 1885; Immelman, *Men of Good Hope*, pp. 248–9.

18 Stedman Jones, *Outcast London*, pp. 81–88.

19 *Cape Argus*, 1 April 1876.

20 *Cape Times*, 8 December 1884. In the match factory the women were on piece-work. The newspaper commented: 'The girls are slow, but it saves them from penury'; *Excalibur*, 25 June 1886, 2 July 1886; *Cape Times*, 3 May 1883.

21 *CPP*, A3–1883; *CPP*, C1–1891, 'SCR on Colonial Industries'. *Cape Times*, 2 July 1883, 'Steam Confectionery Works'; The *Cape Times*, 17 March 1884, reported that the jam-making and pickling industries were in their infancy. The *Evening Express* ran a series of useful articles on Cape Town's industries: 16 September 1884, wagons, leather, boots and shoes, saddlers, furniture; 22 September 1884, jewellery, cigarettes, mineral water; 22 October 1884, coach building; 27 October 1884, soap-making and laundry works; 3 November 1884, tin manufacturing; 7 November 1884, sweetmeats; 24 January 1885, box-making; 29 January 1885, aereated water manufacturing; 5 February 1885, a match factory; 18 February 1885, the Kloof pottery works; 2 March 1885, iron foundry, candle manufacturing.

22 *CPP*, A18–1873; Warren, 'Municipal Politics', p. 41.

23 *Cape Times*, 29 August 1876; *Cape Argus*, 29 August 1876.

24 *Cape Argus*, 29 August 1876.

25 *Cape Times*, 14 September 1882, 12 December 1884, 27 August 1886.

26 *Cape Times*, 29 April 1878, 'Report of the Free Dispensary'; *Cape Argus*, 19 February 1876, 'Temperance Meeting'. For two comments suggesting that the dominant class thought that there was little or no poverty in Cape Town, see *Cape Times*, 6 October 1876, 26 February 1880; Barnett-Clarke, *Thomas Fothergill Lightfoot* provides useful information on charity.

27 CA, HBC 242, 'Records of the Free Dispensary', *Cape Times*, 26 July 1880, 'First Impressions of Cape Town by an Ulster Irishman'.

28 *Proceedings of the South African Teachers' Association during the year 1869* (Cape Town, Saul Solomon, 1870), pp. 30–2.

29 *CPP*, A19–1877: see pp. 42 and 56 for specific references to 'dirty habits'' and 'ignorance'; *Cape Argus*, 30 January 1875, letter from 'M.A.', 8 January 1876, 'In the Slums'.

30 Williams, *Poor Law*, pp. 96–7; Stedman Jones, *Outcast London*, pp. 193–4, 196, 271.

31 *CPP*, A19–1877, p. 62.

32 *Ibid.*, p. 64.

33 *Cape Times*, 2 August 1877.

34 *Cape Times* 17 September 1879, letter from 'A.P.'.

35 *Cape Times*, 17, 29 September 1879, 10, 11, 14, 15 November 1879.
36 *Cape Times*, 27 September 1879, letter from 'Blood'. See also letters from 'No Humbug' and 'T.M.'; 11 October 1879, letter from 'Dangerous Impulse'.
37 *Lantern*, 20 August 1881.
38 *Lantern*, 3 September 1881.
39 *Cape Times*, 19 October 1878. Williams, *Poor Law*, pp. 136–40 for discussion of the concept of social control; M. J. Daunton, 'Public Place and Private Space: The Victorian City and the Working-class household', in Fraser and Sutcliffe (eds.), *Urban History*, pp. 218–23: in Britain adolescent street life was also defined as delinquency and vigorously suppressed; *CPP*, A1–1881, 'SCR on the Porter Reformatory Bequest'; *Cape Times*, 25 December 1876, 5, 9 January 1878.
40 Barnett-Clarke, *Thomas Fothergill Lightfoot*: several benefit societies were established by Lightfoot; J. Pearce, 'The Origins of the Temperance Movement in Cape Town in the 1880s' (Honours thesis, UCT, 1985); Lewis, *Between the Wire and the Wall*, p. 14. Van Heyningen, 'Poverty'.
41 *CPP*, A19–1877; *CPP*, A1–1881.
42 *Cape Times*, 10 November 1879, sub-leader.
43 CA, HBC 242, 'Records of the Free Dispensary'.
44 *Lantern*, 24 March 1883. Stedman Jones, *Outcast London*, pp. 179, 193–6.
45 *Cape Times*, 26 February 1880.
46 *Lantern* 26 August 1882.
47 *Cape Times*, 28 June 1882.
48 *Cape Times*, 27 June 1882. For other awful examples of crowded living conditions see 1, 4 July 1882.
49 *Cape Times*, 30 June 1882; and see Lombaard, 'Smallpox' and Van Heyningen, 'Public Health' for further details of events surrounding the smallpox epidemic.
50 *Lantern*, 9 September 1882, 7 October 1882. For a detailed analysis of Mayhew's descriptions and views on London's poor see G. Himmelfarb, *The Idea of Poverty* (New York, Alfred A Knopf, 1983), pp. 307–400, esp. pp. 312–23.
51 *Cape Times*, 6 July 1882; see also 29 June 1882.
52 *Cape Times*, 26 February 1880.
53 The quotation is from the *Cape Times*, 19 July 1882; see also 15, 17, 20 July 1882, 17 August 1882.
54 *Cape Times*, 17 August 1882. Lombaard, 'Smallpox', pp. 117–118.
55 *Cape Times*, 21 August 1882, 4, 12 October 1882.
56 *Cape Times*, 11 September 1882.
57 Swanson, 'Sanitation Syndrome'; *Cape Times*, 29 January 1883.
58 *Cape Times*, 22 July 1882.
59 *Cape Times*, 19 April 1883.
60 CA, LC 5, 'City Tramways'.
61 *Cape Times*, 6 May 1881, 6, 9 September 1882.
62 *CPP*, G2–1888, 'Report of the Committee on Convicts and Gaols', pp. 9, 390, 400, 408; *CPP*, G13–1888, 'Report of District Surgeons for 1887', p. 13; *CPP*, G47–1893, 'Report on the Management and Discipline of Convict Stations and Prisons for the Year ended 1892', pp. 6, 10, 12, and 18 which show that

segregation in Cape Town gaols was far more complete than in 1888; *CPP*, A17–1891, 'SCR on the Porter Reformatory'; *Cape Times*, 4 April 1906.

63 Van Heyningen, 'Public Health', esp. pp. 45–103.

64 H. Deacon, 'Racism and Reform: The Colonial Insane on Robben Island 1846–1880' (unpublished paper presented to the British African Studies Association, September 1992), p. 21.

65 Van Heyningen, 'Public Health', p. 127; Lombaard, 'Smallpox'.

66 *CPP*, G16–1883 and G17–1883: reports on the New and Old Somerset Hospitals for the year 1882.

67 Van Heyningen, 'Public Health', pp. 143, 235.

68 *CPP*, G9–1884, 'Reports of the Colonial Medical Committee and Vaccine Officer, and on the Hospitals under Government Control, for the year 1883'; CA, Medical Committee (MC) 30, Letters despatched 1872–1888, Secretary to Colonial Secretary, 12 July 1882, 28 December 1883; *Lantern*, 8 December 1883, 12 April 1884.

69 CA, MC 30, Secretary to Colonial Secretary, 22 June 1883.

70 *Excalibur*, 4 October 1889, quoting Dr J. W. Matthews.

71 *Cape Times*, 24 August 1883.

72 *Cape Times*, 4 July 1883.

73 *Cape Times*, 31 August 1883.

74 *Cape Times*, 4, 7 September 1883, 15 August 1884.

75 *Cape Times*, 3, 7 September 1883.

76 *Zuid–Afrikaan*, 2 February 1884; Ryan, 'Ohlsson', pp. 26 and 99: O'Reilly, on a platform of 'Northward Expansion and Protection', was elected in 1888; *Cape Times*, 27, 28 April 1883, 29 March 1883 (which includes St Leger's leader), 9 February 1884.

77 *Cape Times*, 8 January 1884.

78 CA, CHB 89, 'Resolutions, letters and petitions from Harbour Board Employees', 30 April 1886, 1, 12 May 1886: these employees included platelayers and fitters attempting to ward off a second reduction in their pay, seemingly without success. The optimistic attempt by artisans in the building trade to reduce the working day from ten or nine-and-a-half hours to nine did little better in 1885: *Cape Times*, 7, 19, 20 October 1885, 4 November 1885; see also 1 August 1884, petition re. Salt River workers.

79 *Cape Times*, 3, 5 March 1884, 1 August 1884.

80 *Lantern*, 16 August 1884; *Cape Times*, 2, 4, 5 August 1884; *Cape Argus*, 2, 4 August 1884; CA, 1CT 6/170, 'John Titus and seven others', 18 August 1884. John Titus was a forty-six-year-old Jamaican. 'Long Dick's' real name was Robert Williams. The other alleged leaders were James Mandes, George Roberts, August Brown and John Alvery, all West Indians and aged between twenty-four and thirty. CA, Attorney General (AG) 2861 gives the Titus quotation.

81 *Cape Argus*, 2 August 1884.

82 *Cape Times*, 11 August 1884.

83 *Lantern*, 14 June 1884, 10 January 1885.

84 *Cape Times*, 12 August 1884.

85 *Cape Times*, 11 August 1884.

86 *Cape Times*, 20 August 1884.

87 *Cape Times*, 21 August 1884.

88 *Cape Times*, 22, 26, 29 August 1884.

89 *Cape Times*, 26 August 1884: Lightfoot was speaking at a special town council meeting.

90 *Cape Times*, 6, 26 August 1884, 5 September 1884; *Cape Argus*. 5 September 1884.

91 *Cape Times*, 22 July 1886; *Excalibur*, 23 July 1886.

92 *Cape Times*, 23, 28, 29 July 1886, 16 November 1886.

93 *Cape Times*, 18 August 1886.

94 *Cape Times*, 24 July 1886, 6 August 1886.

95 *Lantern*, 11 July 1885, 13 February 1886; *Cape Times*, 11 June 1888.

96 Turrell, *Capital and Labour*, pp. 135–54; Ryan, 'Ohlsson', pp. 22, 26.

97 K. Elks, 'Crime, Community and Police in Cape Town, 1825–1850' (MA thesis, UCT, 1986); Van Heyningen, 'Public Health', chap. 4. Bradlow, 'Cemetery Uprising'; *Cape Times*, 25 December 1876, 5 , 9 January 1878 for examples of fracas between police and Malays; 10 November 1877, article on the city police.

98 P. Burke, *Popular Culture in Early Modern Europe* (New York, Harper & Row, 1981), pp. 203–4.

99 D. Pinnock, 'Stone's Boys and the Making of a Cape Flats Mafia', in Bozzoli (ed.), *Class*, pp. 418–35 – the quotation is from p. 422; G. Stone, 'The Coon Carnival' (unpublished paper, Abe Bailey Institute of Interracial Studies Cape Town, 197–), is one of the few attempts to analyse the carnival in the kind of way that Burke (see above) has analysed carnivals in early modern Europe. Stone puts the beginning of the Carnival in 1888. That may have been the first occasion when Coloured participants wore coon make-up, but a *Cape Times* report of 1 January 1886 would seem to suggest that year as a more appropriate 'first', although street parades on a smaller scale on New Year's Day went back to at least the 1820s.

100 CA, AG 2881, 'Preliminary Examinations', Case 7, 17 January 1886; *Cape Times*, 19, 21 January 1886; *Cape Argus*, 18, 19 January 1886; Van Heyningen, 'Public Health', chap. 4.

101 *Cape Times*, 22 January 1886.

102 *Cape Argus*, 18 January 1886; *Cape Times*, 22 January 1886.

103 *Lantern*, 30 January 1886.

104 *Cape Times*, 18 February 1887, 9 August 1888, 25 January 1889; *CPP*, A9–1888, p. 1.

105 J. Easton, *Four Questions of the Day* (Cape Town, Juta, 1888), pp. 90, 95, 105, 113, 115.

106 *Cape Times*, 9 August 1888.

107 Wiebe, *Search for Order*, p. 88; Davison, *Marvellous Melbourne*, pp. 236–8; Gillettt and Macmahon, *History of Hull*, pp. 327–8; P. Boyer, *Urban Masses and Moral Order in America 1820–1920* (Cambridge, MA, Harvard University Press, 1978), pp. 127–8.

108 *Lantern*, 8 September 1883, 16 February 1884, 8, 29 March 1884, 3 May 1884, 11 July 1885, 14, 28 May 1887.

109 *Lantern*, 6, 13 October 1888.

110 *Lantern*, 27 August 1887, 21 January 1888, 29 June 1889.

111 Stedman Jones, *Outcast London*.
112 Stedman Jones, *Outcast London*, pp. 129–51, 281–7; Boyer, *Urban Masses*, pp. 128–9, 149; Davison, *Marvellous Melbourne*, pp. 144–50, 237–88.
113 *Lantern*, 8 August 1884; *Excalibur*, 4 October 1889. See also *Cape Times*, 24 July 1886 for a similar classification of the poor.
114 Lorimer, *Colour*, pp. 100–6.
115 Stepan, *The Idea of Race*.
116 W. Gresswell, *Our South African Empire* (London, Chapman & Hall, 1885) vol. II, p. 209; J. J. Aubertyn, *Six Months in the Cape Colony and Natal* (London, Kegan Paul, 1886), p. 235; J. Mackinnon, *South African Traits* (Edinburgh, James Gemmell, 1887).
117 J. Ewing Ritchie, *Brighter South Africa* (London, T. Fisher Unwin, 1892), p. 52; S. Cumberland, *What I Think of South Africa; Its People and Its Politics* (London, Chapman & Hall, 1896), p. 10.
118 *Cape Times*, 21 January 1896; Shaw, *Some Beginnings*, p. 17.
119 *Cape Times*, 24 July 1896.
120 Cited in F. Van Heyningen, 'Prostitution and the Contagious Diseases Acts: The Social Evil in the Cape Colony', *Studies* vol. V (1984), pp. 105–6.
121 *Lantern*, 29 June 1889. See also L. Chisholm, 'The Pedagogy of Porter: The Origins of the Reformatory in the Cape Colony, 1882–1910', *JAH*, 27, 3 (1986), 481–95. Cell, *White Supremacy*, p. 4, makes the point about the alternatives to segregation for White supremacists.
122 Bundy, ' "Vagabond Hollanders" '; Van Heyningen, 'The First Aim of Every Government' (unpublished paper, UCT, 1980); and 'Social Evil', p. 89.
123 *Cape Argus*, 21 December 1892, 10 January 1893, 24 September 1895, 6 June 1896; *Cape Times*, 24 July 1896.
124 *Cape Times*, 2 March 1886; Giliomee, 'Afrikaner Capital', pp. 66–9. Davenport, *Afrikaner Bond*, pp. 79, 98, 309; F. Wilson, 'Farming, 1866–1966', in Wilson and Thompson (eds.), *Oxford History* vol. II, p. 124.
125 Dale, 'The Cape and its People', p. 10.
126 *CPP*, G6a–1890, 'SGE Special Report', p. 2.
127 *Cape Times*, 7 December 1889.
128 *Cape Times*, 14, 15, 19 February 1889, 8 July 1890.
129 *Lantern*, 16 July 1887; *Excalibur*, 15 July 1887; CA, 1CT 3/442, 'Resident Magistrate Cape Town: Records in Civil Cases', July 1887, Case No. 1235.
130 *Cape Times*, 11 February 1890, police court; *Cape Argus*, 26 January 1891.
131 Schreuder, ' "Civilising Mission" '. Davenport, *Afrikaner Bond*, pp. 118–23, 181; Lewsen, *John X. Merriman*, p. 132; Giliomee, 'Afrikaner Capital', p. 66.
132 *Cape Times*, 23 November 1881, 10 November 1882, 8 February 1884. See also Lewsen, *John X. Merriman*. For reports on the two trials see the *Cape Times*, 8 November 1887, 17 January 1888.
133 *Cape Times*, 7 December 1889.
134 *Cape Times*, 2 November 1880, 9 February 1883, 19 June 1883, 27 February 1884.
135 Giliomee, 'Afrikaner Capital', p. 66.
136 *Cape Times*, 30 December 1889; *Cape Argus* 12 May 1891, 5 February 1892, letter from 'Perplexed', 19 February 1893; Lewsen, *John X. Merriman*, p. 146.

6 PROBLEMS OF PROSPERITY REVISITED

1 Wiebe, *Search for Order*, pp. vii–viii.
2 Andrews, *Buenos Aires*, pp. 60, 204–5. Andrews argues that this contention is also true of Sao Paolo, and, in general, of what happened in the United States of America.
3 *Cape Argus*, 28 January 1896.
4 *CPP*, G39–1893, pp. 12, 17, 24, 36, 37, 76. Although, unlike in 1875, the 1891 census does not give details for Cape Town specifically, *CPP*, G6–1892, pp. 298–313 does show White and Black (largely Coloured), in the same artisan occupations in the Cape as a whole. Of the 11,005 people listed as general labourers, 958 were White.
5 *Cape Argus*, 14 June 1895.
6 *Cowley St John's Parish Magazine*, July 1889, letter from F. W. Puller, pp. 105–7. See also August 1896, pp. 185–9, and the *Cape Argus* articles on 'Unexplored Cape Town', cited below, notes 22, 92.
7 The quotation is from the *South African Licensed Victualler's Review* (*SALVR*) 2 June 1892. See also Wits University Library, manuscripts, Vidler papers, A724 for another impressionistic view of the approximate division of labour, this time from a visiting British mayor (of Rye, Sussex), L. A. Vidler. He wrote: 'All the manual work here is done by coolies who are a most dishonest set especially to newly arrived English.'
8 *CPP*, G39–1893, pp. 20–1, 34, 37, 38, 115, 152–4. See p. 88 *re* separate gangs at the docks.
9 *CPP*, A6–1906, p. 53 (J. J. Hill confectioners), p. 80 (United Tobacco Company), pp. 142–3 (Garlick's clothing factory); Cell, *White Supremacy*, p. 124.
10 SBA 1/1/28, IR CT, 1890; HA, GM to LO, 6 August, 1 October 1890.
11 *SALVR*, 19 May 1892; CA, LC 126; HA, GM to LO, 6 August, 6 September 1890.
12 HA, GM to LO, 6 February 1889, 10, 24 December 1890; HA, GM to LO, half-yearly report (HYR), 10 February, 5 August 1891.
13 HA, GM to LO, 7 August 1895; HYR, 9 August 1893.
14 *CBB*, 1906, pp. xx, xxii; Mabin, 'Colonial Capitalism', p. 278; Davenport, *Modern History*, p. 490; HA, GM to LO, 3 September 1890.
15 *CPP*, A19–1888, A22–1889, A22–1892, A20–1893, A6–1894, A25–1896, A33–1898, A35–1899, A20–1900, A33–1902: 'Table Bay Harbour Loan Acts'; *CPP*, A36–1899, A9–1900: 'Public Works Loans Acts'; A42–1902, 'New and Additional Railway Works Act'; *CBB*s for 1891 and 1902, 'Imports and Exports via Cape Town'.
16 SBA 1/1/31 IR CT, 1897, 1898, 1899; HA, GM to LO, HYR, 13 August 1902, 8 August 1900; S. L. Orman, 'Sir D. Graaff, Businessman and Politician' (Honours thesis, UCT, 1983), p. 81; Immelman, *Men of Good Hope*, p. 274.
17 CA, LC 5, 38, 84, 121, 211; *CPP*, A21–1895, 'Caledon Street Tramways Co., Limited Act' and A22–1895, 'Metropolitan Tramways Company Act', Acts that established rival tramway companies; N. Kagan, 'The Growth and Development of the Municipality of Green Point and Sea Point' (Honours

thesis, UCT, 1975), pp. 15–41; SBA 1/1/30, 1895 and 1/1/32, 1898, 'List of Liabilities, Combrinck and Company'; HA, GM to LO, HYR, 9 August 1893.

18 *CPP*, G6–1892, pp. 470–1; *CPP*, G19–1905, 'Cape Census for 1904', pp. 524–525.

19 HA, GM to LO, HYR, 13 February 1895; SBA 1/1/199, IR CT, 1902; SBA 1/1/32, 1899, 'Liabilities, Gardens Syndicate'. *Cape Times*, 1 May 1906; *CPP*, G6–1892, pp. 62, 70; *CPP*, G19–1905, p. 78.

20 The statistical calculations are based largely on the censuses for 1875, 1891, 1904 and 1911. They were influenced by previous work on the censuses in E. Batson (ed.), *Reports and Studies Issued by the Social Survey of Cape Town* vol. SS1 (Cape Town, UCT, 1941), esp. pp. 5–6. Batson also used municipal birth and death registers for the period 1894 onwards. For further details of my calculations see Bickford-Smith, 'Commerce', pp. 274–7. On Jewish immigration see M. Shain, *Jewry and Cape Society* (Cape Town, Historical Publications Society, 1983), p. 75. Also CA, Colonial Office (CO) 5763–5769, 8850–8888, 'Naturalisation papers'. On Indian immigration see E. Bradlow, 'The Cape Community during the Period of Responsible Government', in B. Pachai (ed.), *South Africa's Indians*, pp. 132–78. On the slow rate of Afrikaner urbanisation see Welsh, 'Towns', p. 204.

21 *CPP*, G19–1905, pp. xlvi, 78–9.

22 *Cape Times*, 5 October 1888; *Cape Argus* 4, 10 January, 3 February 1893, series of articles entitled 'Unexplored Cape Town', and 26 October 1895, editorial, which draws comparisons between Cape Town and the London revealed by the *Bitter Cry of Outcast London*; *Cowley Evangelist*, July 1893, 'St Philip's Mission', which discusses its setting in District Six.

23 *Cape Times*, 27 June, 11 August 1891; CA, 3CT 1/7/1/1, 'Mayoral Minutes' for the period 1891–1902; V. Bickford-Smith, '"Keeping Your Own Council"', The Struggle between Houseowners and Merchants for Control of the Cape Town Municipal Council in the Last Two Decades of the Nineteenth Century', *Studies*, vol. V, (1984), 189–208.

24 HA, GM to LO, 24 July 1882, 22 April 1891 for details of Cape Town's business revolution; Davison, *Marvellous Melbourne*, pp. 21–30.

25 Lewsen (ed.), *Correspondence 1870–1890*, p. 210; P. Lewsen (ed.), *Selections from the Correspondence of J. X. Merriman 1890–1898*, (Cape Town, VRS, 1963), pp. 68, 141. SBA IR, Liabilities Section, 1880 and 1885. See also Orman, 'Graaff'.

26 *Cape Times*, 20 September 1897, letter from S. Bartlett, 14 April 1898, 'Ratepayers Meeting'. *Cape Argus*, 15 February 1899, letter from Moses Fletcher; *South African News*, 21 August 1899, letter from C. Bernstein and I. Purcell which pointed out that the central business district elected all eighteen councillors.

27 SBA 1/1/32 IR CT, 1899, 'Liabilities Section, Gardens Syndicate'; *South African Review*, 21 July, 18 August 1899; SBA 1/1/31 IR, 1897, 'Liabilities Section, Combrinck and Company'; CA, 3CT 1/1/40, 19 April 1892.

28 *CPP*, A26–1890, 'Cape Town Municipality Amendment Act'; Bickford-Smith, 'Commerce', p. 285.

29 *CPP*, A8–1897, 'SCR on the Cape Town Municipal Act Amendment Bill', pp. 4–5; *CPP*, A26–1893, 'Cape Town Municipality Act'.

30 *Cape Times*, 14, 28 September 1897.

31 CA, 3CT 1/7/1/1 (and following), 'Mayoral Minutes'; Picard, *Grand Parade*, pp. 90–114; Marshall, 'Cape Town', p. 74; Briggs, *Victorian Cities*, pp. 154–65.

32 *SALVR*, 30 June 1892.

33 HA, GM to LO, 13 February 1895 shows that this transformation took place at a rapid pace between 1892 and 1895; *Cape Argus*, 25 January 1895; E. E. K. Lowndes, *Every-day Life in South Africa* (London, S. W. Partridge, 1900), p. 29.

34 Marks, ' "White Supremacy" ', pp. 395–7.

35 Davenport, *Afrikaner Bond*, pp. 127–38.

36 Lewsen, *John X. Merriman*, pp. 146, 154; Trapido, ' "Friends of the Natives" '.

37 *CPP*, G38–1890, 'Report on the Management and Discipline of Convicts and Prisons for 1889'.

38 *Legislative Council Debates 1891* (Cape Town, Murray & St Leger, 1892), pp. 32, 69.

39 *Ibid.*, pp. 167–9; *South African News*, 9 February 1904; CA, Cape Supreme Court (CSC) 1/1/1/40 'Jury List 1894', and subsequent volumes for subsequent years; *Cape Times*, 8 November 1879, 'Supreme Court'.

40 *Cape Argus*, 10 April 1895.

41 Davenport, *Afrikaner Bond*, pp. 132–8.

42 Giliomee, 'Afrikaner Capital', pp. 66–8.

43 *CPP*, G9–1891, 'Education Commission, First Report', esp. pp. 5–33 and 213; *CPP*, G3–1892, 'Education Commission, Third and Final Report'.

44 *CPP*, G9–1891, pp. 117, 124; *CPP*, G39–1893, p. 44; *Cape Times*, 24 April 1892.

45 *CPP*, G39–1893, pp. 27–9.

46 *CPP*, G9–1891, pp. 58–63, 121–2, 151–7.

47 *Cape Argus*, 1 June 1892, 'Education Commission'.

48 See, for instance, editorials in the *Cape Times*, 29 January, 12 November 1890.

49 *Cape Argus*, 9 June 1892.

50 *Cape Argus*, 29 May 1896; *Cape Times*, 8 January 1890, 'Native Education'.

51 *CPP*, G39–1893, evidence of Thomas Muir; *Cape Argus*, 9 June 1892 for Dale's 'farewell report'.

52 *Cape Argus*, 17 January, 20 June 1894.

53 *CPP*, G3–1894, 'Labour Commission Report', p. ix; *Cape Argus*, 23 January, 20 June 1894.

54 *Cape Argus*, 4, 10, 18 January 1893; *CPP*, A5–1896, 'SCR on the Training of Apprentices and Industrial Schools', pp. 6, 26, 28, Appendices viii–xi; *CPP*, C1a–1894, 'SCR on the Destitute Children Relief Bill'; *CPP*, G3–1892, p. 42; *Cape Argus*, 4 July 1895, 'House of Assembly'.

55 *Cape Argus*, 23 January 1894.

56 Most useful in tracing the process of *de facto* segregation taking place in Cape Town schools are the School Inspection Reports. See especially CA, SGE 2/1,

1893 and SGE 2/154–155, 1905. For details on individual schools see Bickford-Smith, 'Commerce', pp. 312–13; *Cape Argus*, 1, 30 June 1892, 23 January 1894; *CPP*, A35–1905, 'School Board Act'.

57 *Cape Argus*, 23 January 1894.

58 *Cape Times*, 28 February, 7 December 1889, 12 March 1890.

59 Davenport, *Afrikaner Bond*, pp. 147–8.

60 *Cape Times* 5 August 1891.

61 *Cape Argus*, 12 May, 5, 6 August, 13 November 1891, 29 January 1892.

62 Davenport, *Afrikaner Bond*, pp. 147–8.

63 *Cape Argus*, 23 June 1893; Davenport, *Afrikaner Bond*, pp. 152–5.

64 *CPP*, A16–1893, 'To Amend the Constitutional Ordinances'; *Cape Argus*, 29 January 1894.

65 *Cape Argus*, 27 January, 1 December 1893, 29 January 1894; *Cape of Good Hope House of Assembly Debates 1892* (Cape Town, Murray & St Leger, 1892), pp. 171–90; *Cape of Good Hope House of Assembly Debates 1893* (Cape Town, *Cape Times*, 1893), pp. 201–2, 204–5, 208, 211; Ryan, 'Ohlsson', pp. 99–100; Trapido, ' "Friends of the Natives" ', pp. 247–74.

66 Davenport, *Afrikaner Bond*, pp. 112, 148–9, 152, 171, 173–87; Lewis, *Between the Wire and the Wall*, p. 11.

67 *Cape Argus*, 4 January 1894, 28 January 1896. *Cape Times*, 21 December 1898; 'XC', *Everyday Life in the Cape Colony in Time of Peace* (London, T. Fisher Unwin, 1902), pp. 91–2.

68 Stone, *Colonist or Uitlander?*, p. 114. For the Cape government's policy on labour and immigration see *CPP*, C2–1892, 'SCR on the Labour Question', pp. vi–viii; *CPP*, G39–1893, 'Labour Commission', pp. iii–iv, xvi; *Cape Argus*, 16 October 1895, 4 May 1899; *Cape Times*, 7 November 1896, 17 February 1897: only aided immigration for domestic servants after 1894; *South African News*, 29 March 1901: 'Immigration Society to Promote Female Immigration'.

69 *Cape Argus*, 6 April 1892, 14 June 1893. See also *Cape Argus*, 6 April, 2 July 1894, 19 November 1896; *Cape Times*, 23 July, 13 August 1896; *South African News*, 10 April, 25 June 1901.

70 *Cape Times*, 23 July, 12 November 1896; *South African News*, 28 September 1899.

71 *Cape Times*, 17 February 1898, 4 April, 23 May, 1 June 1901; *South African News*, 18 October 1899.

72 *Cape Times*, 20 February 1901.

73 *Cape Argus*, 11 May 1891, 14 March 1893, 2 July 1894; *Cape Times*, 4 February 1896; Shain, *Jewry*.

74 *Cape Argus*, 12 February 1895; *Cape Times*, 23 February 1896.

75 *Cape Times*, 23 May, 11 October 1901; *South African News*, 12 October 1901.

76 Shain, *Jewry*; Bradlow, 'Cape Community'.

77 *Cape Times* 20 December 1922: 'Green Point Common, Playground of Generations'.

78 *Cape Times*, 1, 2 October 1895.

79 *Cowley Evangelist*, August 1899; *Spectator*, 9 February 1901, letter from 'Colored Man' [sic].

80 *Spectator*, 29 June 1901.

81 *South African News*, 19 March 1901, letter from 'Disgusted Native'; *Cape Times*, 15 March, 30 August 1901; *Spectator*, 6 April 1901.
82 *Cape Times*, 21 March 1901.
83 *South African News*, 19 October 1903, letter from Joseph Erhard, 30 May 1904, 'Stone Meeting'; *Cape Times*, 16 May 1901, 20 May 1910.
84 R. Archer and A. Bouillon, *The South African Game* (London, Zed, 1982), pp. 28, 81, 85, 86; *Excalibur*, 17 January 1890; *Cape Times*, 25 October 1898, 24 April 1899; *Cape Argus*, 24 February 1891, 24 February 1892.
85 *Cape Argus*, 30 March 1894 (quotation), 7 April 1894, 23 March 1895; *Cape Times*, 13 November 1897.
86 *Cape Argus*, 14 February 1899. See also 8, 9 February 1899.
87 *Cape Times*, 6 November 1897.
88 *Cape Argus*, 3 April 1895.
89 *Cape Argus*, 14 April, 15 September 1893, 8 March, 7 August 1894; *Cape Times*, 24 July, 5 September 1896, 5 January 1899.
90 *Cape Argus*, 25 April 1891, 21 February 1891.
91 *CPP*, G21–1902, 'Cape Peninsula Commission', pp. 605–6, 632–3; CA, NA 457, 'Commission on Native Location for Cape Town', p. 106; *Cape Argus*, 27 March 1894.
92 *Cape Argus*, 26 January 1893, 2, 3 February 1893; CA, 3CT 1/1/1/41, 'Town Council Minutes', 26 January, 2 February 1893; CA, 3CT 1/1/5/247, 1/1/5/255, 'Appendices to Town Council Minutes', 13 February and 15 December 1893 respectively.
93 CA, 3CT 1/7/1/1 'Mayoral Minutes' 1894–5, pp. 108–9; CA, 3CT 1/7/1/2 1896–7, p. 41; CA, 3CT 1/7/1/2 1897–8, p. 69; CA, 3CT 1/7/1/2 1899–1900, p. 5; CA, 3CT 1/5/1/1/1, 'Special Commitee Minute Book', 12 November 1895.
94 *House of Assembly Debates 1893*, p. 167; *Cape Argus*, 13 July 1893.
95 Davison, *Marvellous Melbourne*, pp. 144–6.
96 CA, 3CT 1/7/1/1/1–2 contain the Medical Officer of Health reports for the 1890s.
97 *Cape Argus*, 7 September 1895; *CPP*, G39–1893, pp. 25–34.
98 *Cape Times*, 3 May 1890; *CPP*, G39–1892, pp. 16–25; *CPP*, A12–1890, 'SCR on Labour', p. 41. *Cape Argus*, 11 January, 5 March 1892.
99 *Cape Argus*, 7 September 1895; Shaw, *Some Beginnings*, pp. 44, 45, 48.
100 CA, 3CT 1/1/1/43, 'Council Minutes', 24 October 1895; CA, 3CT 1/1/1/44, 28 November 1895, 28 September 1896; CA, 3CT 1/1/1/45, 24 June, 22 July 1897; *Cape Argus*, 26 October 1895; *Cape Times*, 12 October 1897, 15 April 1898; *South African News*, 27 December 1902.
101 Maylam, 'Urban Apartheid', 61–2.
102 C. Bundy, *The Rise and Fall of the South African Peasantry* (London, Heinemann, 1979), pp. 116–21.
103 *Cape Times*, 14 April 1898.
104 *Cape Times*, 2, 20 June 1898; *South African News*, 14, 21, 23 August 1899; 24 February, 22, 26 March 1900; *South African Review*, 2 June 1899, denounced the SAWMPU as a 'spurious organisation'.
105 *Cape Times*, 12 August 1898; CA, 3CT 1/1/1/47, 11 August 1898; CA, 3CT 1/5/1/1/2, 'Special Committee Minute Book', 26 August 1898; CA, 3CT 1/7/1/2 1897–8, Appendices, pp. lxix–lxxi.

106 CA, 3CT 1/7/1/2, 9 June 1898; CA, 3CT 1/5/1/1/2, 14 June, 21 July, 27, 26 August, 28 October 1898; CA, 3CT 1/1/1/47, 11 August 1898; *Cape Times*, 27 July, 11, 13 August 1898, 16 August 1898.

107 *Cowley Evangelist*, October 1898, December 1898; CA, 3CT 1/7/1/2 1899–1900, p. 53.

108 CA, 3CT 1/1/1/49, 7, 13 April 1899; *South African News*, 5 June 1899.

109 Swanson, 'Sanitation Syndrome', p. 394. See also *Cape Times*, 2 September 1898; *South African Review*, 10 March 1899.

110 Saunders, 'Ndabeni', pp. 169–70; *CPP*, A30–1899, 'To Amend the Law with regard to Native Locations'.

111 *South African News*, 9 December 1899; CA, 3CT 1/1/50, 25 January 1900; Saunders, 'Ndabeni', pp. 170–1.

112 CA, NA 457, esp. pp. 12, 37–43, 46–52, 72, 87. See also *Cape Times*, 8, 16 August, 7 September 1898; *South African News*, 3 June 1899, 12 March 1901; *Cowley Evangelist*, January 1899, April 1901; CA, 3CT 1/7/1/2, 'Mayoral Minutes',1898–9, p. cii; Saul Dubow, 'Race, Civilisation and Culture: The Elaboration of Segregation Discourse in the Inter-war Years', in Marks and Trapido (eds.), *Race, Class and Nationalism*, pp. 75–6; *CPP*, A3–1900, 'SCR on Harbour Boards', pp. iii, v, 14–15, 165.

113 Saunders, 'Ndabeni', p. 171; Van Heyningen, 'Plague', pp. 66–107; *CPP*, A40–1902, 'Native Reserve Location Act'.

114 *Cape Times*, 15 October, 3 December 1901; Saunders, 'Ndabeni', pp. 175–6; *Cape Government Gazette*, 5 March 1901, Government Notice no. 209, for the information on the plague pass system that kept Africans in the city in 1901. See CA, CHB 262, 'Cape Harbour Board Correspondence', A. Fletcher to R. Hammersley-Heenan, 24 January 1902, which tells of the establishment of a Native Labour Bureau in Cape Town, with the support of the government, to provide 'a steady and constant supply' of African labour to employers.

115 *Cape Argus*, 4 January 1894.

116 *Cape Times*, 23 March 1890.

117 *Cape Argus*, 23 January, 15 February 1894, 22 August 1895.

118 *Cape Times*, 24 September 1896.

7 ETHNICITY AND ORGANISATION AMONG CAPE TOWN'S WORKERS

1 Bickford-Smith, 'Meanings of Freedom'.

2 *CPP*, A16–1880, 'SCR on Friendly Societies', pp. 11, 19, 20.

3 F. Cooper, *On the African Waterfront: Urban Disorder and the Transformation of Work in Colonial Mombasa* (New Haven, Yale, 1987), p. 32.

4 I. R. Phimister and C. Van Onselen, *Studies in the History of African Mine Labour in Colonial Zimbabwe* (Gwelo, Mambo Press, 1978); M. Goldberg, 'Worker Consciousness: A Formulation and a Critique' (unpublished paper, African Studies Seminar, UCT, 1980).

5 *CPP*, G6–1892, pp. 470–1; *CPP*, G19–1905, pp. 524–5; *CPP*, G39–1893, pp. 4, 13, 26, 98–100, 118–19; *Cape Times*, 15, 25 September 1906; *CPP*, A6–1906.

6 *Cape Times*, 13 October 1896; D. Ticktin, 'The Origins of the South African Labour Party, 1880–1910' (Ph.D. thesis, UCT, 1973), p. 23; *South African News*, 7 March 1903; S. O'Sullivan, 'Workers with a Difference: Life and Labour in the Salt River Workshops 1900–1935' (Honours thesis, UCT, 1984); S. O'Sullivan, 'Cameos of Life at the Salt River Works in the 1920s', *Studies*, vol. VI (1988) 96–111; *Cape Argus*, 22 April 1897, for meeting at Groote Schuur.

7 B. Atkinson, *Trade Unions in Bristol* (Bristol, Bristol Branch of the History Association, 1982), pp. 1–3.

8 E. Gitsham and J. F. Trembath, *Labour Organisation in South Africa* (Durban, E.P. and Commercial Printing Company, 1926), pp. 1–2, 14; Ticktin, 'Labour Party', pp. 45–6; A. J. Downes, *Printers' Saga* (Johannesburg, Wallach's, 1952), pp. 1–7; P. C. Van Duin, 'Trade Unionism and the Relationship between White and Coloured Workers in the Cape Town Building Industry, 1900–1930' (unpublished paper presented to the Roots and Realities conference, UCT, 1986), p. 6.

9 *Cape Times*, 11 March, 16, 19 May 1890.

10 *Cape Times*, 6, 23 June, 18 August 1890, 17 February 1897. Ticktin, 'Labour Party', p. 46 talks of a trade and labour council being launched in Cape Town in 1894 and relaunched in 1899. But he does not cite contemporary sources for these findings.

11 **Bricklayers**: *Cape Argus*, 27 February, 4 March 1893, 23 March 1897, *South African News*, 3 January, 21 February, 4 April, 4 July 1903, 16 September 1905; **painters**: *Cape Argus*, 1, 24, 29, 31 March, 7 April 1897; *Cape Times*, 8, 11 March 1897, *South African News*, 28 March, 4 July 1903, 22 September 1905; **printers**: *Cape Times*, 17 November 1896; Downes, *Printers' Saga*, pp. 2–3, says that there was definitely a typographical association in existence in 1889 because a copy of the rules of the association exists for that date. But a revised edition of rules was printed in 1896 when the association may have been revived. **Stonemasons**: *Cape Times*, 15 February 1897, *South African News*, 7 July 1899; **tailors**: *Cape Times*, 26 October 1897; **plumbers**: *South African News*, 20 September 1902; **plasterers**: *Cape Times*, 16, 29 April 1898, *Cape Argus*, 28 October 1895.

12 CA, PWD 1588, 'Lists of Aided Immigrants, 1889–1902'; *CPP*, G39–1893 gives considerable detail about origins and rates of pay of artisans in Cape Town: see pp. 25–6, 34–9, 42–3, 82–91; *South African News*, 8 June 1899, details of Plasterers' Union; 1 July 1899, Typographical Union; 7 July 1899, Operative Masons; 1 July 1899, Operative Plumbers; Ticktin, 'Labour Party', pp. 15–21; D. Blankenhorn, ' "Our Class of Workmen": The Cabinet–makers Revisited', in R. Harrison and J. Zeitlin (eds.), *Divisions of Labour* (Brighton, Harvester, 1985), pp. 24–5.

13 *Cape Times*, 5 April 1889, *Cape Argus*, 4 November 1895.

14 **Plumbers**: *Cape Argus*, 28 October 1895; **tailors**: *Cape Times*, 27, 28, 29 October, 3 November 1897; **plasterers**: *South African News*, 8 June 1899; **printers**: *South African News*, 23 May 1903; **painters**: *South African News* 28 March 1903; **carpenters**: *South African News*, 7, 21 March 1903; **plasterers**: *South African News*, 7 March 1903.

15 R. Harrison, 'Introduction', in Harrison and Zeitlin (eds.), *Divisions of Labour*, p. 8.

16 Harrison, 'Introduction', pp. 8, 14; Stedman Jones, *Outcast London*, pp. 59–60.

17 P. Van Duin, 'Artisans and Trade Unions in the Cape Town Building Industry, 1900–1924', in James and Simons (eds.), *Angry Divide*, pp. 95–110.

18 S. Greenberg, *Race and State in Capitalist Development* (Johannesburg, Ravan Press, 1980), chap. 13; *South African News* 9 May 1903; *Cape Times*, 9 May 1903; *Cape Argus*, 23 March 1897; Cell, *White Supremacy*, p. 137.

19 *CPP*, G39–1893, p. 38.

20 *Cape Times*, 8 March 1897; *Cape Argus*, 8, 24, 31 March 1897.

21 J. Lewis, *Industrialisation and Trade Union Organisation in South Africa, 1924–1955: The Rise and Fall of the South African Trades and Labour Council* (Cambridge, Cambridge University Press, 1984), p. 14. For comments on the shortage of skilled labour or the need or desirability of importing it from Britain see: *Cape Argus*, 27 July 1894, 20 August 1895; *Cape Times*, 19 September 1909; *CPP*, G21–1907, 'Report on Immigration and Labour', p. 12; *CPP*, A6–1908, 'SCR on Imported Contract Labour', pp. 3, 4.

22 *CPP*, G39–1893, pp. 26, 37, 83; *CPP*, A6–1908, pp. 22–30; Davison, *Marvellous Melbourne*, pp. 73–5.

23 CA, Government House (GH) 35/129, 'Report on Labour Question', E. Pillans to the Governor, 18 November 1902; *Cape Times*, 5 February 1897: 'with the present class of labour only one man out of a great many was really a competent man'; 15 January 1903, advertising for 'first-class' bench-hand carpenters and 'six rough carpenters'; 5 January 1904, 'employment of foreigners'; HA, GM to LO, 28 May 1890, *re* new machinery and new skilled labour.

24 Cell, *White Supremacy*, p. 189.

25 P. Butt, 'The Growth and Development of the Master Builders Association in the Cape Peninsula' (M.Sc. thesis, Natal University, 1984), pp. 69–94; A. G. Howard, 'Progress of Architecture in Cape Town since 1876', *South African Architect, Engineer and Surveyor* (May–September 1907), 139–212; J. Rennie, *The Buildings of Central Cape Town*, 2 vols. (Cape Town, Cape Provincial Institute of Architects, 1978), vol. I, 8–15 and vol. II, p. 195. Laidler, *Growth and Government* says the first building of cut stone in Cape Town was in 1888.

26 *Cape Times*, 5 January 1904, 'Employment of Foreigners'; *Cape Argus*, 3 August 1892; *South African News*, 8 June 1899. See also Rennie, *Central Cape Town*, vol. I, p. 11.

27 *CPP*, G39–1893, pp. 118–19; Laidler, *Growth and Government*, p. 360.

28 See chap. 6 for details of this state-imposed exclusivity; CA, SGE 2/154–5, 'Anglican School of Industry'.

29 *Cape Times*, 13 March 1907, 'Transvaal Indigency Commission'; *CPP*, A6–1908, p. 22; see also pp. 27–30. For a similar approach by Australian craft unionists see Davison, *Marvellous Melbourne*, pp. 86–8.

30 Simons and Simons, *Class and Colour*, pp. 73–4; Lewis, *Between the Wire and the Wall*, p. 16; Van Duin, 'Trade Unionism', pp. 7–8. Both Lewis and Van Duin cite the Simonses, whose reference is to the *Spectator*, 23 March, 20 April 1901. But these editions refer to the fact that the plasterers were *de facto*

Whites only and would not allow their members to work on the same scaffold as Coloureds or Malays; *South African News*, 8 June 1899.

31 *Cape Times*, 1 October 1896. See also *Cape Times*, 10 February 1897: 'The Malay Mason so called' was not recognised by the 'legitimate tradesman'; *South African News*, 7 July 1899, there were no Black masons; *South African News*, 21 February 1905 and *Cape Times*, 10 October 1908 both discuss the relationship between the appearance of stone buildings and the requisite skills supplied by these masons; *South African News*, 7 July 1899; Davison, *Marvellous Melbourne*, p. 86.

32 *Spectator*, 23 March 1901; *South African News* 8 June 1899, 18 April 1903. See *South African News*, 13 February, 18 April 1903: the plasterers' refusal to work with Black labour led to their disaffiliation from the Trades Council in 1903.

33 *South African News*, 23 April 1901: at a meeting of the union a Coloured carpenter wanted to know if any Coloureds could join and the White chairman said his union would help the Coloureds form their own, or as a branch of the White union; *Cape Times*, 11 March, 16, 19 May 1890, 9 February, 9 March 1903; *Cape Argus*, 3, 14, 15 February, 3, 7, 9, 20, 22 March 1893; *South African News*, 28 March, 22, 23, 24, 26 April, 6, 22 May 1901, 31 January, 7, 21 February, 7, 14, 21 March, 18 April 1903; Davison, *Marvellous Melbourne*, p. 88. Particularly skilful work was required in cabinet-making for which cabinet-makers were imported: *Excalibur*, 9 August 1889. See also *Cape Times*, 5 January 1904, 'Employment of Foreigners'; *CPP*, A6–1908, p. 61 comments on the particular skills possessed by British carpenters.

34 *Cape Times*, 8 March 1897; *Cape Argus*, 10 April 1893, 23 March 1897; Harrison, 'Introduction', p. 1.

35 *Cape Argus*, 23 March 1897.

36 *Cape Argus*, 27 February, 4 March 1893, 23, 24 March 1897; *South African News*, 9 May, 13, 27 June, 4, 6, 11 July 1903.

37 **Bricklayers**: *South African News*, 29 July, 16, 30 September 1905, 17 February, 31 March 1906; **painters**: *South African News*, 16, 22, 30 September 1905, 24 February, 17, 24 March 1906, 7 April, 12 May 1906. For the origins and principles of the General Workers' Union see *South African News*, 19, 24 July 1905 for the constitution of the GWU. The GWU had considered organising parallel unions for Whites and Coloureds for strategic reasons. For origins of the SDF see *South African News*, 11 July 1903: the SDF was formed in 1902.

38 *Cape Times*, 26, 27, 28, 29 October, 3 November 1897; *South African News*, 3, 4, 6, 24 April 1901.

39 *Cape Times*, 17 November 1896, 15, 22 January, 2, 3, 4, 6, 9, 10, 18, 19, 20, 22 February, 1 July 1897; Downes, *Printers' Saga*, pp. 6–7; J. Zeitlin, 'Engineers and Compositors: A Comparison', in Harrison and Zeitlin (eds.), *Divisions of Labour*, pp. 186–215: British compositors were careful to proclaim their opposition to *underpaid* female labour, rather than women *per se*, echoing the emphasis on craft rather than colour exclusivity of Cape Town unionists who also opposed female labour.

40 *South African News*, 1 July 1899.

41 *Cape Argus*, 14 May 1892, 29 August 1895; *Cape Times*, 15 January 1897.

42 CA, GH 35/40, Governor to Joseph Chamberlain, 23 April 1901; Van Duin, 'Artisans'.

43 *South African News*, 4 April 1901.

44 *Cape Times*, 9 February 1897.

45 *Cape Times*, 23 September 1897.

46 *Cape Times*, 10 December 1889.

47 *Cape Times*, 8 January 1889; *Excalibur*, 11 January 1889.

48 *CPP*, A12–1890, p. 41; *Cape Argus*, 21, 22 December 1891.

49 *CPP*, C2–1892, pp. 73–6. The quotation, from the evidence of Johannes Veldtman, 'Headman and Recruiter', is from p. 76.

50 CA, CHB 11–13, 'Minutes of the Table Bay Docks and Breakwater Management Committee'; CHB 11, 3, 10 May 1878; CHB 12, 9 April 1880; CHB 13, 8, 12, 22 July 1881; *Cape Times*, 24 April 1880.

51 CA, CHB 262, 'Labourers Barracks Correspondence'.

52 *CPP*, G39–1893, pp. 19, 25, 79–80; *Cowley Evangelist*, November 1893; Pretoria Archives, *South African Native Affairs Commission 1903–1905* vol. II, p. 84.

53 *Cape Argus*, 25 July 1892, 2 June 1894, 10 April 1897; *Cape Times*, 14 December 1896, 8 March 1897.

54 CA, CT 6/226, 'Preparatory Examinations', May 1892, case of Nqute, Jack, 'Office' and 'Rabits Hana'.

55 *Cape Argus*, 29 April 1892: the men were on wages of from 30s to 50s a month, but they could earn 6d an hour overtime, i.e. for night work. This presumably explains why night work was preferred to day work; CA, 1CT 6/234, May 1893, case of dock labourers charged under the Masters and Servants Act of 1873; *Cape Argus*, 1 May, 2 May, 2 August 1893.

56 CA, 1CT 6/281, June 1896, case of Matthew Mahoney versus Mteto and eight others; *Cape Argus*, 6, 9, 25 June 1896; *Cape Times*, 10, 26, 30 June, 21 July 1896.

57 CA, CHB 262, 'Labour Barracks'. See Table 3.

58 *South African News*, 16 February, 14, 15 March 1901; CA, CHB 268, 'Docks Location'; Van Heyningen, 'Plague'.

59 *Cape Times*, 15 October, 3 December 1901; CA, CHB 262, 'Cape Harbour Board Correspondence', A. Fletcher to R. Hammersley-Heenan, 24 January 1902; *Cape Government Gazette*, 5 March 1901, Government Notice No. 209.

60 *Cowley Evangelist*, 1903, p. 90, 'Native Acting Songs'.

61 S. Dubow, 'African Labour at the Cape Town Docks, 1900–1904', *Studies*, IV (1981), pp. 108–34; V. Bickford-Smith, 'Black Labour at the Docks at the Beginning of the Twentieth Century', in *Studies*, vol. II (1980), pp. 75–125.

62 Dubow, 'African Labour'; CA, CHB 262, 'Correspondence': Bickford-Smith, 'Commerce', pp. 409–10 gives details; Saunders, 'Ndabeni'; *Cape Times*, 21 October 1901, letter from Mangena.

63 Saunders, 'Ndabeni'; Van Heyningen, 'Plague'; CA, CHB 262, Secretary TBHB to Secretary Chamber of Commerce, 24 August 1901; Bickford-Smith, 'Commerce', p. 402; B. Nasson, *Abraham Esau's War: A Black South African War at the Cape, 1899–1902* (Cambridge, Cambridge University Press, 1991).

64 *Cape Times*, 16, 18 November 1901; CA, CHB 262, 'Superintendant Docks Location to Engineer-in-Chief', TBHB, 25 November 1901.
65 *Cape Times*, 5 August, 24 November 1896, 4 February 1897.
66 *Cape Times*, 16, 22 May 1901.
67 *CPP*, G39–1893, pp. 4, 5, 15, 68, 80–1, 98–9, 118; *CPP*, C1– 1891, pp. 24, 25, 46, 57, 65, 70, 90, 91, 95; *CPP*, A29–1899, 'SCR on the Employment of Women in the Civil Service', pp. iii–v, 1, 44–5; *Cape Times*, 21 July 1896 talks of the great extent of 'wife labour' in Cape Town; 31 August 1896: women employed in the dairy industry; *CPP*, C4–1904, 'SCR on Colonial Industries', pp. 25, 32, 33, 38, 46, 70, 96, 106; *CPP*, A6–1906, pp. 4, 5, 8, 55, 56, 74, 80–90, 114, 118, 124–5, 128.
68 *Cape Argus*, 23 June 1892, 7 November 1894, 9 July 1897; *Cape Times*, 29 September 1897.
69 *Cape Times*, 12 October 1896, letter from 'One who Speaks from Experience'.
70 CA, PWD 2/8/20, 'Mrs Lancaster's Forms of Contract', Agent General of Cape to the Commissioner of Crown Lands and Public Works, 28 November 1889; *Cape Argus*, 29, 31 December 1891, 4 January 1892, 27 November 1895.
71 *Cape Times*, 1, 2 October 1896, 21 September 1897, 17 October 1898; *Cape Argus*, 26 September 1892: the servant accused of theft in this case had only been receiving 6s a month.
72 *Cape Argus*, 31 December 1891, letter from 'Paterfamilias'.
73 *Cape Times*, 17 May 1901.
74 CA, 3CT 1/1/5/229, 'Appendix to Cape Town Council Minutes', January 1890, Skead Cowling and Company to the Cape Town Council; *Cape Argus*, 12 January 1892.

8 A DARKER SHADE THAN PALE?

1 Crais, *White Supremacy*, pp. 77, 83–5, 182; H. Ludlow, 'Missions and Emancipation in the South Western Cape: A Case Study of Groenekloof (Mamre), 1838–1852' (MA thesis, UCT, 1992); Nasson, *Abraham Esau's War*; Bickford-Smith, 'Meanings of Freedom'.
2 H. Den Besten, 'From Khoe Khoe Foreigner Talk via Hottentot Dutch to Afrikaans: The Creation of a Novel Grammar', in M. Putz and R. Derven (eds.), *Wheels within Wheels* (Frankfurt, Verlag Peter Lang, 1989), pp. 207–49; A. Davids, 'Words the Slaves Made: A Socio-historical-linguistic Study', *South African Journal of Linguistics*, 8, 1 (1990), 1–24.
3 Bickford-Smith, 'Meanings of Freedom' gives more details on the emergence of the Coon Carnival and on celebrations of the anniversary of emancipation, 1 December. D. B. Coplan, *In Township Tonight: South Africa's Black City Music and Theatre* (London, Longman, 1985), p. 39 states that performance clubs that paraded through the streets of Cape Town were formed in the aftermath of the visit to the city of McAdoo's American Jubilee singers in 1887. But it would seem that performance clubs pre-dated this visit, and that their growth in numbers was merely boosted by it. V. Erlman, ' "A feeling of Prejudice": Orpheus M. McAdoo and the Virginia Jubilee singers in South

Africa' *JSAS*, 14,3 (1988), 331–50 gives a fascinating account of the McAdoo singers' visit to South Africa in the 1890s, what and where they performed, and suggests links between the singers and the Ethiopian movement.

4 Kennedy, *At the Cape*, pp. 14–15.
5 D. Birmingham, 'Carnival at Luanda', *JAH*, 29, 1 (1988), 93–103. Quotations are from 100 and 102. For the musical influences on Cape Town's Carnival see Coplan, *In Township Tonight*, pp. 8–38.
6 *Cape Times*, 4 January 1886.
7 Cited in Winberg, ' "*Ghoemaliedjies*" ', pp. 25–6. This is Winberg's translation, and I am grateful to her for permission to cite this extract and the two below.
8 *Ibid.*, p. 30.
9 Birmingham, 'Carnival in Luanda', 102.
10 Winberg, ' "*Ghoemaliedjies*" ', p. 18.
11 *CPP*, G39–1893, pp. 117–20, 140–1.
12 *Evening Express* 27 October 1884; *Cape Times*, 3 May 1888.
13 Grant, 'Bokkoms', pp. 31–64.
14 *Lantern*, 3, 10 May 1884; *Cape Argus*, 18 January 1893.
15 *Cape Times*, 9 January 1880; *Cape Argus*, 20 September 1893; *Lantern*, 9 March 1889; *CPP*, G39–1893, p. 69.
16 CA, 1CT 6/175 and 6/192, 'Preparatory Examinations', July 1884, case of James Williams, and September 1886, case of Frederick Punter respectively.
17 CA, 1CT 6/226, 'Preparatory Examination', May 1892, case of Nqute, Jack, 'Office' and 'Rabits Hana'; *Cape Argus*, 3 April 1897.
18 *Cape Times*, 28 December 1896, 24 November 1897; CA, AG 3009, 'Preliminary Examination', June 1896, case of James Hendricks: Hendricks talked of fighting with a 'Kafir'; CA, CHB 266 'Docks Location', Superintendent to the Secretary TBHB, 19 August 1901, Assistant Superintendant to Secretary TBHB, 29 September 1901; CHB 268, Mangena to Superintendant of Docks Location, 20 January 1902.
19 *Cape Times*, 29 November 1901; *CPP*, A28–1898, 'Liquor Law Amendment Act'.
20 *Cape Argus*, 8 March 1902.
21 *CPP*, A36–1902, 'Betting Houses, Gaming Houses and Brothels Suppression Act'. See chap. 6 above.
22 Cited in S. Trapido, 'The Emergence of Liberalism and the Making of "Hottentot Nationalism", 1815–1834' (unpublished paper presented to the Institute of Commonwealth Studies Postgraduate Seminar, University of London, 1990), p. 32.
23 Cited in Crais, *White Supremacy*, p. 186.
24 *CPP*, A22–1871, 'SCR on the Masters and Servants Act Amendment Bill', Appendix B.
25 This point has been made by M. Adhikari, 'The Sons of Ham: Slavery and the Making of Coloured Identity', *SAHJ*, 27 (1992), 95–112.
26 Following Bozzoli, 'Class', p. 9.
27 Lewis, *Between the Wire and the Wall*, pp. 12–14, 22, 24.
28 *Ibid.*, p. 24.

29 The quotation is from *CPP*, A4–1878, Appendix G, p. ix. See also *Cape Times*, 19, 25 July 1878.

30 *Cape Times*, 15 November 1878.

31 *Cape Times*, 18 December 1878.

32 *Cape Times*, 27 February 1880, letter from 'Ismael'; 3 November 1880, from Abdol Kadier; 19 March 1881, letters from Abdol Burns and 'A Moslem'; 25 March 1881, letter from Abdol Carter, (possibly Kadier again); *Lantern*, 30 August 1879, letter from 'Magmoet'; 7 February 1880, from Abdol Gemarodien; 9 September 1882, letter from Mogarh-Naheer; 23 September 1882, letter from Abdol Soubeyan.

33 *Cape Times*, 3 November 1880. The letter from 'Civis' appeared in 1 November 1880.

34 *Lantern*, 23 September 1882.

35 *Lantern*, 9 September 1882.

36 *Cape Times*, 18 August 1882, 6 December 1883.

37 The quotation is from the *Cape Times*, 13 June 1885. For other correspondence on the issue see *Cape Times*, 19, 24 October, 4 November 1882, 27, 28 August, 6 October 1883, 28 March 1884, 30 April, 25 November 1885.

38 *Cape Times*, 14 November 1885.

39 Davids, 'Politics and the Muslims of Cape Town', pp. 191 and 194; Van Heyningen, 'Public Health', pp. 151–220.

40 *Lantern*, 9 November 1889.

41 *Cape Argus*, 26 August 1892.

42 Lewis, *Between the Wire and the Wall*, pp. 10–11.

43 It seems likely that the men described as John, W. or James Currey/Curry by contemporary newspapers are the same person, who has mistakenly been given different names by the journalists who attended the various political meetings at which he was present. By the end of the 1890s James Curry appears as the consistent name in the newspaper reports and correspondence columns; and this is the spelling that Gavin Lewis uses in *Between the Wire and the Wall*, pp. 36, 56, 81.

44 *Lantern*, 26 December 1891.

45 *Cape Argus*, 16 August 1892.

46 *Cape Argus*, 14 September 1892.

47 *Cape Argus*, 18 January 1893: this edition also contains biographical details on Effendi.

48 *Cape Argus*, 23, 26 January 1893.

49 *Cape Argus*, 18 January, 20 May 1893.

50 *Cape Argus*, 17, 23, 24 January 1894. See also *CPP*, G9–1891, p. 96, for Abdol Burns' evidence that a friend's child had been turned away from the Normal School and the 'Dutch' school in New Street.

51 *Cape Argus*, 29, 30 January 1894.

52 *Cape Argus*, 16 July 1894; Lewis, *Between the Wire and the Wall*, p. 11.

53 *Cape Argus*, 22 August, 9, 10 September 1895. For Shaw's other activities see 1, 2 May 1893, 15 March 1894, 6, 9 June 1895, 25 June 1896.

54 Nasson, *Abraham Esau's War*.

55 *Cape Times*, 3 August 1898; Lewis, *Between the Wire and the Wall*, p. 11.

56 *Cape Times*, 1 and 8 August 1898 for Anderson attracting Coloured support.

See 11 August 1898 for the election result which shows Anderson being elected with the fewest number of votes, possibly another reason for his wooing of enfranchised Coloureds.

57 *Cape Argus*, 16 April 1897.
58 *Cape Times*, 2, 4 November 1897.
59 *Cape Times*, 6, 7, 9, 13 September 1898.
60 *Cape Times*, 2 October 1897.
61 *Cape Argus*, 2 October 1895, *Cape Times*, 27 April 1898; Lewis, *Between the Wire and the Wall*, p. 17, has some more details on Roberts.
62 *Spectator*, 8 February 1902; *Cape Times*, 30 April 1898, 5, 7 July 1902.
63 *Spectator*, 29 December 1901, 22 February 1902; Lewis, *Between the Wire and the Wall*, p. 11.
64 Cited in Nasson, *Abraham Esau's War*, p. 191. See also p. 42.
65 *Cape Times*, 9 January 1901; Nasson, *Abraham Esau's War*, pp. 32–4, 38–63.
66 Nasson, *Abraham Esau's War*, pp. 162–4.
67 *Spectator*, 14 January, 23 March, 18 May 1901. For more details on Peregrino and his newspaper see C. Saunders, 'F.Z.S. Peregrino and the "South African Spectator"', *Quarterly Bulletin of the South African Library*, 32 (1977–8), 81–90, and Lewis, *Between the Wire and the Wall*, pp. 16–18.
68 *Spectator*, 4 May 1901; Lewis, *Between the Wire and the Wall*, pp. 17–20.
69 *Cape Times*, 13 April 1901; *Spectator*, 18 October 1902.
70 Lewis, *Between the Wire and the Wall*, p. 15; Goldin, *Making Race: The Politics and Economics of Coloured Identity in South Africa* (Cape Town, Maskew Miller Longman, 1987), p. 20.
71 *Cape Times*, 26 April 1898.
72 Lewis, *Between the Wire and the Wall*, p. 20. See also pp. 7–28.
73 Goldin, *Making Race*, p. 13.
74 *Ibid.*, p. 35; Grant, 'Bokkoms', p. 71. The *Cape Times* gives detailed descriptions of the 'respectable' carnival performances on Green Point Common.
75 *South African News*, 14, 15 March 1901; Saunders, 'Ndabeni'; Van Heyningen, 'Plague'.
76 Bozzoli, 'Class', pp. 26–7.
77 *South African News*, 4 April 1901, letter from S. Joshua.
78 *South African News*, 19 March 1901.
79 *Cape Times*, 7, 9, 12, 17, 18 July 1902; Saunders, 'Ndabeni', pp. 178–84.
80 A. Odendaal, *Black Protest Politics in South Africa* (Totowa, Barnes & Noble, 1984), p. 31.
81 *Cape Times*, 20 March 1901.
82 *Spectator*, 10 August 1901; Saunders, 'Ndabeni', p. 179.
83 CA, CO 7605, Colonial Medical Officer of Health to Colonial Secretary, 21 May 1902. See also 'Memorandum by W. E. Stanford', 10 June 1902.
84 *South African News*, 24 February, 3 March 1900, 16 October 1902. Somewhat ironically, Sellar had chaired a meeting of the SAWMPU in favour of a location in 1900. But he himself had favoured a site virtually in the city centre.
85 *Cowley Evangelist*, 1902; CA, GH 35/84 'Ethiopian Movement'.
86 Saunders, 'Ndabeni', pp. 184–7; N. Barnett, 'Ndabeni 1901–1910: Towards a Social History' (Honours thesis, UCT, 1985); B. H. Kinkead-Weekes,

'Africans in Cape Town: The Origins and Development of State Policy and Popular Resistance to 1936' (MA thesis, UCT, 1985); Odendaal, *Black Protest.*

9 CONCLUSION

1 Bozzoli, 'Class', p. 21.
2 Fredrickson, *White Supremacy*, p. 260.
3 *Cape Times*, 12 August 1902.
4 Trollope, *South Africa*, p. 3.
5 Cell, *White Supremacy*, p. 134.
6 Evans, *Black and White*, p. 296.
7 *Cape Times*, 13 September 1904, 7 March 1905. There is a great deal about Alexander in Shain, *Jewry.*
8 *Cape Times*, 6 March 1909.
9 *APO*, 21 May 1910.
10 *South African News*, 24 August 1906, 'Coloured Unemployed'; 29 August 1906, letter from 'L. Sopa'; CA, CHB 262, N. R. Veldsman to the Secretary of the Harbour Board, 27 August 1906; *Cowley Evangelist* 1906, pp. 259–60; CA, 3CT 1/5/1/1/4, 'Minutes of an Interview accorded by His Worship the Mayor to a deputation representing the Natives of Uitvlugt Location . . . on Wednesday, 29th August, 1906'.
11 A useful new overview of South African politics in the twentieth century is contained in N. Worden, *The Making of Modern South Africa: Conquest, Segregation and Apartheid* (Oxford, Blackwell Publishers, 1994). For Coloured politics and identity in the twentieth century see Lewis, *Between the Wire and the Wall* and Goldin, *Making Race*. Much of the following summary of events is gleaned from these sources.
12 See Western, *Outcast Cape Town* and S. Jeppie and C. Soudien (eds.), *The Struggle for District Six: Past and Present* (Cape Town, Buchu Books, 1990).
13 Worden, *Modern South Africa*, pp. 85, 104, 115–16, 128–31. For more detail see Lewis, *Between the Wire and the Wall* and Goldin, *Making Race*.

Bibliography

MANUSCRIPT SOURCES

CA STATE ARCHIVES DEPOT, CAPE TOWN

AG   Attorney General's Department, Preliminary Examinations
CGR   Cape Government Railways, Staff Registers
CHB   Papers of the Table Bay Harbour Board
CO   Colonial Office, correspondence files and naturalisation papers
CSC   Cape Supreme Court, records of proceedings in criminal cases in Cape Town
GH   Government House files
HBC   Archives of the Cape Town Free Dispensary
HOS   Archives of the Superintendent, Old Somerset Hospital
IAC   Immigration and Labour Department
LC   Limited Companies, Registered under Acts 23 of 1861 and 25 of 1892
MC   Medical Committee, correspondence files
NA   Native Affairs Department
PWD   Public Works Department
SGE   Archive of the Superintendent-General of Education, Cape Colony
1CT   Resident Magistrate for Cape Town
3CT   Town Clerk, Cape Town Municipality

HA HENRY ARCHIVES, CAPE TOWN

Extracts from the correspondence between the General Manager of the Standard Bank, Cape Town, and London Office, in the possession of J. A. Henry, Newlands, Cape Town

SBA STANDARD BANK ARCHIVES, JOHANNESBURG

IR CT   Inspection Reports for Cape Town Branch

WITWATERSRAND UNIVERSITY LIBRARY, ARCHIVES SECTION

Records of the Church of the Province of South Africa
L. A. Vidler Papers

J. W. JAGGER LIBRARY, UNIVERSITY OF CAPE TOWN

John Garlick Papers

OTHER PRIMARY SOURCES

APO
Cape Argus
Cape Government Gazette
Cape Monthly Magazine
Cape Times
Cowley Evangelist
Evening Express
Excalibur
Lantern
South African News
South African Licensed Victualler's Review
South African Review
South African Spectator
Zuid-Afrikaan

OFFICIAL PUBLICATIONS

CAPE COLONY

CBB *Cape of Good Hope Blue Books and Statistical Registers*, 1875–1910
CCP *Cape Command Papers*:
       Ordinance 1, 1839, 'For the creation of a Municipal Board for Cape Town
       and the vicinity thereof'
       Ordinance 1, 1840, 'Act for establishing a Municipal Board for Cape Town'

       Cape of Good Hope House of Assembly Debates
       1892, Cape Town, Murray & St Leger, 1892
       1893, Cape Town, *Cape Times*, 1893
       1905, Cape Town, *Cape Times*, 1905

       Cape of Good Hope Legislative Council Debates
       1875, Cape Town, Saul Solomon & Co., 1875
       1876, Cape Town, Saul Solomon & Co., 1876
       1878, Cape Town, Saul Solomon & Co., 1878
       1879, Cape Town, Saul Solomon & Co., 1880
       1891, Cape Town, Murray & St Leger, 1892
       1899, Cape Town, *Cape Times*, 1899
       1905, Cape Town, *Cape Times*, 1905

       *Votes and Proceedings of the House of Assembly, Sixth Session, Fifth
       Parliament*, Cape Town, Saul Solomon & Co., 1878

CPP *Cape Parliamentary Papers*
       A1–1860, 'SCR on Cape Town Municipal Bill'
       A1–1861, 'Act to Re-establish a Municipal Board for Cape Town'
       G24–1863, 'Report of a Commission of Enquiry into the Government
       Education System'
       A7–1865, 'SCR on Cape Town Municipal Amendment Bill'
       C2–1865, 'SCR on Somerset Hospital'

G20–1866, 'Cape Census for 1865'

A1–1867, 'The Cape Town Municipality Amendment Act'

A22–1871, 'SCR on Masters and Servants Act Amendment Bill'

A13–1873, 'Petition of Coloured Persons, Inhabitants of Cape Town and Neighbourhood'

A18–1873, 'Masters and Servants Act'

G27–1874, 'Blue Book on Native Affairs for 1873'

A2–1875, 'SCR on the Cemeteries Bill'

G1–1876, 'Report on Schools Inspected for 1875'

G32–1876, 'Report on education for 1875'

G42–1876, 'Cape Census for 1875'

G50–1876, 'Report of Table Bay Dock and Breakwater Management Commission for 1875'

A19–1877, 'SCR on Sanitary Arrangements of Municipalities'

G1–1877, 'Report ... Colonial Defence Commission'

G47–1877, 'Report on Cape Immigration for 1876'

A4–1878, 'SCR on Rogge Bay Nuisance'

A5–1878, 'Act for the Establishment of a Colonial Yeomanry Force'

A10–1879, 'SCR on Cape Town Municipal Bill'

A15–1879, 'SCR on the Oranjezicht Purchase Bill'

A16–1879, 'SCR on Public Health Bill'

A23–1879, 'Vagrancy Act'

A26–1879, 'SCR on Labour'

A34–1879, 'Letter from Mr Stevens on Removal of Native Women and Children from Cape Town'

A39–1879, 'Immigration Act'

A42–1879, 'Return showing the Number of Native Men, Women, Boys and Girls, Respectively, Applied for by the Inhabitants and Contracted by Government'

A43–1879, 'Number of Kafirs Introduced into the Western Districts during and after the Late Galeka and Gaika War'

A7–1880, 'SCR on the Table Bay Harbour Board'

A16–1880, 'SCR on Friendly Societies'

G6–1880, 'Report on the New Somerset Hospital for the Year 1879'

G11–1880, 'Report on the Old Somerset Hospital for the Year 1879'

G75–1880, 'Report of the Commission to Inquire into and Report upon the Workings of the Education Acts in Force in this Colony, 1879–1880'

A1–1881, 'SCR on Porter Reformatory Bequest'

A10–1881, 'Return of Number of Registered Voters in Electoral Districts'

A13–1881, 'SCR on Cape Town Municipal Bill'

A42–1881, 'Petition for the Removal of Kafirs'

A27–1882, 'Police Offences Act'

A44–1882, 'Cape Town Municipality Act'

A3–1883, 'SCR on Colonial Agriculture and Industries'

A15–1883, 'SCR on the Pass Laws of the Colony'

A24–1883, 'SCR on the Beer Excise Duty Bill'

A26–1883, 'SCR on the Native Locations Act'

G2–1883, 'Reports by Bernard V. Shaw on the Police and Gaol Establishments of the Colony'

G4–1883, 'Report and Proceedings on Native Laws and Customs'

G16–1883, 'Report on the New Somerset Hospital for the Year Ending 31 December 1882'

G17–1883, 'Report on the Old Somerset Hospital for the Year Ending 31 December 1882'

G29–1883, 'Report on the Robben Island General Infirmary for the Year Ending 31 December 1882'

G36–1883, 'Report on Customs Tariff, 1882'

G119–1883, 'Report of the Board of the Porter Reformatory'

G120–1883, 'Return of the Estimated Strengths of the Police and Gaol Establishment for the Financial Year 1883–1884'

G9–1884, 'Reports of the Colonial Medical Committee and Vaccine Officer, and on the Hospitals under General Government Control, for the year 1883'

G58–1884, 'Reports of the Immigration Agents at London, East London and Cape Town for 1883'

A8–1885, 'SCR on Brewer's Petition'

A9–1885, 'SCR on the Cape Town Municipal Act Amendment Bill'

A28–1885, 'Cape Town Municipality Act'

G10–1885, 'Reports of the Colonial Medical Committee, the Vaccine Officer and on the Government and Public Hospitals and Asylums for the Year 1884'

A11–1886, 'SCR on the Pass Laws'

A9–1888, 'SCR on Cape Town Sanitation and Water Supply'

A19–1888, 'Table Bay Harbour Board Loan Act'

A12–1888, 'SCR on Convict Stations and Prisons Bill'

G2–1888, 'Report of the Committee on Convicts and Gaols'

G13–1888, 'Report of District Surgeons for 1887'

A9–1889, 'SCR on the Friendly Societies Act'

A11–1889, 'SCR on Cape Town and Kimberley Police Force'

A22–1889, 'Table Bay Harbour Board Loan Act'

A8–1890, 'SCR on Cape Town Municipality Bill'

A12–1890, 'SCR on Labour'

A26–1890, 'Cape Town Municipality Amendment Act'

G4–1890, 'Blue Book on Native Affairs'

G6a–1890, 'SGE Special Report'

G38–1890, 'Report on the Management and Discipline of Convicts and Prisons, for 1889'

A17–1891, 'SCR on the Porter Reformatory'

C1–1891, 'SCR on Colonial Industries'

G9–1891, 'Education Commission, First Report'

A21–1892, 'SCR on the Liquor Act'

A22–1892, 'Table Bay Harbour Board Loan Act'

C2–1892, 'SCR on the Labour Question'

G3–1892, 'Education Commission, Second Report'

G3–1892, 'Education Commission, Third and Final Report'

G6–1892, 'Cape Census for 1891'

G37–1892, 'Report of the Fisheries Committee'

G50–1892, 'Reports on the Management and Discipline of Convict Stations and Prisons during the Year 1891'

A16–1893, 'To Amend the Constitutional Ordinances'

A20–1893, 'Table Bay Harbour Board Loan Act'

A26–1893, 'Cape Town Municipality Act'

C1–1893, 'SCR on Railway Management'

G29–1893, 'Report of SGE for 1892'

G39–1893, 'Labour Commission'

G47–1893, 'Reports on the Management and Discipline of Convict Stations and Prisons for the year ended 1892'

A6–1894, 'Table Bay Harbour Board Loan Act'

C1a–1894, 'SCR on the Destitute Children Relief Bill'

G3–1894, 'Labour Commission Report'

A21–1895, 'Caledon Street Tramways Co. Limited Act'

A22–1895, 'Metropolitan Tramways Company Act'

A5–1896, 'SCR on the Training of Apprentices and Industrial Schools'

A25–1896, 'Table Bay Harbour Board Loan Act'

A8–1897, 'SCR on the Cape Town Municipal Act Amendment Bill'

A28–1898, 'Liquor Law Amendment Act'

A33–1898, 'Table Bay Harbour Board Loan Act'

A38–1897, 'Railway Loan Act'

C2–1898, 'SCR on the Fishing Industry'

A13–1899, 'Return Showing Number of Natives Dismissed since 1 January 1899 . . . Salt River . . .'

A17–1899, 'Return of Number of Labourers Proceeding to the Different Labour Centres'

A22–1899, 'SCR on the Harbour Boards Bill'

A29–1899, 'SCR on Employment of Women in the Civil Service'

A30–1899, 'To amend the Law with Regard to Native Locations'

A35–1899, 'Table Bay Harbour Board Loan Act'

A36–1899, 'Public Works Loans Act'

A3–1900, 'SCR on Harbour Boards'

A9–1900, 'Public Works Loans Act'

A20–1900, 'Table Bay Harbour Board Loan Act'

G6–1901, 'Reports and Proceedings of the Plague Advisory Board'

A13–1902, 'SCR on the Cape Town Municipal Amendment Bill'

A28–1902, 'Cape Town Municipal Amendment Act'

A33–1902, 'Table Bay Harbour Board Loan Act'

A36–1902, 'Betting Houses, Gaming Houses and Brothels Suppression Act'

A40–1902, 'Native Reserve Location Act'

A42–1902, 'New and Additional Railways Works Act'

G21–1902, 'Cape Peninsula Commission'

C4–1904, 'SCR on Colonial Industries'

A35–1905, 'School Board Act'

C2–1905, 'SCR on Colonial Industries'

G19–1905, 'Cape Census for 1904'
A6–1906, 'SCR on the Factory Act'
A10–1906, 'SCR on the Poor White Question'
G21–1907, 'Report on Immigration and Labour'
A6–1908, 'SCR on Imported Contract Labour'

T R A N S V A A L   C O L O N Y

South African Native Affairs Commission, 1903–1905, 3 vols.

U N I O N   O F   S O U T H   A F R I C A

UG32–1912, *Census of the Union of South Africa, 1911*
UG34–1914, *Report of the Tuberculosis Commission*
UG54–1937, *Report of the Commission of Inquiry regarding the Cape Coloured*
            Population of the Union

S E C O N D A R Y   S O U R C E S

Adam, H. and Giliomee, H., *The Rise and Crisis of Afrikaner Power*, Cape Town, David Philip, 1979
Adhikari, M., 'The Sons of Ham: Slavery and the Making of Coloured Identity', *SAHJ*, 27 (1992), 95–112
Anderson, B., *Imagined Communities, Reflections on the Origins and Spread of Nationalism*, London, Verso, 1983
Andrews, G. R., *The Afro-Argentines of Buenos Aires 1800–1900*, Madison, University of Wisconsin Press, 1980
Archer, R. and Bouillon, A., *The South African Game*, London, Zed, 1982
Arnold, J. M., *Abdullah Ben Yusuf or the Story of a Malay as told by Himself*, Cape Town, J. H. Rose and J. M. Belinfante, 1877
Arnold, J. M., *Kind Words and Loving Counsel to Malays and other Moslems*, Cape Town, Murray & St Leger, 1879
Aspeling, E. G., *'The Cape Malay': An Essay by a Cape Colonist*, Cape Town, W. A. Richards & Sons, 1883
Atkinson, B., *Trade Unions in Bristol*, Local history pamphlets, nos. 51–4, Bristol, Bristol Branch of the History Association, 1982
Aubertyn, J. J., *Six Months in Cape Colony and Natal*, London, Kegan Paul, 1886
Bank, A., *Decline of Urban Slavery at the Cape, 1806 to 1834*, Cape Town, Centre for African Studies, 1991
  'The erosion of Slavery at the Cape, 1806–1834', in Crais and Worden (eds.), *Breaking the Chains*
Ballantyne, R. M., *Six Months at the Cape of Good Hope*, London, Nisbet, 1878
Barnett, N., 'Ndabeni 1901–1910: Towards a Social History', Honours thesis, UCT, 1985
Barnett-Clarke, H. P., *The Life and Times of Thomas Fothergill Lightfoot, BD Archdeacon of Cape Town*, Cape Town, Darter, 1908

Batson, E. (ed.), *Reports and Studies issued by the Social Survey of Cape Town*, vol. SS1, Cape Town, UCT, 1941

Beinart, W., 'Worker Consciousness, Ethnic Particularism and Nationalism: The Experience of a South African Migrant, 1930–1950', in Marks and Trapido (eds.), *Race, Class and Nationalism*, pp. 286–309

Beinart, W., Delius, P. and Trapido, S. (eds.), *Putting a Plough to the Ground: Accumulation and Dispossession in Rural South Africa 1850–1930*, Johannesburg, Ravan, 1986

Bickford-Smith, V., 'Black Labour at the Docks at the Beginning of the Twentieth Century', *Studies* II (1980), pp. 75–125

'Dangerous Cape Town: Middle Class Attitudes to Poverty in Cape Town in the late Nineteenth Century', *Studies* IV (1981), pp. 29–65

'"Keeping your own Council": The Struggle between Houseowners and Merchants for Control of the Cape Town Municipal Council in the Last Two Decades of the Nineteenth Century', *Studies* V, (1984), 189–208

'Commerce, Class and Ethnicity in Cape Town, 1875–1902', Ph.D. thesis, Cambridge University, 1989

'Slavery, Emancipation and the Question of Coloured Identity', *Collected Seminar Papers on the Societies of Southern Africa in the 19th and 20th Centuries*, vol. 19, No. 45, (1993), 17–25

'Meanings of Freedom: Social Position and Identity among ex-Slaves and their descendants in Cape Town, 1875-1910' in Crais and Worden (eds.), *Breaking the Chains*

Bird, W., *The State of the Cape of Good Hope in 1822*, Cape Town, Struik, 1966

Birmingham, D., 'Carnival at Luanda', *JAH*, 29, 1 (1988), 93–103

Birmingham, J. W., *Black New Orleans 1860–1880*, Chicago, Chicago University Press, 1973

Blankenhorn, D., '"Our Class of Workmen": The Cabinet Makers Revisited', in Harrison and Zeitlin (eds.), *Divisions of Labour*, pp. 19–43

Bolt, C., *Victorian Attitudes to Race*, London, Routledge & Kegan Paul, 1971

Boyer, P., *Urban Masses and Moral Order in America 1820–1920*, Cambridge, MA, Harvard University Press, 1978

Bozzoli, B. (ed.), *Labour, Townships and Protest: Studies in the Social History of the Witwatersrand*, Johannesburg, Ravan, 1979

(ed.) *Town and Countryside in the Transvaal: Capitalist Penetration and Popular Response*, Johannesburg, Ravan, 1983

(ed.) *Class, Community and Conflict: South African Perspectives*, Johannesburg, Ravan, 1987

'Class, Community and Ideology in the Evolution of South African Society', in B. Bozzoli (ed.), *Class*, pp. 1–43

Bradlow, E, 'Cape Town 100 Years Ago: A "Somewhat Ragged" Place', in *Cape Times Centenary Supplement*, 27 March 1976, pp. 3–7

'Cape Town's Labouring Poor a Century Ago', *South African Historical Journal*, 9 (1977), 19–29

'The Cape Community during the Period of Responsible Government' in Pachai (ed.), *South Africa's Indians*, pp. 132–78

'Emancipation and Race Perceptions at the Cape', *South African Historical Journal*, 15 (1983), 10–33

Bradlow, M. A., 'Islam, the Colonial State and South African History: The 1886 Cemetery Uprising', Honours thesis, UCT, 1984

Briggs, A., *Victorian Cities*, New York, Pelican, 1963

Buirski, P., 'Mortality Rates in Cape Town 1895-1980', *Studies* V, (1983), 125–66

Bundy, C., *The Rise and Fall of the South African Peasantry*, London, Heinemann, 1979

'"Vagabond Hollanders and Runaway Englishmen": White Poverty in the Cape before Poor Whiteism', in Beinart, Delius and Trapido (eds.), *Putting a Plough to the Ground*, pp. 101–28

Burke, P., *Popular Culture in Early Modern Europe*, New York, Harper & Row, 1981

Butt, P., 'The Growth and Development of the Master Builders Association in the Cape Peninsula', M.Sc. thesis, Natal University, 1984

Cell, J. W., *The Highest Stage of White Supremacy*, Cambridge, Cambridge University Press, 1982

Checkland, S. G., 'An Urban History Horoscope', in Fraser and Sutcliffe (eds.), *Urban History*, pp. 449–66

Chisholm, L., 'The Pedagogy of Porter: The Origins of the Reformatory in the Cape Colony, 1882-1910', *JAH*, 27, 3 (1986), 481–95

Clarke, C. G., 'A Caribbean Creole Capital: Kingston, Jamaica (1692–1938)', in Ross and Telkamp (eds.), *Colonial Cities*, pp. 153–170

Cohen, A. P., *The Symbolic Construction of Community*, London, Routledge & Kegan Paul, 1992.

Cole, A., *The Cape and the Kafirs: Or Notes of Five Years' Residence in South Africa*, London, Richard Bentley, 1852

Cole, J., *Crossroads: the Politics of Reform and Repression 1976–1986*, Johannesburg, Ravan Press, 1987

Colls, R., 'Englishness and the Political Culture', in Colls and Dodd (eds.), *Englishness*, pp. 29-61

Colls, R. and Dodd, P. (eds.), *Englishness: Politics and Culture 1880–1920*, Beckenham, Croom Helm, 1986

Cooper, F., *On the African Waterfront: Urban Disorder and the Transformation of work in Colonial Mombasa*, New Haven, Yale University Press, 1987

Coplan, D. B., *In Township Tonight: South Africa's Black City Music and Theatre*, London, Longman, 1985

Crais, C., *White Supremacy and Black Resistance in Pre-industrial South Africa*, Cambridge, Cambridge University Press, 1992

Crais, C., and Worden, N. (eds.), *Breaking the Chains: Slavery and Emancipation in the Nineteenth Century Cape Colony*, Johannesburg, Wits University Press, forthcoming

Crossick, G., 'Urban Society and the Petty Bourgeoisie in Nineteenth Century Britain', in Fraser and Sutcliffe (eds.), *Urban History*, pp. 307–26

Cumberland, S., *What I think of South Africa; Its People and its Politics*, London, Chapman & Hall, 1896

Cuthbertson, G., 'The Impact of the Emancipation of the Slaves on St Andrew's Scottish Church, Cape Town, 1838–1878', *Studies* III (1984), pp. 49–63

Dale, L., 'The Cape and its People' in Noble (ed.), *The Cape and its People and other Essays*, pp. 2–20

Daunton, M. J., 'Public Place and Private Space: The Victorian City and the Working-class Household', in Fraser and Sutcliffe (eds.), *Urban History*, pp. 218-23

Davenport, T. R. H., *The Afrikaner Bond 1880–1911*, Cape Town, Oxford University Press, 1966

'The Consolidation of a new Society: The Cape Colony', in Wilson and Thompson (eds.), *Oxford History*, vol. I, pp. 272-33

'The Beginnings of Urban Segregation in South Africa; the Natives (Urban Areas) Act of 1923 and its background' *Occasional Paper No. 15*, Grahamstown, Institute of Economic Research, 1971

South Africa: A Modern History, 4th edition, Johannesburg, Macmillan, 1991

Davids, A., 'Politics and the Muslims of Cape Town: A Historical Survey', *Studies* IV, (1981), 174–220

' "The Revolt of the Malays": A Case Study of the Reaction of the Cape Muslims to the Smallpox Epidemics of Nineteenth Century Cape Town', *Studies* V, (1983), 46–78

'Words the Slaves Made: A Socio-historical-linguistic study', *South African Journal of Linguistics*, 8, 1, (1990), 1–24

Davison, G. J., *The Rise and Fall of Marvellous Melbourne*, Melbourne, Melbourne University Press, 1978

Deacon, H., 'Racism and Reform: The Colonial Insane on Robben Island 1846–1880', unpublished paper presented to the British African Studies Association, September 1992

De Kiewiet, C. W., *History of South Africa: Social and Economic*, Oxford, Oxford University Press, 1957

Den Besten, H., 'From Khoe Khoe Foreigner Talk via Hottentot Dutch to Afrikaans: the Creation of a Novel Grammar', in Putz and Derven (eds.), *Wheels Within Wheels: Papers of the Dutsburg Symposium on Pidgin and Creole Languages*, Frankfurt, Peter Lang, 1989, pp. 207–49

Dictionary of South African Biography, 4 vols.

vol. I, Johannesburg, Nasionale Boekhandel Beperk, 1968

vol. II, Cape Town, Tafelberg-Uitgewers, 1972

vol. III, Cape Town, Tafelberg-Uitgewers, 1977

vol. IV, Durban, Butterworth & Co, 1981

Dodd, P., 'Englishness and the National Culture', in Colls and Dodd (eds.), *Englishness*, pp. 1–28

Downes, A. J., *Printers' Saga*, Johannesburg, Wallach's, 1952

Dubow, S., 'African Labour at the Cape Town Docks, 1900–1904', *Studies* IV, (1981), 108–34

'Race, Civilisation and Culture: The Elaboration of Segregation Discourse in the Inter-war Years', in Marks and Trapido (eds.), *Race, Class and Nationalism*, pp. 71–94

Racial Segregation and the Origins of Apartheid in South Africa, 1919–1936, London, Macmillan, 1989

Duff Gordon, Lady, *Letters from the Cape*, Cape Town, Maskew Miller, 1925

Du Plessis, I. D., *The Malay Quarter and its People*, Cape Town, Balkema, 1953

Dyos, H. J. (ed.), *The Study of Urban History*, London, Edward Arnold, 1968

Dyos, H. J. and Wolff, M. (eds.), *The Victorian City*, London, Routledge & Kegan Paul, 1973

Easton, J., *Four Questions of the Day*, Cape Town, Juta, 1888

Ellis Cashmore, E., *Dictionary of Race and Ethnic Relations*, London, Routledge & Kegan Paul, 1992.

Elks, K., 'Crime, Community and Police in Cape Town, 1825–1850', MA thesis, UCT, 1986

Elphick, R., 'The Khoisan to c1770', in Elphick and Giliomee (eds.), *Shaping*, pp. 3–40

Elphick, R. and Giliomee, H. (eds.), *The Shaping of South African Society*, 2nd edition, Cape Town, Longman, 1989

Ensor, J. D., *Sitongo*, Cape Town, A. Richards & Sons, 1884

Erlman, V., ' "A Feeling of Prejudice": Orpheus M. McAdoo and the Virginia Jubilee Singers in South Africa', *JSAS*, 14, 3, (1988), 331–50

Evans, M. S., *Black and White in South East Africa: A Study in Sociology*, London, Longman's, Green & Co., 1916

Foster, J., 'Nineteenth Century Towns: A Class Dimension', in Dyos (ed.), *The Study of Urban History*, pp. 281–300

  Class Struggle and the Industrial Revolution, London, Weidenfeld & Nicolson, 1974

Fraser, D., *Urban Politics in Victorian England*, Leicester, Leicester University Press, 1976

Fraser, D. and Sutcliffe, A. (eds.), *The Pursuit of Urban History*, London, Edward Arnold, 1983

Fredrickson, G. M., *White Supremacy*, New York, Oxford University Press, 1981

Froude, J. A., *Oceana or England and her Colonies*, London, Longman's Green & Co., 1881

General Directory and Guide Book of the Cape of Good Hope and its Dependencies, Cape Town, Saul Solomon & Co., 1875

General Directory and Guide Book, Cape Town, Saul Solomon & Co., 1882

Gibson, A. G. S., *Sketches of Church Work and Life in the Diocese of Cape Town*, Cape Town, South African 'Electric' Printing and Publishing Co., 1900

Gillett, E. and MacMahon, K. A., *A History of Hull*, Oxford, Oxford University Press, 1980

Giliomee, H., 'The Growth of Afrikaner Identity', in Adam and Giliomee (eds.), *Rise and Crisis*, pp. 83–127

  'Aspects of the Rise of Afrikaner Capital and Afrikaner Nationalism in the Western Cape, 1870–1915', in James and Simons (eds.), *The Angry Divide*, pp. 63–79

Gitsham, E. and Trembath, J. F., *Labour Organisation in South Africa*, Durban, E. P. and Commercial Printing, 1926

Goldberg, M., 'Worker Consciousness: A Formulation and a Critique', unpublished paper, African Studies Seminar, UCT, 1980

Goldin, I., *Making Race: The Politics and Economics of Coloured Identity in South Africa*, Cape Town, Maskew Miller Longman, 1987

Grant, D., 'Bokkoms, Boycott and the Bo Kaap: The Decline of the Rogge Bay Fishing Industry between 1890 and 1920', MA thesis, UCT, 1991

Green, L., *Growing Lovely, Growing Old: The Story of Cape Town's Three*

Centuries – the Streets, the Houses, the Characters, the Legends, Traditions and Folklore, the Laughter and Tears, Cape Town, Howard Timmins, 1975

Tavern of the Seas, Cape Town, Howard Timmins, 1975

Greenberg, S., *Race and State in Capitalist Development*, Johannesburg, Ravan, 1980

Gresswell, W., *Our South African Empire*, London, Chapman & Hall, 1885

Guelke, L., 'Freehold farmers and frontier settlers, 1657–1780', in Elphick and Giliomee (eds.), *Shaping*, pp. 66–108

Harries, P., 'Mozbiekers: The Immigration of an African Community to the Western Cape, 1876-1882', *Studies* I, (1979), 153–64

'Plantations, Passes and Proletarians: Labour and the Colonial State in Nineteenth Century Natal', *JSAS*, 13, 3 (1987), 372–99

Harrison, R., 'Introduction', in Harrison and Zeitlin (eds.), *Divisions of Labour*, pp. 1–19.

Harrison, R. and Zeitlin, J. (eds.), *Divisions of Labour*, Brighton, Harvester, 1985

Hattersley, A. F., *An Illustrated History of South Africa*, Cape Town, Balkema, 1969

Henry, J. H., *The First Hundred Years of the Standard Bank*, Oxford, Oxford University Press, 1963

Hennock, E. P., 'The Social Compositions of Borough Councils in the large Cities, 1835–1914', in Dyos (ed.), *The Study of Urban History*, pp. 315–36

Himmelfarb, G., *The Idea of Poverty*, New York, Alfred A. Knopf, 1983

Hobart Houghton, D., 'Economic Development, 1865–1965', in Wilson and Thompson (eds.), *Oxford History*, vol. II, pp. 1–48

Hofmeyr, I., 'Building a Nation from Words: Afrikaans Language, Literature and Ethnic Identity, 1902–1924', in Marks and Trapido (eds.), *Class, Race and Nationalism*, pp. 95–123

Howard, A. G., 'Progress of Architecture in Cape Town Since 1876', *South African Archictect Engineer and Surveyor's Journal*, May–September, (1907), 139–212

Iliffe, J, 'The Creation of Group Consciousness: A History of the Dockworkers of Dar Es Salaam', in Sandbrook and Cohen (eds.), *African Working Class*, pp. 49–72

The African Poor, Cambridge, Cambridge University Press, 1987

Immelman, R. F. M., *Men of Good Hope*, Cape Town, Chamber of Commerce, 1955

James, W. G. and Simons, M. (eds.), *The Angry Divide: Social and Economic History of the Western Cape*, Cape Town, David Philip, 1989

Jackson, J. J., *New Orleans in the Gilded Age: Politics and Urban Progress 1880–1896*, Baton Rouge, Louisiana State University Press, 1969

Jeppie, S., and Soudien, C. (eds.), *The Struggle for District Six: Past and Present*, Cape Town, Buchu Books, 1990

Judges, S., 'Poverty, Living Conditions and Social Relations – Aspects of Life in Cape Town in the 1830s', MA thesis, UCT, 1977

Kagan, N., 'The Growth and Development of the Municipality of Green Point and Sea Point', Honours thesis, UCT, 1975

Karasch, M., 'Rio de Janeiro: From Colonial Town to Imperial Capital (1808–1850)', in Ross and Telkamp (eds.), *Colonial Cities*, pp. 123–51

Kennedy, D., *Kennedy at the Cape: A Professional Tour through the Cape Colony, Orange Free State, Diamond Fields and Natal*, Edinburgh, Edinburgh Publishing Company, 1879

Kilpin, R., *The Romance of a Colonial Parliament*, London, Longman's, Green & Co., 1930

King, A. D., 'Colonial Cities: "Global Pivots of Change"', in Ross and Telkamp (eds.), *Colonial Cities*, pp. 7–32

Kinkead-Weekes, B. H., 'Africans in Cape Town: The Origins and Development of State Policy and Popular Resistance to 1936', M.Soc.Sci. thesis, UCT, 1985

Kirk, T., 'The Cape Economy and the Expropriation of the Kat River Settlement, 1846–1853', in Marks and Atmore (eds.), *Economy and Society*, pp. 226–246

Krauss, F., 'A Description of Cape Town and its Way of Life, 1838–1840', *Quarterly Bulletin of the South African Library*, 21 (1966–1967), 2–12, 33–49

Laidler, P. W., *The Growth and Government of Cape Town*, Cape Town, Unie-Volkspers, 1939

Lamond, M. F., 'A Consideration of the Cape Town Elite at the end of the last Century', Honours thesis, UCT, 1985

Le Feuvre, P., 'Cultural and Theological Factors affecting relationships between the Nederduitse-Gereformeerde Kerk and the Anglican Church in the Cape Colony 1806–1910', Ph.D. thesis, UCT, 1980

Legassick, M., 'The Making of South African "Native Policy" 1903–1923: The Origins of Segregation', unpublished paper, University of London, Commonwealth Studies Institute Postgraduate Seminar, 1972

Lewis, G. L. M., *Between the Wire and the Wall: A History of South African 'Coloured' Politics*, Cape Town, David Philip, 1987

Lewis J., *Industrialisation and Trade Union Organisation in South Africa, 1924–1955: The Rise and Fall of the South African Trade and Labour Council*, Cambridge, Cambridge University Press, 1984

Lewsen P., 'The Cape Liberal Tradition – Myth or Reality?', *Institute of Commonwealth Studies Collected Seminar Papers,* 1, (Oct 1969–April 1970), London, Institute of Commonwealth Studies, 72–88

John X. Merriman, New Haven, Yale University Press, 1982

Selections from the Correspondence of J. X. Merriman 1870–1890, Cape Town, Van Riebeeck Society, 1960

(ed.), *Selections from the Correspondence of J. X. Merriman 1890–1898*, Cape Town, Van Riebeeck Society, 1963

Linnegar, J. D., 'From Village to Municipality: A History of Wynberg to 1903', unpublished Honours thesis, UCT, 1975

Little, A. I., *History of the City Club, Cape Town*, Cape Town, *Cape Times*, 1938

Lombaard, A., 'The Smallpox Epidemic of 1882 in Cape Town with some Reference to the Neighbouring Suburbs', Honours thesis, UCT, 1981

Lorimer, D. A., *Colour, Class and the Victorians*, Leicester, Leicester University Press, 1978

Ludlow, H., 'Missions and Emancipation in the South Western Cape: a Case Study of Groenekloof (Mamre), 1838–1852', MA thesis, UCT, 1992

Lowndes, E. E. K., *Every-day Life in South Africa*, London, S. W. Partridge, 1900

Mabin, A. S., 'The Making of Colonial Capitalism: Intensification and Expansion in the Economic Geography of the Cape Colony, South Africa, 1854-1899', Ph.D. thesis, Witwatersrand University, 1977, revised 1984

Mabbutt, J. A. (ed.), *The Cape Peninsula*, Cape Town, Maskew Miller, 1952

Mackinnon, J., *South African Traits*, Edinburgh, James Gemmell, 1887

Marais, J. S., *The Cape Coloured People*, Johannesburg, Witwatersrand University Press, 1968

Marks, S., 'Khoisan Resistance to the Dutch in the 17th and 18th Centuries', *JAH*, 13, 1 (1972), 55–80

'Natal, the Zulu Royal Family and the Ideology of Segregation', *JSAS*, 4, 2 (1978), 172–194

' "White Supremacy": A Review Article', *Comparative Studies in Society and History*, 29, 2 (1987), 385–97

Marks, S. and Atmore, A. (eds.), *Economy and Society in Pre-Industrial South Africa*, London, Longman, 1980

Marks, S. and Rathbone, R., 'Introduction', in Marks and Rathbone (eds.), *Industrialisation*, pp. 1–44

Marks, S. and Rathbone, R. (eds.), *Industrialisation and Social Change in South Africa*, Harlow, Longman, 1982

Marks, S. and Trapido, S., 'The Politics of Race, Class and Nationalism', in Marks and Trapido (eds.), *Race, Class and Nationalism*, pp. 1–70

Marks, S. and Trapido, S. (eds.), *The Politics of Race, Class and Nationalism in Twentieth Century South Africa*, London, Longman, 1987

Marshall, M., 'The Growth and Development of Cape Town', MA thesis, UCT, 1940

Maylam, P., 'The Rise and Decline of Urban Apartheid in South Africa', *African Affairs*, 89, 354, (1990), 57–84

Mayson, J. S., *The Malays of Cape Town*, Manchester, Cave & Sever, 1855

McCracken, J. L., *The Cape Parliament 1854–1910*, Oxford, Clarendon, 1967

Meltzer, J. L, 'The Growth of Cape Town Commerce and the Role of John Fairbairn's *Advertiser* (1835–1859)', MA thesis, UCT, 1989

Miles, R., *Racism*, London, Routledge & Kegan Paul, 1989

Nasson, B., *Abraham Esau's War: A Black South African War in the Cape, 1899–1902*, Cambridge, Cambridge University Press, 1991

Newton, R., *Victorian Exeter 1837–1914*, Leicester, Leicester University Press, 1968

Newton-King S., 'The Labour Market of the Cape Colony', in Marks and Atmore (eds.), *Economy and Society*, pp. 171–207

Noble, J., *Descriptive Handbook of the Cape Colony: Its Composition and Resources*, Cape Town, Juta, 1875

The Cape and South Africa, Cape Town, J. C. Juta, 1878

(ed.), *The Cape and its People and other Essays*, Cape Town, J. C. Juta, 1869

Odendaal, A., *Black Protest Politics in South Africa to 1912*, Totowa, Barnes & Noble, 1984

Orman, S. L., 'Sir D. Graaff, Businessman and Politician', Honours thesis, UCT, 1983

O'Sullivan, S., 'Workers with a Difference: Life and Labour in the Salt River Workshops 1900-1935', Honours thesis, UCT, 1984

'Cameos of Life at the Salt River Works in the 1920s', *Studies* VI (1988), 96–111

Pachai, B. (ed.), *South Africa's Indians*, Washington, University Press of America, 1979

Pama, C., *Bowler's Cape Town: Life at the Cape in Early Victorian Times, 1834–1868*, Cape Town, Tafelberg, 1977

Pearce, J., 'The Origins of the Temperance Movement in Cape Town in the 1880s', Honours thesis, UCT, 1985

Phimister, I. R. and Van Onselen, C., *Studies in the History of African Mine Labour in Colonial Zimbabwe*, Gwelo, Mambo Press, 1978

Picard, H. W. J., *Grand Parade*, Cape Town, Struik, 1969

Pinnock, 'Stone's Boys and the Making of a Cape Flats Mafia', in Bozzoli (ed.), *Class*, pp. 418–35

Pirie, G., 'South African Urban History', *Urban History*, (1985) 18–29

Pleck, E. H., *Black Migration and Poverty: Boston 1865–1900*, New York, Academic Press, 1979

Proceedings of the South African Teachers' Association during the Year 1869, Cape Town, Saul Solomon, 1870

Purkis, A. S., 'The Politics, Capital and Labour of Railway Building in the Cape Colony, 1870–1885', Ph.D. thesis, Oxford, 1978

Rabinowitz, H. N., *Race Relations in the Urban South 1865–1890*, New York, Oxford University Press, 1978

Rankin, D. C., 'The Politics of Caste: Free Coloured Leadership in New Orleans during the Civil War', in R. R. MacDonald, J. R. Kemp and E. F. Haas (eds.), *Louisiana's Black Heritage*, New Orleans, Louisiana State Museum, 1979

Rennie, J., *The Buildings of Central Cape Town*, 2 vols., Cape Town, Cape Provincial Institute of Architects, 1978

Rex, J., *Race and Ethnicity*, Milton Keynes, Open University Press, 1986

Rex, J. and Mason, D., *Theories of Race and Ethnic Relations*, Cambridge, Cambridge University Press, 1989

Ritchie, J. E., *Brighter South Africa or Life at the Cape and Natal*, London, T. Fisher Unwin, 1892

Rose Innes, J., *Sir James Rose Innes 1855–1942*, Cape Town, Oxford University Press, 1949

Rosenthal, E., *Fishorns and Hansom Cabs: Life in Victorian Cape Town*, Cape Town, AD. Donker, 1977

Ross, R., *Cape Of Torments*, London, Routledge & Kegan Paul, 1983
  'Cape Town (1750–1850): Synthesis in the Dialectic of Continents', in Ross and Telkamp (eds.), *Colonial Cities*, pp. 105–21
  'Structure and Culture in Pre-Industrial Cape Town: A Survey of Knowledge and Ignorance', in James and Simons (eds.), *Angry Divide*, ch. 4
    (ed.), *Racism and Colonialism: Essays on Ideology and Social Structure*, Leiden, Martinus Nijhoff, 1982

Ross, R. and Telkamp, G. J. (eds.), *Colonial Cities: Essays on Urbanism in a Colonial Context*, Leiden, Martinus Nijhoff, 1985

Rudé, G., *Ideology and Popular Protest*, London, Pantheon Books, 1980

Ryan, M., 'Anders Ohlsson, Brewer and Politician: 1881–1894', Honours thesis, UCT, 1976

Sandbrook, R. and Cohen, R. (eds.), *The Development of an African Working Class*, London, Longman, 1975

Saunders, C., 'F. Z. S. Peregrino and "The South African Spectator" ', *Quarterly Bulletin of the South African Library*, 32 (1977–8), 81–90

'The Creation of Ndabeni: Urban Segregation and African Resistance in Cape Town', *Studies* I (1979), 165–93

'Africans in Cape Town in the Nineteenth Century: An Outline', *Studies* II (1980), 15–41

Saunders, C. et al. (eds.), *Studies in the History of Cape Town*, 6 vols., Cape Town, UCT, 1979–88

Schreuder, D. M., 'The Cultural Factor in Victorian Imperialism: A Case Study of the British "Civilising Mission" ', *Journal of Imperial and Commonwealth History*, 4, 3 (1976), 283–317

Scobie, J. R., *Buenos Aires: From Plaza to Suburb 1870–1910*, New York, Oxford University Press, 1974

Shain, M., *Jewry and Cape Society*, Cape Town, Historical Publications Society, 1983

Shaw, G., *Some Beginnings: The Cape Times* (1876-1910), Cape Town, Oxford University Press, 1975

Shell, R., 'Rites and Rebellion: Islamic Conversion at the Cape, 1808 to 1915', *Studies* V (1983), 1–45

Shorten, J., *Cape Town*, Johannesburg, Shorten, 1963

Simons, J. and R., *Class and Colour in South Africa 1850–1950*, London, International Defence and Aid Fund, 1983

Simpson, V., *My Reminiscences*, London, Longman's, Green & Co., 1926

Smith, R. T., 'Race and Class in the Post-emancipation Caribbean', in Ross (ed.), *Racism and Colonialism*, pp. 95–120

Society for the Propagation of the Gospel in Foreign Parts, *Historical Sketches: 'Cape Town'*, Westminster, 1908

Solomon, W. E. G., *Saul Solomon*, Cape Town, Oxford University Press, 1948

Stave, B. M., 'In Pursuit of Urban History, Conversations with Myself and Others: A View from the United States', in Fraser and Sutcliffe (eds.), *Urban History*, pp. 407–27

Stedman Jones, G., *Outcast London*, Harmondsworth, Penguin, 1976

Stepan, N., *The Idea of Race in Science: Great Britain 1800–1960*, London, Macmillan, 1982

Stone, G., 'The Coon Carnival', unpublished paper, Abe Bailey Institute of Interracial Studies, Cape Town, 197–

Stone, J., *Colonist or Uitlander? A Study of the British Immigrant in South Africa*, Oxford, Clarendon Press, 1973

Swanson, M., 'Reflections on the Urban History of South Africa: Some Problems and Possibilities, with Special Reference to Durban', in H. L. Watts (ed.), *Focus on Cities: Proceedings of a Conference Organised by the Institute for Social Research, at the University of Natal, Durban, 8–12 July, 1968*, Durban, Institute for Social Research, University of Natal, 1970, pp. 143–9

'The Sanitation Syndrome: Bubonic Plague and Urban Native Policy in the Cape Colony, 1900-1909', *JAH*, 18, 3 (1977), 387–410

Ticktin, D., 'The Origins of the South African Labour Party 1880–1910', Ph.D. thesis, UCT, 1973

Trapido, S., ' "The Friends of the Natives": Merchants, Peasants and the Political and Ideological Structure of Liberalism in the Cape, 1854–1910', in Marks and Atmore (eds.), *Economy and Society*, pp. 247–74

'The Emergence of Liberalism and the Making of "Hottentot Nationalism", 1815–1834', unpublished paper presented to the Imperial and Commonwealth Studies Postgraduate Seminar, University of London, 1990

Trollope, A., *South Africa*, London, Chapman & Hall, 1879

Turrell, R. V., *Capital and Labour on the Kimberley Diamond Fields, 1871–1890*, Cambridge, Cambridge University Press, 1987

Vail, L. (ed.), *The Political Economy of Tribalism in Southern Africa*, London, James Currey, forthcoming

Van den Berghe, P. L., *Race and Racism: A Comparative Perspective*, New York, Wiley, 1978

Van der Spuy, P., 'Slave Women and the Family in Nineteenth-century Cape Town', *SAHJ*, 27 (1992), 50–74

Van Duin, P. C., 'Skilled Labour, Trade Unionism and Racial Attitudes in Cape Town, 1900–1914', unpublished paper, Leiden, 1985

'Trade Unionism and the Relationship between White and Coloured Workers in the Cape Town Building Industry, 1900–1930', unpublished paper presented to Roots and Realities conference, UCT, 1986

'Artisans and Trade Unions in the Cape Town Building Industry, 1900–1924', in James and Simons (eds.), *Angry Divide*, pp. 95–110

Van Duin, P. C. and Ross, R. (eds.), *The Economy of the Cape Colony in the Eighteenth Century*, Leiden, Centre for the History of European Expansion, 1987

Van Heyningen, E., 'The First Aim of Every Government: The Making of the Cape Colony Public Health and Amendment Act of 1897', unpublished paper, UCT, 1980

'Refugees and Relief in Cape Town, 1899–1902', *Studies* III (1980), 64–113

'Cape Town and the Plague of 1901', *Studies* IV (1981), 66–107

'Prostitution and the Contagious Diseases Acts: The Social Evil in the Cape Colony, 1868–1902', *Studies* V (1984), 80–124

'Public Health and Society in Cape Town, 1880–1910', Ph.D. thesis, UCT, 1989

'Poverty, Self-help and Community: The Survival of the Poor in Cape Town, 1880–1910', *SAHJ*, 24 (1991), 128–143

Van Onselen, C., *Studies in the Social and Economic History of the Witwatersrand 1886–1914*, 2 vols., Johannesburg, Ravan, 1982

Vienings, T., 'Stratification and Proletarianisation: The Rural Political Economy of the Worcester District, 1875–1910', Honours thesis, 1985

Walker, A., ' "Boer" and "Boesman", "Folk" and "Fyand": Attitudes to Race in *Ons Klyntji,* 1896–1906', Honours thesis, UCT, 1990

Walvin, J., *Black and White*, London, Allen Lane, 1975

Warren, D. P., 'Merchants, Commissioners and Ward Masters: Politics in Cape Town, 1840–1854', MA thesis, UCT, 1986

Watson, G., *Passing for White*, London, Tavistock, 1970

Welsh, D., 'The Growth of Towns', in Wilson and Thompson (eds.), *Oxford History of South Africa*, vol. II, pp. 172–243

The Roots of Segregation: Native Policy in Colonial Natal 1845–1910, Cape Town, Oxford University Press, 1971

Western, J., *Outcast Cape Town*, Cape Town, Human & Rousseau, 1981

Whittingdale, J., 'The Development and Location of Industries in Greater Cape Town', MA thesis, UCT, 1973

Wiebe, R. H., *The Search for Order*, London, Macmillan, 1967

Williams, K., *From Pauperism to Poverty: The Poor Law 1870–1914*, London Routledge & Kegan Paul, 1981

Wilmot, A., *A History of the Cape Colony for use in Schools*, Cape Town, J. C. Juta, 1871

Wilson, M. and Thompson L. (eds.), *The Oxford History of South Africa*, 2 vols., Oxford, Oxford University Press, 1969–1971

Winberg, C., 'The "Ghoemaliedjies" of the Cape Muslims: Remnants of a Slave Culture', unpublished paper presented to the English Department Seminar, UCT, 1991

Wohl, A., 'Unfit for Human Habitation', in Dyos and Wolff (eds.), *The Victorian City*, pp. 603–24

Worden, N., *Slavery in Dutch South Africa*, Cambridge, Cambridge University Press, 1985

The Making of Modern South Africa: Conquest, Segregation and Apartheid, Oxford, Blackwell, 1994

Worger, W. H., *South Africa's City of Diamonds: Mine Workers and Monopoly Capitalism in Kimberley, 1867–1895*, Craighall, AD Donker, 1987

Wright, H., *The Burden of the Present: Liberal–Radical Controversy over Southern African History*, Cape Town, David Philip, 1977

'X.C.', *Everyday Life In the Cape Colony in Time of Peace*, London, T. Fisher Unwin, 1902

Zeitlin, J., 'Engineers and Compositors: A Comparison', in Harrison and Zeitlin (eds.), *Divisions of Labour*, pp. 186–215

Index

Other books in the series